Globalizing International Political Economy

Globalizing International Political Economy

Edited by

Nicola Phillips

First published 2005 by
PALGRAVE MACMILLAN
Houndmills, Basingstoke, Hampshire RG21 6XS and
175 Fifth Avenue, New York, N.Y. 10010
Companies and representatives throughout the world

PALGRAVE MACMILLAN is the global academic imprint of the Palgrave
Macmillan division of St. Martin's Press, LLC and of Palgrave Macmillan Ltd.
Macmillan® is a registered trademark in the United States, United Kingdom
and other countries. Palgrave is a registered trademark in the European
Union and other countries.

ISBN 978-0-333-96505-4   ISBN 978-1-137-20416-5 (eBook)

DOI 10.1007/978-1-137-20416-5

This book is printed on paper suitable for recycling and made from fully
managed and sustained forest sources.

A catalogue record for this book is available from the British Library.

Library of Congress Cataloging-in-Publication Data
Globalizing international political economy / edited by Nicola Phillips.
      p.   cm.
  Includes bibliographical references and index.
  ISBN 978-0-333-96504-4 (cloth)
  1. International economic relations.   2. Globalization—Economic
  aspects.   I. Phillips, Nicola, 1971–
  HF1359.G628 2005
  337—dc22   2005043738

10   9   8   7   6   5   4   3   2   1
14   13   12   11   10   09   08   07   06   05

Contents

v

Acknowledgements

This book, like most others, found its origins and inspiration in a series of conversations with a number of friends and colleagues. I owe the start of the concrete train of thought that led eventually to this project to a conversation with my then colleague at the University of Warwick, Shaun Breslin. Although the approach I have developed here is, I suspect, very different from the one he himself would take, I am grateful to him for generously allowing me to pick up and run with the ideas that arose in our early conversations.

The process of developing my thoughts, refining the approach and shaping the project itself involved further lengthy conversations with a range of other people, including and most notably Tony Payne, who is also the author of one of the chapters. Characteristically, and as ever, he asked all the right questions at all the right times, offered extremely valuable thoughts and commentaries throughout the process, and also found the time and energy to read drafts of all the chapters. While I take more than full responsibility for what follows, it has been enriched enormously by his collaboration and I am most grateful for the keen interest and enthusiasm he has brought to the project right from the start.

The final product, I am afraid to say, has been an excessively long time in the making. In the face of a number of very disappointing and frustrating setbacks and delays, I am grateful to my collaborators for their truly impressive patience and forbearance. I am also indebted to them for their enthusiasm for the project itself and their extremely hard work on various drafts of their individual contributions. I hope that I have been able to do justice to their efforts, both in the way the published volume now looks and in my final editorial interventions in each chapter. Steven Kennedy of Palgrave Macmillan has also shown great patience as I have struggled to move this project towards publication, and I appreciate very much his consistent interest in it as well as his thoughtful suggestions and advice. I am grateful also to the anonymous referees upon whom he called for views at various points, and who provided thought-provoking reactions.

The bulk of the work on this project was facilitated by the Hallsworth Research Fellowship that I have held at the University of Manchester for the past couple of years, and I have benefited enormously from the research support that the Department of Government there has provided. The final draft of the manuscript was pulled together and despatched to press in the early part of a visiting fellowship which I was fortunate to hold at the Instituto Tecnológico Autónomo de México (ITAM) in Mexico City, in connection with the International Studies Department's Centro de Estudios y Programas Interamericanos (Centre for Inter-American Studies and Programmes) and sponsored by the Ford Foundation. I am most grateful for both the research support provided by this grant, the very stimulating intellectual environment in which to work, and the warmest hospitality that colleagues have offered me.

Mexico City   NICOLA PHILLIPS

Notes on the Contributors

Mark Beeson is Senior Lecturer in International Relations in the School of Political Science and International Studies, University of Queensland, Australia. His latest edited book is *Contemporary Southeast Asia: Regional Dynamics, National Differences* (Palgrave Macmillan 2004).

Stephen Bell is Associate Professor and Head of the School of Political Science and International Studies at the University of Queensland, Australia. He is author, most recently, of *Australia's Money Mandarins: The Reserve Bank and the Politics of Money* (Cambridge University Press 2004).

Jean Grugel is Professor in the Department of Politics, University of Sheffield, UK. Her most recent book is *Democratization* (Palgrave Macmillan 2002). She is presently editor of the journal *Bulletin of Latin American Research*.

Robert O'Brien is LIUNA/Mancinelli Professor of Global Labour Issues and Associate Director of the Institute on Globalization and the Human Condition at McMaster University in Canada. His most recent book is an introductory IPE text with Marc Williams entitled *Global Political Economy: Evolution and Dynamics* (Palgrave Macmillan 2004).

Anthony Payne is Professor of Politics at the University of Sheffield, UK. He is managing editor of *New Political Economy* and is author, most recently, of *The Global Politics of Unequal Development* (Palgrave Macmillan 2005).

Nicola Phillips is currently Hallsworth Research Fellow at the University of Manchester in the UK. She is an editor of *New Political Economy* and joint editor of the *International Political Economy Yearbook* series (Lynne Rienner), and is author, most recently, of *The Southern Cone Model: The Political Economy of Regional Capitalist Development in Latin America* (Routledge 2004).

Fredrik Söderbaum is Associate Professor at the Department of Peace and Development Research (Padrigu) at Göteborg University, Sweden, and Associate Research Fellow at the United Nations University/Comparative Regional Integration Studies (UNU/CRIS), Bruges, Belgium. His most recent book is entitled *The Political Economy of Regionalism: The Case of Southern Africa* (Palgrave Macmillan 2004).

Andrew Walter is Senior Lecturer in International Relations at the London School of Economics, UK. His most recent publication is 'Implementation in East Asia', in B. Schneider (ed.) *The Road to International Financial Stability: Are Key Financial Standards the Answer?* (Palgrave Macmillan/ODI 2003).

List of Abbreviations

APEC	Asia-Pacific Economic Cooperation
BIS	Bank for International Settlements
CPE	Comparative Political Economy
EU	European Union
FDI	foreign direct investment
GATT	General Agreement on Tariffs and Trade
IFI	international financial institution
IMF	International Monetary Fund
IO	*International Organization*
IPE	International Political Economy
IR	International Relations
ISA	International Studies Association
MNC	multinational corporation
NAFTA	North American Free Trade Agreement
NGO	non-governmental organization
NPM	new public management
NR/NRA	new regionalisms/new realist approach
NRA	new regionalism approach
OECD	Organisation for Economic Cooperation and Development
PED	political economy of development
RIPE	*Review of International Political Economy*
TNC	transnational corporation
UN	United Nations
UNDP	United Nations Development Programme
UNU/WIDER	United Nations University/World Institute for Development Economics Research
WHS	Weberian historical sociology
WOA	world order approach
WSF	World Social Forum
WTO	World Trade Organization

Chapter 1

'Globalizing' the Study of International Political Economy

Nicola Phillips

Despite its pretensions to 'global' scope and relevance, the study of International Political Economy (IPE) remains entrenched in a highly specific and narrow set of theoretical, conceptual and empirical foundations. IPE has unfolded on this basis in ways which have narrowed, restricted and constrained the field of study, to the extent that the 'global' applicability of its central debates and perspectives is open to considerable question. This narrowness takes two principal forms. The first is that the empirical scope of IPE research has remained predominantly confined to the 'core' triad of advanced industrialized economies, in ways which are both discordant with the intellectual project underpinning IPE and signally problematic for its pursuit. The second is that the development of IPE theory has privileged a set of assumptions which emerge from the distinctive political economies and experiences of core economies, states and regions, and from their specific context of 'early industrialization'. As a consequence, many of the theoretical and conceptual frameworks currently on offer in IPE are of limited utility and relevance once taken out of their roots in the 'core', and many of the key debates are compromised in their ability to encompass and account for the *whole* of the global political economy and the nature of its constitution, even where they purport to do so.

These, stated succinctly, are the arguments and concerns which animate this volume. Its aim is to demonstrate how these twin dimensions of narrowness in IPE permeate and mould the principal debates in the field, and to offer a detailed consideration of how we might go about overcoming them. The founding contention is that

1

we need to initiate a process of rethinking and rebuilding IPE in order to move towards a field which is of more intrinsic applicability to the study of global political economy and *all* of its constituent regions and processes, rather than remaining, as at present, a field which is strikingly for and about the advanced industrialized world. In a nutshell, the pressing need is to 'globalize' the study of IPE. In our view, this challenge lies at the heart of what should surely be the next phase of the field's development, and we aim with this volume to take a first step towards meeting it.

The task of this introductory essay is to unfold these arguments more fully and lay out in more detail the case for 'globalizing IPE', before I pass the baton to the authors assembled here for their considerations of specific debates in the field. But it is important to pause at the very outset and be clear what this volume is and is *not* about, and indeed how it differs from some other treatments of closely related themes that have recently emerged and are under way. This work has been concentrated in International Relations (IR), rather than IPE more specifically, and has been addressed directly to what are perceived to be the limited empirical scope and theoretical inadequacy of that discipline. It arises from a growing frustration with IR's continuing adherence to the disciplinary identity that historically was articulated for it – that is, as a discipline not only concerned centrally with the study of the great powers, but also, moreover, developed *for* this purpose (Waltz 1979). The result, it is claimed, is a discipline which is deficient in its ability to cater for, and to, the international relations of those countries and regions not encompassed in this category.

Although the growing critiques have yet to be taken fully on board within IR, they have successfully established two principal lines of argument. The first is that what is generally termed the 'Third World' has been systematically and unjustifiably excluded from the purview of mainstream IR, and that IR theory is generally unsuited to its analysis (Ayoob 1998; Neumann 1998; Tickner 2003a; Thomas and Wilkin 2004). This sort of work has issued valuable calls for greater attention to these parts of the world in IR and the greater incorporation of pertinent issues – such as development, civil conflict or autonomy – into the overarching concerns of the field. At the same time, and perhaps more usefully, it has called attention to the ways in which key concepts in IR – such as war, sovereignty and power, among many others – are conceived differently by scholars resident in and preoccupied with the Third World. The reworking of these concepts in tune with the distinctive realities that prevail in 'non-core' areas is thus advocated as a means of laying the foundations for, as Arlene Tickner (2003a: 324) puts it, 'incorporating third world thinking into IR', and thus overcoming the systematic marginalization and demeaning of this scholarship in the mainstream of the discipline. In this work, then, the emphasis has fallen on the more sustained study of IR *and* the Third World, on bringing the Third World more centrally *into* IR, on how the Third World is to be studied within IR. The underlying assumptions are that the Third World represents a single distinctive and coherent category, constitutes a discrete unit of analysis and requires a separate line of enquiry within the broader field. The strategy, in this sense, is strikingly reminiscent of one noted and much excoriated by feminist IR theorists in their own context: one of 'add the Third World and stir'.

The second interesting, and related, line of argument that has recently gained ground is that the study of IR in an Anglo-American setting bears little relevance for the study of IR in different parts of the world. The focus in these accounts is usually on the ways in which Anglo-American IR is 'exported' to contexts in which it sits only uneasily. It is unable to account for the realities and pressing issues in the international relations of 'other' parts of the world, and remains remote from the sorts of theoretical and conceptual frameworks that are needed for studying these specific forms of international relations. Highly important and perceptive contributions along these lines have been offered in the contexts of China (Chan 1999; Wenli 2001; Xinning 2001; Breslin 2002), Latin America (Puig 1980; Perina 1985; Tickner 2002, 2003b; Tussie 2004), Africa (Dunn and Shaw 2001) and on occasion, as noted above, the 'Third World' in its putative entirety. The pressing project for most of these scholars is to build a discipline of IR and a body of IR theory *for* particular countries or regions, in a manner which calls forth a disaggregation of IR into a number of region- or country-specific versions of the discipline. In other words, the project here is one of developing a discipline of IR which is organized around a number of hubs, rather than the hub–spoke version that currently prevails and serves unhelpfully to perpetuate an Anglo-American intellectual hegemony.

The Globalizing IPE project is clearly sympathetic to the concerns that have motivated these lines of scholarship. At the same time, it takes clear issue with a number of the assumptions on which they are built and with the sorts of remedial strategies they advocate. With respect to the first, 'add the Third World and stir', approach, there are two key problems. One is the notion of a discrete category which can be labelled the 'Third World'. Such a nomenclature has come under sustained attack across the areas of the social sciences, even in those that have traditionally identified most with a concept of the 'Third' or 'developing' world and been most dependent on it for their *raison d'être*. It would be tedious to rehearse all these arguments here, but they can be distilled into the contentions that the label 'Third World' is part of a distinctly Cold War terminology that depended for any force it once had on the existence of a Second, socialist, World (now defunct); that the developmental trajectories of many parts of the world over the twentieth century have made a single category of 'Third' or 'developing' world impossible to identify, let alone deploy as a unit of analysis; and that the binary division of the world into 'developed' and 'developing' is premised on a teleological, linear and finite understanding of development that is entirely inappropriate to the understanding of the economies and societies supposedly encompassed in either category. The terms 'North' and 'South' offer few improvements on these problems, not least because they suggest a geographical demarcation that has never existed, and exists still less in a global political economy supposedly characterized by transnational structures and processes. Anthony Payne's (1999, 2005) full dissection of the terminology deployed in the study of development, along with the essays recently collected together by Mark Berger (2004) around the theme of *After the Third World?*, attest amply to the vast difficulties occasioned by a stubborn clinging to these outdated ways of carving up the world.

The other difficulty is that this line of enquiry remains wedded to the equally suspect premise of Third World exceptionalism. This premise underpinned much of traditional development theory, not to mention the assertion of a distinctive intellectual and disciplinary identity for something called 'development studies'. The contention, in a nutshell, is that 'developing' areas of the world require separate analysis, unique theoretical constructs and distinct analytical strategies, including if and when they are brought into a broader discipline.

This is also a premise which afflicts the second line of argument – that we need to build country- or region-specific forms of IR and a multi-hub discipline. This in some ways constitutes a much more sophisticated reflection on what needs to be done in order to break with the highly context-specific characteristics of mainstream IR, inasmuch as it recognizes one of the central contentions of the present volume: that 'adding and stirring' is simply not enough. Rather than thinking solely about what needs to be brought *into* IR and IPE, we need also to think about what we need to do *to* IR and IPE themselves in order to overcome the theoretical or empirical problems we identify. This said, there are serious questions to be raised about the contention that the way forward is some form of multi-hub discipline. It is certainly indispensable that we pay closer attention to the place and position of specific countries and regions in the international system or the global political economy, and it is certainly the case, illustrated forcefully by the contributors to this volume, that a greater comparative focus is essential for the project of Globalizing IPE. Yet there is a sense in which a region-specific strategy represents too much of a regression to the premises of exceptionalism which international political economists, in particular, have fought hard to try to discard. We are still left, in other words, with a problem of 'parochialism' in IPE, to borrow Holsti's (1985) well-known description of the myopic introspection and narcissism of US IR. Can the best means of mitigating the parochialism of US or Anglo-American IR and IPE be the construction of a similar parochialism rooted in sub-Saharan Africa, the Caribbean or the Middle East?

Most of all, both of these lines of scholarship posit a set of arguments which are, in themselves, insufficient, and which in fact become the more problematic when taken into the realms of IPE. One could go further and argue that they miss a set of key points, inasmuch as they fail to question the extent to which the IR (or IPE) conducted within and for the 'great powers' – in IPE terminology, the advanced industrialized world – achieves its purposes. In other words, the assumption is that mainstream IR and IPE are entirely appropriate and fruitful within the context in which they are rooted and for which they are predominantly articulated, but deficient once removed from that context. The empirical preoccupation and theoretical entrenchment of both IR and IPE in the study of the advanced industrialized powers is certainly in ample evidence, as we have noted here, as is the difficulty with which they accommodate the study of the world outside this small grouping. But the consequences of this theoretical and conceptual narrowness are not felt solely in a neglect of the 'developing' regions or countries of the world and in the poverty of the purchase offered on their study. They are felt equally in the limitations it foists upon analysis of the advanced industrialized world itself and, moreover, upon understandings of the nature and functioning of the global political economy.

The two issues identified in this last sentence are related. On the one hand, it is largely assumed in mainstream IPE that a range of key issues and processes in the global political economy – such as democratization, development, political change, (in)equality, (in)justice, poverty, culture and so on – are of little or no relevance to the advanced industrialized world, and therefore are largely neglected. Not only does this neglect impoverish understanding and analysis of core aspects of the contemporary global political economy; it also fundamentally misunderstands the ways in which these issues and processes are in fact as intrinsically relevant, in different ways, to the advanced industrialized world as to the so-called 'developing' world. The political economy of the advanced industrialized world itself, in this sense, is frequently only inadequately captured in much of mainstream IPE, and many issues and concepts of core relevance to it are afforded insufficient attention. On the other hand, a focus on the advanced industrialized world has inflicted on mainstream IPE a pervasive deficiency in its treatments of the issues and processes that *are* deemed to be the proper preoccupations of international political economists, such as globalization, global governance, finance, production, transnational corporations (TNCs), transnational relations and so on. The global political economy operates as a system in which, in highly uneven and unequal ways, the various parts of the world and various political economies are drawn into the structures and processes that define it. These key issues and processes, concomitantly, are of intrinsically 'global' articulation, significance and constitution, not phenomena that are encased within a very particular political economy of advanced industrialization and to be understood purely within that frame of reference. The empirical preoccupation of mainstream IPE with this particular political economy, and the rooting of the project of theorizing within this context, thus yields only partial and ultimately unsatisfactory insights into the nature of these key structures, processes and issues around which the field of IPE crystallizes and focuses its energies.

In short, it is not only in its understandings of the 'Third World' that an IPE built around and for the advanced industrialized world is impoverished; it is compromised also in its theoretical and empirical purchase on the advanced industrialized world itself. Moreover, it is an IPE which offers only unsatisfactory understandings of the nature of the global political economy and the key structures and processes on which it rests.

What is required, then, is a project for IPE that aims to rethink and rebuild the field so that it can be more 'globally' applicable in its reach and more able to accommodate the diverse parts of the global political economy – *including* the advanced industrialized world in which mainstream IPE continues to be theoretically, conceptually and empirically mired. The project of Globalizing IPE is therefore not about 'IPE and the developing world'. Its aim is not to develop an IPE *for* the 'non-core' areas of the world. Nor is its aim to advocate or develop a single framework that can account for all things, at all times, in all places. Rather, it advocates a necessary uprooting of IPE from the narrow and limiting context in which it has unfolded, and the development of a field of study that is more able to account for the *whole* of the global political economy and the forms of diversity within it, and thus to offer fuller and more satisfactory understandings of the structures and processes that comprise the contemporary world order than those currently on offer. The argument, in other words, is that it is necessary, and possible, to build an IPE which can stretch more easily and more fruitfully across the complex range of countries, regions, structures, actors and issue areas in the global political economy. What this involves is not only an empirical broadening to widen the focus outside the 'core' parts of the world and their experiences, but also, crucially, a serious reflection then on the theoretical implications of this broadening and the ways in which we might act on them in order to 'globalize' the study of IPE.

Let us, then, take a step back and lay out in more detail the dominant characteristics of IPE and their origins, and the rationale on which the 'Globalizing IPE' project rests.

IPE and its discontents

The field of IPE finds its intellectual provenance in two, largely distinct, traditions. The first is the discipline of IR, the second is the broader intellectual enterprise of classical political economy. It is generally accepted that IPE, as we know it today as a field of academic study with its own scholarly community, journals and conferences, emerged at the beginning of the 1970s. Its genesis is usually ascribed to the article Susan Strange published in 1970 in the British journal

International Affairs, in which she lamented what she saw to be the mutual neglect of international relations and international economics, and issued a robust call for a synthesis of insights from these two fields (Strange 1970). Her target audience was mostly the IR community, which she saw to be regrettably blind to the inextricable linkages between economics and politics in world affairs. She was not the first to recognize these linkages; indeed, it was not only in IR but also in Economics that much of the early work emerged which laid the ground for the subsequent development of IPE. Through the 1960s, growing attention in Economics to the phenomenon of interdependence, particularly from Richard Cooper (1968), was instrumental in inspiring the later work on the same theme in IR. Early interdependence scholarship, indeed, reflected in a preliminary way two of the founding propositions of what subsequently crystallized as IPE. On the one hand, it propelled to some prominence in IR the notion that the boundaries between the domestic and the international were blurred, building on analytical currents which already emphasized the importance of domestic politics in the study of international relations. As the study of interdependence advanced in IR over the course of the 1970s, notably in the work of Keohane and Nye (1977) and Rosenau (1980), understanding and theorizing the relationship between the national and the international became a significant preoccupation in the discipline (Gourevitch 1978). The early interdependence work also presaged the founding premise of IPE that attention to both economics and politics was crucial in analyses of international economics and international relations, a theme picked up by Strange (1970) in her call for what, at the time, she called a 'theory of international economic relations'.

With these forerunners, then, Strange's early article is widely credited not only with setting out a founding agenda for a field of IPE, but in so doing, according to Robert Cox (2004: 307), 'reviv[ing] the idea of political economy'. What it should also be credited with, however, is rooting IPE firmly within the discipline of IR. Strange's aim was to do away with a general clinging to 'the comfort of separatist specialization' that she perceived in the social sciences generally (Strange 1996: xv), but her elaboration of a project for IPE took aim very directly at IR and what she saw to be its manifold deficiencies. While she noted the poverty of Economics in a similar spirit, it was the IR community that she directed her considerable energies to shaking up. It was IR that was 'allowing the gulf between international economics and international politics to grow yearly wider and deeper and more unbridgeable than ever before', and it was to IR that the 'damage' would be done if a theory of international economic relations was not developed forthwith (Strange 1970: 307, 310). The thrust of Strange's founding statements, in this sense, was a revival of an idea of political economy *within IR*, and their effect was to anchor what became IPE firmly within that discipline. Despite its supposed straddling of the divide between IR and Economics, IPE does not enjoy any particular currency or following in the latter. Indeed, the concept of political economy that informs IPE and that which informs the study of political economy in Economics are very different, as even a cursory glance at the respective political economy journals – say, *New Political Economy* or *International Organization* from IPE, and the *Journal of Political Economy* from Economics – would amply reveal. While much of the mainstream *methodological* apparatus of mainstream IPE is borrowed from Economics, its primary *theoretical* apparatus is inherited from IR, as were many of the scholars that came to populate this 'new' field. In short, IPE is a field of study housed within IR and pursued by scholars employed, for the most part, within academic departments of politics and/or international relations. It is also its relationship to IR that constitutes international political economists' overriding preoccupation and point of reference in thinking about how the field of IPE is actually or desirably defined. What keeps us awake at night, as it were, is 'whether [IPE] is a sub-field of International Relations, or whether it is something broader and more inclusive' (Underhill 2000a: 805).

Those who advocate the 'something broader and more inclusive' are usually invoking the second intellectual tradition on which IPE is founded: that of classical political economy. When approached from this angle, IPE can be said to enjoy a much longer and more prestigious lineage than that suggested by IR-centric accounts of its development. In classical political economy, the liberal ancestry is associated with the figures of Adam Smith, David Ricardo, John Maynard Keynes and others, and the line then traces down through such influences as Friedrich Hayek and Milton Friedman. The radical political economy tradition founds itself upon the work of Karl Marx and the subsequent extensions of Marxist ideas that gave rise to Leninist notions of imperialism, Latin American structuralism, dependency theory and world systems theory, through to the newer 'critical' currents in IPE that emerged in the 1980s, developed primarily by Robert Cox, which sought to combine a neo-Marxist political economy with the political sociology of Antonio Gramsci. It has been in these classical political economy traditions that much of modern IPE, as it has evolved since the early 1970s, has found its clearest intellectual influence, in the sense that it was in these traditions that most faithful expression was given to a notion of *political economy*. The central metatheoretical and analytical battles in IPE revolve around how that notion is to be formulated, theorized and analysed. While the liberal political economy tradition was largely hijacked in the twentieth century by the development of neoclassical economics and the disciplinary parting of the ways that occurred between Political Science and Economics, the radical tradition remained defined by its enquiry into the intrinsic inseparability of the political and the economic (Underhill 2000a: 812). In this sense, while liberal political economy drew a classical distinction between politics and economics (states and markets, public and private) and sought to interrogate the close interaction between these supposedly separate spheres, the radical tradition remained wedded to the development of what it advocated as a purer and more integrated 'political economy', which denied the possibility of the theoretical or methodological separation of the political and the economic that was posited in the liberal tradition.

In some ways, the diversity of its intellectual origins has always been one of IPE's great strengths. It has generated a multidisciplinary openness, a 'theoretical heterodoxy' and a vibrant set of metatheoretical, theoretical and conceptual debates that are not matched elsewhere in the social sciences (Murphy and Nelson 2001). At the same time, it has been one of its weaknesses, in the sense that its boundaries can be notoriously hard to establish. As in all academic disciplines, international political economists have displayed an anxiety to assert for their field a clear intellectual and disciplinary identity, in a way which would offer a robust retort to those in IR, particularly, that deem IPE to be little more than a sub-field of their own discipline. Witness the exchange between Stephen Krasner and Susan Strange (both 1994) in the inaugural issues of the *Review of International Political Economy* (RIPE). Yet the dominant manner in which this has been done in IPE has led, somewhat paradoxically, to a marked rejection of potentially constructive engagement with other fields – particularly, I would suggest, comparative political economy (CPE), comparative politics and 'development studies' – and thereby, in fact, to limit the degree of multidisciplinary openness that can be said to characterize the theoretical constructs that predominate in the field. Many of the chapters in this volume demonstrate clearly the manifestations of this narrowness in the key IPE debates, and show how a greater openness to relevant insights from other contiguous areas of the social and political sciences can offer significant resources for the project of Globalizing IPE.

The important point to make for now is that, as a result of this diversity, there remains very little consensus on what IPE is actually about, and what its core concerns, characteristics and contributions are or should be. A particularly incisive overview of the terrain of IPE offered by Craig Murphy and Douglas Nelson (2001) sees it as dominated by two schools which are largely separate and 'non-communicative' with each other. These two schools advance rather different responses to these questions concerning the proper identity of the field, as well as the nature of its relationship with IR. Murphy and Nelson associate the first school with 'mainstream' IPE, dominated by scholars and scholarship in the USA and epitomized by the journal *International Organization* (IO). The second they identify as the 'British' school, which in fact is a rather broader church that clusters around a British–Canadian nexus and includes scholars from Australia and some continental European countries as well as others scattered across other parts of the world. A rigid distinction between these two schools in geographical terms is rather hard to draw. Murphy and Nelson readily concede that there are a number of prominent scholars resident and working in the USA that would form part of the British school (including Murphy himself), and *vice versa*. Yet the intellectual distinction is highly apposite.

They characterize the IO school as concerning itself primarily with the overarching metatheoretical and theoretical 'great debates' – the protracted conversations (or furious disputes) between the dominant approaches to the study of IPE: between liberalism, Marxism and statism; between neorealism, neoliberal institutionalism and constructivism, and so on (Murphy and Nelson 2001: 403). One of the characteristics of IPE broadly is its essentially discursive character, certainly when compared with the sort of IR work that features in the dominant IR journal in the USA, *International Studies Quarterly*. Yet, over time, the IO school has been at increasing pains to adopt for IPE the 'language of science' and thus to lay claim to the sorts of social scientific legitimacy deemed to be demanded by the mainstream of US political science (Murphy and Nelson 2001: 404). This language of science has consisted essentially of an asserted reliance on formal methods drawn from the discipline of Economics, and above all an attachment to the methods and theories associated with rationalism.

To this we must add a further and crucial characteristic: that mainstream IPE developed in the USA as a means of addressing a set of questions of very particular relevance to the USA itself, namely the problem of hegemony and the position of the USA as the global hegemonic power. Mainstream IPE thus developed into 'a discourse constructed around a particular view of the hegemonic state' (Payne 1998: 254), and as such was marked by an innate parochialism in its concerns and its identified remit.

Meanwhile, Murphy and Nelson argue, the diverse units of the British school are pulled together by a commitment to *critical* scholarship and a considerably less pronounced anxiety about – not to say, a rejection of – the strictures of orthodox social science. British school IPE is characterized by a concern with 'direct analysis of issues in the world as they appear' (Murphy and Nelson 2001: 404), such as globalization, finance, trade, inequality, poverty, production, gender, race and so on. It is also most certainly the case that British school IPE has been somewhat less parochial in its horizons, and indeed many of the chapters in this volume find in it significant capital for the project of Globalizing IPE. Equally, however, British school IPE has tended to turn its back entirely on the sorts of mainstream IPE associated with the IO school, rejecting the particular methodological and theoretical inclinations on which the latter is, at least rhetorically, constructed. US-based and British school IPE have, in this sense, evolved largely separately from each other, identified little with one another as parts of the same enterprise, and spoken largely to their own audiences rather than to each other.

The key point, however, is that the characteristics of these two schools (and the differences between them) have been shaped in large part by their associations with the distinct intellectual progenitors of modern IPE. There is a striking correlation of the IO and British schools with, respectively, the IR-centred and political economy-centred traditions that I identified earlier. The development of IPE in the USA has been premised on the central concerns of IR (the states system and relations between states, of whatever nature), has taken as its theoretical pillars the dominant IR theories (realism, neoliberalism, Marxism, constructivism and so on), and has been associated with IR scholars who have either turned their hand to IPE or else have sat somewhere at the intersections. Frequently, these scholars continue to refer to themselves as scholars of IR even while their work epitomizes the IO school of IPE (such as Robert Keohane, Stephen Krasner and Helen Milner, among others). The critically oriented British school, conversely, has put down much firmer and more self-conscious roots in the intellectual traditions of political economy, often of the radical variety. The primary theoretical innovation to spring from these roots has been the critical IPE school – as it is often labelled, the field of 'new political economy'. The primary IPE journals associated with the British school are explicitly heterodox in their orientations. Both *New Political Economy* and RIPE have sought to associate themselves with a much wider field and audience than those to which the mainstream (IO school) of IPE is generally inclined to address itself. RIPE's basic premise in fact rejects the existence of a 'mainstream', deeming this to exist only 'in the eye of the beholder' (Blyth and Spruyt 2003: 608). *New Political Economy* has gone further to proclaim its identification with a broader *political economy* (as opposed to IPE) of the sort espoused in classical and radical social science (Gamble *et al.* 1996).

What is striking about this debate between the IO and British schools in IPE, and between 'mainstream' and 'critical' scholarship, is that it directly echoes a debate of longer standing in IR. Since Stanley Hoffman (1977) first called attention to the fact that IR was essentially and intrinsically an 'American' social science (echoed in Holsti's observation of hegemonic parochialism), there has been a sustained assault on the dominance of US social science and US conceptions of what the discipline of IR should look like, from IR scholars resident, primarily, in the UK. Steve Smith, in a series of articles (2000, 2002) and in his presidential address to the International Studies Association (ISA) in 2001, has systematically revealed the ways in which the hegemony of US IR has acted to stipulate what is, and what is not, considered to be legitimate social science, and to police the boundaries of the discipline in ways which have excluded non-rationalist, non-positivist scholarship from recognition within the mainstream (see also Waever 1998; Crawford and Jarvis 2001; Jørgensen 2003). Similar sorts of observations on US dominance of both IR and IPE were made, again in presidential addresses to the ISA and elsewhere, by Susan Strange (1995).

US intellectual hegemony in the field of IPE clearly matters. For our purposes, it matters most in its definition of what are, and are not, the core concerns for IPE, for these derive mainly from the firm association of the mainstream with US-based IR. Smith's (2002: 82) observation that, for mainstream IR, the only inequalities of concern are those of a political and military nature is certainly revealing of its influence on mainstream IPE. In contrast with the much closer focus on structural inequality invited and facilitated by the critical inclinations of the British school, mainstream IPE has retained many of the characteristics of mainstream IR in its concern primarily with issues and theories of relevance to the advanced industrialized powers. Herein lies one of the core reasons for the failure of IPE, as yet, to develop as a field of genuinely 'global' relevance, and its continuing tendency to remain empirically and theoretically focused on the advanced industrialized world.

The final point I wish to make about the intellectual influences on the development of IPE brings us out in exactly the same place. It is that, despite the vast differences between the two schools they have respectively informed and the sorts of IPE scholarship they have engendered, the evolution of both the political economy and the IR tradition have been strikingly consonant with one another in one very crucial respect. Both have been associated with the establishment of a clear – ultimately compromising – distinction between the various levels of analysis in the study of politics and political economy. In the IPE born of *both* the IR and the political economy traditions, in other words, the inclination has been strongly towards forms of analysis and theorizing in which it is deemed possible, and proper, to distinguish clearly between the national and international/global levels of analysis. The contemporary academic enterprise of studying political economy has been cast clearly on that basis, as have most understandings of the intellectual identity of IPE itself.

In this sense, the development of IPE has represented a departure from the ways in which questions about political economy were addressed and understood in the classical political economy traditions of the nineteenth century. Classical political economy crystallized around what Andrew Gamble (1995) has identified as three 'key discourses': namely, a 'practical', policy-based one preoccupied with the best means of driving and regulating wealth creation; a 'normative' one concerned with the forms the relationship between state and market should take; and a 'scientific' one which focused on how political economies actually operate. Political economy thus comprised a number of different areas of enquiry but cohered as an endeavour with a 'distinctive intellectual character' (Gamble 1995: 518). Over the 1970s and 1980s, the emergence of IPE as an identifiable disciplinary area and the further crystallization of CPE meant that this classical tradition was largely left behind in favour of a field of enquiry organized effectively by levels of analysis. That is, the field of political economy came to be divided not into a set of intrinsically interrelated 'discourses', as in its classical era, but rather into increasingly differentiated camps identified by their core preoccupation with national- or international-/global-level analysis. CPE concerns itself essentially with 'the conceptual frameworks used to understand institutional variation across nations' (Hall and Soskice 2001a: 1); IPE identifies itself as concerned with the international or global levels of analysis and, indeed, with the study of *the* international (or global) political economy, understood as separate from the national political economies to which CPE lays claim. For international political economists, Strange (1997: 182–3) claimed, the appropriate focus of attention is the 'whole system': the wood rather than the trees. We are and should be, she says, 'more interested in the webs of structural power operating throughout the world system than in comparative analysis of discrete parts of it, bounded by territorial frontiers dividing states'. Thus, national political economy fell to the comparativists, international/global political economy was claimed by international political economists, and only rarely have the twain met again in any constructive manner (Phillips 2004).

These tendencies in IPE reflect the historical evolution of IR, and indeed are reinforced in continued parallel trends in the latter. Since the publication of Kenneth Waltz's (1959) path-breaking statement of neorealist IR theory, the discipline of IR has been organized around the three levels of analysis that Waltz called forth as the foundation for his theory of international politics – the individual, the state and the international system (also Waltz 1979). Notwithstanding some of the valiant attempts that we noted earlier to afford the study of domestic politics more intrinsic representation in theories of IR, the discipline has consequently been marked by a pronounced bifurcation of the study of domestic politics and the study of international politics, according to which 'domestic society and the international system are demonstrably different' (Caporaso 1997: 564). The unfortunate consequences of this bifurcation have been increasingly recognized in IR as creating a 'great divide' which stands in urgent need of bridging, giving rise to a spate of calls for the closer integration of international politics and domestic politics across the discipline (Caporaso 1997; Clark 1998, 1999; Russett 2003). Nonetheless, IR, like IPE, has generally remained defined by its identification with a supposedly distinct, 'international' level of analysis. As with IPE, the comparative study of politics and the study of particular parts, as well as the study of domestic politics, are still generally deemed to be of limited interest or relevance in the study of international relations.

Organizing the field of IPE in this fashion has carried a number of unhappy consequences for its evolution (Phillips 2004). First, the identification and privileging of a supposedly distinctive inter-national and global level of analysis has favoured a leaning towards excessively structuralist and 'systemic' conceptions of what the central concerns of IPE are. These tendencies were illustrated clearly in Strange's concern with the wood over the trees in her understanding of the proper orientation of IPE. It is an understanding which has also pervaded the way the field has been articulated and the manner in which it has unfolded, including in the evolution of its dominant theoretical constructs. Structuralist tendencies have always been characteristic of many of the dominant theoretical frameworks in IR (particularly realism, neorealism and Marxism), and also of the key political economy traditions; indeed, a notion that 'special explanatory weight' should be granted to economic structures and processes has always constituted the distinctive method and approach associated with political economy (Gamble 1995: 517). Yet they have been exacerbated in modern IPE by the dominant contemporary preoccupation with the issue of globalization. The treatment of globalization in IPE has been strikingly diverse and the field of globalization studies often ferociously divided, but they have rested broadly on the central contention that political economy can no longer be understood entirely in national or domestic terms. The analytical and conceptual toolbox offered by state-centric social science is unequal to the task of understanding the structural reorgan-izations that globalization implies of capitalism, development, governance or politics, depending on one's chosen focus and concern. This much is surely indisputable. Yet this position has also sustained a much more precarious contention about the actual or desirable parameters of IPE itself, namely, that the nation-state is no longer a fruitful or advised focus of analysis and that, accordingly, Strange's 'discrete parts' of the world system are left appropriately to compara-tive politics, CPE and that even more marginalized of endeavours, 'area studies'.

Thus, the countries and regions – the 'trees' – that comprise the global political economy *and are fundamentally constitutive of it* have generally been ignored, such that we are left with a noticeably disembodied and decontextualized field of enquiry. Moreover, the emphasis on structure and 'system' – or, to use the language of critical

IPE, 'world order' – has generally not been accompanied by the study of the *whole* of the structure, system, or order. The 'trees' are implicitly considered to be only 'developing' countries and regions, while the 'whole system' approach is entirely consistent with, and indeed requires, a theoretical and empirical focus on the advanced industrialized powers. In other words, it is not that trees are ignored *per se*, but rather that only certain trees are deemed to be of interest, namely, those which are seen to determine the nature and form of the wood. This arises in part from IPE's particular focus on the advanced industrialized world, inherited from IR; in other part, it is facilitated by the dominant economistic approach to the study of globalization which focuses on a set of economic processes and issues that are concentrated and find particular salience in this context. It is widely recognized that the bulk of 'global' economic activity is essentially trilateral in nature and that the vortex of global economic processes is located in the triadic 'core' of North America, Europe and Japan (Zysman 1996; Hirst and Thompson 1999). The key point, however, is that these processes and their specific manifestations in these 'core' regions are frequently assumed, implicitly or otherwise, to define 'the system' in its entirety. On this basis, they are also considered to be fully amenable to generalization. In studies of the wood, in other words, the trees are generally, wrongly, considered to be all of the same type. There is limited or no recognition of the specificity of structures and processes within these core regions, nor of the problems associated with extrapolation from them, nor of the limitations of building general theories of IPE on the very distinctive foundations of these few cases.

The second unhappy consequence, related to the first, is that much of mainstream IPE has thus continued to struggle with the central metatheoretical question of the relationship between structure and agency. Most of the dominant bodies of theory in IPE, both radical and liberal, do indeed advance a clear conceptualization of this relationship, but it is generally one entirely in keeping with the central structuralist predilections of the field. This conceptualization is ultimately an unsatisfactory one in that it frequently has precluded an adequate account of agency in the study of political economy and world politics. Much of IPE has thus been charged with carrying 'excessively determinist connotations' (Payne 1998: 266), which go a long way to obviating the need for attention to the constituent parts of the structure, and to constructing strikingly apolitical analyses which afford little space to agency and agents. It is this structural determinism which, according to many IPE theorists, particularly of a critical persuasion, needs urgently to be remedied by the injection into IPE of an appropriate concern with agency. Yet it is not simply that agency and politics require greater attention; rather, the most pressing theoretical challenge for IPE revolves around understanding the relationship between structure and agency. In this respect, IPE has much in common with many other areas of the political and social sciences, which themselves continue to grapple with the question of the relationship of structure and agency and the appropriate means of theorizing it. Indeed, a range of influential frameworks have been put forward in attempts to meet this challenge, among which social constructivism (Wendt 1999) and the various versions of 'structuration' theory (Giddens 1984; Cerny 2000) would possibly be the most salient.

Yet the metatheoretical question of structure and agency is also that which fully defines the enterprise associated with new political economy (Cox 1987; Gamble 1995; Gamble *et al.* 1996). The crucial point here is that the calls from these quarters for an appropriate meshing of structure and agency are related intrinsically to the central understanding of *political economy* that is advocated as the foundation for IPE. In other words, the question of structure and agency is essentially a question about the nature of political economy; the more appropriate theorization of the structure–agency relationship and its more effective deployment in our analytical strategies are crucial for overcoming the economism and structuralism that are identified as pervading the mainstream of the field. A theoretical and analytical meshing of the study of structure with due attention to agency, therefore, is for critical IPE the surest means of recapturing what we heard Cox refer to as an 'idea of political economy' as the necessary foundation for the field and the enterprise it represents.

The third consequence, as set out in the earlier statement of the arguments that animate this volume, is that the bulk of IPE has been of only limited utility in studying the *whole* of the global political economy. The tendency to focus on only a small handful of trees is theoretically, conceptually and empirically problematic in that, in the first place, it neglects large swathes of the world outside the political economy of the advanced industrialized powers, and offers few resources for their understanding, analysis and theoretical illumination. In the second place, it is problematic in the sense that it places highly unfortunate limits on the purchase IPE offers on the study of core themes such as globalization, inequality, justice, capitalist development, regionalization, civil society and so on. Third, and as a result, mainstream IPE offers only restricted and unsatisfactory insights into the political economy of the advanced industrialized world itself, its position in the global political economy and the processes, structures and politics that are deemed to be constitutive of it.

The organization of the volume

This volume thus constitutes a first attempt to elaborate and put some flesh on the bones of these arguments, and to consider how we might go about 'globalizing' IPE. It is organized around a number of the key debates in the field, namely, those concerning globalization, governance, states, models of capitalism, finance, transnational relations, democratization and regionalism. Each of the authors has been asked to consider three specific issues in the areas of which they have expert knowledge. First, they have been asked to explore the terrain of the debate in question and the way it has unfolded, giving particular attention to the theoretical, conceptual and empirical assumptions and inclinations on which its evolution has rested. Second, they have been asked to consider the problems and limitations that these characteristics may have implied for the manner in which the debate has been conducted. Third, they have been asked to reflect upon how these limitations might be overcome, and the paths that they see as most appropriate to the task of 'globalizing' IPE in this light. I will then gather together some of the key insights and common themes from the chapters in my concluding reflections on the steps we might take towards achieving a more 'globalized' field of study.

Chapter 2

Globalization Studies in International Political Economy

Nicola Phillips*

It is often heard said that the study of globalization and the study of IPE are, to all intents and purposes, one and the same thing. This may be because, as Ben Rosamond (2003: 661) has noted, most of the claims to disciplinary distinctiveness that IPE makes are 'bound up with what are commonly understood to be the key processes and effects of globalization'. It may be because, as others have observed (Higgott 1999: 23), IPE seems to be uniquely well-placed among the social sciences to grapple with the complexities and enormity of globalization. Whether or not one would concur with a proposition that IPE developed specifically *in order to* accommodate the emerging necessity of dealing with globalization, much of the intellectual and theoretical purchase to which it lays claim is undoubtedly associated with its multidisciplinary credentials and supposed openness to the array of perspectives necessary for understanding globalization processes. In short, these arguments go, globalization put IPE on the map. It may also be, turning the argument around a little, that globalization fits neatly, and rather pleasingly, with the self-professed inclinations of many international political economists to concern themselves with the nature of the 'system', and thereby legitimates the particular project and particular territory that have been staked out for IPE. In all of these ways, globalization studies has been moulded into a form that is useful for defining the enterprise of IPE, justifying its dominant orientations and validating its claims to disciplinary relevance.

* I am grateful to Tony Payne for his helpful reactions to a draft of this chapter.

20

Whether a tendency to conceive of globalization studies as largely the same thing as IPE is well-placed is an important question, but one which there is not the space to address fully here. What matters is that it is frequently perceived to be so, and indeed that the concept of globalization permeates *all* of the various debates that currently predominate in the field. What this means is that the manner in which globalization debates are conducted provides a highly instructive lens through which to view and highlight some of the predominant characteristics of the ways in which IPE, as a field of enquiry, has been articulated. In this sense, it is significant that even globalization studies suffers from many of the shortcomings that we identify in this volume as lying at the heart of IPE itself. Indeed, we find in the literature a generous smattering of claims that, as James Mittelman (2000: 227) has put it, 'globalization is not really global': claims that the world economy is not globalized but rather internationalized or perhaps regionalized; that economic activity associated with globalization occurs primarily among the triad of advanced industrialized economies; or alternatively that large swathes of the world experience globalization as a process of marginalization from the global political economy rather than integration into it. But, at the same time as all of these observations have much to recommend them, they go only so far towards capturing the dominant inclinations and biases that characterize the field of contemporary globalization studies. We must pay close attention, in addition, to the theoretical and conceptual apparatus which has accompanied the study of the empirical manifestations of globalization and suffused the primary areas of debate within globalization studies. In this endeavour, we discover again that the origins of globalization studies and the primary defining theoretical traditions are rooted in the experiences of a very small part of the world, or, better put, in the very particular political economy that prevails among and knits together advanced industrialized economies, societies and states. The result is that, despite the quite astonishing volume of literature on globalization and the enormous intellectual and academic resources that have been invested in its study, globalization debates in IPE, on the whole, retain a very sterile quality when taken outside this particular context. By extension, they frequently offer only impoverished and limited perspectives on globalization itself.

My aim in this chapter is to take stock of the current state of globalization debates in IPE, and to consider ways in which their relevance and insight can be made more 'global' in their reach.

Given the nature of the debates in question, inevitably the discussion will intersect with many themes that will be taken up in more detail in later chapters. I have taken care to avoid excessive overlap in what follows; rather, I attempt, where it is necessary or fruitful to make incursions into the specific remits of other chapters, to do so in a way which complements those analyses. The chapter starts by offering an overview of the main contours of globalization debates in IPE. It goes on to demonstrate the ways in which globalization studies offers limited purchase on the nature and significance of globalization in the areas of the world not captured within the advanced industrialized triad, and equally to consider the ways in which these problems impoverish our understandings of globalization *generally*. This is approached through a consideration of what I identify as three of the key problem areas within globalization studies, namely, those associated with the tendency towards economism, the treatment of inequality and the treatment of agency and resistance. (The key debates concerning governance and states are addressed fully in the following two chapters.) Finally, I consider how some of these shortcomings might be ameliorated in a way which makes globalization studies more sensitive and amenable to the study of the *whole* of the global political economy, and indeed more hospitable to international political economists with a wide variety of thematic and regional interests.

The terrain of globalization debates in IPE

Theoretical backcloths

The limitations of globalization studies in IPE arise, to an important degree, from their disciplinary origins and the dominant theoretical influences that have been brought to bear on the unfolding of the debates. In an immediate sense, globalization studies in most of mainstream IPE is directly an outgrowth of the study of 'interdependence' which dominated IR around the same time as IPE was itself crystallizing as a field of study. This took its lead from parallel work on interdependence in the discipline of Economics, associated, as mentioned in the previous chapter, with the noted economist Richard Cooper (1968). His particular concern was with the ways in which effective multilateral management of the world economy was essential for the maintenance of the process of international economic integration and the achievement of the prosperity and development assumed to attach to that process. Interestingly, Cooper's work left a substantially more significant imprint on neoliberal institutionalist scholars in the US IR community than in his own discipline of Economics (Strange 1988: 20). His work was important in calling forth in IR, during the 1970s, a range of theoretical perspectives on international organization and the management of the international order, ranging from regime theory to hegemonic stability theory and the notion of interdependence itself. The character of this interdependence school, in both IR and Economics, left a significant imprint on the study of globalization in what became IPE, inasmuch as the pedigree of mainstream globalization studies and the dominant conceptualization of globalization itself were unmistakeably liberal in character.

The hallmarks of this liberal theorizing of globalization cluster around the classical separation of politics and economics (corresponding with the other binary formulations of states and markets, and public and private), a belief in the rationality and efficiency of markets and, concomitantly, a perception of a 'logic' of market integration. In the first place, mainstream liberal IPE features a pronounced economism in analyses of globalization, arising in significant part from the strong influence of neoclassical economics and, within that, the assumptions that derive from the predominant deployment of general equilibrium models (Watson 2003). Globalization is deemed to constitute a multifaceted process of accelerating market integration. It is seen to be driven by an economic logic tightly associated with technological change, and as such is seen to constitute a set of processes which are located progressively beyond the reach of political control mechanisms. Moreover, it is considered desirable that this should be the case. Simplifying a range of complex arguments, the core proposition is that markets operate most effectively when unencumbered by political constraints and state intervention, but also that globalization itself carries a range of consequences for states which themselves act to weaken the capacities of states and governments to exercise meaningful control over or intervention in global market processes. The analytical separation of politics from economics in liberal political economy in this sense facilitates the elaboration of a very particular debate about the nature and significance of globalization – one which relies on a conception of globalization as a process that occurs as a result of a logic of market integration, and which conceives of a 'governance' of globalization as oriented essentially towards the maximization of market efficiency in the interests of growth and development.

Yet we should take care not to overstate the degree of optimism that prevails in liberal accounts of globalization, nor indeed the extent of perceptions of its benign impact. Indeed, many overviews of liberal theories of globalization, particularly those with a critical purpose, tend to 'over-egg the pudding' not only in their depictions of the liberal faith in market rationality and efficiency, but also in their portrayal of the homogeneity of the liberal school. In fact, despite the common underlying propositions and theoretical principles, liberal thinking on globalization is by no means as inflexible or unified as is often assumed (Hurrell and Woods 1995: 452). Particularly in the 'early' globalization literature of the 1980s and early 1990s, there was undoubtedly a strong streak of myopic faith in market-led growth and development. Nevertheless, the bulk of the engagement of liberal scholars in debates about the impact and significance of globalization has been oriented to considering a range of problems that globalization poses and engenders, an orientation particularly evident in the literature emerging by the end of the 1990s. These problems range from the challenges of provision of public goods in a global political economy (Cerny 1995; Kaul *et al.* 1999; McGinnis 1999) to the inequalities generated by adjustment to the new economic challenges of a globalized world economy and the political tensions generated by this adjustment (Reich 1991; Bhagwati 2004), the nature of the international financial architecture necessary to deal with the exposure occasioned by financial globalization and to manage the financial crises that may result (and have resulted) therefrom (Eichengreen 1999; Kahler 2000; Stiglitz 2002), the sorts of domestic institutional and economic arrangements necessary to ensure effective implementation of reforms and safeguards (Williamson and Kuczynski 2003), and the sorts of (global) governance mechanisms that might be necessary to deal with an array of issues relating to environmental protection, the protection of labour standards, poverty alleviation and so on (Prakash and Hart 1999; Kahler and Lake 2003). By the early 2000s, the tone of liberal analysis had thus noticeably changed, to the extent that forceful neoliberal advocacy of globalization was usually couched in discussions of, as Jagdish Bhagwati (2004: 6) puts it, 'the governance that must accompany globalization once one recognizes that it is generally a benign force for social agendas'.

Yet three points are important to note in this context. The first is that the problems thrown up by globalization, and standing in need of effective governance for their alleviation, are considered to be of a transitional nature. They are seen as associated with the short-term dislocations generated by structural change and economic restructuring; consequently, political action needs to be oriented to mitigating and offsetting these transitional dislocations and their consequences. The faith in the intrinsically benign character of globalization and its *long-term* capacity to reduce or eliminate socio-economic inequality, generate sustained growth and increase the efficiency of resource allocation and distribution remains intact as the guiding normative premise and conceptual foundation. The second is that these transitional problems are all considered to be negative *externalities* associated with economic globalization, capable of being addressed effectively while the process of market integration continues unabated. Even then, these transitional externalities are seen to be by no means inevitable. Despite recognitions of what Bhagwati (2004: 33) calls 'globalization's occasional dark side', most defences of both globalization and the neoliberal policy agenda continue to attribute its failure to produce the anticipated developmental outcomes to *internal* policy failures: to incomplete implementation of reforms, corruption, economic mismanagement and so on (Williamson 2003). Hence a central contradiction in liberal accounts of the impact of globalization on growth and development: while the determinants of good economic performance are deemed to lie in the global economy and prospects for growth and development to rest on effective insertion into it, growth and development remain conceptualized as inherently national processes and failures to achieve them are almost invariably understood to stem from internal and endogenous factors (Phillips 2005).

The third issue is the recurring tension between the recognition of the need for political management of negative externalities of globalization, on the one hand, and, on the other, the project of dismantling of many of the political mechanisms that might serve such a purpose. A strong and interventionist state is deemed a significant obstacle to the realization of a benign market-led globalization and, indeed, globalization is understood to erode and 'hollow out' state capacity; conversely, the effective exercise of political authority is considered essential to the implantation of appropriate policy conditions in national economies and, moreover, to the management of the political and economic issues thrown up by engagement in a globalizing world economy (Hurrell and Woods 1995: 453). Hence, in an updated version of the 'orthodox paradox' noted as central to structural adjustment in the 1980s – in which states became responsible for the reforms that ensured their own dismantling or rolling back, and a strengthening of states was crucial for this purpose (Kahler 1990) – liberal accounts of globalization continue to struggle with the contradictions within their arguments concerning the impact of globalization and the tensions within the policy prescriptions that arise therefrom.

The second, opposing, set of theoretical perspectives in globalization studies can be grouped under a 'critical' heading. This represents a strikingly broad church of scholars. A good number (but not all) of these perspectives derive at least some of their primary theoretical influence from Marxist and neo-Marxist political economy. As in liberal thought, theoretical influences on the globalization debate from these Marxist quarters are various and varied, but feature a number of salient recurring themes. The first is the insistence that the study of globalization is, in essence, the study of global *capitalism.* What we currently refer to as 'globalization', it is contended, constitutes the latest phase in the historically continual development of capitalism *as a global system*, and the character of this latest phase can only be grasped through an understanding of the internal globalizing logics of capitalism itself and a historicized approach to its analysis. In contrast with the liberal focus on the countries and economies that are deemed collectively to be the 'engine' of globalization – a point to which we will return in greater detail shortly – the array of perspectives associated with Marxist and critical IPE seeks to understand the ways in which all of the various economies, societies and classes of the world are intrinsically drawn together in the global capitalist system. This project, as is well-known, found noted expression in the neo-Marxist scholarship associated with dependency and world systems theories, which advanced the seminal propositions that capitalism existed as a 'world system' integrating the core, semi-peripheral and peripheral parts of this system, and that development and underdevelopment existed essentially as two sides of the same coin.

Clearly, this old terminology and the understanding of development it advanced were much critiqued and substantially superseded in the ensuing decades, even while the *concepts* of both dependency and the world system have remained important in much of the critical theorizing that prevails within globalization studies (James 1997; Wallerstein 2004). But what has persisted most visibly, and found particularly helpful expression in critical theories, is that globalization, and the particular world order with which it is associated, rests fundamentally and inescapably on structures of *inequality*. These are conceived variously as relating to economic inequalities, inequalities of power, inequalities of opportunity, the establishment of the hegemony of certain social groups or classes over others, and so on. Global capitalism, in this view, relies intrinsically on a structure of exploitation and domination, both of the 'periphery' by the 'core' and of labour by capital. Inequality, immiseration and marginalization are consequently seen not as negative externalities that arise as transitional and short-term management issues; rather, they are *structural* dislocations that are *intrinsic* to the functioning of global capitalism, and the political challenges they generate are consequently very different from those perceived by liberal globalization theorists.

The second unifying contention of the array of Marxist and critical IPE perspectives is that politics and economics cannot meaningfully be separated. This was noted in the introductory chapter as a commitment to a genuine *political economy* that recovers the classical tradition associated with Marx himself, deemed to have been submerged by the growing tide of liberal and neoclassical economics. Adam Smith's understanding of capitalism as based intrinsically on markets and market relations is seen to obscure the fundamental character of capitalism as a system of *class* relations, social relations, or production relations, depending on the favoured terminology. It is true, as several have pointed out (Brenner 1977; Morton 2004), that not all Marxist or critical analyses themselves avoid this 'Smithian' bias towards market-based conceptualizations of capitalism; nevertheless, Marxist and critical political economy analyses of globalization found themselves without exception on the notion that a separation of the political and the economic is fundamentally misplaced, both theoretically and analytically. The task before us, therefore, is to construct genuine theories of 'political economy' and conceptualize on that basis the specific manifestations of the social relations that constitute contemporary globalization.

Third, and finally, Marxist and critical scholarship is united by the full recognition of the political and ideological nature of globalization, as well as the ways in which it rests fundamentally on structures and relationships of power. All of the various perspectives that I have, not unproblematically, grouped together in this category are notable for their insistence on the intrinsically political and ideological nature of contemporary globalization, and the structures of power, variously conceived, that both underpin and define it. In this sense, a liberal notion of market rationality is roundly rejected as the driving force of capitalist globalization. Many Marxist analyses lay emphasis on the logic of capitalist expansion, and hence are frequently deemed, like the strong hyperliberal thesis, to be excessively determinist and economistic. Yet a good deal of Marxist and neo-Marxist scholarship concerns itself with the power relations that are seen to be intrinsic to capitalism and, particularly in more recent IPE scholarship, with an analysis of ideas and ideology in the global political economy. This analysis of ideology and ideational power in the constitution of world order belongs most obviously to the critical IPE scholarship that seeks to draw together neo-Marxist political economy with neo-Gramscian political sociology, and owes a good deal also to the newer constructivist currents that have come to be salient within IR. Ideological power is conceived as an important dimension of broader and varied forms of structural power that define and permeate the global political economy (Cox 1987; Strange 1988), and the range of structures of power that entrench the hegemony of a single state, group of states, or transnational class structure (Gill 1990; Rupert 1995).

Yet, beyond these broad lineaments of a common perspective on globalization from Marxist and some neo-Marxist thought, it should be noted that the huge body of scholarship on globalization that would define itself as 'critical' is enormously diverse, heterogeneous and, indeed, disparate. What has been identified by James Mittelman (2004) as 'Critical Globalization Studies' is bound together only by very tenuous ties. Lacking a primary unifying theoretical influence, any common ground that could be said to unite a critical school within globalization studies is significantly more methodological than theoretical. Mittelman (2004: 219) himself notes that critical globalization scholars 'are not wedded to any single worldview' and goes on to amass an impressive list of their interests and backgrounds. The unifying theme, he suggests, is a particular approach to constructing knowledge about globalization, which rejects a positivist methodology and epistemology and seeks to expose the interests that are served by particular forms of knowledge and the purposes to which knowledge is put. Thus, in Cox's (1981: 128) famous dictum, 'theory is always for someone, for some purpose' and critical scholarly enquiry is to consider carefully 'what is being theorized... who is theorizing and from where' (Slater 1998: 646).

This post-positivist orientation has been long-established and its path well-trodden in IPE, largely as a result of the precision lent by Cox and others to the distinction between problem-solving and critical theories – the former taking the world order as given and asking a set of questions about problems *within* this world order; the latter being committed to a historicized interrogation of the nature of particular world orders, how they come into being and how emancipatory change might be achieved (Cox 1981). The question that has been addressed rather less clearly is what sort of research agenda this methodological commitment might generate. Thus Mittelman (2004: 224–5) identifies the central ingredients of a critical approach in globalization studies as being:

(a) reflexivity (an awareness of the relationship between knowledge and specific material and political conditions);
(b) historicism (an incorporation of time and history into analyses of globalization);
(c) decentring (an incorporation of perspectives on globalization from both its epicentres and its margins);
(d) crossovers (engagement with other areas of the social sciences and other branches of knowledge); and
(e) strategic transformations (consideration of counter-hegemonic projects in order to achieve a new moral order and a 'democratic globalization').

Defined in this way, a critical research agenda in globalization studies is clearly hospitable to a very broad church of scholars, who may or may not identify themselves with the neo-Marxist and neo-Gramscian theoretical influences of critical IPE. It can accommodate those who define a critical agenda as essentially a normative one, engaging with the sorts of questions that Mittelman identifies as associated with 'strategic transformations' (Falk 1995, 1999; Scholte 2000a), along with those who seek to advance a wide range of alternative theoretical agendas (such as postmodernism, postcolonialism, feminism, ecologism, constructivism and so on). At the same time, it could also surely be said that Critical Globalization Studies is often more clearly defined by what it rejects (liberalism and positivism), and that it struggles to approximate a coherent body of *thought* given the extent of the diversity it accommodates. Clearly, though, its aim is not to take up a discrete position within globalization debates, but rather to provide a methodological, conceptual and normative framework for a particular sort of analysis, and in this it has made pivotal contributions to globalization studies in IPE.

Schools of thought in globalization debates

These diverse theoretical influences on globalization studies inform the various perspectives that have been brought to bear on the study of globalization, but nevertheless do not straightforwardly underpin the various positions within the associated debates. Instead, the different 'schools of thought' in globalization debates cut across the scholarship associated with these various theoretical influences. Perhaps the most influential classification of these schools is that advanced by Held *et al.* (1999), in which they distinguish between a 'hyperglobalist', a 'sceptical' and a 'transformationalist' school. Let us then take this classification as a useful starting point.

The first, 'hyperglobalist', position refers largely to the hubris surrounding the globalization of the world economy as perceived at the start of the 1990s. Many scholars, most especially those inhabiting business schools or writing at least partly for a popular market, were moved to pronounce variously a 'first global revolution', the 'end of the nation-state', the advent of a genuinely 'borderless world', the 'end of sovereignty', the arrival of 'one world' and a 'global village', the 'death of distance', the advent of the 'information age', the construction of genuinely 'global' markets and, most (in)famously, the 'end of history' (*inter alia*, Ohmae 1990, 1995; King and Schneider 1991; Reich 1991; Camilleri and Falk 1992; Fukuyama 1992; Cairncross 1997; Greider 1997). Much of the hyperglobalist school is thus associated with hyperliberalism, both in the celebration of globalization and its benign effects, and in the analytical assumptions that underpin its central observations of the triumph of markets over states, the shift of the locus of authority in the global political economy into private (rather than public) spheres, the efficiency of market-led allocation of resources and market-led development, and the inexorability of global integration. As Held *et al.* (1999: 3–4) have been quick to point out, however, the hyperglobalist terrain has also been occupied not only by scholars working from a liberal theoretical and ideological position, who deem these processes to be desirable and beneficial, but also by rival radical scholars who consider them to represent the triumph of the oppressive and exploitative global capitalist system. In either perspective, the key to the hyperglobalist approach lies in a form of 'market triumphalism', a state of affairs to be celebrated within one ideological camp or excoriated within the other.

This over-excited commentary gave way to 'sceptical' refutations of these hyperglobalist theses. One branch of this sort of analysis sought to challenge the very notion of globalization, if this was taken to refer to the advent or existence of genuinely 'global' markets. Paul Hirst and Grahame Thompson were the most obvious proponents of this sort of argument in the mid-1990s. They contended that, in fact, the latest historical phase of globalization represented little more than an extension of a long-running process of 'internationalization', and that the contemporary world economy conformed less with the ideal type of a 'global' economy than an 'internationalized' one (Hirst and Thompson 1999). Their strategy was to marshall serious empirical evidence to dispute a series of conventional contentions about globalization, arguing, by this means, that levels of integration in the 1990s were by no means unprecedented (using the pre-1914 era of the gold standard as their point of comparison); that patterns of foreign direct investment (FDI) remained largely 'triadic' (that is, confined to North America, Europe and Japan); that transnational corporations (TNCs) did not warrant the label 'transnational'; that capital was not as mobile as generally assumed; that the world economy, and particularly the advanced industrialized economies, could not be classified as 'open' by any useful measure; and so on. Others' analyses chimed closely with these arguments, emphasizing that what we referred to as 'globalization' was in fact closer integration between only a handful of advanced industrialized countries and amenable only to an idea of 'regionalization' (Zysman 1996).

Much sceptical analysis thus sought to use these arguments to dispute the existence of globalization or to reject the primacy afforded to it. Yet it also encompassed softer versions which aimed instead simply to temper the degree of exaggeration and excitement that characterized much of the hyperglobalist literature, rather than to launch a full-scale assault on the very validity of a concept of globalization. In this vein, the aim was to dismantle some of the most misleading 'myths' about globalization – to demonstrate that globalization processes in fact were, and remain, very uneven and much more limited than often acknowledged. Such an approach led, for example, to an unpicking of exaggerated and sweeping claims about the extent of capital mobility (Watson 1999), refutations of arguments claiming the 'death' of national economies (Wade 1996a), and attempts to dispute the existence of such a thing as a 'global' corporation (Doremus *et al*. 1998).

Overlapping quite considerably with this sceptical literature, particularly in its 'softer' versions, is what Held *et al*. (1999) chose to call the 'transformationalist' school. It deems globalization to involve a 'massive shake-out of societies, economies, institutions of governance and world order', and consequently to represent new and powerful processes of transformation. At the same time, it refutes the hyperliberal notion of convergence on a 'single world system', pointing instead to the processes of 'stratification' in which 'some states, societies and communities are becoming increasingly enmeshed in the global order while others are becoming increasingly marginalized' (Held *et al.* 1999: 7–8). In this sense, the transformationalist position could be said to constitute some sort of 'middle ground' between the hyperglobalist and sceptical schools of thought. Both are deemed to miss key points about the nature of contemporary globalization: the former, its polarizing, fragmentary and fundamentally unequal effects, as well as the intrinsically uneven character of the processes associated with it; the latter, the centrality of globalizing processes which exist *alongside* the persistence of national and regional patterns of economic and political enmeshment and exchange.

A mainstay of this 'transformationalist' middle ground is an insistence on rejecting the economism of many analyses of globalization, whether of liberal or Marxist provenance. The emphasis falls on an understanding of the political character of globalization and the politics of globalization processes, typified by observations that globalization arises as a result of political decisions on the part of states and other actors, that globalization is shaped by the restructuring of politics and political power, that the nature and impact of globalization are as much political as economic in character, and that globalization is inherently contingent rather than driven by a teleological economic inevitability (*inter alia*, Amoore *et al.* 1997; Gills 1997; Clark 1999). Thus, for Randall Germain (2000b: xiv), globalization must be conceptualized as an 'endogenous social phenomenon'; for Ian Clark (1999: 52), it is to be understood intrinsically as 'a number of changes within the state, and not simply as a range of external forces set against it', and thus as representing in itself a 'state form'. Yet other variations on the theme are at pains equally to resist a 'politicism' in analyses of globalization. Colin Hay and David Marsh (1999a: 6) argue persuasively that globalization must be seen to consist of a set of processes that are incapable of being understood properly when *either* the political *or* the economic is analytically privileged. They advocate, on this basis, a drive to *re*politicize the study of globalization, in the sense that globalization debates are considered to have been depoliticized by the emphasis on the 'logic of inevitability' that has come to pervade the study of economic globalization. However, they argue usefully that the problem lies not with economism in the study of globalization – on which basis it could be argued that a good deal of analysis is effectively taking aim at the wrong target – but rather with the *particular conception* of the political that has been bequeathed to IPE (and consequently globalization studies) by realism (Hay and Marsh 1999a: 7). For them, the project thus needs to be one of not only rehabilitating but also reframing notions of 'the political' in globalization debates. That is, the study of politics involves 'the identification and interrogation of the distribution, exercise and consequences of power', politics here being understood as a *process* which 'has the potential to exist in all social locations, since all social relations can be characterized as relations of power' (Hay and Marsh 1999a: 13).

This leads directly to the second key pillar of this broad position in the debate: namely, an emphasis on agency and an appropriate meshing of structure and agency in analyses of globalization. The political dimensions of globalization, in this view, cannot be understood simply in terms of questions about the impact of globalization on states and policy-making which is generally the thrust of mainstream economistic analyses. Nor can they be limited in this way to the public realm, in a manner which overlooks the ways in which the private and the personal arenas are also intrinsic to the political landscape of agency (Elson 1998; Steans 1998, 1999) and the important new forms of 'private authority' in the global political economy (Sinclair 1994; Cutler *et al.* 1999; Hall and Biersteker 2002). Rather, globalization debates need to take adequate account not only of politics and agency, but also of the full range of political agents and arenas in which agency is exercised. In this sense, due attention needs to be afforded to the politics of resistance and engagement, phenomena such as transnational social movements and global civil society, the nature of both private and public spheres of power, and the full array of agents that are active within, affected by and fundamentally constitutive of globalization processes and world order.

Finally, the transformationalist school has been the most hospitable to an explicitly normative agenda in globalization studies. Most of this scholarship groups together as reactions to the prejudicial and negative consequences of globalization, emphasizing its 'discontents' or 'delusions' (Gray 1998; Sassen 1998), and encompasses work from various theoretical quarters on varied aspects of globalization processes relating to democracy, accountability, equality, development, justice, ethics, citizenship, participation, representation and so on (*inter alia*, Falk 1995; Pauly 1997; Armijo 1999; Hurrell and Woods 1999; Castles and Davidson 2000; McMichael 2000; Murphy 2003; Held 2004).

What becomes clear, then, is that each of these three schools of thought in globalization debates houses analysis of very different theoretical genesis and conceptual orientation. Orthodox liberal and orthodox Marxist accounts jostle with each other on the hyperglobalist terrain, generating fundamentally different interpretations of the nature and significance of contemporary globalization, but often sharing economistic and determinist streaks at the heart of their analyses. The sceptical school opens its doors to those of a critical persuasion as well as those liberals who would lament the failure of contemporary globalization to augur genuinely global markets. The transformationalist school intersects closely with the enterprise Mittelman defined as Critical Globalization Studies and derives much of its orientation from critical theoretical approaches, whether of a neo-Marxist or neo-Gramscian IPE inclination or of the many other varieties of critical approach that were outlined, necessarily briefly, above. Yet it can also accommodate neoliberal perspectives that seek to venture away from the economism that is often seen to permeate a good deal of liberal analysis in order to focus on the political character of globalization processes (Cerny 2000) and, as we have seen, normative work emanating from a wide variety of theoretical and ideological quarters. To this extent, Held *et al.* offer a fruitful starting point for thinking about the various positions within the debate about how, empirically and conceptually, we should understand globalization.

Yet it would also seem that, since the publication of their work at the end of the 1990s, a new school of thought has started to emerge in globalization studies which could be said to constitute a 'fourth wave' in the debate. Having gone through the sceptical phases of the globalization debate and a period of sustained exposure of the deleterious consequences of neoliberal globalization for development, justice and equality, this new body of scholarship is essentially concerned to defend globalization. In this sense, it seeks to move beyond *both* the excessive and myopic optimism of the hyperliberalism of the early 1990s and the excessive pessimism and fatalism of Marxist strands of the hyperglobalist school, as well as offering a riposte to those condemnations of globalization that have abounded in critical scholarship. This, indeed, is the key to this new dimension of globalization debates: the defence of globalization has been ventured from both the right (Bhagwati 2004) *and* the left (Kitching 2001). In many ways, in addition, it represents a convergence with much of the critical and normative debate about globalization, inasmuch as, *on both sides*, it is concerned with how to achieve a more socially equitable globalization and harness its potential benefits, and indeed deploy globalization itself as a means to achieving social justice. In both, a nationalist frame of reference, as well as nationalist means of achieving these goals, is roundly rejected. The emphasis across liberal, Marxist and critical analyses of globalization on what the governance of globalization can and should look like has thus, in this latest phase, been harnessed to a defence of globalization itself.

Perhaps, then, we could usefully term this emerging school of thought the 'global reformist' school. This term would distinguish it, in the way the associated analyses seek to distinguish themselves, from excessive 'hyperglobalist' excitement as well as what they would deem to be the excessively nationalist and regionalist inclinations of the sceptical school. Framed in this way, it would also cut across the strands of critical globalization studies that are concerned fundamentally with the governance of globalization and emerging forms of global governance. It may well be, with its further crystallization, that this latest phase in the debate will bring the debates about globalization, on the one hand, and global governance, on the other, into even tighter association with one another.

The 'global' reach of globalization debates

We have surveyed at some length the expansive contours of globalization debates in IPE. Yet a striking characteristic across the terrain of the debates is that they remain heavily imbued with the theoretical and conceptual traits that arise from their origins in, association with and continuing focus on the small collection of advanced industrialized economies that are seen to comprise the 'core' of the global economy. To make this claim is not unduly to dismiss the range and quality of work within globalization studies on parts of the world not encircled within the triadic core of most powerful states and economies. On the contrary, I intend to give full due to this work in identifying the existing scholarship from which a more 'global' globalization studies might take its initial lead. Rather, the argument here is that globalization studies *for the most part* remains mired theoretically, conceptually and empirically in the study of the advanced industrialized world, and that this characteristic of globalization studies has prejudicial implications for understandings of globalization itself.

In good part, the particular theoretical derivation and narrow empirical focus of globalization debates arise from their roots in liberal IR and economics. As noted in Chapter 1, the realist and liberal influences in IR have long marked it out as a study of the 'great powers', and this orientation found continued reinforcement with the scholarship on interdependence in the 1960s and 1970s. The interdependence debate, along with the parallel debates about the internationalization of the world economy in what was crystallizing as IPE, were concerned, at root, with a very particular set of international economic and political relations between a small number of advanced industrialized countries, a focus later picked up by globalization debates in IPE in their concern with the structural processes that knit those states, societies and economies together. Following their seminal statement of a notion of 'complex interdependence' in the 1970s, Robert Keohane and Joseph Nye (2000: 115) acknowledged this point explicitly in a later article:

> We used the concept of complex interdependence in the 1970s principally to describe emerging relations among pluralist democracies. Manifestly it did not characterize relations between the United States and the Soviet Union, nor did it typify the politics of the Middle East, East Asia, Africa or even parts of Latin America.

It is worth noting, in passing, their characterization of this focus: that it did not extend to the *politics* of those *regions*, rather than that it did not extend to the manner in which the countries of those regions were inserted into particular sets of international relations. The 'even' before Latin America is also rather puzzling. But those are quibbles: the point is that the concept of globalization and the theoretical influences brought to bear on it were, by Keohane and Nye's own acknowledgement, applicable to a very particular reality that prevailed among a very limited number of states and economies. Yet the interdependence school was presented, and treated, as a significant theoretical lens on international relations, not the international relations of the advanced pluralist democracies. While a concept of 'globalization' might have been expected to widen the foundations on which it was built – perhaps necessarily as the nature of the world economy changed – in fact globalization studies has remained concerned, overwhelmingly, with both the international and transnational relations between advanced industrialized states and societies, on the one hand, and, on the other, the economic processes that are seen to knit them together.

This focus weaves its way through not only dominant liberal accounts of globalization but also many of the critical approaches that we have surveyed. Indeed, the very positing of a condition of globalization arises from a set of ideas and meanings – a dominant 'discourse' about the world – which have their origins in very particular 'Western' or 'core'-based understandings of the contemporary period. There are, as critical theorists are quick to point out, a specific set of interests and political positions that are served by the entrenchment of this particular discourse as the 'common-sense' of contemporary politics. It is thus revealed how, as Colin Hay and Matthew Watson (1999: 419) put it, 'it is a distinctively Western common-sense which is being taken as the norm here; one which elevates the experience of a "shrinking world", itself shared mainly by only a limited number of (mainly) Western individuals, to the status of *the* globalisation experience'. The political uses to which this common-sense and the rhetorical device of a 'naturalized' globalization are put – and, indeed, for which they are devised – serve further to reinforce this dominant common-sense. We are bound to question the use of the term 'Western' in this context, as there are countries, regions and cultures of the world that are identified as 'Western' (such as those associated with Latin America) but would not fall within the particular political economy of globalization that we identify here as prevailing in the advanced industrialized world. Equally, there are a significant number of non-Western countries, regions and societies, particularly in Japan and some other parts of Asia, that would be included in the triadic core, the experiences of which inform and delimit the dominant conceptualizations of globalization. Perhaps, then, the argument is better formulated (although rather more clumsily) as relating to a set of dominant theoretical, conceptual and empirical assumptions emanating from the advanced industrialized world, which encompasses parts of the Western cultural and socio-political world as well as parts of its non-Western counterpart.

This is not to say, as I insisted earlier, that these sorts of understandings of globalization are unrecognized or unquestioned in the expansive debates. There are many instances of important work which seeks to reject this empirical reliance on the advanced industrialized world and challenge understandings of globalization which derive from this dominant common-sense. Nevertheless, what is striking about much of the literature which seeks to study globalization 'outside' the advanced industrialized world is that it does so in a way which, on the one hand, is oriented largely to questions about the 'impact' of globalization, as if globalization were an external force which affects the countries, regions, societies, economies and states in question, rather than to questions about their place and constitutive insertion into the globalizing world economy. This is significantly different from the way in which the political economy of globalization is understood in the context of questions deemed germane specifically to the advanced industrialized world. The parts of the world 'outside' this advanced industrialized grouping are not merely affected by globalization; they are fundamentally constitutive of it, and an understanding of their constitutive nature and role is critical to an adequate understanding of globalization processes. On the other hand, and moreover, the pronounced tendency is to seek to demonstrate how any entity not considered to fall within the political economy of the advanced industrialized world *differs* from those 'core' cases in its relationship with globalization. This is a point made by Shaun Breslin and Richard Higgott (2000: 343) concerning the study of regionalism, and pursued by Fredrik Söderbaum in his chapter in this volume, but it applies with interesting force also to globalization. In essence, the Western common-sense to which Hay and Watson alluded is taken to be the 'norm', and the aim is to expose difference, deviation and variation from it, even while the broader critical aim is often to demonstrate the weaknesses of extrapolation from that 'norm' and challenge the associated wisdom.

Why then, and in what ways, are these issues and tendencies problematic for the study of globalization in IPE? This question is best addressed through an illustrative examination of some of the most salient problems that manifest themselves in globalization debates.

Analytical economism

It has been widely noted, including in this chapter, that economism remains the hallmark of academic discourse and theorizing about globalization. In orthodox neoliberal as well as Marxist and neo-Marxist accounts, the emphasis tends to remains firmly on the material foundations of globalization processes. It is acknowledged, implicitly and explicitly, that economic globalization carries consequences for politics, culture and social life, but in the main these dimensions are considered to relate to the *impact* of globalization rather than its intrinsic character, the manner of its constitution and the nature of its central processes. Moreover, theories of globalization in IPE remain heavily influenced by neoclassical economics and the assumptions of teleological inevitability that arise therefrom. The economism of globalization studies is significant for a range of reasons. They include, as will be highlighted in this and other chapters, the neglect of a wide range of political, normative, social and cultural questions which, it is maintained in critical analyses, are crucial to an adequate understanding of globalization. Yet a further key point, which is much less frequently recognized, is that an economistic bias in analyses of globalization often leads directly to and reinforces the focus on the political economy of the advanced industrialized world. In a good deal of analysis, a focus on structural transformations in finance, production and trade signifies, in essence, a focus on the small part of the global political economy where those processes find particular salience and momentum.

In this regard, statistics abound which indicate the concentration of global economic activity among economies of the advanced industrialized triad (for overviews, see Perraton *et al*. 1997; Held *et al*. 1999; Hirst and Thompson 1999; Scholte 2000a). Undoubtedly, since the 1970s, there has been an explosion in capital flows to so-called 'emerging markets', membership of the world trading system has expanded equally significantly, liberalization and deregulation have been disseminated and pursued widely, and so on. Yet, apart from the aforementioned concentration of this activity, economistic understandings of globalization are premised on realities that pertain very particularly to the arenas of this concentration. That is, they are predominantly about the significance of large TNCs, tertiary production that is highly capital- and technology-intensive, trade structures dominated by services and tertiary products, highly integrated financial markets and so on – all characteristics specifically of advanced capitalism. Studies of investment and production focus on a small number of mammoth corporations and the associated salience of mergers and acquisitions, these corporations being drawn overwhelmingly – in the case of the very largest ones, exclusively – from the countries of the Organisation for Economic Cooperation and Development (OECD). Likewise, not only are around two-thirds of total FDI flows concentrated within the OECD, but analyses of FDI and trade also emphasize the enormously increased importance of intra-firm trade (Stopford and Strange 1991), which again is a characteristic of the small number of TNCs concentrated in the advanced industrialized world.

There is clearly some mileage, therefore, in Mittelman's afore-quoted observation that 'globalization is not really global', or the recognition that complex interdependence 'even today...is far from universal' (Keohane and Nye 2000: 116). But we do well also to enter-tain the Braudelian recognition that 'a world economy is a bounded social totality which may or may not be world-wide in scope' (Germain 2000a: 73) and consider the implications of this proposition for our understandings of globalization. In other words, to stipulate too demanding a definition of globalization, as do Hirst and Thompson in their efforts to dispute the existence of something that might qualify for the label, and to argue that globalization must be genuinely 'global' – defined as universal and worldwide – in its reach and salience, is undoubtedly to miss crucial aspects of globalization processes and their significance. In this regard, we return to the argument set out in Chapter 1 of this volume: that the study of the advanced industrialized world is in no sense invalid or invalidated by the argument that IPE is impoverished by the tendency to focus *exclusively* on it and, moreover, to construct its primary theoretical apparatus on these excessively narrow and limiting foundations.

Yet the important question concerns the extent to which these arguments get globalization studies off the hook, so to speak. At the same time as the advanced industrialized economies constitute the motor of globalization processes, other economies and regions of the world are integrated into those processes in highly complex ways and exist within the global 'system' constituted by those processes of structural (neoliberal) transformation. The argument, then, should not be (simply) that globalization is not global, but rather that a theoretical and empirical preoccupation with these 'mainstream' experiences of globalization processes offers only a limited terrain on which to think about the nature and significance of globalization. Equally, leaving to one side the experiences of globalization of huge swathes of the world as we focus on and theorize on the basis of 'a' dominant 'world economy' implies leaving to one side the extensive range of questions about the unevenness of globalization and the struc-tures of inequality which it generates or, depending on one's point of view, on which it rests. The dominant economism in globalization studies thus stipulates a very specific view of what globalization is – those processes in those parts of the world that indicate deepening market integration and constitute a condition of advanced capitalism – and defines different experiences of globalization as in some way isolated from those core processes or simply reflective of a less 'advanced' stage of capitalist development or integration into the mainstream of global economic activity. The liberal reliance on a notion of linearity and teleology in development trajectories finds clear expression in mainstream globalization debates.

In response to some of these shortcomings, there have been some enormously valuable investigations into *specific* political economies of globalization, which have straddled the various regions and countries of the world (among *many* others, Bernard and Ravenhill 1995; Breslin 2000; Hirst and Thompson 2000; Payne and Sutton 2001; Rupert 2000; Taylor and Vale 2000; Robinson 2002; Rosamond forthcoming). One strand of this body of work has been concerned to distinguish national and regional models of capitalism from one another, and identify the ways in which globalization processes are mediated by different economic, political, cultural and institutional settings. Another strand has been more associated with the aforementioned tendency to distinguish the 'developing world' from the advanced industrialized world and highlight issues of inequality, injustice and marginalization, both between these parts of the world and within the countries and regions in question. In mainstream IPE, the latter scholarship is undoubtedly considered to be of secondary interest to the analysis of advanced capitalist contexts and, as noted, is understood to refer to the *impact* of globalization rather than its fundamental constitution. Yet, while these sorts of context-specific analyses are indispensable, they tend, as noted earlier, to rest on a premise of excessive exceptionalism and to advance an analytical strategy which serves further to ring-fence the study of political economies outside that of the advanced industrialized triad.

In the endeavour of constructing a globalization studies which privileges neither excessive exceptionalism nor inappropriate generalizations and extrapolations from a highly specific, 'core'-based analysis, several lines of analysis have sought to conceptualize the ways in which various parts of the world are drawn into a globalizing world economy, and thus to advance understandings of how global capitalism operates as an integrated system. Significantly, they dispense with the idea that the world is divided into two categories of countries or regions; instead, they offer perspectives on how the divisions are social rather than territorial, how classes are increasingly transnational in character, and how traditional North–South divisions are rendered obsolete by processes of global social and economic restructuring. For instance, there has emerged some very sophisticated analysis of the processes of reconfiguration of production structures, particularly in the growing literature on global commodity chains, the issue of outsourcing and the role of export-processing zones and offshore production sites (*inter alia*, Gereffi and Korzeniewicz 1994; Gereffi 1995; Henderson *et al.* 2002; Heron 2004a, 2004b). This literature has offered particularly useful insights into the ways in which various regions and economies are integrated into global production chains on a very specific basis, most frequently as suppliers of cheap labour or raw materials for manufacturing processes. The moulding of many small economies into 'service economies', particularly in parts of the Caribbean, Central America and sub-Saharan Africa, has also received valuable attention in a similar vein (Mittelman 2000: ch. 5; Hoogvelt 2001; Pantojas-García 2001; Robinson 2002). Other critical scholarship has focused on the developmental and social consequences of TNCs' activity and the implications of labour flexibilization for workers and other groups in society (Amoore 2000, 2002; Elias 2004).

This sort of critical analysis thus seeks to expose systematically the ways in which the entrenchment of inequality constitutes the foundation of globalization – not only between countries but also between groups of people within societies. It is also consequently useful in challenging what are sometimes rather misleading analyses of the 'marginalization' or 'delinking' of various parts of the world or various parts of societies from globalization processes. The argument is that globalization has caused this delinking and marginalization, with devastating developmental consequences; nevertheless, this implies a certain reinforcement of the idea that globalized economic activity is something which prevails within the political economy of the advanced capitalist world. Mittelman (2000: 103), for example, suggests that Mozambique has been 'increasingly marginalized in a rapidly changing GDLP [global division of labour and production] and forced to remain a service economy' (see also Moore 2002). Yet it is precisely with the creation and entrenchment of a raft of service economies that the Mozambican and other economies have been *integrated* into global systems of labour and production. It would thus seem more apposite to observe a process of marginalization from any potential *benefits* of globalization, alienation from the mainstream of technology- and capital-intensive economic activity characteristic of the advanced industrialized economies, and an entrenchment of the obstacles to successful development located within the structures of the global political economy. At least in this particular respect, the process of what is customarily referred to as marginalization relates to the entrenchment of a particular mode of insertion into the global political economy, on developmentally disadvantageous and highly prejudicial terms.

In some respects, debates surrounding global finance have been somewhat better at developing this sort of 'integrated' theorization and analysis of globalization, in the sense that it has become impossible to speak of financial globalization without focusing centrally on the financial crises that have beset various parts of the 'non-core' world since the mid-1990s. Considerable attention has been devoted to the consequences of financial globalization for the emerging economies of East Asia or Latin America, the pros and cons of capital controls, and the whys and wherefores of international financial regulation. In the bulk of orthodox neoliberal accounts of financial globalization, crisis is treated as a negative externality rather than as intrinsically a part of the workings of deregulated financial markets. The blame for financial crises is laid at the door of the shortcomings of internal systems of regulation, domestic politics or particular forms of state intervention in national economies, the implication being that with prudent action by national governments financial volatility can be mitigated and controlled. More generally, while analyses of global finance do take into account areas of the world outside the advanced industrialized triad, nevertheless the focus remains only on those that are significantly integrated into global financial flows. These are concentrated in Southeast Asia and Latin America. Those that are not – such as large swathes of sub-Saharan Africa – are largely ignored. Again, little attention is afforded to the implications of this unevenness, both of levels of vulnerability and levels of integration, or to the forms of inequality that are as intrinsic to globalization as the massive flows of financial capital that pour between the advanced industrialized economies and to the major emerging markets.

It is in these ways – outlined necessarily briefly and illustratively – that an economistic bias in globalization studies determines what is of interest and what is not, and which parts of the world are of interest and which are not, in a manner which reinforces the theoretical and empirical narrowness of the bulk of globalization debates. A privileging of the material foundations of globalization over its social, political or cultural dimensions inevitably invites a selective empirical focus, on the advanced industrialized world in particular but also on those areas of the world and economic sectors that are seen to be in some way 'central' to globalization. On theoretical grounds, moreover, these economistic understandings of globalization can be challenged as misrepresenting the intrinsic character of globalization itself, and entrenching a very particular political economy as the theoretical foundation for globalization debates in IPE.

The treatment of inequality

It was noted in Chapter 1 of this volume that there is a generalized tendency in the mainstream IO school of IPE systematically to neglect issues of inequality, poverty and development. In good part, this arises from the tendency to focus exclusively on the political economy of advanced capitalism and the associated relations between advanced industrialized countries. The myriad issues relating to globalization and inequality have been subjected to far more sustained attention in critical IPE, where the relationship between globalization and inequality has been interrogated theoretically, empirically and normatively. Critical globalization debates and transformationalist perspectives have, as we saw earlier, been pivotal in calling attention to the unevenness and inequity of globalization processes and the neoliberal world order.

Yet the treatment of inequality in globalization studies, in critical as well as orthodox neoliberal accounts, continues to feature a range of shortcomings. These reflect and stem directly from the dominant tendencies in IPE and globalization studies with which we are concerned in this volume. In the first place, in this area of investigation as across the terrain of globalization debates, there remains a pronounced tendency towards a division of the world into 'North' (the advanced industrialized economies) and 'South' ('developing' economies), and to think about inequality largely in these terms. Liberal analyses retain clearly a faith in the capacity of globalization to overcome the marginalization and developmental shortcomings of the 'South'; critical analyses, including those of a Marxist orientation, generally lay the causal blame for these circumstances squarely at the door of globalization itself. Yet, in both cases, there is a tendency to conceive of inequality still in a form of 'North–South' dualism. This point can be formulated in a slightly different way as a tendency to focus on inequality *between* states – that is, to bring to bear distinctly statist understandings of inequality on the globalization debate in a manner which reflects, and in turn reinforces, the territorial and state-centric biases of both globalization studies and IPE.

The implications of these inclinations are felt primarily in two areas. The first, as Andrew Hurrell and Ngaire Woods (1995) point out, is that inequality is understood predominantly as an effect or a consequence of globalization. While they too concern themselves with inequality *between states*, they make the crucial and fruitful point that globalization itself is influenced and structured by inequality. In other words, inequality constitutes and shapes globalization as much as globalization generates and defines the contours of inequality. To illustrate, they draw attention to key inequalities in state strength, international institutions, values and norms, and non-state actors. It could be said that Hurrell and Woods tend to treat inequality primarily as a condition which influences responses to globalization rather than genuinely tracing the ways in which globalization is itself intrinsically structured by inequality. But nevertheless their argument is apposite and important in challenging the liberal focus on inequality as a negative externality associated with accelerating market integration. As a way of drawing the line of enquiry out more fully, we could again make recourse to a range of critical and neo-Marxist analyses, which highlight systematically how neoliberal globalization *depends*, by definition, on the entrenchment of a set of inequalities: between states and economies representing different modes of insertion into the global political economy and occupying different niches in the global production structure, and between social groups or classes.

The second concerns the ways in which a territorialist focus on inequality between states obscures a full understanding of the relationship between inequality and globalization, and indeed the nature of contemporary inequality itself. In overdrawing the division between the rich and powerful states and the poor and weak states, the 'rich' countries of the North become the 'haves' of globalization, and the 'poor' and 'marginalized' of the South become the 'have-nots'. The structures of inequality on which globalization rests are incapable of full understanding through these analytical lenses. As noted, it reinforces a sterile division of the world into two categories, rather than seeking to understand the ways in which the various different parts of the world constitute and are constituted by globalization processes. Moreover, it misrepresents the nature of the primary fault-lines of inequality, in that it privileges a set of territorial distinctions that are increasingly difficult to sustain and consequently of little analytical utility or conceptual insight. While inequalities do exist between national entities, a study of inequality in the context of globalization demands a recognition that the divisions are not primarily territorial or regional, but rather social in character (Robinson 2001, 2004; Hoogvelt 2001).

This insight arises from an understanding of the ways in which capitalism and neoliberalism rest fundamentally, by definition, on a particular set of social relationships. Whether or not couched in the vocabulary of Marxism, neoliberal globalization needs to be understood as entrenching and relying upon the hegemony of capital over labour and a structure of global inequality which reflects this hegemony. One influential line of analysis reflecting this theoretical contention has posited the emergence, on this basis, of transnational class structures, whether a global 'proletariat' (Coates 2000) or a transnational neoliberal elite (Cox 1983, 1987; Gill 1993; Rupert 1995; van der Pijl 1998; Sklair 2000). Put slightly differently, the structures of inequality implied by globalization need to be understood as existing *within* societies, and as much within those societies which the traditional distinction would label 'rich' and 'Northern' as in 'poor', 'Southern' ones. Just as globalization is not something which happens among the advanced industrialized economies, so inequality is not something which exists in the so-called 'developing' swathes of the world; development is, in this sense, a project common to *all* countries, societies and economies (Payne 1999, 2004, 2005).

What these perspectives offer us is, therefore, an exit route from several of the analytical quicksands that have characterized the debate. Those interested in particular 'developing' areas of the world, with tendencies to advance premises of excessive exceptionalism in their analyses of globalization, are cautioned to frame their concerns with inequality, injustice and development as stretching across the various parts of the global political economy. Those scholars, particularly in the liberal mainstream of IPE, who concern themselves narrowly with the advanced industrialized world and the globalizing tendencies of advanced capitalist processes are reminded that globalization represents a system of global reach. It is necessary, for a full under-standing of globalization itself, to give due attention to the structures which pull the various parts of the global political economy together, in differential ways, on differential terms and with differential consequences for various sections of the world's societies.

The treatment of agency and resistance

Issues of agency have been widely recognized as inadequately integrated into the mainstream of globalization studies in IPE. In both orthodox liberal perspectives and orthodox Marxist perspectives, the study of globalization has been marked by a pronounced structuralist bias which has tended strongly to relegate politics and agency to secondary importance. Yet it is not simply that issues of agency have received insufficient attention; at the same time, mainstream globalization studies lacks a clear and satisfactory theorization of the relationship between structure and agency. In this, as noted in the introductory chapter, IPE is perhaps not so different from all other areas of IR and Political Science, which also continue to struggle with the vexed structure–agency question. Indeed, it is in this question that critical IPE has found much of its value and purpose. A call for an appropriate meshing of structure and agency, in IPE generally but also in the study of globalization, has constituted one of the central theoretical propositions of critical IPE (Cox 1987; Gamble 1995; Gamble *et al.* 1996; Payne 1998). It has been founded on a concern to temper the excessive economism and structuralism of mainstream IPE, make the terrain of globalization debates more hospitable to a range of political and normative questions, and thus capture more accurately and fully the *political economy* of globalization. But there is another consequence of the failure adequately to integrate agency and politics in mainstream globalization studies, namely, that untenable biases are thus introduced which act to constrain the applicability of globalization debates outside the advanced industrialized core of the global political economy. These biases, unhappily, are also reinforced by the manner in which questions of agency and politics are treated even within many of those critical analyses which seek above all to draw due attention to them.

In a nutshell, agency remains a distinctly 'Western' – or perhaps 'Northern' – concept in globalization studies. Studies of agency and politics, for the most part, privilege as their basis those agents that are based in the advanced industrialized world and significantly integrated into structures of transnational relations. There exists a tendency thus to generalize understandings of agency that characterize specifically the advanced industrial democracies, which travel only uneasily outside these settings. To illustrate: most studies of agency in globalization studies call forth a notion of 'global civil society' and concern themselves primarily with instances of transnational activism by associated groups. In the case of studies of labour, the focus has fallen on the tentative emergence of a global labour movement or a form of labour internationalism (Stevis and Boswell 1997; O'Brien 2000a). These analyses carry enormous value in their rescuing of labour from a position of 'invisibility' within IPE, which Robert O'Brien (2000b: 89) has highlighted as a 'serious blind spot' carrying significant theoretical and empirical implications. Yet what is striking about analyses of a putative global labour movement is that, for the most part, they privilege distinctly 'Western' understandings of labour and the relationship between labour, capital and states – that is, those which are generally characteristic of advanced capitalism and post-Fordist production strategies. Moreover, the notion of a global labour movement refers almost exclusively to the interactions of a very small number of labour groups drawn overwhelmingly from OECD countries, ignoring that the politics of labour does not universally – or even predominantly – approximate this sort of 'global' articulation (Phillips 2004: 144–5). Given that the putative global labour movement is the result of interaction between *organized* labour groups, and even then only a select number of unions in key sectors, the study of labour in those countries and regions in which only a tiny proportion of the workforce is unionized is systematically neglected.

At the same time, these studies of agency are built on several assumptions concerning the political context in which they act. It is assumed that civil society organizations, whether in the global, national or transnational arenas, are active within an essentially liberal, pluralist and democratic environment, which both allows for and fosters democratic engagement and participation. Perhaps indirectly, these assumptions also facilitate the general optimism concerning civil society activity and transnational relations that prevails in liberal analyses: they are seen, on the one hand, to be signals of a vibrant democratic culture, emerging at the global level as well as existing at the national level; on the other, they are seen to embody a desirable dispersion of political authority away from national states and governments. The latter point clearly applies particularly to economic agents, such as central banks, corporations, financial institutions and so on, to which neoliberal analysis would deem a transfer of authority beneficial and useful for the maximization of market efficiency. The huge bulk of analysis focuses on agents that have a formal articulation within a political system, are recognized as in some way legitimate, and are seen to reinforce the idea of a global democratic culture of participation.

In response to some of these shortcomings, and indeed to events such as the 1999 riots in Seattle and many others since, critical IPE scholarship has sought to emphasize the politics of resistance as a key dimension of globalization. In this scholarship, as in much of that which surrounds more general notions of civil society, there is a clear recognition of the fact that not all resistance movements are progressive or legitimate (Amoore *et al.* 1997; Rupert 2000). As O'Brien notes in Chapter 7, not all of civil society qualifies for the label 'civil', and indeed there has been some attention to the illegitimate and violent nature of many elements of what has come to be conceptualized as the 'global resistance movement'. In addition, some strands of critical analysis have sought, in the spirit of injecting agency more forcefully into globalization debates, to advance a theorization of 'globalization from below' or a 'people-level globalization' (Mittelman 2000; Falk 2003). Such a project, it is argued, allows not only for a greater incorporation of 'non-Western' experiences of globalization but also for a more adequate accommodation of resistance (Mittelman 2000: 6). Yet the bulk of agency-centred analyses of resistance tend visibly to privilege the analysis of those social movements and groups which demonstrate at least a degree of 'global' or 'transnational' articulation and organization; indeed, the central concern is with the emerging transnational or 'global' forms of resistance to globalization.

What this debate reveals perhaps most forcefully, however, is a tendency to conceive of a politics of resistance to globalization as in some way a new and novel phenomenon which found its first real expression, and indeed academic attention, at the end of the 1990s in Seattle. The assertion is that what is new is the contestation of liberal capitalism itself. In the advanced industrialized world this might well be the case, and indeed the 'transnational' character of leftist mobilization is in some respects a new development. It is clearly not the case from a more 'global' perspective, from which we can identify very significant sites of resistance to liberal capitalism throughout the postwar period. Such contestation spawned theoretical innovation (dependency theory), political movements (the New International Economic Order) and alternative economic projects (import-substituting industrialization, the Asian developmental state model and so on). Similarly, the 1980s saw waves of mobilization and so-called 'IMF riots' across the developing world in opposition to the imposition of structural adjustment processes by international financial institutions (IFIs) and neoliberal governments at home and abroad.

In short, the fact that popular protest might have arrived in Seattle at the end of the 1990s does not mean that this was the first instance of genuine challenge to liberal capitalism; nor does it make the associated events 'extraordinary' (Rupert 2000: 1). Such a position can only be sustained by an inappropriately narrow focus on the politics of globalization in the advanced industrialized world, and its infiltration of the debates about agency and resistance in globalization studies reflects precisely this empirical and theoretical focus, in mainstream orthodox spheres as well as across critical ones.

Paths to a more 'global' globalization studies

Many of the avenues for ameliorating the problems identified in globalization studies were allowed to emerge in the course of the discussion. It will have become clear that, in the broadest terms, I consider a critical theoretical and analytical project to provide the most conducive platform from which to push forward a project of 'globalizing' the study of globalization in IPE. I have articulated this project as involving the rethinking of dominant frameworks in globalization studies, such that we can begin to develop a set of theoretical, conceptual and analytical lenses that are capable of capturing the nature and significance of globalization across the various parts of the world that exist within the *global* political economy of capitalism. The starting point is to abandon fully the remnants of a 'North–South'-type division of the global political economy and, moreover, the theoretical and empirical prioritization of the political economy of the advanced industrialized world in defining the disciplinary identity of IPE. The pronounced tendency to cordon off the political economy of advanced capitalism, often with the contention that it is this political economy that is (and should be) the proper concern of international political economists, is neither theoretically nor empirically viable as an approach to the analysis of globalization. Equally, it is necessary to move beyond the parallel parochialism evident in the tendencies similarly to ring-fence – geographically as well as theoretically – the study of areas outside the 'core' of the global political economy by those with particular regional interests. The study of globalization needs also to break the strictures of economism and structuralism, and engage instead with the socio-political nature of globalization processes and their significance, as well as the core issue of the relationship between structure and agency.

It has emerged in the course of the discussion that the readiest resources for undertaking such a task are to be found in areas of critical IPE and Critical Globalization Studies. In particular, I have found significant value in those analyses of globalization which seek, through various theoretical lenses, to conceive of globalization as a system which relies on differential modes of insertion of economies, states, regions and societies into structures of production, finance and trade. Globalization in this perspective is conceived equally to rest on the entrenchment of a social hierarchy of inequality. Varied insights into the social divisions implied by globalization have been tremendously valuable in challenging the ring-fencing exercises noted above, and developing more adequate understandings of the intrinsically socio-political nature of globalization processes themselves. They also contribute to a rejection of the narrow economistic focus on the advanced industrialized world and the processes peculiar to the political economy which defines it. In related ways, the critical focus on the metatheoretical question of structure and agency offers a valuable corrective to the limitations imposed by excessive structuralism in mainstream IPE. I have also emphasized the value of calls for a 'repoliticization' of IPE and the exhortations from critical IPE to bring to bear more fruitfully a genuine *political economy* approach to globalization studies.

Yet this does not mean that critical IPE has been immune from many of the criticisms that have been levelled at the orthodox mainstream; indeed, I have been at pains to demonstrate the ways in which the limitations that concern us stretch across the various theoretical traditions in globalization studies. Critical analyses of globalization exhibit similar tendencies towards a privileging of assumptions derived from the political economy and the experiences of the advanced industrialized world, and frequently remain wedded to the 'common-sense' that emerges therefrom as their analytical point of departure. Nor does this mean, crucially, that liberal or orthodox IPE has been rejected in its entirety. Indeed, it has been noted how recent currents in globalization debates – which I labelled a 'global reformist' school – seem to feature a certain convergence of the concerns that are animating both liberal and radical or critical globalization scholars. While the theoretical lenses and guiding normative premises remain entirely divergent, nevertheless there is a sense in which the debate is crystallizing around a set of common questions relating to the governance of globalization. I have argued, nonetheless, that it is mainstream, orthodox IPE that is most guilty of, responsible for, and indeed constrained by many of the biases that limit the 'global' relevance and insight of globalization debates.

The specific avenues for approaching the project of 'globalizing' globalization studies, then, can be pulled together into four key points.

First, the study of globalization cannot be defined merely as the study of advanced capitalism. Instead, it needs to be formulated as the study of the evolution of capitalism, both in its articulation as a global system and in its diverse national and regional forms. Understanding the former requires a conceptualization of the way in which the system of global capitalism rests on the insertion of its constituent economies, economic sectors, societies and social groups into the structures of the global political economy, on highly unequal terms and in highly differentiated ways. Moving in this way beyond a myopic focus on the political economy of advanced capitalism opens up considerably more theoretical and conceptual space for addressing the political economy of inequality that accompanies and underpins neoliberal globalization processes. These issues have been noted by Craig Murphy and Douglas Nelson (2001: 404) to have preoccupied scholars working within the 'British school' of IPE far more than those working within the orthodox mainstream. Their neglect in the latter has impoverished the 'global' relevance and utility of the perspectives on globalization advanced therein.

Understanding national capitalist systems, in turn, involves a more constructive engagement with CPE and, as Mark Beeson and Stephen Bell note in Chapter 5, a much closer integration of comparative and international perspectives on models of capitalism. Yet the 'models of capitalism' debate remains fascinated by the three models drawn from the points of the advanced industrialized triad, and also retains an excessive nationalist bias which has prevented an adequate analysis of the regional and transnational articulation of capitalist systems (Phillips 2004). There is thus considerable space within globalization studies (as well as in the models of capitalism debate more specifically) for much wider comparative work on the evolution of capitalism, and its various forms of spatial organization, in a globalizing world economy.

Second, the task of rectifying some of the theoretical and empirical biases in globalization studies, and moving towards a theoretical and conceptual apparatus of more 'global' relevance, would be assisted considerably by a reformulation of the ways in which questions of development and inequality are approached. We noted just now that questions about inequality have been insufficiently integrated into the concerns of mainstream globalization studies. But the issue runs deeper, in the sense that these questions, when they have been asked, have generally been framed as questions about the 'developing' world. The strategy, then, involves a number of steps: a refocusing of attention on the ways in which different parts of the world are inserted into a *global* political economy of globalization; an insertion into that conceptualization of the social dimensions of globalization, the ways in which globalization creates and entrenches social divisions which transcend traditional territorial divisions, and the social hierarchy of inequality on which globalization depends; and, on this basis, a reformulation of questions of inequality and development as affecting not the 'developing world' but all countries and societies. In other words, investigations into the relationship between globalization and inequality, or globalization and development, are *not* specialized investigations into the developing world and properly left to area studies scholars. Rather they are relevant, as Payne has suggested, to all of the societies and economies that comprise the global political economy. Questions of development and inequality, framed in this manner, can thus be moved to a position of much greater salience and centrality in the defining concerns of globalization debates.

Third, considerable and valiant strides have already been taken in critical IPE to 'repoliticize' the study of globalization and afford greater privilege to agency in the dominant analytical and theoretical constructs. The critical concern with possibilities for counter-hegemony and emancipatory challenge to the neoliberal world order has usefully moved the study of agency and resistance to pride of place in globalization studies. The tendency in much of mainstream globalization studies to conceive of the politics of globalization as relating mainly to the globalization–state relationship has also been convincingly challenged by critical perspectives. I have argued, nonetheless, that many of these analyses remain mired in particular understandings of agency and politics that derive primarily from the forms that prevail in the advanced industrialized world. Moreover, these understandings invite a particular theorization of the relationship between structure and agency that is limiting and unsatisfactory when addressing the forms of agency and the nature of politics outside the political arenas associated with these understandings. The task, once we have accepted that structure and agency require an appropriate meshing and sought to theorize this relationship appropriately, is to investigate the ways in which different forms of agency exist within different relationships with structures. In other words, empirically the structure–agency relationship is not singular but rather multiple and varied, and a widening of globalization debates would contribute significantly to illuminating and expanding our understandings of agency and politics on this basis.

Finally, the issue of power lies at the heart of the study of globalization, and indeed of attempts to increase the 'global' relevance and insight of globalization debates. Despite the supposed centrality of these questions in IPE, globalization debates have tended, as Mittelman (2000: 5) has observed, to remain strikingly 'silent about hierarchies of power' and, indeed, about the different forms that power takes in different parts of the world. The mainstream tendencies to 'naturalize' globalization, as Hay and Watson (1999: 421) have argued, have similarly obscured 'the embedding of certain forms of privilege', both within societies and between them. The manifold dimensions and manifestations of power in the global political economy are thus central to a vast range of questions about the nature of globalization itself, the governance of globalization, inequality and injustice, social organization, class relations, the global politics of development and so on. Locating power at the centre of globalization debates, of both mainstream and critical persuasions, is pivotal in the task of broadening the study of globalization beyond its limiting and disabling preoccupation with the political economy of the advanced industrialized world.

Chapter 3

The Study of Governance in a Global Political Economy

Anthony Payne*

Governance has lately become one of the most widely deployed concepts in the field of IPE. It is probably second only to globalization in use and abuse. Yet, for all its undoubted fashionableness, it has rarely been authoritatively defined and unquestionably remains inadequately understood as an aspect of the politics of the global political economy. Indeed, Marie-Claude Smouts (1998: 81) has gone so far as to suggest that 'the more seriously the notion of governance is taken, the less content it has'. This is unnecessarily pessimistic, although she was right to note that, like all social science concepts, governance has both 'limitations and a high mythification potential'. With that warning in mind, this chapter has three aims: first, to sketch a portrait of the recent study of governance in – and around – IPE; second, to expose the narrowness of some of the theoretical and conceptual assumptions which have underpinned the various different sub-plots of the governance debate; and, third, to set out the beginnings, at least, of that broader analysis of the present and future governance of the *whole* of the global political economy called for by the editor of this volume in her bid to advance the 'globalization' of IPE itself.

I suggest that a useful initial organizing tool is to distinguish in the literature between what we might call 'projects of governance' and 'theories of governance'. As we shall see, such a distinction is hardly watertight, but making this analytical move at the outset does have the merit of clearing away quite a lot of potential confusion at

* I should like to thank several colleagues in the Department of Politics at the University of Sheffield, as well as, of course, the editor of this volume, for the many invaluable suggestions they made with a view to improving the first draft of this chapter.

a relatively early stage, as well as clarifying immediately several aspects of the politics which inevitably attach to all discussions of governance.

Projects of governance

Much purported discussion of governance is actually designed to advance what are conscious attempts to organize systems of governance in particular economic and political ways. These can be seen – and should be thought about – as distinctive, ideological projects fashioned and pursued by identifiable institutions and interests. The purpose of these literatures is not to analyse the world, but rather to change it. As such, it is a mistake (which many make) to allow them to become too closely entangled with the academic endeavour of analysing and theorizing the changing ways in which we are governed in reality. Three such ideological projects related to governance stand out because of the enormous attention they have received and the political appeal they have generated. Each will be briefly described.

Entrepreneurial governance

In an influential book published in 1992, two American writers, David Osborne and Ted Gaebler, sought to 'reinvent' government for the last decade of the twentieth century. The central theme of their argument was that, for too long, government as an activity had focused on extending control over all aspects of social and economic life, and that this had led to excessive bureaucratic growth, inertia and inefficiency. They claimed that the role of government should be to 'steer, rather than row' and accordingly they condemned the traditional Weberian state as a bankrupt tool designed only for rowing. The old model should instead by replaced by what they called 'entrepreneurial government', based on the following ten principles:

Entrepreneurial governments promote *competition* between service providers. They *empower* citizens by pushing control out of the bureaucracy, into the community. They measure the performance of their agencies, focusing not on inputs but on *outcomes*. They are driven by their goals – by their *missions* – not by their rules and regulations. They redefine their clients as *customers* and offer them choices…They *prevent* problems before they emerge, rather than simply offering services afterwards. They put their energies into *earning* money, not simply spending it. They *decentralize* authority, embracing participatory management. They prefer *market* mechanisms to bureaucratic mechanisms. And they focus not simply on providing public services, but on *catalyzing* all sectors – public, private and voluntary – into action to solve their community's problems. (Osborne and Gaebler 1992: 19–20; emphasis in original)

The essence of the idea of entrepreneurial government was thus that the state should radically withdraw from direct intervention in social and economic life and the associated delivery of services (less rowing) and concentrate instead on overall policy management (more steering). Osborne and Gaebler described this as entrepreneurial government, rather than entrepreneurial governance, but they were deliberately setting out to emphasize control rather than command as the key task of government and, in so doing, they in effect made the important conceptual shift from (old-style) government to (new-style) governance.

In practice, what this was deemed to require was the idealized package of ideas about the redefined role of government which came to be known as the New Public Management (NPM) and which dominated the state reform agenda of most Western liberal democratic countries during the 1980s and 1990s. All the clichés that became so familiar to citizens of these societies in those years – from 'contracting out' to competitive tendering, performance indicators, 'hands-on management' and the like – were embraced within Osborne and Gaebler's formulation of how governance ought to be conducted. As already indicated, the ideological colours of such a programme of reform are not difficult to discern. As Christopher Hood (1991: 5) has argued, NPM was 'a marriage of two different streams of ideas' – one partner being the 'new institutional economics' derived from public choice, transactions cost and principal–agent theory (Arrow 1963; Niskanen 1971), the other being the then latest in 'business-type' management theory for the public sector (Pollitt 1990). One can debate whether these partners were fully compatible ideologically, for, as Hood (1991: 6) again deftly put it, '"free to manage" is a rather different slogan from "free to choose"'. But slogans are what they were and the point is that much discussion of governance in the

OECD world during these two decades was actually advocacy of a predominantly neoliberal recipe for reducing the scope of the state within Western liberal democratic political economies. Only a more muted, social democratic strand in the debate saw that making government more effective was potentially a way of restoring the legitimacy of state intervention in economic and social matters.

Good governance

The World Bank has been responsible for the invention of the associated notion of 'good governance' which has been the means by which much the same thrust has been transmitted to the so-called developing world. The origins of the term's emergence lay in the Bank's realization around the end of the 1980s that structural adjustment of the macroeconomic policies of developing countries along market lines was not enough of itself to ensure rapid growth and development. The transformation had to be even more funda-mental. Specifically, 'getting the prices right' had to be accompanied by 'getting the politics right'. The Bank turned accordingly to the concept of governance, breaking it down into five elements: public sector management; accountability; the legal framework; transparency and information; and civil society (World Bank 1992). Crucially, however, in its vision these aspects of governance had to be assembled in a prescribed fashion. As David Williams (1996: 163) summarized the desired mix:

> The state being held accountable by civil society is necessary for effective public sector management, the activities of the state must be transparent for this to occur, information is necessary both for the accountability of the state, and for the state to carry out its development functions successfully ... The new model of the state requires both a smaller state and one which functions more effectively, providing an enabling environment for private sector growth and poverty reduction.

From these beginnings the imperative of good governance spread quickly throughout the whole international donor community. It opened up space for a new chapter of conditionalities which broke through past inhibitions about interfering in 'politics' and substantially stretched the terrain upon which Western governments and their agencies could plausibly seek to intervene in the affairs of developing countries. All in all, deployment of the concept of good governance has enabled the World Bank and other donors, including key Western states, to acquire an unprecedented capacity to shape the strategic direction of large parts of the world, especially within Africa and to a considerable extent also in Latin America and the Caribbean.

The key to this achievement was the determined advancement of an apparently apolitical notion of governance which, as Martin Doornbos (2001: 98) has pointed out, was 'somehow broad enough to comprise public management as well as political dimensions, while at the same time vague enough to allow some discretion and flexibility in interpretation as to what "good" governance would or would not condone'. His emphasis on the idea of condonement was not accidental since it has manifestly been the World Bank, above all, which has controlled the give-and-take of donor politics. At the same time the claim to apoliticism must also be severely questioned, since once again the character of the overall vision offered by the Bank is recognizably a Western liberal one (Williams and Young 1994). The fact that its functionaries pay lip service to the need to build on the 'indigenous' and to reflect 'cultural values' (Dia 1991) does not for a moment obscure this. As Williams has put it in a telling turn of phrase, it might even be possible to say that governance, in this usage, is 'part Hobbes (disciplining state), part Locke, Smith and de Tocqueville (civil society, property rights, legal system), with a healthy dose of contemporary management theory thrown in (efficiency, quality control, auditing)' (Williams 1996: 170). The mix of elements is again what is striking, for the irony of the 'good governance' programme is that it legitimizes extensive Western state intervention to bring about limited, non-interventionist liberal states in the non-Western world.

Global governance

A third ideological project in the field of governance gathers around calls for more or better or renewed 'global governance'. Again these emerged during the 1990s largely as a consequence of the combination of the ending of the Cold War, the trend towards globalization and the apparent forging of a global civil society. What they generally seek under this rubric is reform and consequential strengthening of the various world organizations, principally the

United Nations (UN) and/or the so-called Bretton Woods institutions by which is meant principally the World Bank and the International Monetary Fund (IMF). The forerunner within this movement was the self-named Commission on Global Governance, a group of senior politicians and public figures brought together in the early 1990s by the former Swedish prime minister Ingvar Carlsson and Shridath Ramphal, former Secretary General of the Commonwealth, with the explicit purpose of suggesting ways of consolidating the presumed revival of the UN in the aftermath of the Gulf War. Its preference for the notion of governance and its particular usage of the term was interesting and revealing. According to the Commission (1995: 2–3):

> Governance is the sum of the many ways individuals and institutions, public and private, manage their common affairs. It is a continuing process through which conflicting or diverse interests can be accommodated and cooperative action may be taken. It includes formal institutions and regimes empowered to enforce compliance, as well as informal arrangements that people and institutions either have agreed to or perceive to be in their interest... At the global level, governance has been viewed primarily as inter-governmental relationships, but it must now be understood as also involving non-governmental organizations, citizens' movements, multinational corporations and the global market. Interacting with these are global mass media of dramatically enlarged influence.

The Commission thus sought to shift attention away from the specificities of the particular powers of international organizations *per se* and reframe global governance as a process founded on accommodation and continual interaction between public and private actors. To this extent its thinking was wholly in keeping with the liberal view of political action discerned in the preceding entrepreneurial and good governance visions. The difference was that the international system of states proved to be a harder nut to crack and the many (broadly social democratic) reform proposals of the Commission generally fell by the wayside.

This has not, however, meant that other bodies and groups have not followed in its wake. A persistent theme in such discussions has been the need to reinstate the liberal international economic order initially put in place at Bretton Woods (Haq *et al.* 1995). This was pursued again with renewed urgency after the Asian financial crisis of 1997–8 (Michie and Grieve Smith 1999). The latest such prospectus has been offered up, with considerable fanfare, by a group of economists linked to the United Nations Development Programme (UNDP). Their organizing insight is that 'today's turmoil reveals a serious underprovision of global public goods' (Kaul *et al.* 1999: xxi), understood in conventional terms as goods that are unlikely to be provided by unregulated markets. The way that the problem is posed inevitably gives away the means by which the UNDP believes it can be solved. It is true, as Craig Murphy (2000: 790) concedes, that 'many of the world's privileged would certainly deny that distributive justice, peace in far away lands, or the protection of the cultural property of the poor [all of which are embraced within the putative UNDP programme] constitute "public goods"'. For all that, the intellectual origins of the theory of public goods go back, as is well-known, to Samuelson (1954), Hardin (1968), Olson (1971) and Kindleberger (1986) and, as a consequence, the UNDP study is irredeemably cast within the framework of liberal economics. Although, to be fair, much advocacy of this sort does lie more at the social democratic end of the spectrum, the truth is that global governance as a programme still falls within the broad embrace of liberal ideology. It also usually lacks a sharp grasp of politics – in particular, the political obstacles that impede its vision – which tends to tar the whole debate with a somewhat amorphous quality. This is perhaps what led Groom and Powell (1994: 81) to conclude some while ago that global governance could be aptly described as 'a theme in need of a focus'.

The argument

The argument that is being made by means of this rehearsal of the main claims of these three diverse, but manifestly connected, projects of governance can swiftly be restated. Notwithstanding their prominence in the mass of writing about governance, these literatures do not constitute the most likely terrain on which we can expect to find the tools of analysis of governance that we seek for a global IPE. The reason is simple: they do not aspire to provide such analytical sustenance. They exist for a different purpose. What these projects represent in their various ways are different strands of the politics of Western liberalism in the 1980s and 1990s, each mapping in its discourse the ongoing tension between a neoliberalism that confidently asserted the limitations of state action and a social democracy that sought to defend and rethink the case for an active state. As such, they should in fact be the very *focus* of a critical IPE of governance, highlighted and exposed for their bounded intellectual and political foundations. We shall therefore return to all of these notions of 'adjectival' governance in the third section of the chapter which aspires to build up the basic elements of an analysis of the way that the inhabitants of *all* countries – including those not living according to the tenets of Western liberalism, as well as the many who are and the many more who are being deeply influenced by its expansionary impulses – are now *actually being governed* under conditions of globalization. In that context entrepreneurial governance, good governance and global governance all need to be recast as important, ongoing political projects, which are themselves parts of the contemporary realities of governance we need to explain.

Theories of governance

The rest of the scholarly literature on governance does at least endeavour to understand and explain practices of governance. That is the sense in which we can describe these writings as theories of governance (Stoker 1998). They endeavour in the main to establish whether what one might call 'actually existing governance' in the 1980s and 1990s is new and, if so, what is new about it and where the 'newness' came from. In other words, the primary goal of this body of work has been to analyse the contemporary realities of governance, not to advance particular programmes of change. Two literatures stand out – both of them in their ways relatively well-developed – representing different (and hitherto largely unrelated) sub-fields of social science, namely, public policy and IR. As will be seen, they have something to offer analytically, which IPE can fruitfully embrace, but they also have significant limitations which mean that they eventually run out of steam as bodies of theory of genuinely 'global' relevance.

Public policy and governance

As a sub-field public policy has lately devoted itself to discussion of what it calls the 'new governance'. Yet it has, for the most part, failed to establish with any precision what it means by the term. It has also found it difficult to stay clear of proselytizing texts, such as that by Osborne and Gaebler, with the consequence that there has often been an uneasy overlap with arguments calling for – as opposed to dissecting – the NPM package. Moreover, there have emerged different schools of governance analysis within different OECD countries, principally Germany, the Netherlands, the USA and the UK. In sum, it is far from easy to sort out what is being said here that is consistent, original and helpful.

The work of Rod Rhodes in the UK is as good as any to take as illustrative. He is clear that 'current usage does not treat governance as a synonym for government'. Rather, 'governance signifies a change in the meaning of government, referring to a *new* process of governing; or a *changed* condition of ordered rule; or the *new* method by which society is governed' (Rhodes 1996: 652–3; emphasis in the original). But how exactly is it to be defined? Rhodes offers what he calls a stipulative definition – governance as 'self-organizing, intergovernmental networks' (Rhodes 1996: 660) – which he says he derives from three other conventional usages within public policy. These are, first, the familiar notion of governance as the operation of a minimal state; second, the more recondite image of governance as a socio-cybernetic system as developed by Jan Kooiman (1993) whereby governance can be seen as 'the pattern or structure that emerges in a socio-political system as "common" result or outcome of the interacting intervention efforts of all involved actors' (Kooiman 1993: 258); and, third, the view of governance as the management of self-organizing networks comprised of any permutation of government, private and voluntary sectors. On these bases, Rhodes (1996: 660) lists the shared characteristics of governance as follows:

(1) Interdependence between organizations. Governance is broader than government, covering non-state actors. Changing the boundaries of the state meant that the boundaries between public, private and voluntary sectors became shifting and opaque.
(2) Continuing interactions between network members, caused by the need to exchange resources and negotiate shared purposes.
(3) Game-like interactions, rooted in trust and regulated by rules of the game negotiated and agreed by network participants.
(4) A significant degree of autonomy from the state. Networks are not accountable to the state; they are self-organizing. Although the state does not occupy a privileged, sovereign position, it can indirectly and imperfectly steer networks.

The model of governance to which Rhodes is drawing attention is clear enough, at least in broad terms, and he and several other British scholars have worked hard to establish the extent to which the UK system of governance (their main preoccupation) now matches up to this description.

As indicated, Rhodes is but one of a number of leading theorists of governance within public policy. We could just as easily have examined the contributions of Renate Mayntz (1993) in Germany or Walter Kickert (1997) in the Netherlands or Guy Peters (2000) in the United States or Jon Pierre (2000) in Sweden. Although different specific definitions of governance would have emerged, the over-arching message would have been broadly the same. This has been well-summarized in a new survey of the field jointly authored by David Richards and Martin Smith who claim that, at the end of the day,

> Governance is a descriptive label that is used to highlight the changing nature of the policy process in the late twentieth century. In particular, it sensitises us to the ever increasing variety of terrains and actors involved in the making of public policy. Thus, governance demands that we consider all the actors and locations beyond 'the core executive' involved in the policy making process. (Richards and Smith 2002: 15)

In other words, the key appeal of the notion of governance to the public policy field is its capacity, unlike the narrower concept of government, to embrace the whole range of institutions, actors and relationships now thought to be involved in the process of governing. All public policy theorists of governance thus draw attention to what they see as the fragmentation of the traditional centralized state apparatus in recent years. They emphasize a blurring of the distinction once drawn between state and civil society and attest to the consequent new complexity and greater pluralism of policy-making in all its spheres and dimensions.

These are all useful insights which can and should be taken up by IPE. But they only carry us so far. For present purposes, the public policy approach to governance is limited by three failings. First, it is focused almost exclusively on the developed, industrial, largely OECD world within which it is presumed that the relevant story is one of a shift of late from government to governance. Most public policy analysts of this genre do not even try to conceive of the character of governance or even government in the completely different forms of state and associated political system widely to be found, say, in Asia or Africa. Whether the favoured classification is 'developmental state', 'presidentialism', 'patrimonialism', 'kleptocracy' or even 'collapsed state' does not matter, for all signal that the political context is decidedly not that of 'uncorrupt' Western liberal democracy. Admittedly, a long-standing academic tradition of 'development administration' has tried to grapple with these realities (Riggs 1964; Schaffer 1969; Siffin 1976; Dwivedi and Nef 1982), but it only rarely connects to the new theoretical concerns of mainstream public policy analysts (for an exception, see Turner and Hulme 1997). Second, the dominant approach too often seems willing to accept the thrust towards neoliberalism – which was the ascendant, but not the exclusive, ideological trend of the 1980s and 1990s – as the given and unchallengeable context within which the supposed shift to governance has taken place. It does not question the political source of the changes it seeks to map, either as a matter of routine or reflex, although in fairness some honourable exceptions should be noted (Gamble 2000; Bache 2001).

Third, and most importantly from our perspective, public policy does not really succeed in explaining why what is identified as governance is expanding. It does not do this principally because it tends to miss out perhaps the most significant level of analysis. This point was made with particular effectiveness by Philip Cerny in a rejoinder to the article within which Rod Rhodes initially set out his theory of the new governance. Cerny (1997a: 1) alleged that, with the exception of two brief citations *en passant* of a leading international relations theorist and a fleeting reference to the role of the European Union (EU), Rhodes had ignored 'a range of complex processes of globalization, transnationalization and internationalization'. He went on to argue that the rediscovery of governance came about 'not because "self-organizing, interorganizational networks" have expanded through a wholesale or ineluctable process but because the wider (global) structural context has itself changed' (Cerny 1997a: 2) in ways that have been much debated in IPE and indeed elsewhere. His point is generally well-taken and means that, in its handling of the new governance, public policy has sometimes 'missed the wood for the trees' (Cerny 1997a: 20). Again, in the spirit of fairness it should be said that this disregard of varying levels of analysis does not apply to public policy analysis across the board, those working on policy-making within the EU constituting an obvious and important exception.

International Relations and governance

IR as a sub-field fell upon the concept of governance at about the same time as public policy. The beginning of the debate can be traced explicitly to the publication in the early 1990s of *Governance without Government: Order and Change in World Politics*, jointly edited by James Rosenau and Ernst-Otto Czempiel (1992). Prior to this moment most attempts to understand 'government at the global level' had been made via rationalist studies of regime formation inspired by the work of Robert Keohane (1984). The central insight of this school was that, over time, states could learn to cooperate in non-zero-sum ways if they formed intergovernmental institutions, or regimes, in particular policy areas. Rosenau, who wrote the extended introductory chapter in *Governance without Government*, was clearly influenced by regime theorizing, although in this work he sought boldly and successfully to move the discussion forward. He set out the idea of governance as a set of 'regulatory mechanisms in a sphere of activity which function effectively even though they are not endowed with formal authority' (Rosenau 1992: 5). Governance thus differs from government in that 'it refers to activities backed by shared goals that may or may not derive from legal and formally prescribed responsibilities and that do not necessarily rely on police powers to overcome defiance and attain compliance'. It is, in other words, 'a more encompassing phenomenon' which 'embraces governmental institutions, but...also subsumes informal, non-governmental mechanisms' (Rosenau 1992: 4). Here lies the similarity with the conventional notion of regimes, except that regimes have generally been seen to exist in certain defined issue areas (Krasner 1983) and governance was used here by Rosenau in a manner which clearly tied the concept to the whole global order. In a later article in the first issue of the journal *Global Governance,* Rosenau returned to these questions, defining global governance as 'systems of rule at all levels of human activity...in which the pursuit of goals through the exercise of control has transnational repercussions' (Rosenau 1995: 13). Finally, by the time this piece had been edited to reappear in his book, *Along the Domestic–Foreign Frontier*, the ultimate Rosenau definition of governance had been refined as 'spheres of authority...at all levels of human activity...that amount to systems of rule in which goals are pursued through the exercise of control' (Rosenau 1997: 145).

Many thought, and no doubt still think, that this was a very loose way of conceiving of the concept. In a direct response to Rosenau,

Lawrence Finkelstein (1995) suggested that it was hard to know what was excluded by such a formulation. He acknowledged, for example, that international crime syndicates, which Rosenau had included in his wide-ranging survey of existing agents of governance, were a factor to be dealt with in IR, only then to ask caustically:

> Does it really clarify matters, however, or facilitate the research enterprise, to toss them in a hopper along with states, intergovernmental organizations, nongovernmental organizations, and Moody's Investor's Service? (Finkelstein 1995: 368)

Finkelstein's own approach was to insist that governance was 'an activity', not a system; it should be 'concerned with purposive acts, not tacit arrangements' (Finkelstein 1995: 4, 5). This was plausible, if no less vague than Rosenau, but only led in the end to the unoriginal claim that 'global governance is doing internationally what governments do at home' (Finkelstein 1995: 5). The main problem with this line of analysis, as Marie-Claude Smouts (1998: 82) was quick to point out, is that it 'overlaps with multilateralism', which has served for a long while as a perfectly adequate way of coming to terms with what is done by international organizations (Ruggie 1983).

In fact, the appeal of Rosenau's working approach to governance was precisely its breadth. It was not at all, as alleged, a matter of bringing together different types of actors in some great 'spaghetti bowl' (another of Finkelstein's metaphors), but rather of sensitizing analysts of the changing patterns of post-Cold War international relations to the extent of the mix of actors – governmental and non-governmental, public and private, legitimate and illegitimate – which had come to participate in the shaping of systems of global rule. Rosenau captured this very effectively. The problem with his analysis was rather different: it was, as Murphy (2000: 796) has noted, that he was 'less capable of explaining why so much of this creative movement in world politics seems to have added up to the supremacy of the neoliberal agenda both within and across states'. To some extent this lacuna can be filled within IR theory by the incorporation of some of the insights of the constructivist school which has been so prominent of late, especially amongst American scholars (Finnemore 1996b; Ruggie 1998; Wendt 1999). In the vision of constructivists, all actors within international relations have the capacity in their exchanges to influence each other's understanding of their own interests, which means that the norms of those exchanges, the manner of the communication, matters. To follow Murphy again (2000: 797), in the contemporary era 'liberal norms…exert power not due to their inherent validity or rightness, but because they are regularly enacted within certain realms, because some international actors have become convinced of their rightness and validity'. Rosenau, plus a dash of constructivism, might therefore be said to be the best that the IR sub-field can offer to the study of governance.

As an approach it is unquestionably useful. It has identified some of the ways in which international relations appear increasingly to be conducted outside the realist model, emphasizing in particular the growing significance of both new non-state actors and new process such as intermediation, bargaining and networking. As such, it has pointed up some important shifts of behaviour in the international system. The problem is that, for all Rosenau's inventiveness, the mainstream IR approach to governance remains grounded as a body of theory in the liberal institutionalist view of the world from which it originated. That means that it cannot but suffer from the flaws which have been associated over the years with that school of thought, namely that it defines the essence of international relations too narrowly as process and that it ultimately lacks a convincing theory of power by which to explain why outcomes of a certain type keep on occurring.

The argument

As before, the broad argument that is being made in this section can perhaps helpfully be restated. The main theories used in the public policy and IR sub-fields of the social sciences have been trawled with a view to assessing their potential contribution to the building of a broad IPE approach to the study of governance capable of doing service in the genuinely global political economy of the present era. We have given them mixed reviews. They manifestly have substantial analytical insights to offer, but they also come with limitations – namely, the limitations associated with *all* bodies of theory, even those purporting to be purely academic in character, which is that, in the final analysis, they cannot be shorn of their own normative biases. This is the reason why we must acknowledge at this point that our earlier distinction between 'projects of governance' and 'theories of governance' cannot be pushed too far. The difference is that the political positions underpinning the 'projects' are overt and have been deliberately, even unashamedly, espoused. The biases of the 'theories' are often subconscious and are certainly more subtly couched, but they are nonetheless still present. In the context of this chapter, perhaps the most important is methodological, namely a failure to integrate sufficiently agency and structure within their analyses. The truth is that, as fields of study, both public policy and IR have always been excessively preoccupied with agency. This has meant that neither field has ever fully grasped the constraints which systematically bear upon the freedom of manoeuvre of the actors they identify. It is certainly important that that this focus on agency is not lost in too severe an embrace of structuralism, but the argument can easily and plausibly be made that it does need to be related more astutely to an awareness of structural power and an exploration of structural context than has generally been the norm in either of these sub-fields.

IPE and governance

As is well-known, IPE is a notoriously diverse field of study, encompassing mainstream and critical traditions. According to Geoffrey Underhill (2000a: 806), it is, however, held together by a core of shared conceptual assumptions, of which he has highlighted three:

(i) that the political and economic domains cannot be separated in any real sense, and even doing so for analytical purposes has its perils;
(ii) [that] political interaction is one of the principal means through which the economic structures of the market are established and in turn transformed; and
(iii) that there is an intimate connection between the domestic and international levels of analysis, and that the two cannot meaningfully be separated off from one another.

To these should be added a fourth premise already alluded to at the end of the previous section, namely, that in the best critical IPE there should also be an attempt to 'develop an integrated analysis, by combining parsimonious theories which analyse agency in terms of a conception of rationality with contextual theories which analyse structures institutionally and historically' (Gamble *et al.* 1996: 5–6). This is always a hard task, but it is not impossible.

As yet, the IPE literature on governance is best described as embryonic. The field's preoccupation of late has understandably been with the concept and process of globalization where the literature has genuinely been voluminous, as the previous chapter devoted to that theme amply testifies. But, from an agency–structure perspective, globalization is actually the right place from which to begin the analysis of governance. Put more generally, the political economy (structure) must be understood before the politics (agency) can be grasped. To be specific, we need to have a strong sense of the changed structural context brought out within the global political economy by the package of processes encapsulated by the term globalization before we turn to ask: how is globalization governed? This notion of a necessary link between political economy context and associated pattern of governance runs through the one outstanding historical study that has been written about the early phases of the emergence of governance at the global level, namely Craig Murphy's (1994) account of international organization and industrial change since 1850. He shows that world organizations over this period have derived much of their effectiveness from the fact that transnational coalitions of liberal social forces have invested them with the task of promoting the leading sectors of each successive phase of industrialism. As he put it (1994: 9):

> In periods of peace and prosperity they have acted as part of what some social theorists call the 'social structures of accumulation' or 'modes of regulation' that have allowed capitalist industrialism to work as well as it sometimes has. They have also helped industrial societies move out of those times when the system has not worked well – times of economic and geopolitical crisis – by contributing to the rise of the new leading industries of the next era of political order and economic growth.

The method used by Murphy, with its emphasis on the necessary interaction between developments in the superstructure and substructure of global affairs, has much to teach contemporary IPE. In that spirit, the analytical task before IPE can be set as that of mapping and understanding 'the changing governance of a global(izing) political economy'. IPE does not even need its own definition of governance because it can quite satisfactorily use Rosenau's notion of governance as a system of rule. Globalization has its own system of rule. It is just that, at present, we do not understand it very well. There is certainly no single authoritative study of the governance of globalization available at the moment. But the good news is that there do exist fragments of analysis which are relevant and illuminating and which can be assembled into an outline picture. To be specific, I suggest that this picture can be gradually built up by reference to five current areas of debate within IPE, each of which points up an important feature of the contemporary governance of globalization.

The ideological face of governance

Robert Cox, doyen of the critical school of IPE, has insisted for many years that ideational and material dimensions of power need to be understood as 'always bound together, mutually reinforcing one another, and not reducible one to the other' (Cox 1983: 168). Indeed, this insight is one of the distinguishing qualities of critical IPE. We need therefore to recognize that the world order, which is a notion conceptualized by Cox (1981: 152) as 'the way things usually happen', has an ideological, as well as a material, face. The latter, in relation to matters such as control over raw materials, markets, capital and the like, may be the more frequently analysed within IPE, and the easier to quantify, but the former is a vital part of the overall structure of power and, from a governance perspective, arguably even more important because it shapes the way that 'rulers' think about the possibilities of 'rule'. It raises the core Gramscian issue of who or what creates the 'common-sense' of an era, the presumed, taken-for-granted assumptions by which the wielding of power is classically masked.

As will be apparent, this is difficult terrain to research. Cox himself recognized this, at least implicitly, by deploying the French word *nébuleuse* in an attempt to catch the flavour of the way he saw this cloud of ideological forces exerting its impact (Cox 1996a: 301). His elaboration of what this involved in the present era is worth quoting at length:

> There is a transnational process of consensus formation among the official caretakers of the global economy. This process generates consensual guidelines, underpinned by an ideology of globalization, that are transmitted into the policy-making channels of national governments and big corporations. Part of this consensus-formation

process takes place through unofficial forums like the Trilateral Commission, the Bilderberg conferences, or the more esoteric Mont Pélèrin Society. Part of it goes on through official bodies like the OECD, the Bank for International Settlements, the International Monetary Fund, and the G7. These shape the discourse within which policies are defined, the terms and concepts that circumscribe what can be thought and done. (Cox 1996a: 301)

It is no revelation to say that the leading discourse to have been shaped in this way over the past two decades has been neoliberalism. This has unquestionably been the dominant ideology of the globalization phase of world order and is now the ruling orthodoxy of a majority of national governments throughout the world, no matter what varied rhetorical devices they employ to conceal this reality. It embraces within its orbit not only a whole series of practical stances towards markets, taxes, investments and the like, but also more intangible matters like attitudes, values and styles, including those pertaining to modes of governing. As we saw earlier, several explicit projects of governance have arisen out of the neoliberal well and have had their impact on the ways that we are actually governed.

Neoliberal ideas have also unconsciously conditioned the thinking and behaviour of many actors involved in contemporary processes of governance. But it would be an exaggeration to imply that they have not been contested over the past twenty years. As indicated earlier, social democracy has fought a largely defensive battle on behalf of redistribution and continuing state intervention in the social sphere, regrouping lately under the banner of the 'Third Way' (Birnbaum 1999). Similarly, other competing 'models of capitalism' to the Anglo-American variant so revered in the neoliberal handbook have been discerned, and survive, albeit under steady pressure to liberalize (see Beeson and Bell in this volume). These too contribute to the ideological grounding of the theory and practice of governance in the context of globalization. In short, the ideological face of governance, as we have called it, needs to be understood as constituting the very fabric of the picture we are trying to build up.

The global architecture of governance

At the institutional level there has also emerged what Paul Cammack (2002) has lately dubbed a 'global architecture of governance'.

Although the 'global governance' project makes much of the need to extend this apparatus in ways and directions already discussed, it would be a mistake not to acknowledge the extent of the governance which does already exist at the global level. The reference here is not solely or even predominantly to the UN system. The UN has been the embodiment of this aspiration since 1945, even if it largely failed to escape the constraints of superpower rivalry during the Cold War era. Paul Taylor (1999) has shown, however, that during the 1990s it came to demonstrate a renewed activism in peacekeeping, in responding to emergencies and in promoting democracy and 'good governance'. He has argued that this reflects the force of a proactive cosmopolitanism which seeks to ensure that all states are 'well-founded in the light of the standards of the international community'. In his view, this redefines sovereignty as, in effect, 'a licence from the international community to practice [*sic*] as an independent government in a particular territory' (Taylor 1999: 538). If he is right, then the UN has won for itself a substantial role in policing the current terms of entry into the official state-based part of the contemporary system of rule.

Other global bodies have also acquired sufficient regulatory authority further to undermine the state's traditional monopoly of governance. They include, preeminently, the World Bank, the IMF, the World Trade Organization (WTO), the Bank for International Settlements (BIS) and the OECD. Much is written, often in hyperbolic form, about the power of these institutions, and they have become the hate figures of the anti-globalization movement. However, good studies of how they actually operate politically are still thin on the ground. One turns here mainly to Robert Wade's (1996b) analysis of some of the internal mechanisms of governance of the World Bank in the early 1990s, the study of relations between several of the multilateral economic institutions and global social movements by O'Brien *et al.* (2000), Cammack's (2002, 2004) exposition of the intended reach of the World Bank's new so-called 'Comprehensive Development Framework' and Rorden Wilkinson's (2000, 2002) critique of the workings of the WTO. These and other accounts do not generate a neat or simple picture of the way these bodies operate. As international organizations, they are different one from another and they work in different ways at different times according to their own internal politics. There is thus a fluidity to their politics which is often underplayed or even ignored completely. They are also still rooted in the politics of the states which constitute their membership.

Yet it is clear too that these major global institutions do at the same time transcend their statist origins. They represent more than the sum of their parts and certainly command enough resources – of both a material and ideological nature – to qualify as significant agents of governance in their own right.

Multi-level governance

Regions (variously defined) have also been widely identified as new sites of governance. In a frequently quoted remark, John Ruggie (1993: 172) suggested several years ago that the EU might be said to constitute 'the first multi-perspectival polity to emerge since the advent of the modern era'. This claim has been taken up and developed by Gary Marks *et al.* (1996: 342), who deploy the image of 'multi-level governance' to catch the essence of 'a polity creating process in which authority and policy-making influence are shared across multiple levels of government – subnational, national and supranational'. In effect, within the EU, perhaps more than in any other part of the world, states no longer monopolize governance: policy-making is characterized instead by 'mutual dependence, complementary functions and overlapping competencies' (Marks *et al.* 1996: 372) between the supranational, national and subnational actors previously identified (also see Hooghe and Marks 2001). The role played by the growth of sub-state regionalism within the EU model of multi-level governance has been explicitly treated by several authors, notably James Anderson and James Goodman (1995). In a direct evocation of Ruggie, they have described how 'the related building of inter-regional linkages, formal associations of regional bodies, and collective institutional expressions of regional interests at the EU level, are all contributing to a multiple layering of power and to the process of selectively "unbundling" territoriality' (Anderson and Goodman 1995: 620; see Ruggie 1993: 171). What is more, this argument extends generally beyond the idea of a 'Europe of the regions' to provinces, federal states and municipalities in a variety of countries across the world and also, as Saskia Sassen (1995) has suggested, to the 'global city'. For her, cities are now vital parts of 'the global grid of places' (Sassen 1995: 46) and reflect globalization's continuing need for 'strategic sites with vast concentrations of resources and infrastructure' which may no longer be states *per se* but nevertheless still need to be 'situated in national territories' (Sassen 1995: 31).

Much of this strand of analysis does derive from the example of the EU (although it should be noted in passing that the multi-level governance model is far from being the orthodoxy amongst analysts of the EU) and so it is as well to remember that the EU is much more of a special case than a model as far as regionalist trends are concerned. Other, different modes of regionalist governance have emerged in North America and the Asia-Pacific (Payne 2000) and qualify some of the specific lessons, if not the general trend, depicted here. Even this account is perhaps excessively focused on 'core' regions of the world (Söderbaum 2001) and needs to be complemented by more studies of governance within regions such as southern Africa, Southeast Asia and Latin America where one would expect to note distinctive regional patterns shaped by specific, local histories, cultures and structures. What is certainly suggested is that the delimitation of the notion of multi-level governance to the EU framework and the Marks *et al*. definition are at the same time unnecessarily constricting and over-precise. Governance occurs at multiple levels of action in a variety of geographical settings within the contemporary global political economy.

The reorganization of the state

Much – probably too much – has been written in IPE about 'the state and globalization' and another chapter in this volume is charged with surveying this literature. Public policy too has had plenty to say about the changing internal processes of states, as we have seen earlier in this chapter. Yet governance, even within a global(izing) political economy, still derives fundamentally from what states do. In other words, states are written out of the script only at IPE's peril. The point to stress is that states have always varied, and do still vary, *inter alia* in their degree of democracy, level of development, infrastructural power, national indebtedness and regional location. As Michael Mann (1997: 494) has warned, even under conditions of globalization the patterns of change are simply too 'contradictory, and the future too murky, to permit us to argue simply that the nation and the nation state system are *either* strengthening *or* weakening'. A better, more nuanced thesis is that 'the processes of global restructuring are largely embedded within state structures and institutions, politically contingent on state policies and actions, and primarily about the reorganisation of the state' (Amoore *et al*. 1997: 186).

This argument is now expressed in the literature in a range of forms, which are surveyed and discussed fully in the next chapter. Cox, for example, initially referred to 'the internationalization of the state', understood as a process that 'gives precedence to certain state agencies – notably ministries of finance and prime ministers' offices – which are key points in the adjustment of domestic to international economic policy' (Cox 1981: 146). Scholte (1997: 452) has lately suggested that globalization has yielded 'a different kind of state...[which has]...on the whole lost sovereignty, acquired supraterritorial constituents, retreated from interstate warfare (for the moment), frozen or reduced social security provisions, multiplied multilateral governance arrangements and lost considerable democratic potential'. From further to the left Peter Burnham (1999: 43–4) has drawn attention to what he sees as the widespread shift in the politics of economic management in advanced capitalist societies from 'politicised management (discretion-based)' to 'depoliticised management (rules-based)', the latter being characterized by attempts to reduce the former political character of economic decision-making and reposition it as far as possible at one remove from government. Peter Evans (1997: 85), reflecting on 'stateness' in an era of globalization, stresses the centrality of the hegemony of Anglo-American liberal thinking (again) in limiting belief in the efficacy of state action and charts accordingly the recent 'project of constructing a leaner, meaner kind of stateness' lately associated with the 'Third Way' thinking of the Clinton, Blair and Schröder administrations in the USA, the UK and Germany respectively. Linda Weiss (1997: 17) similarly has insisted on the variety of 'state capacities' and has argued that 'adaptation is the very essence of the modern state by virtue of the fact that it is embedded in a dynamic economic and inter-state system'. Although in some states certain policy instruments, particularly those associated with macroeconomic adjustment strategies, may be enfeebled by globalization, others, such as those related to industrial policy, may and do change in all manner of creative ways. One should therefore always look to a country's governing institutions and expect differences according to national orientation and capability.

Reorganized states thus still contribute signally to reorganized governance. The debate about the state must therefore be drawn fully into the debate about governance. As has been quickly demonstrated, it is a rich debate intellectually and there is much to be derived from it. It is proper to note (and object), as Phillips argues in the next chapter, that it has thus far been devoted in the main to discussion of state structures and behaviour in the Western OECD world. Most states in the world, it goes almost without saying, have not been 'restructured' away from social democratic norms, and they too need to be researched. Equally, many states in the world have never rested upon such norms in the first place, and consequently the processes of restructuring of states that are currently under way require careful and specific empirical analysis which takes neither the starting point nor the trajectory – nor indeed the envisaged outcome – of this restructuring as logically 'given' or assumed. This is beginning to happen, especially as critics of imposed 'good governance' are able now to expose the limitations of such an agenda in Latin America (Philip 1999) and East Asia (Beeson 2001), as well as dissect the impact of such external pressures on the way that, say, East African states have actually been functioning (Harrison 2001).

Privatized governance

The dispersal of contemporary governance becomes still more apparent when the lens is extended beyond forms of public authority to the domain of the private. Openness to such a notion was one of the attractive features of the public policy work of writers like Rhodes and is something on which IPE has built. Drawing in good part on Susan Strange's *The Retreat of the State* (1996), Murphy (2000: 794) has recently listed several 'global-level "private" authorities that regulate both states and much of transnational economic and social life', as follows:

- private bond-rating agencies that impose particular policies on governments at all levels;
- tight global oligopolies in reinsurance, accounting, high-level consulting that provide similar regulatory pressure;
- global and regional cartels in industries as diverse as mining and electrical products;
- the peculiar combination of oligopolistic regulation, ad hoc private regulation, and non-regulation that governs global telecommunications and the Internet;
- internationally integrated mafias; and
- a narrow group of economists who define the norms of that profession and thereby regulate the treasury ministries, the most powerful of the intergovernmental agencies, and the private institutions of financial regulation that want to adhere to economic orthodoxy.

His list is far from exhaustive and research into this aspect of governance within IPE has grown quite fast (Sinclair 1994; Cutler 1995; Weiss and Gordenker 1996; Cutler *et al.* 1999; Hall and Biersteker 2002). It is still too early to reach for generalized conclusions, for we do not as yet have anything like a sufficiently full picture, either of the contemporary era or of the past. It is difficult, therefore, to establish how much is really new – for example, most of the 'authorities' identified by Murphy could be said to have had counterparts in the nineteenth century. Enough, however, has been said to have established that, within the study of contemporary governance, the public/private interface has henceforth to be treated as notably fluid and uncertain. It is also worth pointing out here that the very notion of a clear separation between the public and the private is a feature of classical liberal thinking and does not therefore necessarily correspond with due expectation in many countries. Indeed, in many parts of the world it is not at all easy to distinguish effectively between 'public' and 'private' forms or agents of governance. For example, in many countries in Africa and Latin America clientelist behaviour is an accepted norm and often binds 'private' and 'public' actors within an embrace that may well break the rules of Western liberal modes of good governance but nevertheless functions effectively in its particular social context. At the very least we need to be extremely careful in the ways that we approach these questions if a more inclusive, genuinely global understanding of privatized governance is to be reached.

The argument

The argument made in this section is that IPE has been responsible for quite a lot of work which can be gathered together to constitute an approach to the study of governance. The central claim of this work is that in a period of globalization the number and type of sites of governance have multiplied to create a complex, multidimensional, multilayered overall pattern. The explanatory link to the process of globalization is not always or necessarily made – that would be too crude a thesis – but it is rightly stressed within IPE that the package of trends encapsulated by the term globalization has significantly altered the structural contours within which governance as an activity takes place. Certainly in the best work a sense of the interlinking of structure and agency is provided. IPE, in short, has established that globalization is being governed. Although it may not be the case that it is being governed fairly or justly or even efficiently (Scholte 2000a: Part III) – and critical analysts of IPE can be no more acquitted of the charge of bringing their normative values to bear upon their analyses than liberals, conservatives or social democrats – we can at least say that globalization has acquired a distinctive, and increasingly well-understood, apparatus of governance. Of course, much more practical research needs to be done in all parts of the world in order to deliver fully the commitment to a genuinely global portrait of contemporary modes of governance. For all that, the basis has been laid.

Governance and world order

From that basis, however, an important, and as yet unanswered, question arises, namely: what kind of world order, politically speaking, does this apparatus of governance constitute? To be fair, it is a question which IPE cannot at the moment be expected to answer. As Rosenau (1995: 39) has reminded us, this account of 'a dis-aggregated and fragmenting global system of governance' is 'an unfinished story'. It is not just that more research needs to be done (although, as suggested, that is undoubtedly, and always, true), but rather that the pieces have still to fall into a shape which can be easily or consensually classified. It is apparent that the old image of a Westphalian system of states, each ruled from the top down by a government operating largely in command mode, will no longer suffice. Indeed, it probably never did. It is equally apparent that world government remains but a fanciful prospect. What falls in between? We do not know. All we can really offer up at present in an attempt to catch the essence of the new world order is a series of more or less plausible scenarios. This last section of the chapter seeks therefore to highlight briefly some of the component elements of this emergent discussion. It is possible to identify a number of thoughtful and interesting interpretations:

1. '*New liberal internationalism*'. There are those who believe that important steps have already been taken in this direction. They affect to argue that forms of supranational authority, whether as manifested in the UN, the European Commission, the World Bank, the WTO, or the International Court of Justice, have succeeded

in drawing away from states quite significant powers and that, once started, further movement in this direction is likely to be irreversible. In its strongest form, the argument suggests that states are in effect dinosaurs, still alive but their collective fate settled. Sovereignty, the prized ideology of statehood, has already been redrawn in a number of ways and the prospect in due course is indeed the emergence of something that will truly merit being called global governance. In a weaker form it still recognizes the continuing role of states but insists that they must, and will, increasingly accept the behavioural norms set by supranational bodies.

2. '*New medievalism*'. This phrase was first used as long ago as 1977 by Hedley Bull to suggest that one alternative to the system of states might be 'a modern and secular equivalent of the kind of universal political organization that existed in Western Christendom in the Middle Ages' (Bull 1977: 254). This thought was largely forgotten until the phrase was picked up by such writers as Ruggie (1993) and Cox (1996a) to highlight both the variegated nature of the political actors newly operational in international politics and the apparently common ideological discourse of a liberal democratic political economy (*à la* Fukuyama) within which they were having to act. In conceptual terms Ruggie went the furthest in arguing that the term 'new medievalism' was useful precisely because it drew attention to the fact that the world was moving through a transition as significant as that between the medieval and modern eras. As such, it was no longer adequate to view political relations from the single-point perspective characteristic of the age of modernity; instead political and other forms of analysis must open up the 'multiperspectival' nature of reality and take full cognizance of the trends of governance set within such bodies as the EU.

3. '*New transgovernmentalism*'. In a robust response to these visions Anne-Marie Slaughter (1997) has recently set out another view. 'The state is not disappearing', she suggests, 'it is disaggregating into its separate functionally distinct parts. These parts – courts, regulatory agencies, executives, even legislatures – are networking with their counterparts abroad, creating a dense web of relations that constitute a new, transgovernmental order' (Slaughter 1997: 184). While accepting the growing importance of private modes of governance, Slaughter nevertheless argues that they are still no substitute for state power. For her, 'government networks are government for the information age. They offer the world

a blueprint for the international architecture of the 21st century' (Slaughter 1997: 197).

4. '*New regionalism*'. In a series of papers Björn Hettne (1993, 1997a and 1999) has described a world order constructed around a 'new regionalism', which refers in the main to the second wave of regional cooperation and integration schemes which took off after the end of the Cold War. Using Polanyi's terminology, Hettne (1999: 6, 22) has explained this trend as 'a regionalist "second movement"' in which 'the new regionalism represents the return of "the political"; that is, interventions in favour of crucial values, among which development, security and peace, and ecological sustainability are the most fundamental'. As he readily admits, this argument comprises a normative preference as well as the documentation of a trend. The trend is, however, well-established in a range of studies and this picture of regional multilateralism only adds to the richness of the plausible scenarios placed before us.

Governance and world order is the next debate that IPE needs to have in relation to its exploration of the global political economy. As will be apparent, discussion is still at a very early stage and is still affected by that elision between projects and theories of governance which was highlighted at the outset of this chapter. The scenarios which have been advanced thus far and highlighted here are also clearly not mutually exclusive. Each needs to be elaborated with greater care and precision and then tested against much more comparative and differentiated analysis of trends pertaining to governance in all parts of the world, not just the 'core'. Only then will it be possible to see anything like the full shape of the contemporary governance of globalization and to accord it some analytical definition. Governance is one of the realities of politics with which IPE has to grapple and this has only just begun.

Chapter 4

State Debates in International Political Economy

*Nicola Phillips**

The field of IPE, as noted in the introductory chapter, has been characterized since its inception by an anxiety to establish itself as a distinct intellectual and disciplinary enterprise, particularly from IR, CPE and comparative politics. The first platform from which international political economists have sought to assert this distinctiveness has been the rejection of the state-centrism deemed to pervade these other disciplines. This challenge to traditional state-centric analysis has given rise to a rich and valuable collection of theoretical and empirical perspectives on the contemporary world order, and has opened up a new variety of intellectual avenues that were largely foreclosed by the self-identified statist orientation of IR and comparative politics/political economy. Many of the other chapters in this volume attest clearly to this. But the challenge to state-centrism has also meant that the study of states has largely been left to one side in IPE. It is not simply that the study of states has been deemed *passé* in this self-consciously fashionable field. In our justified haste to move away from state-centric social science and its limitations, we have also tended collectively towards an *anti*-statism in the ways we define and pursue our concerns.

The second platform from which a distinctive identity and unique utility have been asserted for IPE is its defining concern with globalization. It is in this area, it is widely claimed, that IPE comes supremely into its own. It is not only lauded by its advocates as the only sub-field in the social sciences which offers the multidisciplinary openness that is essential to the study of globalization; it is also seen

---

* I am grateful to Andrew Gamble, Wyn Grant, Adam Morton and Tony Payne for their very helpful comments on earlier drafts of this chapter.

as constituting the only set of intellectual lenses through which the economic, political, social and ideological intricacies of the globalizing world order can adequately be understood. Thus, for most of its existence, the core and distinctive 'value-added' of IPE has been understood to crystallize around the purchase it offers on the study of globalization and the transformations of contemporary governance that globalization implies.

Together, these hallmarks of modern IPE have constituted the defining influences on *what sorts* of questions about states have been asked, when indeed they have been asked at all. These questions have clustered in the so-called globalization–state debate, revolving around the nature of the relationship between globalization and states in conceptual, empirical and normative terms. In turn, I suggest, the defining influences on *how* these questions about states have been addressed have been three dominant ontological predilections and theoretical biases. The first is a pervasive inclination in IPE towards economism, an inclination which extends across the various theoretical schools of thought and persists in much of the mainstream despite growing calls for 'putting the "P" back into IPE' (Hay and Marsh 1999a, 1999b). The second is functionalism, which again constitutes a strong undercurrent running through the globalization–state debate. The permeation of state debates by these two biases has meant that IPE has had very little to contribute to debates on the *nature* of contemporary states, and that questions of institutions, state–society complexes, legitimacy and sovereignty have, to date, received notably scant attention.

The third inclination is that which underpins the broader arguments of this volume. The study of states in IPE has been dominated by a stubborn empirical focus on the small collection of advanced industrialized states, usually with liberal democratic characteristics. Moreover, the bulk of attempts to *theorize* this relationship in the globalization–state debate have relied both implicitly and explicitly on the experiences of this small handful of states. This reliance has carried a range of implications for the theoretical lenses through which state debates have been approached, and has imbued these debates with a range of biases which have limited their applicability outside the dominant states for which they were originally developed.

This chapter is concerned, first, with advancing and fleshing out these contentions about the study of states in IPE; second, with investigating their implications and setting out their problematic consequences; and, third, with considering how the study of states might more fruitfully be advanced within IPE. It begins by sketching out the evolution of state theory and state debates in other contiguous areas of the social sciences – primarily IR, comparative politics and CPE – before going on to look at the forms the study of states has taken in modern IPE. It must be stressed from the outset that my aim is not, and cannot be, to offer a comprehensive survey or analysis of the evolution of state theory in the social sciences generally, or in any discrete part of them. Rather, it is to offer a thumbnail sketch and critique of some of the dominant state theoretical traditions from which the various theories of IPE have emerged, and the principal perspectives and debates which they have sought to further, improve upon or indeed discard as obsolete.

Key traditions in state theory

Despite disciplinary differences in focus, what is striking about the recent unfolding of state debates in IR and Political Science, particularly in its comparative branch, is that they have advanced largely in tandem with each other. In each case, the controversies have revolved, in different ways and for different purposes, around the appropriate definition of the state in relation to society or social forces and the theorization of this relationship. Specifically, the core concept around which the various theoretical traditions in each discipline have divided is that of 'autonomy'. In other words, state debates have crystallized around the extent to which the state is deemed to be characterized by a high level of autonomy from society and non-state actors, or conversely the degree of autonomy from states that can be said to be possessed by social forces. What John Hobson (2000) has identified as the 'first state debate' has, in this sense, been largely a protracted showdown between society-centric and state-centric approaches to the study of politics and IR. Of the three core traditions in state theory – liberal, Marxist and Weberian – the first two represent what Theda Skocpol (1979) identified as 'society-centred' theories of the state. The third represents a 'state-centred' body of thought which understands the state as a discrete and autonomous entity to be afforded intrinsic analytical interest – an interest of which, it is argued in modern neo-Weberian state theory, it has unjustifiably been deprived by its rival liberal and Marxist theoretical traditions.

For both liberalism and Marxism, the state is fundamentally an 'arena' which represents, reflects *and is inherently constituted by* dominant societal interests or social forces. Liberal state theory, particularly those strands associated with pluralism, is fundamentally concerned with the politics of societal 'input' in liberal democracies, with states conceived as arenas in which competing interests are aggregated and adjudicated. For this reason, it can be said that liberalism – and particularly liberal pluralism – historically 'has mostly been a theory of society rather than a theory of the state' (Dunleavy and O'Leary 1987: 42). Yet the controversies within modern liberal thought have revolved around the *manner* in which societal interests are represented or aggregated by states, and by extension around the manner in which states must consequently be defined. Moreover, the inbuilt and enduring assumption across liberal theory is that, for both the preservation of democracy and the maintenance of market efficiency, the state's role must be confined to guaranteeing individual rights and freedoms (both economic and political), and the centralized, arbitrary or interventionist exercise of state power must be checked by a full range of constitutional, social and institutional constraints. The state is conceptualized as an arena that is defined by its functions of *democratic* representation; consequently, liberal state theory posits a high level of social and societal, rather than state, autonomy.

Marxist state theory shares with liberalism this basic conceptualization of the state as an arena defined intrinsically by the interests it represents. It has also been noted frequently, as with liberalism, that the huge body of Marxist scholarship fails to put forward discernibly concrete, explicit or generally accepted statements of the conceptions and understandings of the state that underpin Marxist thought. It is, as Colin Hay (1999: 153) has remarked, 'difficult to identify any analytically precise Marxist definition of the state as an object of inquiry, let alone one that is commonly agreed upon'. Beyond this, however, the differences with liberalism are often stark. They arise from the central Marxist preoccupation with class as the fundamental basis for social organization, and thus from the theorization of national states as, variously, the coercive expression of the interests of the capitalist bourgeoisie, the arbiters of class conflict, the mechanisms by which the exploitative social (class) order required by capitalism is maintained and sanctioned, or, in Peter Burnham's (2001) formulation, 'political nodes in the global flow of capital'. The common emphasis is on a 'de-fetishized' understanding of the state 'not as a thing in itself, but as a social form, a form of social relations' (Holloway 1994: 26).

To this extent, as Theda Skocpol (1979: 25) noted, the battle between liberal and Marxist state theory has been, and still is, fought largely over whether the arena of the state represents 'fundamentally consensually based legitimate authority, or fundamental coercive domination'. To this we could add a further key distinction, namely, that the bulk of liberal state theory is built on a notion of the state as intrinsically *neutral*, both in its nature and in the manner in which it acts to aggregate political interests or broker relations between them. In Marxist theorizations, conversely, states are anything but neutral, representing instead an institutionalized expression of a particular class interest and the interests of the capitalist system. To this extent, what are normally obscured in liberal state theory – or at least left implicit – are the ideological and political foundations on which both liberal state theory *and* liberal states themselves are constructed, foundations which a range of other theoretical traditions have sought to expose and challenge.

The body of thought associated with German sociologist Max Weber, by contrast, represents the essence of state-centric state theory. The state, in Weber's (1964) famous formulation, is defined by the twin elements of its association with a specific territorial unit and its claim to monopolize the legitimate use of violence within that territory. From these emerge two further intrinsic and defining elements: first, the core requirement that this monopolization of violence be recognized as *legitimate* and the legal, moral and functional authority of the state therefore accepted (Weber 1972); and, second, the existence of what Weber (1978) referred to as an 'ideal-typical' bureaucracy based on 'legal-rational authority'. Among the various characteristics of Weberian bureaucracy are an 'impersonal' staff selected and promoted on meritocratic (rather than political) grounds, hierarchical organization and a clear delineation of the tasks of offices within the bureaucracy that exist independently of the person occupying them. The state was thus to be understood as a set of both institutions and institutional rules – in Skocpol's (1979: 29) later reformulation, as 'a set of administrative, policing, and military organizations headed, and more or less coordinated, by an executive authority'. Consequently, above all, it was seen to be intrinsically autonomous from society and deserving of discrete analysis.

These three traditions in state theory have permeated the various schools of thought associated with both IR and comparative politics/CPE, as well as other disciplines such as Sociology. Since the 1970s, the focal point of state debates in comparative politics, CPE and Sociology has been the 'state autonomy' literature. Dominant liberal and Marxist tendencies to relegate the state to secondary analytical importance were rejected by those seeking to identify the conditions in which states could be and were autonomous – autonomy being defined broadly, with variations, as the ability of state officials to translate their preferences into policy unencumbered by pressures from non-state arenas (Nordlinger 1981) – and, on this basis, to launch a sustained campaign to 'bring the state back in' (Skocpol 1979; Evans *et al.* 1985). This neo-Weberian scholarship found its home particularly within the discipline of Sociology, coming frequently to be referred to as 'Weberian historical sociology' (WHS). The counterpart to the debate in CPE, also deriving its inspiration from Weberian understandings of state autonomy and indeed associated strongly with some of the same scholars, sought to pursue its concerns with the relationship between state and economy by examining the role of strong 'developmental states' in economic development (Hobson 2000: 3). This debate was sparked first by Chalmers Johnson's (1982) original elaboration of the 'developmental state' model for the purposes of explaining industrial policy in Japan, and rose to prominence as it was extended to the study of development and industrialization in East Asia.

We will return to the developmental state later in the chapter; for now it suffices to note that this debate called forth the recognition that Weberian-inspired notions of state autonomy could not afford to neglect societal and social forces. Drawing on insights well-established in political economy into the role of states in constituting markets, as well as the socially constructed nature of states themselves (Polanyi 1944; Ruggie 1982; Katzenstein 1985), the developmental state literature extended the notion of 'embeddedness' to advance a concept of what Evans (1995a) termed 'embedded autonomy'. By this, he sought to denote 'a concrete set of social ties which binds the state to society and provides institutionalized channels for the continual negotiation and re-negotiation of goals and policies'. Thus, the notion of embedded autonomy 'combines the Weberian bureaucratic insulation with intense connection to the surrounding social structure' in a manner that suggests 'isolation is not necessary to preserve state capacity' (Evans 1995a: 50), an understanding he brought to bear on the study of industrial transformation in Brazil, India and Korea. Echoes of the embedded autonomy approach were found in the 'state-in-society' approach in comparative politics (Migdal 1988; Migdal *et al.* 1994), which sought similarly to escape the strictures of Weberian state-centrism. Other related work (notably Hobson 1997, 1998, 2000; Hobden 1998; Hobden and Hobson 2001) has sought to bring WHS more concretely into IR, and fashion from it a new and coherent body of IR theory. This work also aimed to build further upon these notions of embeddedness, challenging what was deemed to be the narrow focus of the embedded autonomy literature on states' developmentalist ties with business and capital, and advancing a notion of 'social embeddedness' as a 'bottom-up' antidote to the 'top-down' understandings of states that permeated other neo-Weberian perspectives. This 'second state debate' thus sought to transcend the sterile opposition between state-centric and society-centric state theory, seeking instead to advance a 'state autonomy *and* society' approach (Hobson 2000: 3).

In IR, the 'first state debate' has taken a slightly different, but parallel, form. In essence, it pitted realist and neorealist theories of IR – and, by extension, their central theorization of the state – against those associated with liberal theories and radical pluralist theories, and was articulated in its clearest form in the context of the study of interdependence in the 1970s (Hobson 2000: 2). As is well-known, neorealist and neoliberal IR theories clashed with each other primarily on matters of whether the central patterns of state behaviour in world politics were associated with confrontation or cooperation and, by extension, whether the primary motivations of state behaviour were to be understood as the zero-sum relative gains associated with neorealism or the positive-sum absolute gains associated with neo-liberalism. This debate received a new injection of vigour with the perceived rise of interdependence as the defining characteristic of relations between states, as a result of which realism and neorealism were largely dislodged by neoliberal institutionalism from their long-held position of primacy in IR theory.

With overlaps with what at the time was crystallizing as the field of IPE, the debate in IR centred largely on neorealist efforts to (re)assert the primacy of nation states, conceived as possessing high levels of autonomy, against the onslaught of analyses of interdependence which sought to challenge this view of states in favour of understanding the array of structures and forces in an increasingly complex world. The conclusion of the latter line of argument – advanced particularly at the time by neoliberal interdependence theorists (most notably, Keohane and Nye 1977) – was that the degree of autonomy from (international) social forces that states could be said to possess was undergoing a process of steady erosion, even though neoliberal IR as a whole, like neorealism, remained strikingly state-centric in its orientation and theoretical apparatus. The running was subsequently taken up by analyses which sought to identify the decline of the state as the primary locus of authority and, furthermore, analytical interest. Many of these came to define their concerns as lying not so much with interdependence *between* states as with the dispersal of authority and power, new forms of international organization and emerging structures of global governance in which states occupied but one, increasingly minor, part (Rosenau and Czempiel 1992; Rosenau 1997).

In one sense, then, the 'first state debate' in IR was about the analytical centrality that should be afforded to states, the degree of autonomy that they were understood to possess from the array of social forces at work in the international arena, and the extent to which the blurring of distinctions between the domestic and the international could be said to be unravelling the internal coherence of the state as an autonomous legal and institutional entity. In another sense, it was about how the *interests* of states were to be understood. On this score, IR theory had long been dominated by a tension between, on the one hand, realism and Marxism, and, on the other, liberalism and neoliberalism. For the former, states' interests were determined by 'external', 'structural' forces – in the case of realism, by the international structure of the states system; in the case of Marxism, by the worldwide structure of capitalism – and consequently were considered 'fixed' or 'predetermined'. For the latter, such a conceptualization represented an unacceptable structuralist and reductionist bias. Strands of neoliberal institutionalism, in particular, sought to build on classical liberal state theory and to inject a theory and analysis of domestic politics into IR, arguing that it was necessary to open up the 'black box' of the state and focus on the *politics* – particularly the distributional politics – of the processes by which state preferences were formed and state strategies designed (Milner 1997a; Moravscik 1998).

Like the parallel 'first generation' debates in other areas of political science, in this sense, mainstream IR theory has been characterized by a pervasive dichotomization of 'state-centric' and 'society-centric' approaches. Unlike these parallel debates, however, mainstream IR theory has been slow to engage with or incorporate recent 'second state debate' currents from other areas of Political Science, Sociology and political economy, or, indeed, to absorb fully the newer WHS interventions in IR itself (Hobson 2000: 3–4). It also remains attached to traditional tendencies to focus on 'the system' (however defined) rather than affording states an intrinsic analytical interest, and on relations between states where states are taken as 'given' entities. At the same time, state theory in Political Science, comparative politics and, to a lesser extent, CPE has been reticent in taking on board and reflecting upon the implications of interdependence and globalization for the nature of states, their institutional coherence, their degree of autonomy and the ways in which their 'embeddedness' should be understood in a global political economy. It is upon these failings of state debates in its neighbouring disciplines that IPE has set out to improve. We turn our attention now to the ways in which this task has been undertaken.

State debates in IPE

While the bulk of state debates in IR and political science have been concerned with the relationship between states and social/societal forces, the hallmark of state debates in IPE has been a preoccupation with the relationship between states and *markets*. In this regard, they build in part upon the long-standing and defining concern with and insight into this relationship in classical and comparative political economy, in both their liberal and their Marxist streams. This focus also arises from the founding rationale put forward for the development of IPE as an identifiable field of study, which responded not to classical political economy but rather to IR. Susan Strange's (1970) call for a greater integration of international economics and international politics was followed by her seminal elaboration of what this field of IPE should look like, which she condensed into the catchphrase 'states and markets' in her book of that title (Strange 1988).

Yet what has been most striking about the ways in which the resulting debates have been conducted in IPE is the pervasive tendency to relegate states to secondary interest within its purview. Given the widespread perception among international political economists that IPE should concern itself primarily with the nature of the 'system' or 'world order' and with the various processes which constitute it (finance, trade, production and so on), state debates have frequently been neglected as second-order preoccupations capable of being left largely to colleagues in other disciplines. Indeed, Strange (1996) subsequently reformulated her definition of IPE to involve more properly the study of '*authority* and markets', which, in her view, captured more appropriately the limited and declining importance of national states in the global landscape of dispersed power and authority. This conceptualization was widely taken on board within the field, and indeed continues to inform most of the intellectual activity which goes on within it. We are apparently to understand from most of IPE, then, that (national) states play little more than a bit part in the global political economy, and also that their study is remote from the central and pressing concerns which define the field.

The same can be said of the place of state *theory* in IPE. Apart from the shortage of solid contributions from IPE to theorizing states, it is striking that mainstream debates – including those explicitly addressing questions about states – are usually conducted without concrete acknowledgement of the theorization of the state from which they work or the implications that this prior, implicit theorization carries for the type of analysis undertaken. In other words, international political economists for the most part have failed sufficiently to expose the understandings of states within which their analyses are rooted and which inform the perspectives and arguments that result therefrom. This empirical and analytical neglect of states and the theoretical failure to elucidate and reflect carefully on conceptualizations of states are all the more striking when set against the backdrop of the vibrant and energetic state debates that continue to rage in other areas of the political and social sciences, with which, for the most part, IPE has been strikingly reluctant to engage.

The globalization–state debate

The area of IPE in which states have been subject to most sustained consideration, as noted earlier, is the globalization–state debate. The dominant approaches in this debate can be usefully divided into three, which Held *et al.* (1999) have identified as 'hyperglobalist', 'sceptical' and 'transformationalist'. These were introduced in the chapter on globalization, but here are useful in the specific context of the positions they represent within the globalization–state debate. The first of these had its heyday in the early 1990s. In its more hyperbolic versions, it advanced a view of globalization as an inexorable, encompassing and irreversible process of global integration which heralded the obsolescence of 'national' entities, not only states but also economies, societies, systems of regulation, modes of governance and so on. The gist of this hyperglobalist 'orthodoxy' is well-known and requires only brief restatement here. Its central contention is that nation-states are ill-equipped to discharge the functions of government and governance under conditions of globalization, their capacity, autonomy, authority and jurisdiction being systematically undermined and constrained by the structural power of markets and global capital. At the same time, the authority, legitimacy and traditional jurisdictions of nation-states are deemed to have come under sustained assault from the array of non-state actors, both public and private, that have come to represent new 'sites of authority' in the global political economy.

While much of this enquiry into non-state actors, transnational relations and dispersed power structures is indispensable to our understanding of global political economy, as O'Brien's chapter in this collection amply shows, nevertheless the cumulative consequence of the globalization orthodoxy and the scholarship on non-state authority has been an association of the hyperglobalist school with a sustained anti-statism. There have been important variations in the strength with which the hyperglobalist arguments have been articulated – from Ohmae's (1990) 'borderless world' to Camilleri and Falk's (1992) 'end of sovereignty', Rosenau and Czempiel's (1992) 'governance without government' and Strange's (1996) 'retreat of the state'. Yet, whether associated with liberal versions of the arguments or their Marxist counterparts, the hyperglobalist school is distinguished essentially by its depiction of the triumph and primacy of global markets.

The neoliberal position advances a 'globalization orthodoxy', which relies for its force and coherence on a hypothesis of 'convergence' – a contention, in essence, that 'all advanced industrial economies tend toward common ways of producing and organizing economic life', and that deviations or variations from this norm must be understood to be the product of 'extramarket' distortions (Berger 1996: 1). In its association with liberal understandings of globalization and neoclassical understandings of economic processes, the convergence hypothesis deems the universal availability of technological innovation to the advanced industrialized economies necessarily to imply the generation of convergent rates of productivity and, in turn, the emergence of convergent (neoliberal) sets of institutional and social configurations (Boyer 1996). The focus on 'advanced industrial economies' is glaring in this formulation, and we will come back to this point in due course. What for now is important is that, in fact, the convergence hypothesis has been extended, frequently in blanket fashion, to all the other economies of the world. Indeed, those seeking to advance such a hypothesis have considered themselves to have found even more fertile ground for their arguments in these cases, given the multitude of pressures towards convergence that emanate from the conditionality imposed on national governments by the IFIs and global financial agents, as well as the extent of the dependence on foreign capital flows for national development projects within emerging-market economies. In essence, as Suzanne Berger (1996: 5) puts it, 'convergence came to be synonymous with the global mobility of the factors of production, and above all of finance', deemed by Philip Cerny (1994) to connote an 'embedded financial orthodoxy' which constrains the autonomy and limits the capacity of national states.

The orthodoxy rests in this sense on perceptions of the constraints placed on the viability and efficacy of expansionary fiscal and monetary policies in conditions of high capital mobility, and the risks associated with macroeconomic divergence in this context. The globalization of financial markets is seen to imply a situation in which policies of these kinds generate pressures on governments, both from markets and other governments, to defend or devalue the national currency, with concomitantly serious implications for the foreign reserves position of the economy in question (Andrews 1994). In this sense, the policy strategies prized within a global political economy are those of maintaining stable and flexible exchange rates, determined not by political actors but by markets, and adhering to fiscal discipline in order to effect the kinds of macroeconomic convergence deemed necessary in conditions of capital mobility. At the same time, the risks associated with macroeconomic divergence are deemed to be heightened by precisely this high capital mobility, in the sense that the 'exit options' of mobile capital asset holders are significantly increased (Milner and Keohane 1996). This is associated with the ways in which the attraction of investment is seen to require the removal of controls on capital flows and the restructuring of taxation in connection with financial deregulation and trade liberalization. The consequence of the latter completes the circle, in the sense that taxation is no longer amenable to use for governments' distributive and employment objectives (Rodrik 1997; Rhodes 2001), thereby reinforcing conformity with the neoliberal dictates of fiscal discipline.

Notwithstanding the variety of positions within the hyperglobalist approach, the conclusion is uniformly that states are in decline, or, at least, struggling (ultimately in vain) against the forces precipitating such a decline. This is also the argument advanced in many of the parallel debates in the study of governance in IR and IPE, especially in those relating to global governance which, by definition, seek to escape the strictures of realist state-centrism in their analyses of the new forms and agencies of governance in world politics. It chimes particularly closely with the conclusion reached in much of the literature associated with the liberal ideological *project* of global governance that Payne identified in the previous chapter. In both of these versions of the argument, the 'empirical' contention that states are generally in decline as a result of globalization processes is equally an ideologically founded contention that they *should be* in decline. In other words, what Evans (1997: 70) has described as the 'pervasive belief that the institutional centrality of the state is incompatible with globalization' is essentially, and crucially, an ideological statement of the desirability of this incompatibility in order to assure the primacy of markets and enforce the social and political orders deemed to be necessary for their effective operation (Phillips 2004: 221).

The sceptical and transformationalist positions in the globalization–state debate have unquestionably been effective in challenging the hyperglobalist approach and, indeed, in dismantling its dominance of the debate by the end of the 1990s. The 'globalization sceptics', the most noted of which have been Paul Hirst and Grahame Thompson, have constructed their critique on two principal arguments, both of which rely on an injection of concrete empirical evidence into analyses of globalization. The first is that the very existence of something called globalization is open to serious question. What are viewed as entirely ahistorical accounts of globalization have been deemed to miss the point that contemporary patterns of trade and investment indicate little more than a continued process of internationalization, and indeed that the world economy had become no more internationalized by the start of the twenty-first century than it had been in other historical periods, notably the pre-1914 era (Hirst and Thompson 1999). The idea that contemporary globalization represents the latest phase in a long-running historical process was unquestionably an important insight for the globalization–state debate. Yet this version of the sceptical approach did ultimately obscure many crucial and unique facets of contemporary structural change and in this sense often served as a hindrance to the task of understanding and explaining this 'latest' phase and form of globalization.

A rather more effective second argument in the sceptical church has assailed both the convergence hypothesis and the dichotomization of the global and the national upon which the hyperglobalist approach rests. It has contended instead that, as John Zysman (1996: 181) put it, 'the national institutional foundations of the several market systems are neither washed away nor compressed into homogenous convergence by growing interconnectedness, or at least not yet'. These sorts of arguments echo similar ones in parallel CPE debates, particularly those associated with models of capitalism. In both contexts, notions of convergence have been challenged by careful analyses of the myriad manifestations of national divergence in, for example, state strategies and capacities (Boyer and Drache 1996; Crouch and Streeck 1997; Weiss 1998), domestic state institutions (Weiss 2003) and modes of corporate governance and 'business systems' (Whitley 1992a, 1992b; Ruigrok and van Tulder 1995; Hollingsworth and Boyer 1997a; Doremus *et al.* 1998), among many others.

The transformationalist school deploys many of the same sorts of arguments in order to challenge the convergence hypothesis underpinning the globalization orthodoxy. As indicated in Chapter 2, it perceives a 'massive shake-out of societies, economies, institutions of governance and world order' – that is, globalization *does* represent new and powerful processes of transformation – but at the same time refutes the notion of convergence on a 'single world system'. Moreover, it points to the processes of 'stratification' in which 'some states, societies and communities are becoming increasingly enmeshed in the global order while others are becoming increasingly marginalized' (Held *et al.* 1999: 7–8). In this sense, it coincides neatly with what has been called the 'middle ground' in the globalization–state debate – that is, between the hyperglobalist and sceptical positions. According to this interpretation, states must be understood not in the sterile terms of a strengthening/weakening dichotomy of the sort advanced between the other two schools of the debate, but rather as undergoing variegated processes of adaptation and transformation. The relationship between states and globalization must also be understood, from this middle ground, as one of symbiosis. States are critical to the 'authoring' and propulsion of globalization itself, and globalization processes, as well as global markets, are both embedded within and dependent upon states (*inter alia*, Helleiner 1994; Panitch 1996; Amoore *et al.* 1997; Evans 1997; Scholte 1997; Weiss 1998).

These insights have been marshalled for the purposes not only of understanding the nature and internal dynamics of globalization processes themselves, but also of taking aim at the central tendency in the globalization orthodoxy to treat states as essentially undifferentiated from one another. Orthodox perspectives in the debate endeavour to identify *the* relationship between globalization and *the* state, assuming in the process that states can be treated as a single and uniform category and understood as subject to a uniform set of structural influences. The CPE debates about the global–national interaction have been quick to pick this up and argue, as we have seen, for an understanding of enduring national specificity and contingency, often in a manner which suggests that there is really very little that does or should alter fundamentally the ways in which we understand individual states. In transformationalist middle-ground approaches in the globalization–state debate, there has naturally been a much more conscious effort to locate analysis of states within the context of the transformative impact of globalization. At the same time, it is maintained that there is no such thing as 'a' relationship between globalization and 'the state', and that careful differentiation between states is necessary in order to establish whether the assumptions of the globalization orthodoxy and the convergence hypothesis hold any analytical water.

Some of the legwork in this respect has been done by those keen to point out that not all states are in fact engaged by or integrated into globalization processes, and by extension that the main impacts of globalization are not inclusion and convergence, as assumed by the globalization orthodoxy, but rather exclusion and divergence. These arguments were considered in the earlier chapter on globalization. By far the strongest challenge to convergence perspectives, however, has been mounted by a body of robust recent scholarship that clusters within the field of CPE. It seeks to identify considerable deviation from the globalization orthodoxy in economic policy orientations and the social configurations that underpin distinct political economies. On this basis, the aim is not only to identify particular and peculiar relationships (plural) between globalization and states (also plural), but also, in so doing, to dispute the mechanistic understandings inherent in the globalization orthodoxy of how markets work.

The empirical evidence amassed in this regard has been impressive. Geoffrey Garrett's (1998, 2000a) work on the OECD countries has demonstrated the significant divergence in fiscal and taxation policies and the persistence of expansionary expenditure patterns which run directly counter to the predictions of orthodox understandings of the sources of competitiveness and the conditions which are, and are not, attractive to global flows of investment capital. Martin Rhodes's (2001) work on Europe has reached similar conclusions concerning welfare and employment policies. He has also demonstrated that 'old' corporatist bargaining structures are in many places more, rather than less, important in the management of the structural pressures associated with globalization. Colin Hay (2000a, 2004a, 2005), again looking at Europe, has sought also to challenge the predictions of convergence by assembling extensive empirical data across a wide range of policy areas. On this basis, he has drawn a range of broader conclusions which posit a 'dual convergence' around liberal and coordinated forms of market economy, challenge the assumptions about the determinants of FDI and capital markets, and reveal that, in fact, restructuring processes in Europe are considerably more consistent with a trend towards regionalization than one of globalization. Layna Mosley's (2003) work advances similarly arresting conclusions about the investment preferences and decisions of capital market participants. Like Hay, Rhodes and Garrett, she takes aim convincingly and with detailed empirical ammunition at the contention that international financial integration is inimical to social democratic welfare policies in 'developed' countries, extending this line of enquiry to demonstrate that, despite somewhat greater constraints, national governments in 'developing' countries retain 'some measure of choice' in the face of capital market pressures (Mosley 2003: 3). In both contexts, she argues, echoing Helen Milner, that domestic distributional considerations are as important as external financial market pressures in determining governments' policy choices.

These are highly salient contributions to a growing body of literature that seeks to challenge the convergence hypothesis and has left a deep imprint on the globalization–state debate. Their primary utility has been felt in their reformulation of the questions that we ought to ask about states, and indeed about globalization itself. They suggest forcefully that a focus on the putative decline of states is premised on a misplaced concern with the *degree* of state intervention rather than the *type* of intervention and the *nature* of the active strategies pursued by states. Thus the apposite question is not about *how much* 'stateness' exists but rather *what sorts* of stateness emerge as a result of the variegated impact of globalization (Phillips 2004: 222).

It is perhaps striking that most of these pivotal contributions have been developed more from within CPE than IPE, or at least by people who would identify themselves as working at the intersection of these two fields. In IPE, the endeavour to address precisely this question of what forms of state emerge has been found primarily in two areas. The first, within critical IPE, is in Robert Cox's seminal notion of the 'internationalization of the state'. He seeks in this regard to identify a 'global process whereby national policies and practices have been adjusted to the exigencies of the world economy of international production' (Cox 1987: 253) in which precedence and salience are accrued by 'certain state agencies...which are the key points in the adjustment of domestic to international economic policy' (Cox 1981: 146). The task before us is therefore, Cox suggests, to understand the nature of the state forms that emerge from this process, in a manner which reflects the 'different positions of countries in the world economy' and the ways in which 'changes in forms of state will be conditioned by both the social structure of accumulation... and...the structure of world order' (Cox 1987: 253, 298). This framework has been deployed to very valuable effect in investigations of the neoliberal trajectories of particular national or regional political economies (Bieler 2000; van Apeldoorn 2002; Morton 2003; Shields 2003). But it is nonetheless striking that there have been only rather scanty attempts thus far to deploy it for the purposes of investigating the *institutional* evolution of particular states in various contexts, notwithstanding some valuable exceptions to this generalization (A. Baker 1999).

The second salient contribution, emerging from neoliberal IPE, is Cerny's (1997b) notion of the 'competition state'. His starting point is the presumed crisis of the postwar welfare state model and its obsolescence under a process of 'marketization' designed around the core imperative of international and transnational competitiveness. Cerny's view of the result is a conventional neoliberal one: a 'residual' form of contemporary state which is essentially associated with 'neoliberal monetarism' and only a tangential role in the provision of welfare. The competition state model thus overlaps in some ways with other similar formulations advanced by CPE scholars, such as Peter Evans's (1997) 'leaner, meaner' variety of stateness that has emerged as a result of the overload on states occasioned by this postwar model, and Bob Jessop's (2002) 'Schumpeterian post-national workfare regime' that, similarly, he deems to be in the process of superseding the 'Keynesian welfare national state'. Yet, considerably more than these other perspectives, Cerny's arguments in fact take us a long way back towards the globalization orthodoxy in their explicit assumption of the 'erosion of capitalist diversity'

(Cerny 1997c) and the intrinsic validation of the convergence hypothesis. The only substantial difference between the competition state model and the convergence hypothesis lies in Cerny's sustained attention to the nature of the state *form* that emerges and his attempt thus to lend some conceptual and empirical substance to some of the balder and more banal offerings of the globalization orthodoxy.

These, then, are the principal contours of the globalization–state debate as it has unfolded in IPE, with some acknowledgement of the ways in which proximate debates in other areas of the social sciences have impinged upon it. I indicated at the outset that I wish to highlight three specific and pervasive problems with the debate as it has evolved thus far: economism, functionalism and the focus on advanced industrialized states.

Economism

The globalization–state debate has been constructed on the basis of two prior, implicit, theorizations: of states (to which we will turn shortly) and of globalization itself. Globalization is understood on the whole as an intrinsically economic process, and is both theorized and framed empirically on that basis. The consequently 'apolitical' nature of much of the globalization debate in IPE has been widely remarked upon, and calls for injecting politics more forcefully into the study of globalization have been plentiful. Focusing on the relationship between globalization and states is, it often appears, widely thought to rectify the problem, the assumption being that if one focuses on what are essentially political units, then necessarily one is no longer guilty of analytical economism. Yet this strategy does not modify the overarching economistic conception of globalization on which the globalization–state debate is then built – it is a form, perhaps, of 'economics (globalization) meets politics (states)'. In other words, it is only in its impact on states that the economic process of globalization is generally understood to acquire political characteristics and achieve political expression.

This sort of economistic bias is most marked in the hyperglobalist school of thought. In the neoliberal globalization orthodoxy, it arises from the reliance (both acknowledged and implicit) on the principles of neoclassical open economy models (Mosley 2003; Watson 2003; Hay 2005). These give rise not only to excessively mechanistic assumptions about the behaviour of capital, as noted earlier, but also to an inappropriately homogenizing account of the relationship between globalization and states. Both of these traits are evident in analyses which afford virtually no interest to states and concentrate instead on the behaviour of markets, extrapolating from these the 'relationship' between globalization and states. They are equally evident in more conscious attempts, such as Cerny's, to understand the form of state that the economic 'logic' of globalization engenders. Economism is also the hallmark of Marxist hyperglobalism. In this approach, it takes the different form of a tendency towards economic determinism and a heavily structuralist account of politics, in which states, state strategies and, indeed, the class relations they represent derive from the processes and imperatives of global capitalist accumulation. Although the nature of the capitalist 'logic' deployed from a Marxist position varies from that identified by neoliberal hyperglobalists, a claim that a 'logic' of economic (capitalist) globalization exists, and a determinist argument that states are essentially subordinated to it and intrinsically defined by it, are nevertheless common to both.

From the intersections of the transformationalist middle ground and critical IPE perspectives, the central recognition of the importance of politics in the study of globalization has left a significant mark on the debate. Yet even in these perspectives there remain two clear undercurrents of economism. The first is that refutations of the convergence hypothesis have tended to concentrate on economic policy, strategies designed by states for achieving economic competitiveness, and patterns of economic performance. As a result, questions about the institutional form of states, the role of political actors within states and the structures of social relations in which states are embedded have tended to be left aside. Naturally, there are important exceptions to this generalization, some of which we have already noted in the work of Hay, Rhodes, Mosley and others. Yet, particularly in IPE but also in much related work in CPE, it appears largely to be assumed that the form of state and the nature of state–society complex flow directly from the nature of the policy regime, and thus do not in themselves require a great deal of sustained or specific analysis. A neoliberal policy regime is assumed to engender a distinctively neoliberal set of social and political relationships and an institutionally minimal form of state; a policy model associated with continental European welfarism will foster an equally 'appropriate' state and state–society complex. Nevertheless, the difference between such concepts as the competition state and the unquestionably richer critical refutations of the convergence hypothesis is that the latter are much less homogenizing in their thrust and much more receptive to the notion that forms of state may be multiple and are necessarily contingent.

The second manifestation of economism appears in the neo-Marxist inspiration of the bulk of critical IPE, and thus in the form of economic determinism that underpins it. Cox's notion of the 'internationalization of the state', in this sense, derives its understandings of states largely from their position in the world economy and the social structures of capitalist accumulation, both global and domestic. The 'politics' of the process are essentially derived from the socio-economic realities of capitalism, as are Cox's discussions of the institutional reconfigurations of states that capitalist globalization is seen to require and generate. Certain critiques of this economism in critical IPE read largely as unsympathetic critiques of political economy itself (such as Shaw 2000: 84), but the general point that critical IPE tends strongly to reduce the state to an expression of economic and socio-economic dynamics is certainly apposite. The point that carries even greater force is the failure of neo-Marxist political economists, including Cox, to engage substantially with Marx's theory of the *state*, as opposed to his work on the socio-economic structures of global capitalism. The reliance on Gramsci, for the most part, has served only to inject (or perhaps subsume) a valuable element of political sociology into the political economy equation, but this has not added up to a concrete theory of the state as the foundation for critical IPE. Cox's work, in this sense, has been observed as having 'left the state where it had been in Keohane and Nye: a still-national entity operating in conditions of macroeconomic interdependence, now redefined as those of the world market economy and capitalist hegemony' (Shaw 2000: 85). Shaw's critique of Cox and other critical theorists should be tempered by a recognition, highlighted in the earlier pages of the chapter, that Marx's work in fact yields no concrete theory of the state. Nevertheless, he is unquestionably persuasive in his observation that the main difference between neoliberal approaches and Coxian critical approaches is in their conceptualizations of *structure*, not of states.

Functionalism

We have noted several times now the pronounced concentration in the globalization–state debate on questions of state capacity. For the most part, the notion of state capacity is understood as policy-related, referring to the capacity of states autonomously to formulate and implement their policy preferences. As we have seen, in much of the traditional 'state autonomy' debate in Political Science and some of CPE, autonomy was primarily taken to refer to autonomy from social and societal actors in policy-making processes. In the globalization–state debate in IPE, notions of autonomy refer instead to states' relationship with markets. In other words, questions about state capacity focus on the extent to which their policy-making autonomy is or is not constrained by globalized market forces and the demands of competitiveness these are assumed to imply. It is not simply, then, that notions of state autonomy from societal and social forces are ignored, although manifestly this is often the case. What is more important is that they are usually 'assumed away' in arguments which identify the internationalization not only of state structures but also of their accountability and representative functions. A mainstay of the globalization–state debate, in both orthodox and critical perspectives, is the contention that states are increasingly centralized, insulated and 'technocratic', and accountable primarily to global market forces rather than national societies.

The core questions in the debate about state capacity are approached in a way that privileges functional understandings of the forms of state that are forged by globalization. This frequently tips over into an overt functionalism – that is, the (inherently circular) use of functional outcomes as *explanations* of the phenomena in question. The focus on functionality and the functionalist bias link with economism in the sense that, across the bulk of the globalization–state debate, states are defined and theorized with almost exclusive reference to *economic outcomes*. In matters relating to forms of state, both neoliberal and critical (including Coxian) perspectives conceive of the state as undergoing a process of adaptation to the challenges of achieving global economic competitiveness; the resulting forms of state are understood in a functional sense as the consequence of that adaptation. For neoliberals, this is conceived as the achievement of economic efficiency and competitiveness; for critical international political economists, it is represented by consistency with the demands of 'market civilization' and 'disciplinary neoliberalism' (Gill 1995). Either way, states are defined as functional, or dysfunctional, according to the economic outcomes of their adaptation to the demands of the new global economy. Not only is functionality thereby 'selected for' (Hay 2004b), but states are also *theorized* primarily on the basis of their functionality, or lack of it. Questions of state capacity have been approached in largely the same way. Capacity is identified and judged according to outcomes: if a state achieves economic competitiveness, efficiency and robust economic performance levels, or indeed if its policy outputs deviate substantially from what are presumed to be the requirements of the global financial orthodoxy, it is considered to be possessed of high levels of capacity and autonomy.

Functional*ism* is rather more implicit in these perspectives, but nevertheless runs through them as a notable undercurrent. In a sense, it arises somewhat 'by default' as a result of the generalized failure to consider or advance clear understandings of the processes by which outcomes are produced. Across the globalization–state debate, the competitive outcomes of state adaptation to the demands of globalization are the focus of analysis, and strikingly little has been offered in the way of explanations of how those outcomes are generated or achieved. Likewise, attempts to analyse the form of state (usually singular) that emerges from these processes concentrate virtually exclusively on identifying what that state form looks like, rather than the causes of it and the concrete processes by which it is forged. Much of the process of adaptation, particularly in neoliberal analysis, is presented apparently as automatic, as the state responds in a mechanistic and possibly 'rational' manner to a set of external imperatives. There are, of course, very robust exceptions to this general functionalist tendency, and indeed the need to escape it has frequently been intoned. Mosley (2003: 15), for example, is concerned directly with identifying the 'causal mechanisms underpinning government policy selection', and pays particular attention to the ways in which financial market participants evaluate government policies and make investment decisions on this basis. Hay and Rosamond (2002) have explored the ways in which *ideas* about globalization lead to a 'discursive construction of economic imperatives' by policy-makers. Critical IPE theorists have also attempted more than many others to avoid this pitfall and to explain the political and social processes by which state forms evolve, notably in the identification of the 'conveyor belts' by which the dictates of disciplinary neoliberalism are transmitted to national states. Yet we are still aware of an underlying argument in these critical IPE currents that the 'internationalized' form of state emerges as a result of its functionality for global capitalism and the capitalist interests that represent it, and therefore is explained by and theorized on the basis of this functionality.

The focus on advanced industrialized states

The most salient problem with the study of states in IPE is precisely the one at the heart of this volume, and the problems of functionalism and economism intersect closely with it. The narrow focus on advanced industrialized states has both empirical and theoretical dimensions, and has acted significantly to limit IPE's purchase not only on the study of states generally, but also on the study of states outside the dominant 'core' group of countries.

Two tendencies are immediately obvious. The first has been noted throughout this chapter: the mainstream globalization–state debate has tended to concern itself with identifying 'the' relationship between globalization and 'the' state, and on that basis to develop generalizable conceptualizations of what happens to the state under the impact of globalization. The explanation for this is fairly easily located in the structuralist and determinist bent of much of contemporary IPE, which has meant that much more effort has been expended in understanding globalization than in understanding states. However, on closer examination, this is only part of the story. More important is the second tendency: the implicit reliance on understandings of the nature of advanced industrialized states, and the specific nature of modern, Westphalian statehood that these represent, in the enterprise of studying and theorizing all contemporary states. This arises in part, again, from the dominant structuralist conceptions of what IPE is, and should be, about. Interest has been confined to that small handful of powerful states that are deemed to define the global political economy, recalling from Chapter 1 that these are the only 'trees' that are generally considered to be of note and importance in the study of the global system. This bias is also the hallmark of contemporary IR. It arises in other part from the notable fact that all of the key traditions in state theory presume not only the existence of an institutionalized and sovereign – that is, modern – state, but also, as Leftwich (2000: 78) has pointed out, the existence of 'an advanced or, least advancing, industrial capitalist societ[y]'. Specific approaches carry particular embellishments: in Weberian approaches, for example, the attributes of advanced, institutionalized and functioning bureaucracy are both assumed and, indeed, essential for the Weberian theorization of the state to have any meaning; in liberal approaches, there is the additional assumption that the state will also be democratic in nature and the political system essentially pluralist.

What this theoretical legacy has meant for the globalization–state debate is not only that the empirical study of states has been limited, for the most part, to those of the core 'triad', but also that the dominant conceptualizations of states have been developed specifically in relation to those states, even while they are presented as generalizable conclusions about 'the' contemporary state form. The functionalist bias also comes forcefully into play here, in the sense that the focus on advanced industrialized states reflects clearly an analytical selection for functionality. The competition state and similar models, for example, have been developed solely on the basis of and for the analysis of advanced industrialized, liberal democratic states. Moreover, the competition state model, and the broader globalization orthodoxy into which it fits, are built on a peculiarly 'Anglo-American' understanding of competitiveness and its sources – emphasizing state retrenchment, neoliberal flexibilization and a very particular relationship between state and market – that does not apply easily even to the continental European case (Hay 2005). Its limitations are even more pronounced when the Asian model of development and others are brought into the picture.

Entirely similar observations can be made of another dominant framework – that of the regulatory state. The regulatory state model has been developed primarily by scholars working in public policy, comparative politics and European politics traditions, but has also found a foothold in IPE debates. It was developed initially for and has been applied mostly to the study of Anglo-American and European states (McGowan and Wallace 1996; Wilks 1996; Burnham 1999; Moran 2003), but has also been applied to a number of Asian states (Jayasuriya 2001) and others such as the Chilean case (Muñoz 1996). Broadly, it refers to a process by which economic management becomes 'depoliticized' and 'proceduralized'. It is characterized by an increasingly rules-based and technocratic approach to economic governance, in which the functions of such a state are seen to be twofold: first, to underpin markets, and, second, to address market failures through the provision of various rights and goods (McGowan and Wallace 1996: 562). In IPE perspectives on the regulatory state, this drift in the developmental trajectory of states towards primarily regulatory, rather than planning or interventionist, functions, is presented as a generalized, *and functional*, one occasioned by the demands of the globalizing world economy.

Furthermore, despite its allegedly wide relevance, many versions of the regulatory state argument are premised upon an ideological assertion of what the functions and roles of states should be. Thus, like the competition state, the regulatory state model is not solely (or always) a descriptive construct within which to analyse those functions. While there is no necessary or prior association of a regulatory state with a particular model of capitalism, it is nevertheless clear that regulatory modes of governance are more intrinsically compatible with neoliberal ideological inclinations than with many others, and more relevant to the particular associated forms of state– society relations than to those in evidence in other systems. It is also clear that, *particularly* in neoliberal discourses, regulation has been encouraged by the policies of expenditure reduction allied to neoliberal preferences for market solutions, at the same time as other forms of intervention are made less attractive by the policy constraints imposed by globalization (McGowan and Wallace 1996: 564; Wilks 1996: 541). Like the competition state model, in this sense, important strands of the regulatory state debate are shot through with functional and ideological biases.

The broad applicability and utility claimed for the regulatory state model become highly questionable in the context of the institutional evolution of states. It is very far from clear that most states are possessed of the institutional or legal apparatus necessary to sustain a 'regulatory state', or equally of the extent of depoliticization – in the Weberian sense of bureaucratic independence, of the judicial system or in the policy-making process – necessary for conformity with the tenets of the regulatory state model. Across much of Latin America, for example, privatization generally took place without previous preparation of the state to assume the role of regulator of competition, and the regulatory bodies that were subsequently established were most often characterized by institutional weakness, administrative ineffectiveness, extensive politicization and a pronounced absence of autonomy or independence from government. Consequently, the politics of post-privatization in Latin America constituted less an example of a decisive shift to regulatory governance (as in the European and UK cases) than an example of the 'chronic inability of Latin American states to fulfil a regulatory function' (Fleury 1999: 76; my translation). This chronic inability is manifested across many other states notable for comparatively low levels of institutionalization and bureaucratic development and comparatively high levels of politicization, corruption and clientelism.

The developmental state model is, of course, rather different in the sense that its applicability is explicitly acknowledged to be quite specific – initially to Japan and later for a number of the Asian 'tigers'. However, it has sometimes been broadened out to refer to a range of states outside Asia (such as by Woo-Cumings 1999; Amsden 2001), including Brazil, Mexico, Chile, Argentina, France, India, China and Turkey. The inclusion of some of these cases (such as Argentina) seems tenuous at best. There are also questions to be asked about the extent to which some of these states approximate a developmental state *per se*, as opposed to exhibiting developmentalist streaks in their policy orientation and ideological inclinations. In the Chilean case, for example, Kurtz (2001) has spoken of 'state developmentalism without a developmental state'. It is most certainly the case, in addition, that no Latin American state has ever resembled the ideal-type Asian developmental state or enjoyed the sorts of autonomy, 'embedded' or otherwise, that are characteristic of the latter (Leftwich 2000: 152–70; Phillips 2004: 227–8). Yet the most relevant point for our purposes here is that the developmental state model sits alongside the Anglo-American and continental European models as the primary frameworks developed for the purposes of analysing the core 'triad' of advanced industrialized nations. That is, these frameworks mirror the tripartite classification of the central 'models of capitalism' usually deployed in the corresponding debate. The extension of the developmental state model to other cases is entirely consistent with the pronounced tendency to assume implicitly that all other states can be slotted into one of the three available models of capitalism, or indeed into such constructs as the competition state and regulatory state models.

A further manifestation of the focus on advanced industrialized states in the globalization–state debate is found in the body of work that concentrates its energies on refuting the hypothesis of convergence. Much of the best of this scholarship (such as that of Garrett, Hay and Rhodes) has concerned itself primarily with the Western European or the OECD contexts. The central arguments that states and state strategies are by no means as constrained as the globalization orthodoxy might like to suggest are entirely persuasive in these settings, but are problematic when they are presented, as often they are, as broad conclusions about the nature of globalization and its significance for states. The implications of globalization look very different in regions such as sub-Saharan Africa, the Caribbean, or Eastern and Central Europe, among many others, where foreign capital occupies a very different place in economic development processes, issues of credibility and competitiveness present much greater challenges, and other constraining conditions are put in place by the much greater prominence of multilateral agents such as the IMF and World Bank. While this has been widely recognized, much of the literature has tended somewhat simplistically to conclude that 'developing countries' or 'emerging markets' will exhibit far greater degrees of convergence and conformity with the dominant, Anglo-American, policy orthodoxy (for example, Mosley 2003). In other words, while the focus on the distinctive pressures and constraints is unquestionably pertinent, it is the corollary contention of convergence on Anglo-American neoliberalism that is problematic. It would be hard to sustain such a contention even in Latin America and the Caribbean, the regions possibly most hostage to US interests in this regard and certainly those in which there has been most conformity with orthodox neoliberalism.

Most importantly of all, however, it is the very starting point that matters. To put it simply, states themselves look very different in most parts of the world from the 'modern', sovereign, institutionalized forms they take in the European and Anglo-American settings. The impact of globalization will depend not only on the nature of globalization itself, or on the perceptions and preferences of investors with regard to different investment destinations, or on relative levels of existing and potential economic competitiveness. Rather, it will depend also on the nature of states themselves, particularly with regard to their institutional characteristics and their levels of political, institutional and social – aside from policy-related – capacity. This point does not need to be laboured, and indeed has been recognized frequently by those concerned to identify the reasons for the failures of the good governance agenda in various parts of the world (Philip 1999; Beeson 2001; Clapham 2002). It has also been the foundation of the truly huge literature in comparative politics on the multiplicity of types of state and forms of statehood – from 'collapsed' and 'failed' states (Zartman 1995; Doornbos 2002; Milliken and Krause 2002) to 'quasi-states' (Jackson 1990), 'post-colonial', 'enclave' and 'small' states (Katzenstein 1985; Clarke and Payne 1987; Payne and Sutton 1993), neo-patrimonial, corrupt and clientelist states (Médard 1982; Bayart 1993; Szeftel 2000), 'biased' states (Philip 2003), 'predatory' states (Levi 1981, 1989; Evans 1995b), 'soft' states (Myrdal 1970), 'developmental' states (Johnson 1982), 'bureaucratic–authoritarian' states (O'Donnell 1973), and so on. Regardless of the sheer magnitude of this comparative work and the enormous intellectual enterprise associated with it, its imprint on IPE and the globalization–state debate has been only very slight – notwithstanding a handful of honourable exceptions (Bilgin and Morton 2002; Morton and Bilgin 2004).

Yet all this is not solely a question of narrow empirical scope. It is also an important theoretical issue. The three key traditions in modern state theory, as noted, are themselves of questionable utility in analysing those states which do not exhibit the type and degree of modern statehood that all the major theoretical traditions take as given. In much of mainstream IPE, as also noted, there is a failure to elucidate the theorizations of states that inform much of the analysis. This is manifested in a pronounced – implicit – liberal bias which runs though the dominant treatments of states, both in the bulk of mainstream IPE and in the globalization–state debate. The upshots have been manifold, but revolve around a profoundly problematic application of the classical liberal separation of state and market, state and society, and public and private. Scholars from non-liberal traditions have taken issue with all of these dichotomies on theoretical grounds. Marxist political economists, for example, have argued that the presentation of state and market as inherently separate spheres leads us up a blind alley in the study of globalization. Analysing the impact of globalization 'on' states is deemed fundamentally mistaken given that states are intrinsically pivotal to the reproduction of capitalist globalization. If states are understood as the 'political nodes in the global flow of capital', recalling Burnham's formulation, it is considered possible not only to escape the economism outlined earlier but also to construct a more genuine 'political economy' than that offered by orthodox IPE in its treatment of states and markets as independent variables (Burnham 2001: 11). The fundamentally mis-placed separation of state and society and state and market has also been central, in different ways, to the 'middle ground' approaches in the globalization–state debate and to WHS-inspired theories of state–society relations and embeddedness. On empirical grounds, these separations have been upbraided for their very limited purchase on socio-political realities in much of the world. The Asian region, for example, has provided particularly fertile ground for challenges to the liberal parameters of mainstream debates.

Reframing the study of states in IPE

The central argument in this chapter has been that state debates in IPE are both empirically and theoretically impoverished. The avenues for developing a more satisfactory study of states in IPE are to be found both in IPE itself and, moreover, in a greater engagement with state debates in a range of other sub-fields. In IPE itself, the necessary first step is a greater awareness of the three core problems that we have identified in this chapter and greater reflection on the implications they carry for the debate. This invites a reorienting of the conceptual premises on which the debate is constructed and a rethinking of the central questions that are asked. In some ways, indeed, starting by addressing the economistic biases opens up interesting possibilities for addressing the other two problems identified here. We have noted the established recognition in some streams of IPE of the need to inject 'politics' much more forcefully into analyses of globalization and the globalization–state relationship. Much of the work associated with this ongoing project has focused on issues of agency, in response to the generalized neglect of agency-centred variables occasioned by the structuralist economism that pervades the debates. Critical IPE, in particular, takes as its central project the elaboration of theory and analysis that give due weight to both structure and agency, in order, as Payne (1998: 266) has put it, to 'free' mainstream IPE from its 'excessively determinist connotations'. This opens up fruitful avenues specifically for a more satisfactory study of contemporary states. Dispensing with the sorts of economic determinism that are characteristic of both Marxist and liberal approaches in the globalization–state debate allows for and, indeed, compels much greater attention to variation, contingency and specificity in the institutional structures of states, the nature of state strategies and the types of state–society linkages that prevail in *particular* political economies. In this way, we are invited both to dispense with an excessively functionalist focus on economic outcomes and an underlying analytical selection for 'functional' states, and in so doing to engage in wider empirical research on the nature of contemporary states.

The most promising avenue for undertaking this task lies, in my view, with Cox's notion of the internationalization of the state. We noted earlier on that it has been deployed only infrequently for studying the developmental trajectories of individual states, or states within particular regions. A more careful and sustained application of Cox's framework to the individual and comparative study of particular states and their relationships with globalization suggests itself as a fruitful means of overcoming the identified narrownesses of state debates. Cox's framework is the more valuable as it permits a means of charting that precarious middle course between the twin priorities of, first, developing theoretical frameworks that can say something general and broadly significant about the nature of contemporary states and the significance of globalization and, second, achieving an appropriate recognition of specificity and contingency. What we should *not* end up doing is abandoning the project of general and comparative theorizing in an attempt to be appropriately sensitive to individual states or regional groupings of states, or falling into the premises of exceptionalism noted in Chapter 1. Building on Cox's framework, in the manner advocated above, permits the development of a concrete theorization of both the relationship between globalization and states and the nature of states in the contemporary global political economy. At the same time, Cox notes very explicitly that the form the internationalization of the state – or indeed an 'internationalized' state – will take depends upon the external positioning and the internal characteristics of the state itself. Such a framework is consequently amenable to the meshing of the theoretical and empirical endeavours involved in the study of states, and indeed the meshing of structural and agency-centred analysis that we have previously called for.

The need for more – and more *genuinely* – comparative work in IPE has been widely noted, and is one of the running themes in this volume. Without wanting to discount very valuable exceptions, it is striking that the comparative exercise in much of IPE has tended, to date, to correspond tightly with the tripartite classification of the 'dominant' models of capitalism in the global political economy. Often, for these reasons, it has involved little more than a comparative analysis of the distinct political economies associated with the core triad of 'models' (such as Weiss 2003). Nor, of course, should we discount the sophistication and value of much of this work on these particular political economies, but the point remains that the empirical focus and selection of comparative cases have tended to remain limited to the 'core' countries and regions of the world, and thus the 'global' relevance of the debate has remained noticeably constricted. Broadening the empirical scope of state debates, however, involves more than the customary judging of other political economies in relation to the three dominant models, which are almost uniformly taken to be the points of reference for assessments of both 'convergence' and 'divergence'. Rather, within the overarching framework of Cox's internationalization of the state, IPE can fruitfully reach further into the vast literatures on state forms across the world in comparative politics, CPE and development studies in order to develop more considered theoretical and conceptual frameworks within which to understand states and statehood across the various regions of the world. It is in this way that a useful corrective can be found to some of the critiques of Cox's framework that we noted earlier on, particularly to the charge that it is considerably more oriented to theorizing structure than to theorizing states themselves. The engagement with CPE and comparative analysis which we have highlighted here as potentially advantageous is *theoretical* in purpose as much as empirical, and is potentially of considerable value in the project of building more satisfactory theorizations of states in IPE.

However, an attempt to broaden the empirical remit of state debates also acts immediately to reveal the limitations of the theoretical frameworks currently available to us in IPE. As noted, the vast majority of these theories were developed on the basis of and for the purposes of analysing the advanced industrialized democracies, and their limitations become clear as soon as we attempt to take them outside their historical home. Moreover, there is a clear assumption in IPE that the study of advanced industrialized states requires a different set of theoretical and conceptual instruments from those necessary for the analysis of 'developing' states – an assumption which must also be attributed to the premise of 'exceptionalism' on which the field of development studies traditionally has constructed itself. The only bodies of theory of influence in IPE that have sought explicitly to integrate a genuinely 'global' study of states are those associated with dependency and world systems theory. These are useful inasmuch as they point us towards the issues of structural inequality and the intrinsically integrated nature of the global capitalist system. Nevertheless, their utility for state debates is limited by their propagation of the sorts of structuralist and socio-economic determinism we identified as characterizing a number of other approaches in IPE. Furthermore, these bodies of theory posited a clear distinction between peripheral dependent states and the advanced capitalist core states and thus reinforced the premises of exceptionalism that, we have argued, underpin the segregated study of states in IPE.

Yet the fields of development studies and comparative politics have considerably more theoretical, as well as empirical, insight to offer, particularly in the vigorous attempts to theorize the full gamut of state forms in the various regions of the world and in the area of comparative institutional analysis. In IPE, the latter theme has been picked up very usefully by Linda Weiss (2003), and deserves full attention and sustained further development. Moreover, recent currents in development theory point clearly towards a constructive engagement with parallel currents in critical IPE. What has been identified as a 'new' political economy of development (PED) (Hettne 1995a; Payne 1998) is premised on an endeavour to overcome the long-standing and pervasive dichotomization of endogenist and exogenist theories of development, and instead to construct a body of theory that charts a genuinely middle course between them. As put pithily by Björn Hettne (1995a: 262), 'there are ... no countries that are completely autonomous and self-reliant, and no countries that develop (or under-develop) merely as a reflection of what goes on beyond their national borders'. The elaboration on this basis of a new PED thus coincides in its central propositions with critical theories of IPE. In critical IPE, the task is framed as one of meshing structure and agency; in PED, it is framed as one of meshing exogenist (structuralist) and endogenist (individualist) understandings of development processes (Phillips 2004: 27). Closer engagement between these two currents, both in general and in the study of states, thus opens up a variety of useful possibilities for integrating the study of developing states more fully into IPE. More to the point, it offers a valuable starting point for building a body of theory which is able to accommodate and cultivate a genuinely 'global' empirical focus.

Turning to comparative politics, CPE and development studies is, in this sense, a useful starting point for remedying the neglect of institutions and state–society complexes in IPE state debates, as well as for broadening their theoretical relevance and empirical scope. They are also valuable in addressing an equally neglected dimension of statehood – that of legitimacy and authority. Indeed, their perspectives on state–society relations and political legitimacy (and illegitimacy) in various settings intersect closely and can very usefully be combined with IPE debates on the nature of authority in a global political economy. For further insights on these matters, however, IPE can usefully turn to a range of approaches that have infiltrated IR in recent years, namely, those associated with WHS and neo-Weberian theory. It is striking, in fact, that to date WHS should have been much more influential in IR than in IPE, despite significant common ground with critical IPE and the middle ground in the globalization–state debate. While critical IPE finds its inspiration in a different set of theoretical traditions, many of the mainstays of the approaches are very similar. Both, for example, locate their distinctive challenge to mainstream neorealist and neoliberal theories in their capacity to offer a theory of *change* and their insistence on methodological historicism; both are premised on notions of 'multi-causality', which posit the existence of multiple sources and forms of power; both are concerned with 'multi-spatiality' and the interrelationships between societies, states and international systems; both seek to understand the intrinsic enmeshment and 'partial autonomy' of states and social forces; and both hinge on the structure–agency issue (compare Cox 1987 and Hobson 1998). IPE and WHS also intersect closely on the theorization and understanding of 'embeddedness', and WHS offers significant possibilities for broadening the relevant empirical work in IPE.

Finally, the issue of sovereignty remains considerably neglected in IPE, despite a sizeable and important body of recent research on the transformation of sovereignty in IR (such as Jackson 1990; Jackson and James 1993; Spruyt 1994; Krasner 1999, 2001; Osiander 2001; Sorenson 2001; Lake 2003). In some ways this neglect is not surprising, given the functionalist biases that run through state debates in IPE, but its remedy is a crucial dimension of constructing a fuller and more satisfactory approach to the study of states. Of the four dimensions of sovereignty identified by Steven Krasner (1999) – domestic, international legal, Westphalian and interdependence sovereignty – state debates in IPE have engaged only with the latter, which refers essentially to 'the ability of public authorities to control transborder movements' (Krasner 1999: 9). This line of enquiry has generally been deployed in the hyperglobalist school in the globalization–state debate, and indeed has produced useful fodder for contentions of state decline. The focus on interdependence sovereignty has also reinforced the functionalist bias in much of the globalization–state debate.

Yet globalization has affected all four dimensions of sovereignty in fundamental ways, and IPE is uniquely well-placed to contribute to the analysis of the multifaceted transformation of sovereignty wrought by globalization. Issues of Westphalian sovereignty – relating to the exclusion of 'external' actors from domestic authority con-figurations (Krasner 1999: 20–5) and, in this sense, the increasingly blurred delineations of internal and external, national and global – are directly germane to vigorous debates in IPE on globalization, governance and the structural power of financial markets and other unaccountable forces. Issues of international legal sovereignty are similarly central to IPE debates about global governance and the authority of non-state forms of institutionalized authority. Moreover, attention to domestic sovereignty – that is, the organization of authority within states and the control exercised by those holding authority

(Krasner 1999: 11–12) – is in fact facilitated by the greater engagement, advocated above, with comparative politics and CPE perspectives on authority, legitimacy and embeddedness, as well as the seminal Weberian and neo-Weberian contributions on these issues. Closer engagement with these debates would contribute significantly to existing IPE scholarship and, moreover, invigorate substantially the contribution of IPE to the study of contemporary states.

Chapter 5

Structures, Institutions and Agency in the Models of Capitalism Debate

Mark Beeson and Stephen Bell

Capitalism has become the dominant form of economic organization across most of the world. Its ultimate supremacy looked far from assured during some parts of the twentieth century; at the beginning of the twenty-first, the principal focus of attention for policy-makers and scholars alike has become not whether countries will become capitalist, but what *type* of capitalist economies they will develop. Indeed, as economic rather than strategic rivalry has become a more immediate source of international competition since the end of the Cold War (Luttwak 1990), it has become increasingly clear that there are a number of important variations on the overall theme of capitalist development. Much of the unfolding and increasingly sophisticated debate about 'models' of capitalism that has emerged as a consequence has concentrated on the distinctive national qualities that capitalism has assumed in different parts of the world, differences that are often taken to confer specific competitive advantages.

Important as such insights are, the contemporary literature in this burgeoning field has tended to concentrate on the established industrialized economies of Western Europe, the USA and Japan. Much less attention has been given to countries outside this 'core'. This focus on the experience of the developed world has reinforced what we describe as a 'voluntaristic bias' in understandings of contemporary capitalism and the fate of nations. This is a perspective which privileges the role of agency, particularly the self-made efforts of individual nation-states to integrate effectively into an increasingly global capitalist economy. Too often, the assumption

116

is that successful capitalist development is ultimately a question of adopting a technically optimal set of policies, or establishing 'good governance', and that a lack of development is attributable to domestic policy failures and institutional inadequacies. What is missing from such nationally and agency-focused analyses is a recognition and consideration of the structures and institutions that influence the substance of capitalist development and the performance of capitalist economies at the international as well as the domestic levels.

Crucially, it is the general absence in the models of capitalism literature of adequate understandings of structure that most limits its utility for the study of capitalist systems outside the advanced industrialized economies. Developing countries and nations in transition from centrally planned to market-based economic orders must seek to integrate with a *preexisting* international economic order – one dominated by the developed economies and powerful international economic forces, supported by an array of influential international institutions which effectively control economic opportunities and set the regulatory framework with which developing countries must contend, often on highly unfavourable terms. These structures and institutions, which create or entrench the structured social relations that shape economic outcomes across the globe, must be part of any explanation of contemporary capitalism and development, particularly one which pretends to be of general relevance in the study of the contemporary global political economy.

Our starting point in this chapter, then, is the contention that, unless the debate about models of capitalism can account for capitalisms in parts of the world outside the handful of cases on which the literature has been built, and explain the forces that have shaped their distinctive national economic outcomes, it will remain of limited utility. The discussion proceeds in three sections. The first presents an overview of the distinctive qualities of capitalism itself, briefly outlines its historical development and its central dynamics, and considers the contemporary academic debate about national models of capitalism. The second section of this chapter looks in more detail at the theoretical and policy implications of the international expansion of capitalism for understanding capitalist development across the global political economy. The final section considers, in this light, the ways in which the debate might profitably be taken forwards.

The evolution of capitalism within nations

In the four or five hundred years from its original development in Great Britain to its contemporary status as the first genuinely global system of economic organization, the characteristics and physiognomy of capitalism have changed greatly. Yet, at the same time, there are a number of key continuities that define capitalism and must be present for any economic system to be considered capitalist. Of these, the following are crucial: profit-driven and market-governed resource allocation and commodity production; private ownership and control of the means of production and investment; the dominance of commodified wage labour; and individualistic, acquisitive behaviour (Hunt 1979). This is a formulation that draws primarily on Marxist scholarship; followers of Max Weber might also stress the importance of a distinctively modern form of legally enshrined and calculable *rationality* in the development and operation of capitalism (see Sayer 1991 for a comparison of these perspectives). There is nothing natural or inevitable about any of these features: indeed, for most of human history very different patterns of economic organization have predominated, largely because of the centrality to capitalism of states and, more broadly, politics. As Polanyi (1957: 140) pointed out, 'the road to the free market was opened and kept open by an enormous increase in continuous, centrally organized and controlled interventionism'. In other words, market-based capitalist systems have always been dependent upon states actively to create and maintain the conditions that allow their continued existence: without such support and state-sponsored regulation, capitalism could not exist (Heilbroner 1985).

One of the key reasons why capitalism requires the regulatory support of states with the capacity, if required, to enforce a particular political or social order is that capitalism is a class-based system. For social theorists drawing on a 'radical' or Marxian tradition, the existence of class-structured societies and the concomitant dynamic of class conflict are central components of capitalism. Class differentiation is a consequence of the fact that under capitalism the 'means of production' – land, capital, factories, technology, intellectual property and so on – are privately owned. Thus one class of people, the proletariat, has to sell its labour to the other, the capitalists or bourgeoisie. This structured demarcation helps explain both capitalism's dynamism and what Marxists take to be its ultimately unsustainable nature. On the one hand, deploying Marx's terminology, the appropriation by capitalists of the 'surplus value' created by the 'free' labour they employ is an important if not central mechanism of 'capital accumulation' and the reinvestment in productive activities that is so crucial to capitalist expansion. Value, in the Marxist understanding, is created through human labour in the production of commodities; surplus value is the increased value that commodities acquire through the application of human labour which the capitalist then appropriates. On the other hand, however, human beings find themselves in an entirely novel, market-based relationship with each other, such that labour itself has become a commodity (Giddens 1984).

In relation to the shaping of the transnational structures that continue to shape the system in which material civilization is realized, Europe has played a crucial historical role. Not only did capitalism have its origins in Western Europe, but this mode of economic organization and Europe's other great invention – the sovereign state – were subsequently exported to, or imposed upon, the rest of the world (Buzan and Little 2000). One of the reasons that capitalism emerged in Western Europe during the Middle Ages, it is argued, is that specific institutions were developed which encouraged capitalistic economic behaviour (North and Thomas 1973; Weber 1974). Crucial in this were the monetary and property rights systems which secured the position of the emergent capitalist class and encouraged the growth of trade between expanding medieval towns. Whatever the merits of this sort of functionalist reasoning, however, it is difficult to transpose this model to other places and times where very different circumstances have prevailed, particularly in light of the strongly contrasting nature of 'early' and 'late' industrialization (Gerschenkron 1966). The very fact that capitalism had *already* become dominant in Europe meant that countries that followed in its wake faced a different array of constraints and opportunities. Not only did the economies of the core enjoy significant 'first mover' advantages (Chandler 1990) in securing a lucrative and strategically important presence in key industries, but they were able to use their enhanced political influence to create an international regulatory structure that protected their interests.

We shall examine this latter development in more detail later in the chapter. The point to emphasize for now is that the economic and political dominance of the core has meant that all subsequent debates about the nature of capitalism and its historical position have tended to be refracted through European – and Eurocentric – lenses.

There are a number of important points to be made in this regard. First, as Frank (1998) has argued, this Eurocentrism has obscured the fact that there were important centres of economic activity in existence *outside* Europe before the European states and capitalists began their outward expansion. Indeed, for much of recorded history, Europe was a marginal player in trade relations between parts of Asia, Africa and the Middle East. Even so, the primary focus of analytical attention by scholars attempting to understand the evolution of an increasingly international economic system has been Europe and 'the rise of the West' (North and Thomas 1973). Second, while class issues and class-based forms of power remain central to the developed world, despite the growth of post-material and identity politics, the picture is rather more complex in the so-called developing world and is not well-captured in the understandings of class – or indeed state or society – that have been deployed for the analysis of the older capitalist economies. While class issues are frequently important dimensions of social mobilization where processes of industrialization and urbanization have occurred (Rueschemeyer *et al.* 1992), in much of the developing world the penetration of capitalist social relations is mixed with more traditional forms of economic relationships. At the level of what Braudel (1992: 28) described as 'material civilization', or the perennial, predominantly rural patterns of existence that continue to characterize the bulk of humankind's lived experience, the penetration of market forces and the emergence of capitalist social relations remains in some respects, and in some settings, relatively embryonic. Third, as Arif Dirlik (1999: 318) points out, this preoccupation with the European exemplar, and the tendency to measure other parts of the world in terms of their ability to replicate the European model, have distorted the way developmental processes have been understood and caused many to lose sight of the fact that 'the narrative of capitalism is no longer a narrative of the history of Europe'.

The expansion and consolidation of capitalism

Capitalism is driven by the endless pursuit of new sources of growth and profit. At an individual level, this may be attributed to acquisitiveness. In a modern institutional context, however, the expansive drive of capitalism has been reinforced by the dynamics of corporate competition and the need to maximize shareholder value. As Heilbroner (1985: 142) observes, 'the paths of capitalist nations by no means run on parallel tracks; and yet in all variations, the trajectory of capitalism is immediately recognizable as a movement guided by the imperious need for profit'. Despite this ubiquitous imperative and the contemporary context of 'globalization', capitalism has nevertheless evolved in ways that are nationally specific. In order more fully to comprehend these forms of national contingency, it is necessary to sketch briefly some of the more important changes that occurred in the evolution of capitalism over the course of the twentieth century.

In this respect, Dore *et al.* (1999) trace trends in capitalist convergence and divergence in the leading economies, covering issues such as financial and corporate control, managerialism and recent shifts towards shareholder capitalism. Of great significance also has been the secular shift from an international economic system predicated on trade to one that is increasingly dominated by strategies of transnational production and a growing separation between, on the one hand, the 'real' economy of goods and services production and, on the other, the 'money' economy dominated by an increasingly powerful, if not dominant, financial sector. In the nineteenth century, as Hoogvelt (2001: 14) points out, world trade grew eleven times more quickly than world production. Moreover, world trade was just that – Africa, Asia and South America were all major players in an international trading system. Indeed, the 'Third World' accounted for 50 per cent of world trade in 1913, compared to only 22 per cent today. One of the central causes of this dramatic increase in trade was European imperialism. Although there is a good deal of debate about the causes and consequences of imperialism, it emerged in important part as a response to the inherent (and historical) tendencies of capitalism to cyclical booms and busts (see Goldstein 1988), offering one way of resolving the difficulties caused for Europe by these cycles through outward expansion and exploitation (Hobsbawm 1987: 45). New markets, raw materials and cheap labour offered a means of maintaining profitability and the process of capital accumulation and reinvestment that has always been fundamental to capitalism and its possibility of flourishing.

Over the course of the twentieth century, this picture of predominantly European exploitation of colonial empires changed profoundly as both the structure of international economic activity altered and new centres of power emerged. One of the most important long-term developments has been the emergence of TNCs that dominate and organize international economic activities (Dicken 1992). Trade has become increasingly intra-industry and intra-firm, and overwhelmingly destined for the markets of the developed economies. Whether under a version of the (now rather dated) notion of a labour cost-driven 'new international division of labour' (Frobel *et al.* 1978) or because of the corporate search for other favourable factors of production (low taxes, world class research, corporate alliances, market access and so on), the trend towards open markets, disaggregated production and 'slicing up the value chain' has both reinforced the structural power of mobile capital over immobile labour and allowed a number of countries to accelerate the industrialization process and develop successful (if somewhat dependent) export industries. For example, the success enjoyed by a number of East Asian countries, the region's general openness to the increased flows of foreign investment associated with the new production strategies, and its general export orientation have seemed to stand in stark contrast with the experiences of Africa or Latin America. Indeed, much of Africa has largely been bypassed by flows of trade and investment and remains locked in a regime of commodity dependency. In the case of Latin America, policies of import substitution and greater self-reliance did not generate the kinds of outcomes found in East Asia (Ellison and Gereffi 1990); indeed, even following much-accelerated trade and financial liberalization during the 1990s, Latin American countries have failed to replicate the East Asian experience. There is also much concern about the developmental potential of many former Soviet bloc countries, where the transition to capitalism in Russia, in particular, has been associated with the rise of a new class of oligarchs who frequently have links to organized crime (Brady 1999).

The other crucial development in the structure of the contemporary global economy that warrants mention is the rise of financial capital. As discussed by Walter in this volume, since the start of the 1980s financial capital has become prominent, if not dominant, primarily because the USA unilaterally abandoned the system of regulation and managed exchange rates that had underpinned the Bretton Woods system for the first few decades after the Second World War (Block 1977; Helleiner 1994; Eichengreen 1996). Despite the obvious role of agency in the transformation of the Bretton Woods institutions, the net effect of this period, which led to the exponential growth of financial markets and flows of mobile capital, has been to make financial capital a more central 'structural' component of the contemporary international system (Gill and Law 1989; Andrews 1994). Significantly, the growing structural power of the financial sector has underpinned the creation of a 'rentier regime', in which 'the values of finance capital have won precedence over all others' (Greider 1997: 296). A key aspect of this has been the rise of 'financialization', variously manifested as the growth in scale and power of international financial markets, together with the rise of 'shareholder capitalism' and the growing exposure of individuals and governments to equity market gyrations (Boyer 2000; Williams 2000). One consequence has been a strong policy emphasis on monetary stability and low inflation, generally achieved through interest rate hikes, which has come to take precedence over other policy alternatives, including expansionary programmes to boost employment or promote industrial development. Put differently, the interests of financial capital have become structurally embedded in the international financial and national economic architectures which constrain the public policy options of even the most powerful states. For smaller developing economies, however, the constraining effects of large-scale and highly mobile flows of financial capital on options available to national policy-makers are considerably greater and their effects on individual economies can be profound, as demonstrated vividly by the East Asian financial crises of the late 1990s (Winters 2000) and indeed the Argentine crisis from 2001.

The other issue that the rise of financial capital illustrates is just how influential a number of key actors have become in setting the 'rules of the game' within which all national economies are embedded. The role of the original Bretton Woods institutions – the World Bank, the IMF and the General Agreement on Tariffs and Trade (GATT), now the WTO – has changed over time, but they, along with the USA, remain key actors in the management of the international system (Eichengreen and Kenen 1994). Indeed, the influence of the US government and state bodies within these institutions and, consequently, over the running of the international economic system should not be underestimated (Arrighi 1994; Sen 2003; Woods 2003). The postwar institutional architecture was a product of US hegemony and reflected a desire to create a particular *liberal* world order, one consistent with the normative judgements of predominantly US policy-makers about the most appropriate course and content of economic activity in the international system. As such, the system was designed to further the larger economic and strategic interests of the USA (Panitch 2000; Beeson and Capling 2002). Significantly, the normative and economic vision that under-pinned this liberal perspective has been championed by the very same institutions that have emerged to manage the increasingly interdependent international system (Cox 1987). In the longer term, the net effect of this order has been also to promote the interests of an increasingly internationalized business class and to consolidate the authority of a range of intergovernmental and non-state actors (Strange 1990; Cutler *et al.* 1999; Hall and Biersteker 2002). However, the postwar order that emerged under US hegemony also permitted the development of relatively distinctive *national* capitalisms, and it is to these that we now turn our attention.

National capitalisms

Within what Ruggie (1982) famously described as a system of 'embedded liberalism', individual nations were incorporated into a broadly liberal international order that simultaneously allowed a significant degree of domestic economic autonomy and internal protection. It is important to remember that the early phase of US hegemony was marked by a relentless, Manichean struggle with communism in general, and the Soviet Union in particular, to which all other issues were subordinate and subordinated (Cronin 1996). In such circumstances, the Cold War allies of the USA were given significant latitude in questions of economic management: even illiberal or state-dominated capitalism was better than no capitalism at all. This environment, in which economic development occurred within increasingly connected but still comparatively insulated domestic spheres, fostered the distinctive forms of national capitalisms that have been at the centre of much contemporary theorization (Porter 1990; Albert 1991; Boyer and Drache 1996; Crouch and Streeck 1997; Hollingsworth and Boyer 1997a; Hall 1999; Soskice 1999; Coates 2000; Hall and Soskice 2001b). As noted at the start of the chapter, the bulk of this work has focused solely on the advanced economies, and almost uniformly confines itself to the identification and analysis of a triad of capitalist models: the Anglo-American (neoliberal) model, the continental European ('Rhineland' or 'welfare') model, and the Asian (developmental state) model. Our contention is that we need to broaden the comparative basis for such work and, in so doing, recognize clearly that analysis of such national trajectories needs to be explicitly linked to the larger geopolitical and economic structures that constitute the liberal international order that US hegemony effectively created over the postwar period (Latham 1997). Simply put, we need to develop a theoretical perspective that can account for the different ways in which capitalism has developed both in 'core' settings like the USA, Germany and Japan *and* in others such as Korea, Chile or South Africa.

How best to explain this key characteristic of national variation between capitalist models? Some writers have looked to cultural factors at least as partial explanations of national variation (Lodge and Vogel 1987), whilst others, even those who admit its importance, worry that culture has become something of a 'giant residual category' (Migdal 2001: 241). For their part, Marxists have either tended to deploy overly generic theoretical categories and causal theories (such as analytical distinctions between 'core' and 'periphery' capitalisms), or, in more detailed empirically based work, have developed penetrating class-based comparative analyses of processes such as democratization (Rueschemeyer *et al*. 1992). Yet probably the most influential approaches to the study of 'competing capitalisms' (Beeson 1999) have emerged from comparative institutional analysis. This is not surprising in that it has been differential institutional configurations that have largely defined the nature and extent of the national variations with which we are concerned. It is also the case that institutional approaches can also be combined as synthetic elements with other explanatory models, such as Marxism (see Coates 2000).

A central insight of the institutionalist literature on models of capitalism is that the nature of existing institutions in any social context places limits on the mode of economic governance that can emerge or predominate by providing the 'rules of the game of human interaction' (North 1990: 384). Although there is a good deal of debate about the role and nature of institutions in a variety of political science, economic, historical and especially sociological literatures, there is general agreement that they are socially constituted arrangements that endure over time and play a crucial role as bearers of embedded rules, norms and enforcement practices in regulating social behaviour (Beeson 2002; Bell 2002). Significantly, although institutions are created by human action, once established they are also seen to shape it. People know how to behave in particular social situations because they have learned the 'rules' and appropriate behaviours that govern or constitute such activities (Searle 1995: 27).

This is important because the precise form institutions take in any location will not only help to shape patterns of day-to-day behaviour, but also impart a degree of 'path dependency' to social action (Mahoney 2000). By this is meant that contemporary and future social outcomes are to a significant degree conditioned by the actions of the past. This is an especially important consideration when we remember that the complex pattern of interrelated phenomena we label 'capitalism' is, first and foremost, an institutionalized expression of a *social* relationship. As a consequence, institutional differences and the embedded norms they represent help to account for some of the important and enduring differences between national systems of economic organization (Zysman 1994).

There are a number of possible forms such coordination may take at the national level, with concomitantly different emphases on the importance of market forces, social obligations or the role of the state (Hollingsworth and Boyer 1997b: 11). In the so-called 'Anglo-American' economies – the USA, Britain, Canada, Australia and New Zealand – much greater emphasis is placed on the role of the market as the key form of governance determining the production and allocation of goods and services. Latin American capitalism is in the broadest sense 'neoliberal' in nature, but various national (and subregional) capitalist economies exhibit characteristics which preclude its full inclusion in the Anglo-American category. For example, the 'Southern Cone Model' (Phillips 2004), while market-oriented in its broad thrust, is characterized by an absence of the institutional structures capable of sustaining the highly regulatory and juridical forms of economic coordination found in the Anglo-American model, resting instead on much more fluid and informal forms of political relations and, where they exist at all, highly politicized regulatory and economic institutions. In a number of East Asian countries, by contrast, social obligations and complex networks of societal and state-centred relationships may be more important influences on individual behaviour than markets or self-interest. Likewise, the more inclusive or 'corporatist' political structures that have characterized a number of European social democracies represent a distinctive way of responding to the challenges of global economic integration that diverges from the neoliberal or Anglo-American orthodoxy (Schmitter 1979; Katzenstein 1985; Grote and Schmitter 1999). Indeed, it is important to emphasize that different institutional settings may cause the very definition of self-interest and even 'economic efficiency' to vary from context to context, placing major constraints on the type of activities and economic structures that are likely to emerge as a consequence (Orrù *et al.* 1991; Granovetter 1992).

One useful way of conceptualizing these national and regional variations is by considering them as what Hollingsworth and Boyer (1997b: 2) call 'social systems of production'. This formulation offers a broad comparative framework within which to consider what distinguishes political and economic activity in different areas. Of greatest significance, Hollingsworth and Boyer contend, are institutional features like the industrial relations systems, corporate organization, the financial sector, the state and state policies, and the overarching value system that institutions embody. In a similar manner, David Soskice (1999) argues that 'production regimes' are ways of conceptualizing the organization of production through markets and market-related institutions. Production regimes are institutional frameworks of financial, industrial, educational and corporate systems that may be divided into 'business-coordinated market economies' (like Germany and Japan) and 'uncoordinated or liberal market economies' (the Anglo-American countries). Despite the fact that Soskice's analysis remains centred on the major industrialized economies, there are a number of important insights that emerge from this sort of work that have wider ramifications and which can help illuminate the position of other areas.

One of the most important differences between the capitalisms of Japan, Germany and the USA has been the role played by their respective financial sectors. Historically, US capital markets have operated largely independently of government intervention, which has tended to reinforce the distance between government and industry more generally. In Japan, the government has traditionally dominated the allocation of credit to indigenous companies through powerful agencies like the Ministry of Finance. In Germany, by contrast, domestic financial institutions dominate the provision and allocation of credit and reinforce their power by holding substantial stock in German corporations (Zysman 1983). However, in an era when the growth and integration of capital markets have made the idea of discrete national economic spaces less tenable, both Japan and Germany are facing challenges to their distinctive systems. In Japan, the gradual liberalization of the domestic financial system has opened up new opportunities for domestic firms, simultaneously diminishing the influence of the Japanese government and undermining the integrity of Japan's corporate system (Calder 1997;

Hall 2004). In Germany, too, the link between domestic financial institutions, a distinctively national form of capitalism and a concomitant social accommodation is not as robust as it once was (Streeck 1997: 252). The significance of such developments is that even the most powerful core countries are being constrained by changes in the structures of the global economic system in general and finance capital in particular. And yet this sort of nationally focused analysis serves as a powerful reminder that at the domestic or societal level, even within Western Europe, important variations on the theme of capitalist organization endure. Esping-Anderson's (1990) seminal examination of Europe's welfare states reminds us that even among countries with seemingly similar historical backgrounds and levels of economic development, differences in class relations and political alignments have a major influence on the sort of social accommodations that are reached, even where the institutional form appears superficially similar.

The limitation of this sort of analysis for the study of non-core countries is that, even where broadly functioning and solid institutional structures exist, these sorts of Eurocentric institutional templates may not capture the different form institutions take in other parts of the world, or the different purposes to which they may be put. For example, not only are social security systems generally much less developed outside Europe and North America, but even where they do exist they may be controlled and organized in ways that consolidate non-democratic practices. In Singapore and Malaysia, for example, social security mechanisms and funds have been used for a variety of economic and political purposes beyond simple social welfare provision, in ways that are central to maintaining the existing political order (Asher 2002). Despite the insights generated by the institutionalist approach, therefore, there are limits to how easily the European experience or the ensuing conceptual framework can be transferred to other parts of the world. It is for this reason that a wider structurally based analysis is necessary to capture and account for the experiences of countries outside the 'core'.

Capitalisms outside the 'core'

Debates in IPE about the impacts of globalization, as other chapters in this volume illustrate in detail, have thrown up a range of contradictory contentions. On the one hand, there is an intensification of processes associated with globalization, which some observers claim is undermining the power of states and creating an increasingly integrated and global economic order (Ohmae 1995; Strange 1996). On the other hand, the simultaneous persistence of national models of capitalism leads others to argue that such claims are seriously overstated (Wade 1996a; Garrett 1998; Weiss 1998, 2003). How, then, are we to understand the forces that are determining the structure of the international economy, especially as they affect the diversity of national capitalist experiences outside the core economies? More tangibly, are such structures facilitating or constraining capitalist development in the non-core countries, and are they erasing, remoulding or strengthening national models of capitalism?

It should be recognized at the outset that there is much at stake in discussions of economic development, not just for the potential beneficiaries of increased growth rates or rising living standards. During the Cold War period in particular, debates about development were overlaid with the explicit or implicit normative concerns that flowed from intense ideological contestation between the superpowers. It also needs to be remembered that, for the first few decades of the Cold War, the Soviet Union, with its distinctive brand of central planning, was not simply a formidable strategic rival but actually appeared to offer a plausible development alternative. In such circumstances, influential political scientists in the West argued that the establishment of political order should take priority over political emancipation in establishing the preconditions for development (Huntington 1968). Yet what is especially noteworthy is that even in the less ideologically charged post-Cold War environment, critics of the dominant development discourses that emanate from powerful agencies like the World Bank and the IMF claim that there is a desire to manage the increasingly interdependent global economy according to a particular set of criteria that reflect dominant 'Western' (liberal) ideas about economics and the appropriate path to successful capitalist development (Gordon 1994; Cooper and Packard 1997).

At the centre of the liberal economic paradigm has been the Ricardian notion of 'comparative advantage' – that is, the idea that countries should do and produce what they are 'naturally' best at. Thus, it is argued, countries with large populations should develop labour-intensive industries, countries with abundant resources should exploit them, and so forth. Yet critics point out that not only does such thinking threaten to lock developing countries into less valuable economic activities permanently and entrench the structural dominance of the developed world, but it is also unable to account for the remarkable success of countries like Japan, which had no obvious comparative advantage in a range of sophisticated manufacturing industries until government–business cooperation actually *created* one (Tabb 1995). Indeed, the success of Japan and its acolytes in East Asia drew attention to the fact that some states, at least, had the capacity to develop and continuously upgrade a more dynamic form of *competitive* advantage that was a central determinant of how nationally based economic activities were integrated into the wider international system (Wade 1990; Bell 1995). In an increasingly integrated global economy, activist industrial policies were deemed more conducive to the development of domestic industries to exploit lucrative niches, or to the attraction of relatively footloose forms of investment to accelerate the industrialization process.

Japan's 'developmental state', which was emulated with varying degrees of success across much of Northeast Asia, demonstrated not only that it was apparently possible to rise up the international division of labour, but that states could play a crucial role in determining precisely which position would be occupied within it. Indeed, perhaps they always had: it has been argued that developmental states historically played a crucial role in underpinning the rise of the most successful economies from medieval England to postwar Korea (Bagchi 2000; Chang 2002). Japan's pioneering success, and later that of Taiwan, South Korea and Singapore, also highlighted the point that timing is crucial. Not only did Japan in particular exploit the advantages that accrue to 'late' developers able to utilize existing technologies (see Gerschenkron 1966), but it was also able to take advantage of both a secular surge in global economic activity and the particularly favourable geostrategic environment the Cold War provided: there were expanding markets for East Asian goods in the 1960s and 1970s, and the USA was prepared to tolerate authoritarian mercantilism and domestic protection because of its overarching strategic concerns. For the countries of Southeast Asia that attempted to replicate this experience in the 1970s and 1980s, and for the economies of Eastern Europe and Latin America more recently, this benign environment no longer exists. It is in any case proving intrinsically more difficult to break into industries that are already highly competitive and dominated by the established developed economies (Kaplinsky 2000), but the IMF and the World

Bank have also displayed a willingness to exploit their strategic leverage to try and enforce market- rather than state-centred development models on the likes of Indonesia (Beeson 1998) and Russia (Lavigne 1995), as well as Brazil.

The theoretical implications of the East Asian experience in particular, and the evolution of the postwar order more generally, are thus paradoxical and contradictory. Nevertheless, a number of points can still be drawn out. First, the simple bifurcation conceived in some variants of world systems theory between 'core' and 'periphery' – in which the developed industrial economies of Europe, and latterly North America and Japan, systematically exploited the underdeveloped economies of Asia, South America and Africa (Wallerstein 1979) – appears unable to account for the rise of East Asia. For some countries, at least, the structure of the global economy has proved more porous and accommodating than the static, undifferentiated core–periphery model implies. Yet, even so, the Asian financial crisis of the late 1990s has revealed just how fragile and partial was the regional development model, and how ultimately dependent was the region's position in the global political economy, particularly in its Southeastern parts. This implies a second major point: one of the major failings in analysis of the Asian region has been the frequent failure to distinguish between the earlier industrializing states of Northeast Asia with their generally competent bureaucracies, and the states of Southeast Asia, which faced greater developmental challenges and generally had fewer resources to meet them. Revealingly, much of the 'dependency' literature that emerged to account for Latin America's development failures in the 1960s (Frank 1969; Dos Santos 1970; Sunkel 1972; Cardoso and Faletto 1979) still resonates powerfully with some of the Southeast Asian region's most prominent activists and theorists (Hewison 2001).

Indeed, it is precisely this sort of analysis, along with the desire to overcome enduring structural and institutional constraints, that has led countries like Malaysia to pursue greater economic autonomy in order to try and promote economic development (Beeson 2000). Given the impact of recent financial crises in Russia, Asia and South America, this renewed concern with possible regional dependency becomes more comprehensible. Moments of crisis have the effect of highlighting the structured and interconnected nature of the global economy and revealing the most powerful actors within it. In this regard, it has become even more apparent how vulnerable regions outside the core are to the whims of investment fund managers and possible rapid withdrawals of capital. It has also become apparent that states operating in tandem with international institutions continued to play a crucial role in actually facilitating such a process. As Panitch (2000: 14–15) points out:

> the process of globalisation, far from dwarfing states, has been constituted through and even by them. The removal of cross-border flows, the 'Big Bang' which broke down internal barriers within financial markets, massive privatisation of public assets and deregulation in other spheres – all this was accomplished through state action, requiring legalisation and juridification of new relations among economic agents in both domestic and international arenas.

The key point to emphasize here, therefore, is that not only is there an array of newly powerful actors in the global economy, like TNCs and the controllers of mobile financial assets, but their position is reinforced by the actions of states and international institutions actively enforcing the existing rules of the game. Yet this does not mean that there is a simple and unproblematic correlation between US hegemony and the promotion of the interests of US capital. On the contrary, there have been a number of occasions when the US-based financial interests have clashed with those of America's public policy-makers (Woodward 1994). Even during the recent Asian financial crisis, there was a notable split between the position of the US Treasury Department, bent on transforming existent Asian economic systems, and that of the Defense Department, concerned about the strategic implications that might flow from the destabilization of Southeast Asia (Mastanduno 2000).

The most useful way of conceptualizing the structural dominance of financial interests and the interests that support it is by recognizing that, as capitalism has become a global system, the social relationships associated with it have also become transnationalized. Robert Cox (1987: 359) has suggested that a 'transnational managerial class' has emerged which, operating through powerful international institutions like the World Bank and the IMF, has attempted to create a world order that reflects its perceived interests. From a Marxist perspective, globalization is creating both a transnational capitalist class and a 'transnational state' that is driven by the logic of *global* rather than national capital accumulation (Robinson and Harris 2000: 40; also Hoogvelt 2001; Robinson 2004). In short, the powerful actors that effectively shape the governance mechanisms of the international system are embedded within a wider array of rules, institutions and relationships of power that help constitute the structures of global capitalism – structures that continue to exert a constraining influence on the form, substance and prospects of capitalist development in all economies, particularly developing or transitional ones.

Thus, in contrast to those (mainly liberal) theoretical perspectives that account for the level of economic development within an exclusively national framework, we are suggesting that if we wish to understand the relative failure of parts of Southeast Asia, Latin America, Eastern Europe or Africa either to accelerate or to consolidate their developmental projects, we need to recognize the importance of the structural and institutional constraints they confront in an international system dominated by powerful external actors. This is not to suggest that distinctive national political practices and economic structures are no longer significant determinants of economic outcomes across regions and nations. On the contrary, they are. But we have to acknowledge that such models are under pressure and not as distinctive as they once were, even within the established industrial states that have a greater capacity to support them. In much of the developing world, therefore, the difficulty of breaking into an established global production hierarchy in which the rules of international engagement are defined largely to the advantage of the major, established players, and in which *dirigiste* policies are actively discouraged, helps to explain the continuing difficulties that countries experience. Many of these difficulties, in addition, arise from the inconsistencies between the versions of capitalism 'promoted' by the international institutions and associated agencies and the domestic contexts in which they are expected to take root.

Promoting capitalism

We have seen, then, that despite some ubiquitous and universal features, the expansion of international capitalism has assumed different forms in different places and been realized in very different historical circumstances. Significantly, in the aftermath of the Cold War, the capacity for powerful actors and institutions to influence the evolution of the underlying structures of global capitalism has been enhanced. Hardly any part of the globe is now not part of, or seeking greater integration with, the overarching capitalist system. In this context, the disjuncture between the experiences of the core economies and the developing world is highlighted in the reformist agenda laid down by the World Bank and the IMF, with US support. Epitomized by the good governance agenda, discussed at length by Anthony Payne in his chapter, this highly influential discourse emphasizes the importance of national agency rather than international structure, with the key assumption being that effective economic, political and social development is achievable through the state-sponsored implementation of suitable regulatory frameworks and the inculcation of 'appropriate' values amongst target populations more generally (Williams 1999). As Leftwich (1994: 364) perceptively pointed out a decade ago, the good governance agenda is predicated on the assumption that 'there is always an administrative "fix" in the normally difficult affairs of human society'. In such circumstances, overt ideological contestation has been replaced by the rhetoric of 'good governance' and an emphasis on technocratic competence.

More recently, as also highlighted by Payne, it has been argued that even if the requisite degree of enthusiasm for this sort of neoliberal reform agenda actually existed throughout the developing world, it is not clear that such reforms could be implemented successfully, given existing institutional constraints. Yet the difficulty in realizing the good governance agenda, and growing doubts about its efficacy in actually transforming the situation that confronts countries outside the core (Escobar 1995), should not be taken to imply that the role of external agencies is necessarily diminished. On the contrary, China's attempts, for example, to gain accession to the WTO by liberalizing and opening up its domestic economy (Hongyi 2001) highlight how influential the US-dominated Bretton Woods institutions remain, how extensive the spread of capitalism has become and how limited nationally based modes of analysis consequently are. Indeed, the example of China – given its sheer size and strategic importance, its position as *the* pivotal transition economy and its potential role as a major global market – can be used to highlight briefly a number of important issues that are central to our overall approach and argument.

First, despite some salient disagreements amongst its ruling elites about the benefits of globalization and economic openness (Garrett 2001), China has effectively signed up to join an established *capitalist* international order, the governing structures of which were created by the dominant capitalist countries. Second, the manner in which capitalism and capitalist social relations have developed in China is highly distinctive. A focus on national institutions, if sufficiently sensitized to significant contingent differences in the way broadly similar institutions are articulated, can help us to understand how existing institutions can be transformed by processes associated with the expansion of global capitalism. Ding (2000) has demonstrated how members of China's political and economic elite have engaged in a form of 'spontaneous privatization' as ostensibly Chinese-controlled companies expand offshore. Importantly, the precise nature of China's growing number of TNCs is unlike those depicted in the leading comparative capitalisms literature, being neither entirely centrally planned nor completely market-directed. Third, and as a consequence of this distinctive developmental style, China's experience reinforces the idea that a predominantly national focus is no longer appropriate or adequate to capture the complexity of what are increasingly regionally based interactions, both within China itself and between it and its neighbours (Breslin 2000). The emergence of a 'Greater China' that includes both Hong Kong and Taiwan is not simply a function of the increasingly dense webs of economic relationships that underpin this essentially regional phenomenon, but is something also shaped by a complex of often contradictory 'nationalist and geo-economic discourses' that seek to influence the direction of the region's nascent institutionalization (Sum 1999). Put differently, the evolution of capitalism in China reflects a contradictory amalgam of national, regional and transnational factors that range from the narrowly economic and immediate to issues of long-term, geopolitical importance that will ultimately help determine the precise form capitalism takes in China.

At a time when China has effectively given up its claim to represent a major socialist alternative to the capitalist model, and when it actively has sought to join the international economic system on terms dictated by the dominant capitalist powers, then the similarities between broadly capitalist systems would seem to be of far greater significance than comparatively minor variations on the dominant capitalist theme (Strange 1997). This is not to suggest that differences within national jurisdictions will disappear, nor that a process of 'convergence' on some common, economically or socially optimal end-point will necessarily occur in the foreseeable future. What it may mean, however, is that if we wish to understand some of the changes that are occurring within nations and the forces that are shaping them, we may need to look both above and below the level of the nation-state itself. As far as economic analysis is concerned, the most useful points of comparison may now be at the sectoral and spatial, rather than the national, level. As the Chinese example illustrates, not only do regions within and across national borders appear to be increasingly associated with particular forms of production, or what Ruigrok and van Tulder (1995) call 'industrial complexes', but a focus on the production processes themselves, rather than on the particular national context in which they are realized, also seems to provide a useful way of thinking about capitalist development processes that are less tied to specific locations. Gary Gereffi (1995) has demonstrated how 'global commodity chains' are now central components in new forms of economic organization that are driven by TNCs following a transnational production logic – one that has more to do with the demands of global consumer markets and changes to more 'flexible' modes of production than it does with any strictly national considerations. In the highly competitive electronics industries based in East Asia, for example, a process of 'mutual convergence or hybridization' appears to be occurring, in which the Japanese and US firms that dominate production are learning from each other as they reconfigure their regionally based operations (Ernst and Ravenhill 2000: 244). Even in the seemingly less constrained and intangible financial sector, 'global *cities*' have become the major nodes of activity, giving them a global rather than a national orientation (Sassen 1991).

In an international system dominated by the twin forces of relatively mobile economic power in the form of TNCs and finance capital, and an increasingly powerful array of transnational, intergovernmental and private sector organizations underpinned by US hegemony, integration into the global capitalist system on relatively favourable terms depends to a significant degree on the sort of first-mover advantages noted above. Those countries that industrialized early and established a dominant position in the global economic and political hierarchy enjoy enduring *structurally entrenched* advantages that are reinforced by a powerful transnational regulatory framework. Even the first wave of successful 'late' developing countries in East Asia were able to take advantage of fortuitous combinations of economic and strategic structural conditions that no longer exist. And yet, the East Asian developmental experience was no fluke of history. Whatever problems the region may be currently experiencing, its remarkable success demonstrates that effective state capacity in combination with an accommodating configuration of external political, strategic and economic circumstances may make a profound difference in shaping domestic economic activity and determining the way such activities will be integrated with the wider international economy. The significance of national models of capitalism, therefore, lies in their particular mode of insertion into the global political economy and their capacity to manage the process of integration within it. This is central to understanding the diverse and contingent models of capitalism that operate in the contemporary world economy.

Globalizing IPE: structure, agency and development

The key challenge that emerges from the foregoing analysis is to develop a theoretical framework that takes the structures and institutions of the international political economy seriously while at the same time recognizing the importance of contingent factors at the national and regional levels, and even at the level of the production process itself. In this final section, then, we provide the outline of such an approach and link it to a number of important debates that have emerged at the intersection of the IPE and development studies literatures. We suggest that although states are clearly central parts of the evolving international system, those outside the core face an array of constraints that are simply not captured by much of the comparative literature, centred as it has been on the experience of the core economies. In order to achieve a full understanding of the complex dynamics and organization of contemporary capitalism, what emerges most forcefully from our analysis is the need for a foundational theoretical approach that can effectively integrate agency, institutions and wider structures. For this task, we find the approach developed by Robert Cox particularly useful. In a nutshell, his approach to contemporary IPE explicitly attempts to link structure ('objective factors') and agency ('subjective factors') via the mediating influence of institutions (Cox 1987: 29).

For our purposes, structures may be defined as overarching systemic conditions in the international political economy. The structure of capital ownership, the structural power of highly mobile financial capital, or patterns of supply and demand in the world economy can all be thought of as systemic characteristics which condition outcomes and forms of behaviour. For example, the relationship between national economic structure and the pattern of supply and demand in the world economy is one which has proved increasingly disadvantageous to basic commodity exporters as they confront difficult trade conditions and continually declining terms of trade. However, structural forces must be conceived as shaping, rather than wholly determining, behaviour and outcomes: agency and institutional factors will always mediate the impact of structures. Of particular importance to the study of capitalism, both national and global, is the way in which countries operate within a structured and institutionalized terrain which shapes the way in which national economic spaces are integrated into the international political economy. One of the crucial determining factors that influences how this interaction between the broadly conceived national and the international spheres will be played out is agency: simply put, agents or actors face different choices or constraints regarding the way they are incorporated into the existent international system. The other is the role of institutions. North (1990: 4) defines an institution as 'any form of constraint that human beings devise to shape action', and, as noted above, institutions are essentially the formal and informal rules of the game, typically backed by sanctions of one kind or another. Thus, at one level, the institutions in question may be the sort of ubiquitous international institutions established under the Bretton Woods agreement. At another level, they are the highly specific array of national institutions and capacities that ultimately shape how such external forces will be accommodated.

There are also feedback relationships between structures and institutions. For example, the structural power of financial capital in the world economy is underpinned by the institutional rules of the financial markets game. The same general types of relationship pertain with respect to the institutions designed to govern arenas such as the protection of property rights, the terms and conditions of capital investment or the regulation of trade or protection. Hence, it is important to focus on the way such systemic forms or persistent patterns of behaviour become structurally and institutionally entrenched in the evolving capitalist system, and what implications this may have for models of capitalist development in the core and developing regions. Consequently, one of our major arguments is that the structure of the global trade, production and finance regimes is actively reproduced by powerful intergovernmental agencies and institutions, and by increasingly transnational class structures that set the rules of the game in ways that systematically create patterns of advantage and disadvantage in the world economy. While agency is an important determinant of state behaviour (Wendt 1999), and national institutions can be important expressions and causes of differential national economic outcomes (Hollingsworth and Boyer 1997b), unless we recognize the enduring impact of the existent structures and institutions of the global economy it is not possible to account for either the enduring distinctiveness of national and regional forms of capitalism or the continuing development failures outside the core economies.

In order to develop a theory of IPE that can accommodate both structure and agency, we suggest that a degree of theoretical eclecticism is essential. Consequently, two, generally discrete, bodies of scholarship used in combination offer a potentially useful way of conceptualizing capitalist development across very different regions. On the one hand, it is important to emphasize the continuing importance of what is mainly a Marxist theoretical legacy: namely, the importance of wider structural analysis, an insight that is generally overlooked in the preoccupation with the distinct national economies of the core. The most appealing foundations for this crucial understanding of structure can be found, we suggest, in critical IPE. Of particular value for our purposes, in this respect, is Cox's (1987: 7) explicit connection of his schema to an overarching 'world order' centred on a particular hegemonic power (currently the USA) and a hegemonic ideology (currently neoliberalism). Following Cox in this way, we can formulate the task as one of accounting for the very different outcomes that have occurred within this increasingly global framework, the extent of which perhaps threatens even to undermine the consensual nature of that hegemony precisely because development outside the core economies has been so problematic. On the other hand, we need to combine this structural analysis with institutional theory in order to understand and illustrate how the impact of global structures is mediated or shaped by national *and* international institutions. Only by considering national institutions and the wider array of institutions and structures in which national economies operate can we understand the constraints and opportunities that individual nations face. This approach is not only more suited to understanding models of capitalism across the whole of the global political economy, rather than solely in isolated parts of it, but also offers a way of explaining the developmental challenges confronting both the advanced industrialized nations and the populations of the world that live outside the rich 'core' countries.

This is not to dismiss the importance of agency in accounting for the fate of states and nations and their place in the global economic hierarchy. Clearly, some policies are better than others and 'good' governance is better than bad – even if such definitions are inevitably as normative and ideological as they are technical. Likewise, the array of national institutions to which scholars of national models of capitalism rightly draw attention will also affect economic outcomes; whatever globalization is taken to be, it is plainly mediated by nationally demarcated political, social and economic realities. And yet it is also vital to recognize that international economic competition is not played out on the proverbial 'level playing field' in which outcomes – the effectiveness and performance of various models of capitalism, as well as the resulting development trajectories of countries and regions – are determined by the efforts or ingenuity of the competitors. The developing world does not choose to be impoverished or at the bottom of a global order dominated by the first movers in capitalism's inexorable expansion. Unless the structural and institutional factors that limit their development are recognized theoretically and addressed politically, things are unlikely to change.

Chapter 6

Understanding Financial Globalization in International Political Economy

*Andrew Walter**

Understanding the nature of global finance and the origins and consequences of financial globalization is a central task for contemporary political economy, and indeed these questions have received enormous attention (*inter alia*, Frieden 1991; Scharpf 1991; Cohen 1993, 1996, 1998; Kurzer 1993; Eichengreen 1996; Quinn 1997; Garrett 1998; Strange 1998; Simmons 1999). This chapter sets out to assess the contemporary debate surrounding global finance in IPE and advances four main arguments. First, at a basic contextual level, it is implausible to claim that contemporary levels of financial integration remain low by historical standards (Waltz 2000), even though they are not absolutely as high as some have contended. Although it is debatable whether certain countries are more financially integrated today than they were a century ago, it is indisputable that there has been a dramatic increase in the level of international financial integration since the breakdown of the Bretton Woods system in the early 1970s.

Second, it is now reasonably well-established that financial globalization is not – or at least is not yet – the great 'levelling force' implied in some of the earlier literature, where it was seen as an increasingly powerful structural constraint upon national policy autonomy in all countries (Andrews 1994; Cerny 1995). In fact, the extent to which financial globalization constrains state policy varies considerably across both countries and policy areas, depending, as shown in some of the more recent empirical literature (Garrett 1998;

* I wish to thank Nicola Phillips for comments on an earlier draft. Remaining errors are mine.

Quinn 1997; Kitschelt *et al.* 1999), on the specificities of national institutional structures and the characteristics of national political economies.

Third, and conversely, it would be wrong to conclude from this latter literature, which focuses largely on Europe, that financial globalization has in fact had little effect at all. The emerging international financial structure does indeed constrain governments, but does so in a very unequal manner: most of the costs and risks it entails fall largely upon developing countries. Thus financial liberalization continues to be supported by the major industrialized countries, while there are growing concerns across much of the developing world about its impact and implications.

Fourth, the dominant approaches to explaining financial globalization are essentially rationalist ones, and these suffer from important methodological shortcomings. Rationalist approaches locate the origins of financial liberalization in its *a priori*, theoretical consequences for various sectoral or class interests (Frieden 1991). Although the origins and consequences of financial globalization cannot entirely be separated from one another, rationalist approaches place too much weight upon the *ex ante* foreseen consequences of financial integration in explaining policy choices to liberalize capital flows. In fact, in most countries the consequences of financial liberalization have usually been poorly understood, both by international and national policy-makers and by organized interest groups. Yet, at the same time, this does not mean that ideological motivations dominated such policy choices. Non-mainstream approaches in IPE that emphasize the role of 'hegemonic ideas' often exaggerate the extent to which actors are motivated by monolithic world views. Indeed, some are 'hyper-rationalist' to the extent that they associate hegemonic neoliberalism with a conspiratorial world project of finance capital (such as Gill 1995). I argue, rather, that we should give more weight to cognitive failures by actors operating in circumstances of highly incomplete information, including private financial agents, without losing sight of the way in which dominant ideas may work in favour of some actors and groups over others.

In order to elaborate these arguments, the rest of this chapter is divided into three sections. The first briefly discusses definitional and empirical issues surrounding the nature and measurement of financial globalization. The second section turns to an assessment of three main contending approaches to understanding financial globalization: technological determinism, hegemonic power and rationalist interest group explanations. A concluding section discusses the relative merits of the existing dominant approaches in this area and suggests avenues for future research that would broaden the relevance of the debate and applicability of its dominant conclusions.

How extensive is financial globalization?

Many studies of global finance refer to the dramatic increase in foreign exchange and portfolio capital flows in recent years. The triennial BIS survey has shown that, in April 2001, average daily turnover in spot foreign exchange markets was $1.2 trillion and average turnover in derivatives markets was $1.4 trillion (BIS 2002a). In terms of international financial stocks, by the end of September 2001 outstanding international bank loans with maturities of one year or less were estimated to total $4.5 trillion (of which $398 billion was to developing-country entities). By the same date, international bond issues (of all maturities) reached $6.7 trillion; notional foreign exchange derivatives contracts exceeded $17 trillion (BIS 2002b). These measures of financial flows and stocks are sizeable compared to world GDP of about $31 trillion in 2001 (IMF 2001). Nevertheless, they are problematic as measures of financial integration, in part because there is much double counting involved, and in other part because such flows may indicate poorly integrated national financial markets rather than the reverse. For most economists, the 'law of one price' is the preferred measure of market integration. In practice, although there appears to have been some asset price convergence among the advanced industrial countries in recent years, much of this was accounted for by Euro-area asset price convergence; financial asset prices in similar classes continue to differ across borders, not least because of exchange rate volatility and political risk (IMF 1997: ch. 3).

These problems have led researchers to focus upon different measures of financial integration. One of the most influential approaches has been to measure the correlation between national savings and investment. In a world of perfectly integrated financial markets, national investment need not depend upon the flow of national savings since countries can borrow from abroad. Feldstein and Horioka (1980) found that, despite the widespread removal of capital controls by developed countries since the early 1970s, the correlation between national savings and investment remained surprisingly high. More recent empirical work has suggested only a partial breakdown of this relationship for some countries since the 1970s. Nevertheless, it is suggestive of a trend towards greater financial integration among the advanced industrial countries since the early 1970s (see Simmons 1999: 56–61).

Other approaches have measured financial integration by focusing upon the use of capital controls at the national level. In empirical work, this is probably the preferred measure because of its ready availability via the IMF's *Annual Report on Exchange Rate and Monetary Arrangements* (Quinn 1997; Johnson and Tamirisa 1998; Garrett 1998, 2000b; Brune *et al.* 2001). This kind of measure similarly demonstrates a clear trend towards greater financial openness in many countries. Yet it too suffers from various problems. The IMF data are crude and do not distinguish more important from less important forms of exchange control. Nor do they take into account other kinds of barriers to market integration, such as national tax regimes, whilst portfolio capital flows also seem to have led, rather than preceded, the removal of various forms of capital control (Garrett 2000b: 9). Finally, this measure describes national policies rather than the degree of global integration: the removal of capital controls by the USA, Japan and the EU countries has been much more decisive for global integration than have been policy choices elsewhere.

Nevertheless, despite manifest problems with all of the available measures, there is no doubt that global financial integration has increased considerably since the 1970s, although the major industrial economies and a few offshore financial centres and developing countries account for most of this 'global' phenomenon. Almost all developed economies followed the lead of the USA in 1973 in removing capital controls, albeit with substantial delays in many cases. Some important developing countries in Latin America and East Asia also removed many capital controls in the late 1980s and 1990s (Brune *et al.* 2001). Even so, globalization sceptics have argued that the level of contemporary financial integration falls considerably short of that which existed just before 1914, when the most important country, Britain, was exporting annually net savings worth up to 9 per cent of its GDP (Hirst and Thompson 1999: ch. 2). Although this is correct, there are other reasons to believe that the degree of global financial integration is both different from and deeper than that which prevailed before the First World War. First, the ratio of short-term capital flows to long-term flows is much higher today. As Bordo *et al.* (1999: 31–4) explain, investors' preferences for bond rather than equity investments, as well as the dominant intermediary roles of family-owned investment banks, were probably due in part to the much poorer information about foreign investment risk that prevailed before 1914. At this time, long-term bond issues mostly financed railways and raw materials extraction, and ran from the rich European core to developing countries. Second, there was nothing in the pre-1914 period to compare with the way in which, today, deep markets in many different kinds of financial product and many different currencies, including spot and derivative contracts, have flourished and become dissociated from their national origin (and often from fixed investment and trade). Indeed, the actual or potential 'offshore' operation of financial markets has become a defining characteristic of contemporary global finance.

The growth of financial integration over the past few decades has led some to call global finance a 'structure' (Andrews 1994) or a 'cage' (Lindblom 1977). The strong implication is that the scope for national policy agency or autonomy has been considerably narrowed by financial integration. However, in this respect the globalization sceptics have advanced the more persuasive arguments thus far. The reason is simple: although contemporary financial integration is unprecedented, national savings and investment flows continue to dominate cross-border flows. Some careful recent empirical studies have demonstrated that, as a result, there is so far no evidence of a clear trend towards less activist fiscal and monetary policy or any shrinkage of the welfare state and capital taxation (Garrett 1998, 2000b; Kitschelt *et al.* 1999). Despite the increase in the degree of financial integration, it has by no means progressed sufficiently for national policy autonomy to have been erased. Indeed, for the major countries, the shift to floating exchange rates since the early 1970s has probably increased rather than decreased macroeconomic policy autonomy.

It must be emphasized, however, that the great bulk of this evidence is heavily focused on the OECD countries, and on Western Europe in particular. This is primarily because of the better available time-series economic and political data for OECD countries, the dominance of European countries within this grouping – 23 out of the current 30 members are territorially European, and members such as Australia and Canada have European-, or at least Western-, style political economies – and the dominant concern of particular researchers with the fate of the social democratic model. Some might be tempted to argue, looking especially at the fate of Argentina in 2002, that financial globalization does indeed represent nothing but a cage for developing countries. But it remains equally possible that Argentina's problems were more home-grown than structurally imposed from the outside, not least the government's long persistence with the currency board arrangement known as convertibility and the fiscal weaknesses produced by Argentina's federal structure (for accounts, see Manzetti 2002; Mussa 2002).

For low- and middle-income countries in general, the data show that the average ratio of general government final consumption expenditure to GDP rose fairly steadily from 12 per cent in the early 1960s to 15 per cent in the late 1990s, with a small decline from a peak of about 17 per cent in the mid-1980s (see Figure 6.1).

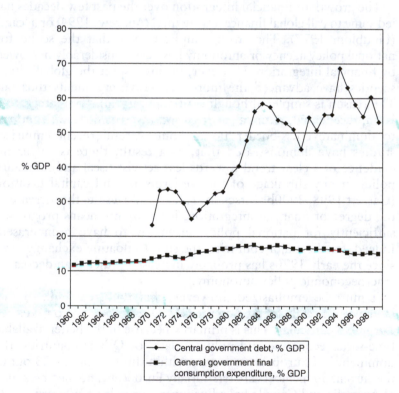

FIGURE 6.1 *Low- and middle-income developing countries: fiscal indicators*

Source: Own elaboration based on data from World Bank, *World Development Indicators 2001*, CD-Rom.

This could be taken to suggest that financial integration has imposed greater constraints on public expenditure since the early 1980s. Yet, conversely, there has also been a continuous increase in government indebtedness in developing countries, which is at odds with the view that financial openness should increasingly constrain deficit spending. This picture is broadly similar to that which prevails in the OECD but, lacking good data and serious cross-country studies, we simply do not know enough about trends in developing countries to be able to say what impact financial integration is having outside the OECD.

What is beyond doubt, however, is that the main costs posed by financial openness for 'emerging market' countries relate to the increased potential for financial crises that it entails. Recent crises in various developing countries over the 1994–2002 period – from Mexico in 1994–5 to East Asia, Russia and Brazil in the late 1990s, and then Argentina in 2001–2 – are powerful testimony to the extent to which the costs of financial globalization have fallen disproportionately upon the larger emerging markets. Banks based in the developed countries, in particular, were more than willing to lend to these countries before mid-1997, but they tended to do so in dollars or yen, often at short maturities. When banks withdrew credits and helped to precipitate the crises, IMF-led international rescue efforts also largely ensured that international banks were repaid, with the exception of some Russian debt.

By contrast, financial openness for the developed countries has allowed them to borrow from international investors by selling domestic currency-denominated financial assets, which does not entail the currency risk incurred by emerging-market borrowers. Consistent with this, Edwards (2001) finds evidence that capital account liberalization boosts growth in high-income countries, but slows it in low-income countries. Those who claim, relying upon textbook economics, that the free flow of international savings is Pareto welfare-improving ignore this basic asymmetry. For the developed countries, perhaps the most obvious cost is the greater difficulty of using pegged exchange rates as an anchor for monetary policy, as the UK, Italy and Sweden discovered in 1992. For the emerging-market countries, the cost–benefit calculation is much more complex and of much greater import. For most of the least developed countries, which tend not to be seen as creditworthy by international banks and investors, the degree of integration with global financial markets remains very limited. This includes most of

China, India and almost all of South Asia and sub-Saharan Africa: in other words, most of the world's population.

The costs of financial integration, then, have been substantial. Yet, as I suggest below, these costs have also been much greater than initially expected, particularly for the emerging-market countries. This poses the question of why the level of financial openness has nevertheless been steadily growing for many developed and developing countries. The puzzle is particularly clear for the emerging-market countries that have suffered financial crises in recent years since, with the temporary exception of Malaysia in 1998, most crisis-hit countries have not reverted to capital controls. On the contrary, these countries have committed themselves to a set of domestic institutional reforms that some argue amount to 'making the world safe for global finance capitalism' (Rodrik 2000). Even Malaysia has been taking steps to improve its standards of corporate governance, accounting, financial regulation and macroeconomic transparency, albeit more quietly than the other crisis-hit countries in the region, and has relaxed its capital control regime (Meesook *et al.* 2001). In the case of Chile, in addition, even though the economy was not directly affected by crisis, the government saw fit in the late 1990s to eliminate the bulk of the system of capital controls that had been in place since 1991, in response to the flagging of investor confidence in emerging markets in general (Soederberg 2002). It is to explanations that seek to resolve this puzzle, then, that we now turn.

Understanding the origins and consequences of financial globalization

Three main approaches to explaining financial globalization may be identified in the existing political economy literature: technological determinism (Strange 1998; Garrett 2000b), hegemonic power approaches (Gill 1995; Gilpin 2001) and rationalist interest group approaches (Frieden 1991; Frieden and Rogowski 1996). Technological determinism explains financial globalization as the product of technological changes that are gradually sweeping aside barriers to the integration of national financial markets. Political factors may help explain the detail and timing of liberalization in particular cases, but essentially this perspective sees financial globalization as driven by factors exogenous to the political system. Not surprisingly, this is the approach adopted by most economists. The other two perspectives place more emphasis on political choice and agency. Hegemonic power approaches argue that financial globalization is a product of dominant political forces. These may be in the form of a hegemonic power that promotes financial liberalization abroad (the USA) and/or in the form of a set of hegemonic ideas ('market neoliberalism') that shapes the assumptions and choices of policy-makers. Rationalist interest group approaches, by contrast, focus not on structural forces and state policy-makers but on the preferences of key societal interest groups. From this perspective, financial liberalization occurs when groups that favour liberalization organize and lobby more effectively than groups that oppose it. Each perspective helps in understanding why financial liberalization has continued to grow since the 1970s. I devote most space to the analysis of this third perspective since, in contrast with the other two, it provides more insight into the particular pattern that international financial liberalization has taken and consequently provides a more propitious foundation for the future development of the debate in IPE.

Technological determinism

As indicated, many authors have argued that the rise of global finance is fundamentally a product of technological change that has undermined the viability of barriers separating domestic financial markets from one another. More specifically, the communications and information technology revolution is seen as the driving factor: 'new technologies make it increasingly difficult for governments to control either inward or outward international capital flows when they wish to do so' (Eichengreen and Mussa 1998a). The dramatic fall in communications and computing costs over the past three decades, continued technological innovation in the form of various derivatives products and the emergence of the borderless internet have all undermined the efficacy of capital controls (Eichengreen and Mussa 1998b; Strange 1998; Edwards 1999; Garrett 2000b). In turn, this has eroded the foundations of post-1930s Keynesian national economic management.

Attempts to maintain barriers between national and global financial markets, the argument goes, only serve to push such markets offshore. Garrett (2000b: 17) cites the example of the Japanese Ministry of

Finance's attempt in the 1990s to outlaw trading in Nikkei index derivatives. In response, market agents (both Japanese and foreign) simply traded these contracts in Singapore, with the same effects on the underlying stock market index as if they had been traded in Tokyo. In this view, then, once governments discover that capital controls do not work they have an incentive to remove them. Indeed, a notable process of competitive financial deregulation has unfolded since the early 1970s, as unilateral liberalizers reap benefits in terms of attracting international financial business. Re-regulation at the global level is theoretically a possibility but suffers from the standard free-rider problem, as there will always be at least one jurisdiction willing to offer a home to offshore financial markets.

This perspective also implies that contemporary financial globalization is different from that of the pre-1914 world. In that era, unsophisticated systems of capital controls could be viable because of the comparatively high costs of and delays in the communication of information, as well as the underdevelopment of financial markets and supporting services in many countries and of derivatives markets in even the most advanced centres. As Broz (1997) has shown, countries like France and Germany, which were less ideologically attached to the 'rules of the game' than was the UK, were able to make unsophisticated capital controls work at various times before 1914. However, not all governments today are convinced that the world is so different from that time or that capital controls can achieve no macroeconomic benefit. Many developing-country governments hold firmly to the view, suggested by their own experience, that capital controls can work (IMF 2000). As just noted, the Chilean government and central bank clearly thought so until recently (Edwards 1999: 74), and the Chinese and Indian governments continue to think so. Furthermore, some prominent mainstream economists have gone against the orthodoxy in arguing that Chilean- or Malaysian-style capital controls have been especially useful in periods of international financial distress (Krugman 1999; Stiglitz 2000, 2002; Kaplan and Rodrik 2001), even though most of these accept that such controls work well only if they are temporary.

There are, nevertheless, other reasons why governments might maintain capital controls after they have lost most of their macro-economic efficacy. One is that capital controls enable policy-makers to achieve other objectives, such as satisfying rent-seeking demands. Johnson and Mitton (2001) have sought to explain the Malaysian attachment to such arrangements in precisely these terms. Another reason is that offered by Garrett (2000b: 41), who suggests that governments may retain capital controls simply to signal to important domestic constituencies that their interests are taken into account. So, for example, one might explain the late removal of capital controls in Scandinavian countries (compared with other OECD countries) by the political importance of service sector unions who favoured monetary policy activism. However, this argument can only explain relatively short delays in liberalization, as these groups should soon learn that such signalling is 'cheap' if the controls have no macroeconomic value.

In summary, technological determinism may help to explain the broad trend towards financial liberalization since the 1970s, but, in relying on exogenous technological factors to explain policy change, this perspective is less able to explain the differential timing of financial liberalization across countries. In addition, it fails to explain why so many countries continue to maintain capital controls of various types. Explanations must therefore either posit cognitive failures by governments to understand the implications of the technological revolution, or draw upon other political economy-based factors that shift the focus away from technology altogether.

Hegemonic power approaches

Robert Gilpin is perhaps the scholar most associated with the argument that an open international financial system depends upon the existence and leadership of a liberal hegemonic power. In this view (Gilpin 1987, 2001), financial globalization today is fundamentally similar to financial globalization a century ago, and in both phases it stems from the promotion of international financial openness by the corresponding hegemonic power – the USA and the UK respectively. In contrast to explanations based on technological determinism, Gilpin's explanation is thus political in nature and focuses on the self-interest and international political power of the hegemon. Helleiner (1994) builds on this explanation in focusing upon the role of the US and UK governments in initiating a process of competitive deregulation in the 1970s. This began with the decision of the UK authorities to allow a lightly regulated 'Eurodollar' wholesale financial market to emerge in London from the late

1950s, promoting the interests of the City of London without jeopardizing domestic monetary control. From the time of the Nixon administration onwards, US governments rapidly removed the restrictions associated with the Bretton Woods system after the collapse of the fixed exchange rate system in 1973.

The key argument of this perspective, then, is that there is a strong hegemonic state interest in promoting the development of this increasingly important service industry, made more acute by the declining importance of manufacturing in the US and UK economies. The mechanism by which initial liberalization by the hegemonic power promotes financial liberalization in other countries varies according to different versions of the theory. One line of argument emphasizes unilateral decisions by other countries since, it is suggested, international financial liberalization, unlike trade liberalization, can flourish with international competition rather than cooperation (Helleiner 1994; Cerny 1995). Another version focuses more closely on coercion and holds that the USA in particular has used various multilateral and bilateral means to promote financial liberalization abroad, above all its dominance within the IMF and World Bank (Wade 1998–9).

Others argue that hegemonic dominance is derived as much from ideological supremacy as from material power factors. The rise of neoliberal economic ideas since the early 1980s has often been associated with US influence over IFIs and especially the liberalizing zeal displayed by the IMF and World Bank since that time (Wade 1996b). Economic ideas, in this view, become another power resource for the hegemonic state, in part because of their 'technocratic' character. The mechanisms by which ideas influence outcomes may vary, and include the policy conditions attached to loans from the IFIs and the circulation of individuals between national central banks, finance ministries and the IFIs in the manner of an epistemic community. More indirectly but in the same vein, the USA's higher education system, particularly in economics, is said to serve as a means by which liberal market ideas are transmitted abroad (especially to Latin America), to the possible long-term benefit of US economic interests. The technocratic elites that have come to dominate government and state apparatuses across Latin America, notably from the time of the 'Chicago Boys' in Pinochet's Chile, have usually held Master's and PhD degrees in Economics from Harvard, Yale, Chicago, the Massachusetts Institute of Technology and similar universities, and often retain strong links with the relevant policy communities in Washington (Centeno 1994; Valdés 1995; Domínguez 1996). These individuals have consistently occupied the highest positions in the political and policy-making elites in Latin American countries, including, recently, those of president (such as Ernesto Zedillo in Mexico and Ricardo Lagos in Chile), economy minister (such as Domingo Cavallo in Argentina) and finance minister (such as Pedro Malan in Brazil).

Other ideational accounts, finally, emphasize a greater separation between the interests of the hegemonic state and those of the private financial sector. At the extreme, the hegemonic project becomes less that of the hegemonic (US) government and more that of '*haute finance*' itself (Gill 1995; also Polanyi 1944). Here, the dominant hegemonic interests are more class- than state-based, even though the dominant state may be seen as having been captured by private financial interests, as depicted in the notion of the 'Wall Street–Treasury–IMF complex' (Wade and Veneroso 1998).

The variety of hegemonic power explanations of financial globalization makes a general assessment of them somewhat difficult. One general problem is that they seem to be insufficient by themselves. Explaining why the US or UK governments would pursue such policies requires an analysis of domestic political factors within these countries, as Eric Helleiner (1994) has recognized. Furthermore, explaining why other countries might choose unilaterally to follow them requires a similar analysis of domestic politics for each case. Even the coercive version of hegemonic power theory cannot avoid the need for attention to these factors, since even when powerful countries put pressure on weaker ones to liberalize the results are in practice varied. In the absence of such analyses, the details of the financial globalization process are left unexplained. Why, for example, in response to US capital account liberalization in 1974 did only Canada and the Netherlands follow with similar liberalization in the same year? Systemic explanations may help explain the accelerating trend towards liberalization after 1973, but they cannot explain the nuances of the pattern.

This lacuna also tends to apply to those approaches that stress the role of hegemonic ideas in explaining financial liberalization. Given the persistence of financial controls in many developing countries, ideational explanations must account for why neoliberal market ideology was less influential in such countries. This in turn requires detailed analyses of the way in which official, educational and training linkages between the USA, Europe and the IFIs, on the one hand, and particular countries, on the other, have varied. It may also be that particular cultures or political systems and institutions are more receptive to liberal economic ideas than others. So far, however, such questions of comparative economic sociology have been left largely unexplored, with only the odd isolated exception, such as Peter Hall's (1989) work on Keynesian ideas in different national contexts.

A further problem with ideational accounts is that they sometimes exaggerate the grip that ideas can have upon political collectives, as opposed to individuals. One prominent example suffices to demonstrate the difficulties here. Chile, after the right-wing military coup of 1973, was often seen as a laboratory for economic neo-liberalism in the developing world, introduced by the Chicago Boys. However, even if it could be said that the Pinochet government was wedded to the doctrines of monetarism and open trade, the same could not be said of policy choices relating to the capital account. Indeed, as we have seen, until the late 1990s Chile stood out prominently as one of the developing countries resisting the removal of capital controls in Latin America. If the Chilean regime could buy some parts of the Washington Consensus but reject a key element of it, this suggests that governments do not treat economic ideologies as complete packages. This example goes against the grain of a 'brainwashing' view of ideologies promoted by some Gramscian analyses (Lukes 1974; Gill 1995) and is in fact more consistent with the view that politicians merely profess to believe in ideas that suit them and the interests they wish to promote. Adoption of certain economic ideologies can be – and frequently is – at least as much a matter of political expedience as ideological conviction. Such an interpretation could apply with force to cases like that of Mexico under President Carlos Salinas, in which political and foreign policy objectives and economic development priorities – including the achievement of the North American Free Trade Agreement (NAFTA) – were arguably more important than ideological inclination *per se* in explaining the conversion to market economics that occurred in the mid-1980s.

In summary, explanations of financial globalization based on notions of hegemony emphasize usefully the role of dominant powers and dominant analytical frameworks. But such approaches raise more problems than they resolve. In explaining financial liberalization, the importance of hegemonic coercion relative to other stimuli to unilateral liberalization remains unclear, and requires much greater comparative analysis and more sustained enquiry into domestic political economy factors than has hitherto characterized the literature. As regards the role of dominant economic ideas, we are still left largely in the dark as to the precise and specific circumstances in which particular neoliberal economic ideas became influential outside the major OECD countries. Finally, on close inspection hegemonic power arguments tend to lose their analytical clarity, since they typically need to be allied with interest group explanations to explain why hegemonic powers pursue financial liberalization and why others follow. We turn finally, then, to this third set of accounts.

Rationalist interest group approaches

As noted above, explanations of financial liberalization based on both technological determinism and notions of hegemonic power need to rely upon domestic interest group analysis to fill in the analytical detail. Yet more formal political economy theories of interest groups have been a relatively recent development in the study of finance. Such theories typically do not challenge the basis of the neoclassical economic view that financial liberalization is welfare-enhancing at the national and global levels. Rather, they employ the tools of neoclassical economics to discern how such liberalization differentially affects identifiable interest groups within society (Frieden 1991; Frieden and Rogowski 1996). This allows these authors to derive the *a priori* preferences of key interest groups relating to financial liberalization. Depending upon the strength of their preferences, such groups will have incentives to lobby politicians. Self-interested politicians, in turn, weigh the electoral costs and benefits of various policies and make decisions on this basis.

How does this approach seek to explain the trend towards financial globalization since the 1970s? Frieden and Rogowski (1996) accept that technological change is a key driver of financial liberalization, but focus upon its distributional consequences. They argue that technological change raised the 'opportunity costs of economic closure' for countries and key interest groups, such as the financial sector itself, multinational corporations (MNCs) and domestic firms seeking cheaper sources of finance (Frieden and Rogowski 1996: 33). This increased the incentives for these sectoral groups to lobby governments to undertake liberalization policies. In addition, as the median voter becomes richer in the process of economic development and acquires more wealth, he or she favours policies that ensure low inflation and also maximize the investment options available to them. This should lead to a shift in median voter preferences towards greater capital account openness over time. In what would, in this view, be considered a virtuous circle, capital account openness should also provide the government with an incentive to pursue low inflation because of the threat of capital exit. If the costs of financial openness fall on individuals, firms and sectors whose political influence is weak (perhaps due in part to relative immobility), there may be little reason for politicians to oppose it.

In contrast with technological determinism, this account accepts that governments may choose to accept increased costs of closure if the electoral gains from liberalization are insufficient. Financial closure remains a viable option, at least in the political short run. This is necessary to the theory since if, as many economists suggest, barriers to integration between national and international financial markets were essentially unworkable, then political coalitions opposed to the liberalization of capital controls could play only a residual role.

To what extent, then, does this theory help explain the pattern of financial liberalization since the 1970s? It is broadly consistent with the fact that financial openness is strongly correlated with the level of development (Brune *et al.* 2001). Export-oriented firms and related labour forces usually favour exchange rate stability over financial openness, since the latter can increase exchange rate volatility. This helps us to understand why, for example, financial liberalization was pursued first in the USA and the UK, where the manufacturing sector was politically less influential than in other countries (Frieden 1991). As Henning (1994) explains, in countries with close bank–industry linkages, as in continental Europe and Japan, a strong political coalition can emerge that favours exchange rate stability. This also helps explain why financial liberalization came later in most of continental Europe and Japan than in the USA and UK. It is also worth noting, as an extension to this argument, that bank–industry linkages also tend to be strong in developing countries, where capital controls have more often been used and where there has been revealed a strong policy preference for exchange rate fixity (Demirguc-Kunt and Levine 1999; Calvo and

Reinhart 2000). Nevertheless, as already noted, big steps towards financial openness were taken in a number of developing countries in the 1980s and 1990s, particularly in Latin America and East Asia. In countries that wished to attract large inflows of foreign direct investment, MNCs' preferences for financial openness may have been an important factor in government decisions to liberalize. As myriad surveys of MNCs have shown, a major concern of investors, even those oriented to domestic markets, has been their freedom to transfer funds and profits.

Another important consideration for developing and transition countries, which typically have shallow domestic capital markets, is that financial liberalization can reduce the cost of funds for creditworthy firms and banks. This factor seems to have been especially important in decisions to liberalize in East Asian countries in the early 1990s (Haggard 2000: ch. 1). This motivation may also apply to governments themselves, as the state is typically the largest debtor within countries and taxation systems are frequently underdeveloped. Italy was among the first to tap the Eurobond market in the 1960s to finance its large infrastructure projects. In the early 1970s, especially in the wake of the oil crisis, many Latin American governments borrowed heavily from international banks. At the time, borrowing through private international capital markets also had the benefit of avoiding the policy conditionality of official sources of finance such as the IMF or World Bank. Although developing-country governments may be cut off from international borrowing in a crisis, this consideration is unlikely to have much weight with incumbent governments which perceive a short-term financial opportunity.

However, although interest group approaches have major strengths and offer an important advance on the excessively general frameworks of the previous two approaches, they also suffer from weaknesses. The first is that, although the Frieden–Rogowski approach helps explain the strong association between the level of development and financial openness, it seems less immediately able to explain the suddenness of the trend towards openness in a number of key developing countries since the late 1980s. Notwithstanding general arguments about technological change, it is unlikely that the opportunity costs of closure for influential firms and sectors increased so suddenly anywhere, not least because of the ineffectiveness of most capital controls. This suggests that we have to look elsewhere to explain the broader trend and its onset.

Second, interest group approaches tend to pay little attention to political and regulatory institutions, which may affect policy outcomes in important ways. One important institution, the central bank, may prefer capital mobility not just because it is usually proximate to the financial sector, but also because it believes openness may constrain deficit spending by governments (Maxfield 1991, 1997, 1998). Governments operating in systems with highly independent central banks may feel they have little influence over monetary policy with or without capital controls, undermining any rationale for retaining them. However, if central banks are required to defend a currency peg or band, as they are in many developing countries, central bankers may be more supportive of capital controls. Openness may also be favoured by bureaucrats in finance ministries, who may see it as a means of resisting populist politicians wishing to engage in deficit spending. In a further complication, Quinn and Inclán (1997: 785–6) argue that, in non-majoritarian political systems, coalition governments have less incentive to impose capital controls because they receive less credit or blame for macroeconomic activism. However, in Japan and Korea powerful finance ministries supported capital controls for many years to facilitate and entrench their influence over domestic credit allocation.

These considerations suggest that once domestic institutions are introduced to supplement interest group analysis, the complexities expand exponentially. Obviously, policies relating to financial liberalization are interdependent in complex ways with policies in other areas, such as those relating to exchange rate and industrial policy. Further complexity can be introduced via consideration of the type of political regime. Implicitly, Frieden and Rogowski assume a democratic pluralist system in which interest groups compete for the attention of elected politicians. Clearly, this may misrepresent the situation typical in most countries, particularly in the developing world. At a most basic level, liberal pluralism is characteristic of only a small handful of contemporary political systems, and the nature of non-democratic or partially democratic systems – often characterized by high levels of centralization and insulation, and low levels of accountability, representativeness and openness to societal input into policy-making processes – means that a focus on interest groups is, from the start, less than illuminating. In some cases, we may need to pay more attention to the preferences of connected family interests (Indonesia, the Philippines) or to those of the army (Thailand, Nigeria, China). Democratization, furthermore, may produce greater political populism and demands for macroeconomic activism, which might push against financial liberalization. It has been argued that this was the case historically in Europe (Eichengreen 1992; also Simmons 1999: 61) and, while not necessarily substantiating the converse argument about democratization, it is clearly the case that much of the financial liberalization that has taken place in Asia and Latin America occurred under variants of authoritarian rule or limited democracy. However, evidence to the contrary has been assembled by Brune *et al.* (2001), who find financial openness is systematically greater in democracies. It can be argued that democratization favours financial liberalization by increasing the influence of the median voter and the middle classes in general over governments as compared to powerful connected interests, and Brune *et al.* again find evidence of this.

Another complexity problem in rationalist interest group approaches is that interest cleavages between groups may be ambiguous or multiple. It is commonly accepted that interests may cleave along class and sectoral lines. According to the standard Heckscher–Ohlin–Samuelson model, in capital-rich economies, capital as the abundant factor gains and labour loses from financial opening. In capital-poor economies, by contrast, labour as the abundant factor gains from the import of capital and domestic capital loses. From this perspective, democratization in major developing countries since the 1980s might have encouraged financial openness by strengthening the voice of labour over capital in the political process. Quinn and Inclán (1997: 776) extend this point to argue that, in capital-abundant economies, right-wing parties will favour financial opening while left-wing parties will oppose it; the opposite result would hold in labour-abundant economies. However, labour preferences may differ according to the level of labour skill, which can in turn affect party policies in complex ways. Whether the left in practice has led financial liberalization in developing countries is unclear.

Others argue that preferences divide primarily along sectoral lines, with both labour and capital in internationally competitive sectors favouring financial openness. This relates to the 'specific factors' model of international trade in economics texts. Within sectors, internationally competitive firms are often strong supporters of financial openness, as they will benefit from lower global costs of capital. Domestic banks may oppose foreign bank entry, but they may support financial opening if this allows them to act as intermediaries between firms and lower-cost foreign funding. This motivated the Thai government to allow Bangkok International Banking Facilities in the early 1990s. Even domestic firms suffering growing competition from MNCs may also support the removal of controls on offshore borrowing to lower their own costs, as did Korean *chaebols* and Indonesian conglomerates.

Moreover, in emphasizing domestic interest cleavages, the Frieden–Rogowski approach ignores international distributional cleavages. This is because, as noted, their approach derives from standard neoclassical economics which holds that, at the international level, financial opening is welfare-improving. Despite the slew of costly financial crises in many emerging-market countries in the 1990s, leading liberalizers such as the USA and UK have gained most and lost least from financial globalization. The size and competitiveness of their financial sectors and MNCs, the comparative strength of their financial regulatory institutions and the discretionary capabilities of their central banks have limited the costs of financial instability at home. In addition, the USA and UK have been able to foster international regulatory cooperation, particularly via the Basle Committee at the BIS, to reduce the regulatory risks of financial globalization (Kapstein 1994; Oatley and Nabors 1998).

A deeper problem with the Frieden–Rogowski approach is that it sidesteps the problem of information and actor cognition. Their approach assumes that economic agents and, by extension, interest groups unproblematically discern their policy preferences and undertake political action based upon them. However, the 'politicization' of public policy does not only depend upon there being different distributional consequences of alternative policies for identifiable interest groups. There must also be a perception by these groups of a clear link between policy and its distributional effects, and such groups must be able to convey their policy preferences to political representatives. Need economic and political agents understand the Mundell–Fleming and Heckscher–Ohlin–Samuelson models that Frieden and Rogowski use to determine distributional conflicts, or is it sufficient that such groups acquire such knowledge inductively? And what should we do when, as is usually the case, alternative underlying economic models are available?

A simple illustration of the problem is the so-called 'unholy trinity', derived from the Mundell–Fleming monetary framework. This is the argument that individual countries can only choose two of the following three policy options: open capital accounts, independent monetary policies and fixed exchange rates (Cooper 1968; Cohen 1993). Although this may hold as a long-run approximation, in the short run governments have often assumed they are not in fact constrained by this trade-off. Governments in a number of East Asian countries in the early 1990s liberalized capital flows while retaining pegged exchange rates and persisting in the belief that this entailed few risks for monetary and, moreover, for banking regulatory policy. As Haggard (2000: 5) found, 'there is evidence in several [East Asian] countries of a basic failure to understand the policy constraints associated with an open capital account'.

A rationalist rejoinder might be that incumbent politicians understood the risks involved but discounted them because they were not relevant to the political short run. However, such calculations would be more likely to pertain to democracies than to countries like Mexico or Indonesia, where entrenched governments nevertheless undertook financial liberalization, to their later cost. The evidence is more supportive of the view that such risks were simply misunderstood by most governments and the IFIs, which were actively promoting capital account liberalization in the developing world in the early 1990s. The domestic banks and firms which pushed for financial liberalization in Thailand and Korea in the early 1990s certainly believed they would gain. But it is now evident, given that many of these firms subsequently became bankrupt, that they did not fully understand the great risks such liberalization entailed.

Lest it be implied that such cognitive failures only occur in developing countries, the same failure was also evident in the pro-market Conservative UK government from 1990, when Britain joined the European Monetary System and thereby pegged the pound to the Deutschmark, until September 1992. Almost until the very moment that the Bank of England was instructed to give up the battle for the pound, the government continued to believe that it could retain some monetary policy autonomy whilst maintaining the Deutschmark peg and a completely open capital account. Of course, it is true that in this case, as in Asian countries, there were domestic political reasons for resisting interest rate increases: in the UK case, these centred on the costs further increases would entail for mortgage-holders. Yet this does not refute the fact that governments believed such policies to be sustainable for much longer than they proved to be.

This suggests that the implications of the knowledge problem have not been fully addressed in the rationalist political economy literature, casting some doubt upon its predictions. As Odell (2002) has argued, in the real world there are likely to be slippages and deep complexities once informational problems and cognitive failures are taken into account. In other words, research in this area needs to take the implications of bounded rationality more seriously.

Reframing the debate

How then does the above discussion relate to the broader project of this book, the quest for a 'truly global' IPE – specifically, in this case, to providing explanations of financial globalization and responses to it that are germane to a wide range of national and regional experiences? I have argued that structural theories, including technological determinism and hegemonic power theories, are better at explaining the broad trend towards financial opening since the 1970s. However, they largely fail to explain the large differences in patterns across countries. Rationalist interest group approaches, supplemented by institutional analysis, provide considerably greater insight into the cross-country pattern of financial liberalization but, perhaps inevitably, do so at the cost of much greater analytical complexity. Nevertheless, greater attention to domestic political institutions and structures is undoubtedly required if we are to understand the large variations that occur between countries. Earlier structural approaches in political economy, in searching for grand theories, were generally uninterested in such variations. They also tended to suggest that circumstances in the poor, developing countries were analytically unimportant. Interest group and institutionalist theories, by contrast, raise many interesting questions about less powerful countries and thereby point us in useful directions for developing a more 'global' IPE.

However, these theories continue to suffer from both theoretical and empirical shortcomings in this respect. Rationalist political economy models typically assume that polities are similar to the pluralist democratic system prevailing in the USA and elsewhere. To be sure, the great strength of formal rationalist models is that they make such assumptions admirably clear. Milner (1997a) confronts the question of whether we should expect autocracies to respond differently to democracies in such models. She argues they should not, since autocrats must still manage distributional conflicts in order to retain power. Nevertheless, we have seen that the kinds of interest groups identified by standard models may differ from those important in authoritarian systems (connected interests, the military and so on). This observation in turn underlines the need for greater attention to be paid to the political realities of individual countries.

Haggard and Maxfield (1996), for example, find that currency crises play a crucial role in inducing developing countries to open their financial account. They argue that countries dependent upon capital inflows to ameliorate the consequences of crises need to signal to international investors that future capital controls will be avoided; in an uncertain environment, investors may view current openness as a credible commitment to such a future policy. They also argue that crises strengthened both domestic and international interests pushing for liberalization. Similarly, the crisis of 1997–8 accelerated financial deregulation in Korea, partly because it increased the influence of the IMF and the US Treasury over Korean policy, but more because it allowed domestic liberal reformers to use the crisis as a means to pursue policies they had long desired. By contrast, Mahathir's decision to impose capital controls in Malaysia in 1998 represented in part the defeat of the liberal reformist clique.

This is not to suggest that detailed country case studies are the only way forward (as in Maxfield 1990, 1991; Haggard *et al*. 1993; Haggard and Maxfield 1996; Loriaux 1996). On the contrary, work such as that provided by Brune *et al*. (2001) may begin to fill the large gaps that exist in our empirical knowledge of policy change in the developing world. Until now, most of the evidence that has been brought to bear on questions of the causes and consequences of financial globalization pertains only to the developed countries. This, as we have said, is largely driven by the much greater availability of comparable cross-country data for the OECD countries than for developing countries, but also by a particular concern amongst Western scholars to investigate the fate of social democracy in Europe. Thus the initial task before us is to expand the scope of empirical research to accommodate more effectively non-OECD systems in the study of global finance, and thereby to generate conclusions about the causes and consequences of financial liberalization, as well as analytical frameworks within which to approach these questions, that are more generally applicable rather than relevant solely to isolated, largely European and OECD, cases.

Finally, IPE in general needs to confront directly the even more difficult issue of how to treat the problem of knowledge and cognition. Political economists have given little attention to the way in which knowledge affects individual decisions in particular contexts, how economic knowledge in particular may be systematically biased in different national and cultural contexts. Continental European economists tend to be more sceptical than their US counterparts about the virtues of *laissez-faire* policy solutions, particularly in the area of financial markets. The growing influence of US ideas in Latin America since the debt crisis of the 1980s, combined with the growth of material US power in the region, may help explain why financial liberalization arrived more quickly there than elsewhere in the developing world. Nevertheless, we have noted that the consequences of financial liberalization were usually poorly understood, by policy-makers and organized interest groups.

When knowledge and cognition are imperfect, as they always are, the roles of ideology and individual biases may be more important than rationalists assume. The failure of the import substitution model in Latin America, the collapse of communism in Europe, and the ideological vacuum this created for the influence of market liberalism, may have been more important for financial liberalization in the developing world than any of the factors identified in rationalist models. The IMF and World Bank have helped to build local technical expertise in central banks and finance ministries of developing countries, favouring financial liberalization. Chronic indebtedness and balance of payments problems may have favoured individuals within governments with financial expertise and foreign academic training. 'Graduation' to developed-country status, symbolized by entry to the OECD, may have played a role in bringing countries like Mexico and South Korea to undertake liberalization, even apart from the leverage that this provided to existing members like the USA.

But this is not a plea for a return to an anti-rationalism in which ideology and perception rule. What is required is a combination of quantitative approaches with more qualitative case-study approaches that are sensitive not only to the role of ideas in particular contexts, but also to the possibility that ideas may be used instrumentally by politicians. What remains most unclear is why certain economic ideas are more influential in some places and times than in others, and the consequences of these variations are highly significant for our understanding of the contemporary dynamics of global finance.

Chapter 7

The Transnational Relations Debate

Robert O'Brien*

The notion that relations between individuals and groups across state borders are significant for understanding international political economy was present at the birth of the contemporary field of IPE. If we trace IPE as a separate area of enquiry back to the early 1970s and the attempt by intellectuals in Western states to understand the economic turbulence of the time (O'Brien 1995: 94–5), we find that transnational relations was a central part of the emerging field. The relationship between politics and economics at the international level was thought to be significant because of the growth of interdependence and the challenges it posed for economic and political management; a central element of interdependence was the activity of non-state actors operating across national frontiers. Yet since the 1970s the transnational relations research agenda has produced mixed results. Its fate has been tied very much to broader theoretical and empirical developments in IR and IPE. It enjoyed some success in periods when integration and interdependence theories were popular (the 1960s and 1970s) and less when realist theories dominated (the 1980s). With the end of the Cold War and increasing focus upon globalization, however, the study of transnational relations experienced a modest revival in the 1990s.

The general argument of this book is that IPE is insufficiently global because (a) empirically, it is mesmerized by the experience of advanced industrialized democracies rather than a wide range of cases, and (b) theoretically, it generalizes from these cases to the whole. The primary argument of this chapter is that the book's

* Helpful critical comments on an earlier draft were provided by William Coleman, Nicola Phillips and Tony Porter.

critique is indeed relevant to the transnational relations literature, but also that some branches of transnational relations do offer hope of moving towards a more *global* political economy analysis. I suggest, in this sense, that whereas many of the other chapters in this volume have sought to advance this project in their particular area of debate by 'bringing in' or engaging more constructively with a range of perspectives from other areas of the social sciences, the resources for so doing in the case of the transnational relations debate are to be found *within* the debate itself. Furthermore, possibilities for globalizing IPE as a broader field of study emerge precisely because of the theoretical and empirical challenges generated by some strands of the transnational relations debate. In both these respects, the recent debate about global civil society opens up particular and considerable room for progress along the lines advocated in this volume. Approaches to transnational relations which focus upon narrow policy networks or fail to differentiate between corporate and civic actors, on the other hand, are less likely to be helpful.

A wide variety of theories and case studies are gathered under the transnational relations umbrella (Keohane and Nye 1972; Risse-Kappen 1995; Willetts 1999; Risse 2002). However, two broad approaches wind their way through various theoretical and empirical manifestations of the debate. In this chapter, they are identified as the 'policy communities' approach and the 'social forces' approach. The former focuses upon the networks of individuals or groups in a particular issue area, whether they are individuals, associations or members of state and interstate organizations. The latter views civic associations in relationship to the broader social forces of which they are a part or which they represent.

The chapter begins by providing a brief overview and initial critique of transnational analysis. It argues that the pluralist category of transnational relations offers a limited critique of state-centric realist theories and that it conflates corporate and civic actors in a distinctly unhelpful manner. Both of these characteristics limit its usefulness. The second section of the chapter surveys policy community approaches to transnational relations, and the third focuses upon social forces approaches. Section four sets out the argument that the recent debates surrounding the concept and practice of global civil society constitute the most fruitful development of transnational studies and offer promising possibilities for globalizing the content and theory of IPE.

Overview and initial critique

To begin, let us briefly consider the overreaching concept of transnational relations and how it relates to the areas of IR and IPE. The concept has varied with the fortunes of dominant approaches in IR and has been hampered by its excessively general nature. A key early contribution, Keohane and Nye's *Transnational Relations and World Politics* (1972), defined transnational relations as 'contacts, coalitions, and interactions across state boundaries that are not controlled by the central foreign policy organs of governments' (Keohane and Nye 1972: xi). In this incarnation, the study of transnational relations has two striking features. First, it is heavily enmeshed in a debate about the limits of state-centric perspectives. Second, transnational relations constitutes a residual category which includes all actors other than states, no matter what their differences might be. Both of these attributes pose difficulties for achieving a genuinely *global* political economy approach.

With respect to the first of these characteristics, the 1970s transnational relations literature is best understood in light of the attempt made by liberal/pluralist scholars in that decade to mount a challenge to the dominant state-centric realist theories of international politics and IPE. Although pluralist approaches had enjoyed some success through the neofunctionalist literature focused upon the European Economic Community (Haas 1958, 1964), they made little impression upon the larger field of IR. Keohane and Nye, who were leading the interest in transnational relations, sought to remedy this situation by developing the concept of 'complex interdependence' as an alternative ideal type to the realist world. In their model, complex interdependence was a world 'in which actors other than states participate directly in world politics, in which a clear hierarchy of rules does not exist, and in which force is an ineffective instrument of policy' (Keohane and Nye 1977: 24). Realist attributes would typify some real-world situations while others, such as economic and ecological interdependence, would be governed by the characteristics of complex interdependence. Transnational relations were a key part of complex interdependence because they were the product of the first of the three characteristics of the ideal type (participation of actors other than states).

Although the transnational relations approach takes issue with the notion that states are the only significant actor in the international system, it is in reality a very limited challenge. At its boldest, the approach claims that understanding state behaviour requires some attention to non-state actors. For example, all of Keohane and Nye's (1972: xi) five main questions for the transnational relations research agenda concentrate on explaining state behaviour. The research questions asked about (1) the effect of transnational relations on government's control over their environment; (2) the implications of transnational relations for state-centric views; (3) the effects on inequality between states; (4) the implications for US foreign policy; and (5) the challenges posed for interstate organizations. Indeed, the fate of transnational relations studies mirrored that of complex interdependence. Keohane and Nye's (1987: 733) retrospective on the fate of the complex interdependence research agenda is instructive: 'the result...has been to broaden neorealism and provide it with new concepts rather than to articulate a coherent alternative theoretical framework for the study of world politics'. Both transnational relations and complex interdependence were eclipsed by realist interpretations as the United States entered the Second Cold War of the 1980s (Halliday 1986). Neorealism became ascendant and the most that liberals hoped for was some form of synthesis whereby a few liberal insights might be incorporated into the dominant realist world view.

Yet, with the end of the Cold War, concern with the process of globalization and the constructivist turn in IR theorizing combined to create a friendly environment for the relaunch of transnational relations studies in the 1990s. A prominent result was Risse-Kappen's (1995) collection of articles designed to bring 'transnational relations back in' to the study of IR. Similar to earlier incarnations, the goal of the study was primarily to understand when transnational actors succeed or fail to influence state behaviour in the foreign policy arena (Risse-Kappen 1995: 5). This critique of state-centrism complemented analysis being conducted on the role of norms in IR, which will be taken up below.

The second hallmark of the transnational relations debate – the division of relevant actors into state and non-state entities – is worth pursuing at some length, for it is central to the arguments of the chapter. It mirrors a pluralist domestic politics approach which views the political arena as being composed of a state and a series of interest groups which compete to influence state policy. Transposed to the international sphere, the world is composed of states and a series of interest groups now relabelled 'non-state actors'. The non-state actors attempt to influence the key central actor – states.

This dichotomy appears even in analyses which attempt to undercut the state/non-state divide. An example can be found in Peter Willetts's (1999) otherwise persuasive argument that a series of actors other than states (TNCs, liberation movements, non-governmental organizations (NGOs), international organizations) are significant in global politics. Although his intent is to oblige students and scholars to take note of a wide variety of actors, the analysis nevertheless returns to a world composed of two main entities – states, on the one hand, and transnational actors, on the other.

The inability to escape this dichotomy creates significant difficulties for the study of transnational relations. Specifically, the dominant pluralist approach is not suited to a global analysis for three reasons. The first is that the pluralist view of political economy is misleading even in its own primary context – that of advanced industrialized states. Over twenty-five years ago, Charles Lindblom (1977: 140–2, 170–88) identified several patterns which undermined pluralist complacency about power differentials. First, those holding institutional authority and power are able to mobilize resources unavailable to others. Second, gross inequalities in wealth provide consistent advantages for some groups over others. Third, the interests of large groups of people remain unorganized and unrepresented, leading to domination by smaller organized interests. Fourth, leaders of associations often use their claim to be representative for furthering their own interests rather than those of the membership. A fifth critique concerns the privileged position of business in the political system. (This last point will be taken up shortly in the discussion of TNCs.)

Pluralist models of politics are also of dubious utility in the purpose for which they were primarily developed: explaining the functioning of US democracy. Whatever their relevance in the 1960s and 1970s might have been, they now seem detached from the modern political economy of the USA. In an environment where less than half the adult population participates in the electoral process, campaigns are dominated by vast sums of money and government authorities have lost the ability to regulate financial affairs in the public interest, explanations and frameworks based on interest group politics fail to capture core characteristics of the central political process. Corporate scandals in the USA (such as Enron and Parmalat) indicate clearly that the regulatory system has been captured by financial interests, and are mirrored in similar scandals in Europe.

The second major issue for pluralist approaches is that their shortcomings are compounded when the model is projected into a more diverse and complex environment. As Nicola Phillips demonstrated at length in Chapter 4, the international system contains many different forms of state, few of which are founded on liberal pluralism. Some may be capable of acting as relatively neutral arbitrators between competing interests, but most do not live up to this model. On the contrary, a great many of them are either ineffective in this regard because of institutional weaknesses or dynamics of 'capture', as noted above, or else because the distinction between 'the state', on the one hand, and 'interests', on the other, is by no means as clear as pluralist approaches would like to suggest. The divergence of state forms has been indicated by a comparative politics literature discussing the distinction between strong and weak states. East Asian development, for example, was facilitated by strong states which enjoyed 'relative autonomy' from business interests (Wade 1990; Evans 1995a) while Latin American states have historically featured neither the levels of state capacity nor the 'relative autonomy' that were the hallmarks of Asian developmental states over the postwar period (Leftwich 2000; Phillips 2004). In retrospect, the East Asian financial crises of the late 1990s raise questions about how autonomous these states actually were from business interests, but the point about diversity in state form remains, as does the point about the need to engage more constructively with comparative analysis of this diversity.

The movement of many developmental states away from relatively autonomous economic projects to a liberal strategy of insertion to the global economy (McMichael 2000) highlights the variety of relationships with external economic forces. A few fortunate states, such as China, are in a strong position *vis-à-vis* foreign investors, but many others must compete to attract investment. This has led to a wide range of state strategies for economic development, from the selling of state sovereignty through tax havens, flags of convenience and offshore production to integration into regional economic agreements and the creation of low-wage labour pools (Palan and Abbott 1996; Payne 2004). Each of these predicaments and strategies calls forth a different relationship between the state and corporate actors which sets the terms for negotiation and distribution of wealth.

A third difficulty afflicting pluralist approaches to transnational relations is one already noted of the broader debate: that they obscure power relations in the global political economy by conflating actors with very different capabilities and roles. Analytically, they reduce the privileged influence of a major global actor – the

TNC – by lumping it in with voluntary civic associations. It is a misleading typology. If typologies or categories are to have some analytical value, then the units of each category should be bound together by virtue of their shared key characteristics or roles. It then becomes possible to make generalizations about the behaviour and significance of the units in those categories. The division between state and non-state actors does not meet this test very well. By definition, all transnational actors share the characteristic of not being states, but what divides them is as great as what unites them.

In particular, a distinction should be made between corporations (especially TNCs) and other actors. Their distinctive internal logic, in the first place, differentiates the goals and actions of TNCs sharply from those of non-profit civic associations pursuing equity or state elites defending their national interests. TNCs were not created to raise labour standards, enhance gender parity, safeguard human rights or prevent environmental degradation. Their task is to facilitate the production and sale of goods and services for the financial benefit of their owners (individuals or shareholders). Some corporations may have longer time horizons because of secure long-term financing and corporations may differ in the basis of their competitive edge (that is, low wage versus quality), but they all must pursue profit as their first priority. They engage in other activities to the extent that their prime goal is advanced.

TNCs also differ from other transnational actors in the structural position they occupy in the global economy. Large TNCs enjoy and benefit from a degree of both structural and relational power that is not available to other transnational actors. On the structural level, Gill and Law (1988) have highlighted the degree to which competition for badly needed investment between and within states results in the tendency to implement policies most desired by TNCs. Since the debt crisis of the 1980s, most developing states have reoriented their domestic economies to attract such capital (McMichael 2000), and the result has been a shift in the balance between capital, labour and the state as neoliberal restructuring projects have advanced for this purpose. Moreover, most of the world's countries are capital-poor and are thus placed in a very different relationship with powerful TNCs than the smaller number of capital-rich advanced industrialized states. Relations of inequality and dependency central to most of the world's population are not accorded a high priority in the dominant pluralistic understandings of transnational relations, notwithstanding the important and long-standing debate on TNCs and development in the field of development studies.

TNCs also exercise considerable relational power, facilitated by their privileged access to state decision-makers. Because of their significance to domestic economies and the extent of their participation in national political life, TNCs are often able to convince states that their particular interests are effectively the interests of the state. The resulting forms of business–state nexus across political systems are clearly evident in the progressively central participation of business actors, alongside governmental and state actors, across such arenas as trade negotiations and talks with the IMF and other creditors. One of the most dramatic instances of this activity was the ability of US TNCs to convince the US government that protection of intellectual property rights through the WTO was a state priority (Sell 1999). This victory allowed TNCs to write the rules of the game for development in key knowledge industries, and sparked ongoing conflict with civic associations and the governments of many developing countries.

Although this chapter argues that failing to differentiate sufficiently between TNCs and other non-state actors is an error, and a pervasive one, some work in IPE does bring these categories together with some success. Sell and Prakash (2004), for example, have suggested that corporations and NGOs adopt many of the same tactics in their political activity, and that the distinction between norm-driven (NGO) and material-driven (TNC) actors is consequently overemphasized. This critique is a useful counter to the idealization of non-governmental actors that is found in the constructivist approaches, but nevertheless runs the risk of downplaying the very different functions, roles and abilities of corporate and civic actors. TNCs need to be understood in their own right, and not primarily in terms of their relationship to state power, as in the transnational relations approach. A TNC's decision to restructure its operations and change its investment strategy will have a significant impact upon local political economies. This is especially true in more vulnerable economic locations. Similarly, conflict and bargaining between TNCs and civic actors may take place with little reference to state power. Examples of this include citizen action to boycott consumer products and corporate codes of conduct constructed in response to citizen activity. Some elements of the dominant transnational relations approach are capable of providing an analysis of TNCs that does not focus solely on their relationship to states. For example, Wells's (1972) chapter in Keohane and Nye's collection does focus upon the TNC and its internal organization. However, the dominant twin tendencies in the transnational relations debate are for studies of TNCs to be pre-occupied with the state–firm nexus (Clark and Chan 1995; Katzenstein and Tsujinaka 1995), and for TNCs to be identified as actors in an excessively generic and generalizing 'non-state' category.

These shortcomings constitute one of the explanations for the relatively slight impact that the idea of transnational relations has had on the fields of IR and IPE, despite providing some significant insights. Given the elasticity of the concept and its coverage of such a wide variety of cases (all non-state actors), there is nothing that holds that subject of study together other than a negative characteristic – they are not states. As a result, studies of TNCs and of civic actors have tended to go their separate ways. Another major reason for the limited impact of the debate in the wider field relates to the drawbacks of espousing an approach which offers such a limited theoretical challenge to dominant theories. The transnational relations approach argues that, in some instances, non-state actors can have an impact on the state system. The object of explanation – the state – remains the same as for traditional realist or liberal approaches to IR. The insight about non-state actors can easily be accommodated by the dominant approaches and then ignored as scholars get back to the real business of explaining state behaviour in a world of states. An interesting example is provided by Stephen Krasner's (1995) contribution to a volume on transnational relations. Viewing the transnational landscape, he concludes that powerful states define the environment in which TNCs operate and that TNCs can have an impact on states when states are relatively weak. The effect of the analysis is to close down discussion rather than open it up to increased dialogue and debate.

Rather than suggesting that there is a state realm and a trans-national realm with non-state actors, it would be considerably more helpful to organize the debate around the identification of three spheres of activity, each with its major actor and logic. The interstate sphere is dominated by states, the global economy by TNCs and global civil society by civic associations. They all attempt to shape the global political economy, but in different ways and to different ends. Each sphere is characterized by inequality between its members and by the presence of other subordinate actors: business associations act in the sphere of global civil society, for instance, and civic associations attempt to influence the structure of the global economy.

This formulation surely offers a more accurate reflection of the distribution of power and responsibility in the global economy than the split between states and non-state actors.

In sum, this initial critique of the transnational relations literature does not argue that it has failed to generate any important insights. It does argue that, because of its inclusion of the corporation as simply an actor among others, the failure to think adequately about issues of inequality and dependency, and the limited extent of its challenge to realist theories, transnational relations in its most established form suffers from many of the shortcomings of IPE debates identified in this volume and is unlikely to contribute to achieving the goals set out in it. In this light, the next two sections look more closely at some recent work on transnational relations where they are viewed alternatively as policy networks or social forces. It should be remembered that while particular analyses can be grouped according to this dichotomy, there is also much crossover between the two approaches. Elements of social movements are, for example, involved in policy communities and problem-solving activities, as well as engaging in confrontation and pushing for deeper systemic change.

Transnational relations as policy communities

The term 'policy community approach' is taken from Coleman and Perl's (1999) work which applies the concepts of policy networks and policy communities from the national public policy literature to internationalized policy environments. Other authors classified here as being part of the policy community approach do not necessarily self-identify with this literature, but they do share a number of its basic propositions. The concept of a 'policy network' refers to the pattern of public–private relations in a particular governance structure (state-dominated, civil society-dominated, or balanced), while the term 'policy community' refers to the participants in the governing structure (bureaucrats, think tanks, NGOs, interest groups, particular firms or business associations) (Coleman and Perl 1999: 694–7). These approaches were developed in the public policy literature of the 1970s and 1980s to cope with an environment in which governance was increasingly extending beyond the state and incorporating other actors. In particular, they reflect the continuing sense that governments are moving away from dealing solely with a broad public or social classes to engaging also with private actors with their own power base (Coleman and Perl 1999: 693). The policy community approach echoes liberal pluralist assumptions about the nature of politics and political power. Interest groups are seen to vie with each other to influence state policy and a number of public–private organizations are created to deal with public policy in a more efficient manner than the state could accomplish on its own. Struggles between social classes thus fade into the background as attention is focused upon the policy-making arena.

Policy community approaches in an international context divide into two principal categories: epistemic communities and network analysis, which we will survey in turn.

Epistemic communities

A subset of transnational relations that seemed to hold out considerable promise in the early 1990s was the study of epistemic communities. Haas (1992: 3) defined an epistemic community as 'a network of professionals with recognized expertise and competence in a particular domain and an authoritative claim to policy-relevant knowledge'. The possession of expert knowledge was deemed to provide the epistemic community with an opportunity to influence decision-makers. These communities, which were usually transnational, facilitated policy coordination between states by providing leaders with crucial information in an environment of uncertainty. The focus on epistemic communities took inspiration from, and contributed to, the constructivist turn in IR. Constructivists argue that knowledge and action are socially constructed and can be shaped to different purposes. The epistemic community literature contributed to this argument by identifying one of the ways that knowledge helped actors define their interests in different ways. It contributed in particular to the study of international regimes by bolstering knowledge-based approaches to regime formation (Hasenclever *et al.* 1997: 149–53). Although the epistemic communities concept enjoyed considerable success in studies of environmental regimes (O. Young 1999: 126), it had faded from view by the end of the 1990s.

One of the weaknesses of the approach was that it was unable to theorize the relationship between these communities and other groups, such as interest groups or social movements. This led some critics to charge that it was normatively biased in favour of expert groups over other possessors of knowledge and understanding (Toke 1999). Other critics have suggested that the approach's 'other groups' problem caused it to miss how expert knowledge groups must engage in coalition-building in order to influence policy (Dunlop 2000). The atrophy of the concept also resulted from the fact that the notion of expert communities influencing state policy was confined to those areas where scientific consensus was widespread. In fact, these areas were (and remain) limited in number, and concentrated in the field where the term first emerged – the study of international environmental issues. In practice, expertise, even scientific expertise, is often divided and can be embedded in different social contexts in various countries. A good example is the disagreement between the WTO, the USA and the EU over the safety of hormone-fed beef. Scientists from each side of the Atlantic may be able to agree about some of the technical issues, but the standards for acceptable risk are set by wider social processes (Skogstad 2001).

When taken into a global context, the epistemic community concept proved to be even more problematic. A core problem was that so much expert knowledge is generated in Western states and universities. This knowledge may not take into account experiences and views from other regions. For example, the epistemic communities that formed around the benefit of capital liberalization in the 1990s were not sufficiently attuned to the reality and vulnerability of developing countries, despite the fact that these communities were constituted by technocratic elites drawn from those countries – although educated in the USA and Europe – as well as the advanced industrialized ones. Similarly, the epistemic community that clusters around the value of intellectual property rights has difficulty extending its consensus outside the OECD due to the differential impact of the protections. The same might be said of labour and environmental standards, which have been pivotal in the international conflicts between so-called 'developing' and 'developed' countries in multilateral trade negotiations. In short, it is difficult to build 'consensual' knowledge in a diverse environment characterized by immense inequality.

Network analysis

Recent years have seen considerable growth in research on the influence of networks of people and organizations interested in particular policy issues. Network analysis serves as a bridge between the epistemic community literature and analysis, as outlined in the following section, which looks at broader social forces. Like the epistemic community literature, network studies focus upon particular issue areas and the role of knowledge and norms. Like social forces approaches, they go beyond knowledge communities to take account of activists, but equally they shy away from the structural analysis and conflicts highlighted in this literature. In this vein, Keck and Sikkink (1998) developed the concept of transnational advocacy networks to capture the activity of activists working across state borders to further particular principled ideas or values. The networks connect individuals across a wide variety of organizations including NGOs, social movements, the media, states and international organizations. Network analysis is central to some constructivist IR theory in that it is the 'norm entrepreneurs' who are seen to shift ideas and norms leading to systemic change. Non-state activists work to foster the emergence of their favoured norms which then may be taken up by states and eventually internalized through a 'norms cascade' (Finnemore and Sikkink 1998). Studies of the international diffusion of human rights have identified transnational advocacy networks as the prime instigators of change toward securing increased respect for human rights around the world (Risse and Ropp 1999).

There are two striking elements in this norm diffusion. The first is the direction of the diffusion. Although some proponents of such analysis argue that networks can act as a site of negotiation between 'developed' and 'developing' countries (Keck and Sikkink 1999), the trend is towards an export of norms from the 'North' to the 'South'. Concerns about human rights, transparency and anti-corruption, environmental protection and non-proliferation of nuclear, chemical and biological weapons are not restricted to developed states, but the form they take when diffused is largely modelled upon Western understandings. Human rights continue to exclude economic rights; poor transparency and corruption are seen to be hallmarks of developing rather than developed countries; non-proliferation enforcement procedures are aimed at Iran rather than Israel. This said, some limited flow of norms in the other direction can be observed. The campaign to cancel the debt of developing countries or the challenge against the immorality of enforcing strict intellectual property rights on life-saving drugs show that, in exceptional cases, it is possible for some developing-country, non-Western or non-'core' norms to achieve significant expression in world politics. Nevertheless, the general trend is for the diffusion of norms of distinctively Western character from the rich industrialized 'core'.

The second striking feature of norm diffusion concerns its content. In a nutshell, norms which challenge neoliberal globalization seem to have a more difficult time diffusing than others. Norms of this nature, such as labour rights, face immense structural obstacles (O'Brien 2004), and the relative lack of success in promoting the norm of safe and fair working conditions in the global economy raises key questions about what type of norms have resonance and which do not. Equally, norms that might lead to economic redistribution from the rich to the poor are less actively supported than those which facilitate liberalization of the global economy. The debate over debt forgiveness is a salient example.

In summary, the policy community approach has advanced our understanding of transnational relations, but it is not well-attuned to global inequalities. Knowledge communities are usually OECD-based knowledge communities. The advocacy networks literature broadens its view to include non-elite groups, but would be enriched by considering the role of broader social forces and developments.

Transnational relations as competing social forces

Transnational relations can also be viewed, in an alternative approach, as a global contest between social forces. The phrase 'social forces' is borrowed from Robert Cox's (1987, 1996b) work and refers to groups of people acting together based upon their perceived interest in relation to a larger social structure. This approach stresses group identities and conflicts around organizing structures such as capitalism (class), patriarchy (gender), industrial development (environmentalism) and state violence (human rights). Social forces are larger in number and have a looser structure than interest groups or policy communities. Advocates of this approach analyse movements, classes and genders, rather than NGOs, interest groups and policy networks.

The two prominent perspectives that are grouped in this approach are concerned with transnational class and global social movements. Again, we will take these in turn.

Transnational class

Although liberal IR and IPE approaches abandoned studies of transnational relations until the mid-1990s, a number of neo-Marxist studies advanced understanding by concentrating their efforts on transnational elites or ruling classes and arguing that the expansion and management of the global economy rested upon elite trans-national networks and institutions. The transnational class approach thus focuses on some of the same subjects as network analysis (such as elite networks), but locates them squarely in the context of overarching structures. In this view, the contest extends beyond particular policies to the nature of the global system itself.

Stephen Gill's (1990) work is illustrative. He argues that US hegemony rested upon a transnational alliance of internationalists in key developing countries (the USA, Western European countries and Japan). The transnationalization of production and finance required a similar transnational alliance of the leading elements of civil society to manage the turbulence unleashed by increasing liberalization. His detailed study of the Trilateral Commission portrays a body actively bringing together internationalist elites in three continents. Its two largest tasks were to extend the liberal economic alliances that stretched across the Atlantic to Japan and to steer US administrations away from unilateralist economic policies that might damage the global economy. In a similar vein, Kees van der Pijl (1998) highlights the role of a series of organizations and networks, dating back over three hundred years, which assisted in coordinating elite interests and responding to challenges from the working class or nationalist-minded elites. He reviews the activities of groups such as the Freemasonry, the Rhodes-Milner group, Bilderberg, the Trilateral Commission, the Pinay Circle and the World Economic Forum (WEF) in providing forums for debating and negotiating elite management of a liberal capitalist global economy. He also argues that hope for transition to a more humane governance rests with cadres of professionals and managers which could act as a brake on the owners of capital.

The transnational class work of the 1980s and 1990s was vulnerable to two criticisms. The first was that it overstated the degree of cohesion between capitalists across states. Comparative political economists – and indeed some globalization scholars – have stressed the enduring differences between Anglo-American, continental European and Asian models of political economy rather than the similarity of ruling-class interests (Hay 2000a; Radice 2000; Beeson and Bell in this volume). Similarly, analysis of the East Asian financial crisis has highlighted the clash between the US state acting on behalf of US TNCs and Asian states attempting to fend off this economic pressure (Higgott 1998). The second criticism was that this work focused excessively upon elites and ignored the widespread resistance to liberal restructuring. Transnational elites appeared all-powerful with little hint that popular activity could challenge or reverse the neoliberal agenda (Drainville 1994). The fixation can be explained by the nature of the task these neo-Marxists set for themselves, inasmuch as they were primarily interested in how power was wielded by those who sought to liberalize the global economy. It can also be explained with reference to their narrow empirical focus on Western Europe and the USA, where progressive forces generally were on the defensive in the 1980s and early 1990s. More recently, however, the focus on elites has been widened to consider broader social forces in response to protests at international economic organizations (Gill 2000).

For the arguments of this volume, the criticism that the empirical work focused very much upon elite networks connecting advanced industrialized states, especially across the Atlantic, is significant. Transnational elite analysis need not confine itself to OECD states and, indeed, would benefit from not doing so. Attention can very profitably be shifted to the networks reaching into and across developing states, particularly in view of the increasing importance of such networks and alliances in understanding the politics of global governance across a range of issue areas (Payne 2005). One could also return to dependency analysis of the 1970s and the notion of a *comprador* elite which supports liberalization and inequality because it suits its domestic interests to do so. In their analysis of dependency and development in Latin America, for example, Cardoso and Faletto (1979) stressed that exploitation of developing countries was not just an external process, but depended upon national elites who also benefited from it. Their analysis reinserted this transnational relationship into domestic class struggle by discussing how the state was used to enforce particular national and international interests. This form of analysis can provide clues as to how transnational elite analysis can be tied back into domestic political struggles across the full range of national settings. Similarly, greater consideration of resistance to neoliberal restructuring in the developing world, as evidenced by the phenomenon of IMF riots or social movement unionism, might have alerted transnational elite theorists to the possibility – and analytical importance – of widespread challenges to the prevailing world order.

Social movements

At the same time as one group of scholars was working on elite class analysis, another was investigating the possibility of transnational and global social movements. Social movements are informal networks based on shared beliefs and solidarity which mobilize around conflictual issues through the frequent use of various forms of protest (della Porta and Diani 1999: 16). They are mass organizations working around a general theme such as peace, environmental protection, women's rights, labour conditions or development. This differentiates them from single-issue interest groups or advocacy networks which rely less on mass mobilization and more on lobbying. Unlike elites, social movements do not have privileged access to decision-makers and must often use alternative forms of political action such as demonstrations and boycotts. In contrast to the transnational elite theories which examine globalization 'from above', social movement scholars are thus investigating globalization 'from below' (Falk 2003). They are interested in the response of non-elites to the building of a global economy and the creation of new sites of authority such as the WTO. In the field of political economy, the contest has tended to revolve around the organizing principles of the global economy and attempts to fight back against neoliberal policies.

Interest in global social movements accelerated following popular protests against the WTO ministerial meeting in Seattle in December 1999. Mainstream media outlets covered the failure of the meeting and publicized the role of demonstrators in complicating its conclusion. This event was followed by similar protests in various countries against the IMF, World Bank and G7. This apparent upsurge stimulated multiple analyses of the colourful protests and their possible implications. Yet the interaction of global social movements and global governance mechanisms predated 1999. The World Bank, IMF and GATT/WTO had been the object of feminist, environmental and labour concern for three decades before bursting on to the television screens in Seattle (O'Brien *et al.* 2000). UN global conferences on the environment, women and development had also facilitated the forging of links and implementation of plans of action between movements across the world.

In similar fashion to some of the global civil society literature, elements of social movement studies posit their subject of study as a solution to many of the world's problems. Thiele (1993), for instance, suggests that transnational social movements may be able to make the world more safe, democratic and sustainable following the failures of realist states and liberal markets. This leaves social movement studies open to the critique that they exaggerate the influence of the groups they examine and substitute their normative preferences for an analysis of reality. However, contributors to the global social movements field have been leaders in the newer and broader debates on global civil society. These debates and the various critiques they have attracted – particularly regarding their assumptions about the nature of community and the existence of transnational solidarity – are the subject of the rest of the chapter.

The global civil society debate

As elements of the transnational relations literature have largely dropped away or broken off into their own areas of study – transnational relations, TNCs, epistemic communities and so on – discussion has increasingly focused upon the concept of a global civil society. Whereas the transnational relations concept refers to an activity (interaction by non-state actors across national boundaries), the term 'global civil society' denotes an arena or space where activity takes place. Specifically, Scholte (2000b: 180) argues that global civil society 'encompasses civic activity that: (a) addresses transworld issues; (b) involves transborder communication; (c) has a global organization; (d) works on a premise of supraterritorial solidarity'. Groups need only fulfil one of these conditions to be part of global civil society. Key to understanding this approach is his view that globalization and the adjective 'global' refer to an environment marked by relative deterritorialization. Deterritorialization is a process where social space and territorial coordinates need no longer be synonymous. The compression of time and space fosters social relations that were previously extremely difficult to engender and sustain. Invocation of the concept of global civil society, however, sparks considerable debate, which has revolved around two core issues: whether a global civil society exists and, if so, what is the nature of the entity under discussion.

The existence of a global civil society

There is little question that, on the empirical level, something which bears resemblance to the global civil society concept exists. Evidence can be gathered by joining 100,000 other people at the meetings of the World Social Forum (WSF) in Porto Alegre or monitoring media coverage of the simultaneous worldwide demonstrations against the US and British plans for war in Iraq in February and March 2003. Yet, on the theoretical level, there is considerable scepticism about whether such activity can and/or should be captured under the label 'global civil society'. Critics have taken issue with all of the key elements of the term – civility, globality and society. The terms 'global' and 'civil society' excite considerable debate not least because they mean different things to different people. For example, Khilnani (2001) points out that the meaning of civil society ranges from an economic sphere free of state intervention, to a social sphere which balances state and market, to a cultural sphere which is defined by particular modes of behaviour (that is, civility). One could also argue that transnational non-state, non-corporate activity is not truly global, often not civil and not part of a society. If a person thinks that global implies universal and equal, then transnational civic activity is clearly not global since many people do not or cannot participate in its activities. Global civil society is dominated by groups from wealthier countries with greater access to resources. However, the notion of deterritorialization outlined above does not contain assumptions of either equality or universality. Global civil society is constantly in a state of flux and need not have utopian standards of equality applied to it before it can be said to exist.

It is also true that the space identified as global civil society contains actors that are not very civil. This is a reflection of the fact that the global arena is not identical to its domestic counterpart. Global space has more limited political authority and a relative lack of policing institutions. Although it goes against the grain of our understanding of domestic civil society, there are groups in global civil society that do lack civility. Civility, which might be thought of as the agreement to manage interaction according to a common set of rules and without recourse to violence, is a hallmark of domestic notions of civil society. Those who choose not to be bound by such rules are considered to be outside the bounds of civil society. In the global system, there is less agreement about common rules and much less enforcement than in most national societies. As a result, there is a greater space for uncivil groups to operate in the global civil society space. Examples include organized criminals, violent ethnic nationalists and terrorist organizations. They are shunned by the majority of civic associations, but they exist in a similar space. The global civil society arena is also occupied by several actors which do not share the characteristics of being non-profit, voluntary, equity-seeking, civic associations. One such group is composed of business associations, which seek to create an environment where corporations can maximize profits. Among these, a prominent example is the International Chamber of Commerce which, in addition to lobbying state and civil society actors, attempts to foster an environment which encourages self-regulation (Schneider 2000).

A further objection to the concept of global civil society is that it is misleading inasmuch as civil society and social movements are formed in relation to particular states. From this perspective, civil society groups can only exist in relationship to their states. Since there is no global state, the argument goes, there can hardly be a *global* civil society or *global* social movements (Germain and Kenny 1998; Brown 2000). The general point that there is no global state is, of course, correct. But there are global governance structures which regulate state, corporate and social activity on a worldwide basis (Hewson and Sinclair 1999). Tarrow (2000), while sceptical of global civil society, nevertheless acknowledges that transnational social movements are most likely to grow in those areas governed by international institutions. Institutions such as the IMF, World Bank and WTO are indeed increasingly the target of a mobilization that has significant deterritorialized attributes (O'Brien *et al*. 2000). The absence of a global state, in short, does not exclude the absence of a global civil society or global social movements.

There are, however, several underlying explanations for such objections to the concept of global civil society. One is global civil society's association with a liberal political perspective and the normative project of a cosmopolitan democracy. In this vein, Archibugi (1998: 222) believes that national and transnational civil societies play a crucial role in building cosmopolitan democracy through democratizing their own states, lobbying for peaceful and lawful international policies and playing a direct role in the management of global affairs. The difficulty this poses is that it suggests that a liberal pluralist model developed in Western states could or should be transposed to the global level, without recognizing the existing structural inequalities between areas of the globe. Advocates of cosmopolitan democracy might argue that it is the solution to inequality, but failure to examine issues such as the role of corporations in the global political economy runs the risk of establishing democratic procedures only for advanced industrialized states. Dominance of Western states, Western corporations and Western civil societies might end up in creating a small league of states with internal peace and prosperity, with the majority of the world's population excluded from both. It is not clear, in this sense, whether cosmopolitan democracy is actually a Western or a global project.

Global civil society also invokes resistance because it suggests that contemporary reality is in a process of changing from a state-based system to a more plural, but as yet undetermined, global governance structure. To use John Keane's (2003: xi–xii) words, it is a big idea that challenges other big ideas about how our global system operates. Since the end state is not yet known, advocates of a notion of global civil society are criticized for racing ahead of reality.

Finally, the debate about transnational or global civil society, as well as the boundaries of community and identity, arises from differences in analytic focus. One set of scholars, critical of the global civil society concept, begins from the state and domestic politics and moves out into the international system. For them, domestic politics is the norm against which other forms should be evaluated. Thus, a global civil society must have the same characteristics as a national civil society; a global social movement must have the same characteristics as a national social movement. A second set of scholars begins with a systemic view and adds the adjective 'global' to new phenomena that resemble (but are not identical to) national concepts. The increasing role of non-corporate, non-state activity in the international system is accordingly labelled global civil society. The 'state-out' view risks making the criteria for global civil society so rigid that it is defined out of existence. The 'system-in' view risks conflating so many forms of activity that probing analysis of the phenomenon becomes difficult and significant differences are ignored.

The differences in view between those starting from a unit or state analysis incorporating transnational relations and those beginning from a systemic analysis utilizing global relations are captured in Figure 7.1. The dark squares represent the state and the smaller

Transnational relations

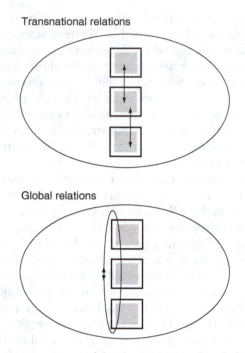

Global relations

FIGURE 7.1 *Contrasting models of transnational and global relations*

shaded squares represent civil society within the state. In the transnational model, groups from one society make connections with a group from another society. This is represented by dark arrows. In the global society model, relations cut across states and intersect in deterritorialized space. This is represented by the stretched oval and small two-way arrows. In the global model, sections of domestic society form a new grouping while remaining tied into the national groupings. Despite these differences in terminology and definition, however, it is possible to identify a common concern among analysts with the transnational, continent-spanning activity of civic actors and their impact upon the global political economy.

The operation of global civil society

A wide variety of scholars have claimed that there is something significant in the transnational operation of civic associations and numerous terms have been developed to label this activity. Prominent terms include international society (Peterson 1992), international civil society (Colás 2001), transnational social movements (Smith *et al*. 1997; Khagram *et al*. 2002), NGOs (Nelson 1995; Charnovitz 1997), global civil society (Lipschutz 1992; Scholte 2000b; Keane 2003), global social change organizations (Gale 1998), global society (Shaw 1994), global social movements (O'Brien *et al*. 2000), transnational advocacy networks (Keck and Sikkink 1998) and world civic politics (Wapner 1995).

Most of these authors are referring to the activity of voluntary, non-profit citizen associations. To differentiate these groups from profit-seeking non-governmental organizations such as TNCs, this chapter uses the term 'civic associations'. The most visible and explicitly political civic associations tend to be those working in high-profile areas such as the environment (Greenpeace, Friends of the Earth) or human rights (Amnesty International). However, there are many other forms of organization. For example, international trade union bodies such as the International Confederation of Free Trade Unions claim a representative (127 million members), as well as advocacy, role. Religious organizations are also very active. In terms of numbers of formal organizations the bulk of activity takes place in relatively uncontroversial and often apolitical forms such as industry associations and scientific knowledge organizations (medicine, sciences, communications) (Boli and Thomas 1999: 41). Aggregating visible NGOs with less visible local activity, one can point to the emergent of fluid social movements around issues such as development, human rights, labour, peace and women's issues.

Although there are many groups and specific agendas, most politically active civic associations would describe themselves as pursuing the objectives of equity or social justice. Equity and justice could be sought in respect to gender relations (women's groups), distribution of resources (development groups) quality of life (environmental groups), or human security (human rights). There are, of course, differences between civic associations, just as there are conflicts between states or corporations. Organized labour is challenged by NGOs claiming to speak on behalf of the informal sector. Women's groups in the developing world have an ambivalent and sometimes conflictual relationship with northern feminist groups. Environmentalists seeking thoroughgoing changes to the doctrine of economic growth are in conflict with more conservative conservationist groups. In short, various NGOs claim to speak on behalf of social movements or constituencies, but the plethora of groups and lack of transparency make it difficult to determine the legitimacy of their claims.

IPE and the global civil society debate

As indicated in the opening paragraphs of this chapter, the body of literature on global civil society raises some significant questions which can help to 'globalize' the study of IPE. These are dealt with in turn.

What are the internal dynamics within global civil society or, if one eschews the global civil society concept, between groups of civic associations?

Proponents of examining global social movements or transnational advocacy networks have noted that global inequality is often mirrored within these groups. A study of social movements' engagements with the World Bank, WTO and IMF highlights the inequality of access and influence among groups. Groups located in the North with ready access to the main organizations, those with funds to support lobbying efforts and those that have a reformist ideology are more likely to be heard than others (O'Brien *et al.* 2000). Activists hailing from states with different levels of economic development are likely to disagree about basic strategy and institutions. For example, Keck and Sikkink (1998: 214–15) point out the conflict between Northern activists, who usually regard the defence of state sovereignty as a ploy to protect state abuses, and Southern activists, who value state sovereignty as a shield against Northern influence.

To think critically about global civil society is necessarily to ask difficult questions about the distribution of power, wealth and influence within that sphere as well as the relationship between global civil society, the state system and the global economy (Amoore and Langley 2004). Because of the imbalances within global civil society, it is often not clear who is speaking for whom and how representation takes place. Inequalities rampant in the global political economy are reproduced in the sphere of global civil society. However, since dominant global civil society norms include equality and justice, and because debate and intellectual persuasion are significant elements of activity in this sphere, there is considerable opportunity to challenge existing patterns of inequality. Activists from Western states are vulnerable to criticisms of imperialist behaviour and are pressured to play different roles.

What is the relationship between global and local activity?

One of the objections to global civil society studies is that they over-emphasize the transnational nature of activity and do not pay enough attention to the local specificity and groundedness of particular cases (Johnston and Laxer 2003). This criticism is stressed by analysts interested in reasserting the primacy of domestic politics and the need to capture the national state before pursing internationalism. The critique has its counterpart in IPE, as noted earlier, when comparativists and others highlight the persistence of national or regional differences in models of political economy. While not negating the contribution of systemic analysis, these are useful reminders to scholars to pay attention to the importance and particularity of local groups and developments. In the context of 'globalizing IPE', it is an argument for paying attention to a variety of experiences across the world.

Which groups are playing a significant role?

There are, of course, many groups operating in global civil society. A pressing question is which groups are potentially playing a significant role, as well as what we might mean by significant in this context. In contrast to most IPE literature which focuses upon OECD states, an interesting aspect of global civil society is that many of the most dynamic, challenging and innovative groups are located in the 'developing' world. This is further grist to the 'globalizing IPE' mill, inasmuch as it invites and is contributing to a reorientation of IPE from firmly *within* the field of study. A good example is the growing work on labour internationalism. After considerable disillusionment with the orientation of labour groups in developing states, a tremendous amount of interest has been generated by the dynamic labour movements of newly industrializing countries such as South Korea, South Africa and Brazil. The emergence of social movement unionism challenges the complacency of labour in developed states and offers an alternative vision to labour groups and intellectuals. Some have even gone as far as to argue that this new form of organization heralds a new model of internationalism (Lambert and Webster 2003).

The growth of the WSF provides a further case that prompts similar conclusions. The WSF first took place in 2001 in Porto Alegre, Brazil, and was designed as a counter-event to the WEF in Davos, Switzerland. The WSF was distinctive in that it was based in the 'South' and dedicated to issues of social protection, and in that its participants were far less privileged than the WEF participants. A key event of the first WSF was a televised debate between participants in the WSF and WEF. The WSF grew in numbers from 10 to over 100,000 people in three years. Similar regional forums were created in Europe, Asia and Africa. In 2004 the Forum moved its physical gathering point from Brazil to India. The WSF is dominated by participants from the developing regions of the world, and by issues of concern to developing countries and peoples (Sen *et al.* 2004). While some Europeans and North Americans participate, they are vastly outnumbered by developing-country participants. This is partially a function of location. The WSF in Brazil is flooded by Brazilian NGOs and Indian NGOs were over-represented at the 2004 Mumbai Forum. It is also a result of the Forum's organization. While the French NGO ATTAC plays a prominent role, the organizing committee is firmly in Southern hands.

Operating with the motto 'Another World is Possible', the agenda of the WSF could also be part of an agenda for a more 'globalized' IPE. Article 4 of the WSF's Charter of Principles states that the alternatives it suggests will 'respect universal human rights, and those of all citizens – men and women – of all nations and the environment and will rest on democratic international systems and institutions at the service of social justice, equality and the sovereignty of peoples' (WSF 2004). These are not the standard IPE topics, but they are of concern to a significant and politically active set of Southern civic associations.

Conclusion: the study of transnational relations in IPE

We have argued in this chapter that the broad concept of transnational relations, in its dominant form, is too incoherent and diffuse to sustain theoretical insight because it groups together actors that are analytically distinct. In particular, the conflation of corporate and civic actors is not helpful. TNCs are such a crucial actor in the global political economy that they require their own space for analysis. Strands of the policy community and social forces approaches to transnational relations lead us into significant debates about global civil society, and our central argument has been that these debates highlight a number of theoretical and empirical insights that can help expand the horizons of IPE.

Theoretically, global civil society discussions:

- *alert scholars to the fact that there is far less consensus on the operating principles of the economy than previously thought*. During the 1990s, civic associations often acted as the unofficial opposition to state and corporate elites. There may have been a 'Washington Consensus' that embraced state elites, but this was not grounded in the civil societies of most states. While cooperation and agreement might have been achieved with international institutions, the implementation of the consensus rested upon weak domestic foundations. In many cases, this domestic consent was withheld and active resistance took place.

- *bring new issues and perspectives to the table*. The realm of global civil society is an exciting space with a profusion of ideas and ideologies. While dependency theory and concepts of imperialism may have been banished from most Western studies of IPE, they continue to inform political action on the ground. There may not be much attention paid to eco-feminism in IPE textbooks, but it is an influential voice at the WSF. This suggests that the theoretical closing of mainstream IPE has been premature and a more pluralistic approach is required. In addition, global civil society advances a counter agenda to liberal economic growth which emphasizes sustainable development, economic justice and gender equality. It suggests that issues of social and economic justice are central to the study of a *global* political economy. This echoes a number of the editor's central arguments, set out in the conclusion to this volume: that issues of development broadly conceived – and in this case the challenges to the development orthodoxy issuing from global civil society – can and should be the central unifying ingredients of a more 'globalized' IPE.

- *highlight the conflict of interest and ideas between people and regions*. Global civil society is extremely diverse with numerous competing strategies and groups. Groups from the same country may espouse social democratic reformism, revolutionary socialism and religious fundamentalism. Cleavages may also appear between groups from different regions as radical change is more appealing to those who have the least. This diversity requires careful study and caution about sweeping generalizations on subjects such as the anti-globalization/global justice movement.

- *reinvigorate utopian visions.* Whereas many Western analysts have developed ideas of the end of history with the triumph of liberal democracy or, conversely, a dark new vision of clashing civilizations, civic actors espouse a wide range of alternative scenarios. Intellectually, this opens our imaginations to new ways of thinking about possibilities for analysis and action. Empirically, global civil society activity helps us think about traditional subjects in new ways. In the area of international trade, for example, civic associations press for ethical trade. This has implications for the production process from corporate codes of conduct to new forms of agriculture and distribution. In terms of finance, alternative arrangements such as microcredit, debt relief and restrictions on speculative capital come to the surface. A wide range of subjects are approached in a different manner with a focus upon increasing economic justice. This again goes some useful way to reorienting the study and practice of IPE.

In sum, the area of transnational relations is a useful complement and challenge to state- or state/firm-centric approaches to IPE. However, as with the field of IPE in general, transnational relations studies have tended to build upon the empirical and theoretical experiences of advanced industrialized political economies. This chapter has argued that attempts to 'globalize' IPE require and contribute to three sorts of amendments to the transnational relations literature. First, the distinctive and dominant role of TNCs must be acknowledged and analytically separated from other forms of transnational relations. Second, differences in interests and understandings generated by the immense disparity in global wealth and power will limit the insights generated by policy community approaches to transnational relations. Third, social forces approaches will need to take more account of radical challenges from outside the OECD. A critical analysis of the burgeoning global civil society literature is one way of beginning to make these changes.

Chapter 8

Democratization and the Realm of Politics in International Political Economy

Jean Grugel

The current preoccupation with democracy and democratization in the international order is not new. Democratic values were grafted on to the principal ideas ordering international society after the Enlightenment. Nevertheless, as Mayall (2000) shows, the democratic ideals that states in the West endorsed rhetorically have only rarely guided their behaviour. This was especially true during the Cold War, when support for democratization was reduced to the status of a decorative motif on an otherwise self-interested agenda. After 1989, democracy, respect for human rights and the importance of the rule of law were enthusiastically reconfirmed by the West as discursive ordering principles for the international system. A so-called 'third wave' of democratization (Huntington 1991) led to the establishment of new systems of rule, based loosely on the introduction of liberal principles and electoral politics into a number of previously authoritarian societies and much of the ex-communist bloc. But the democratic triumphalism evident in the immediate aftermath of the end of the Cold War, when it was assumed that democracy was the natural endgame in international politics, has quickly been eclipsed. Concern about the erosion of democratic institutions in the West through globalization; the impact of the new security agenda on domestic and foreign policies in the USA and Europe; the very evident difficulties of new democracies in the 'developing' world and post-communist countries; the stalling of the democratic impulse, state crisis in parts of Asia and Africa, and actual or threatened interruptions of democratic process in Latin America and the Caribbean; and a growing unease about the undemocratic nature of institutions within international society – all of these raise serious doubts about how far a new democratic era has, in fact, emerged out of the ashes of the Cold War. These are paradoxical times: global politics is marked by a renewed interest in and apparent commitment to democratic principles, while at the same time democracy itself remains more elusive and fragile than ever.

This chapter begins with a brief examination of the emergence and the parameters of the mainstream democratization debate, before moving on to a discussion of how the study of democratization has unfolded within IPE thus far. Because of its focus on world order, the changing roles of states and the interface between market, politics and society, IPE, and especially critical IPE, should provide important insights into the complex processes that both promote and curtail democratization. Nevertheless, it is striking how little serious analysis of democracy and democratization has yet been carried out from within IPE. For one thing, democratization is a notoriously slippery and vague concept. In particular, it is not always clear whether it is used to refer to a system of political institutions or a set of broader social and political changes that reflect and uphold changes to society and the ways in which power is deployed. These are difficulties with which IPE analysts generally have not yet entirely got to grips. But a large part of the difficulty also lies in the way in which the study of IPE itself has unfolded. IPE is held together by an ontological view that the political and economic domains cannot be meaningfully separated (Underhill 2000b). Yet, in practice, it has mainly pursued an economy-driven research agenda. The thrust of IPE since the 1990s has been to identify the various components that make up the present forms of market-led governance. Clearly these are crucial tasks, but IPE must also pay detailed attention to questions of political authority, the (political) struggles for control of states, the processes of (political) contestation and the ideological dimensions of political conflicts. The political world and processes of political interaction cannot and should not be seen as straightforwardly derivative of economic processes or confined to the construction of markets. The assumption that politics and economics are an interwoven whole – the cornerstone of IPE's analytical toolkit – needs to made real by probing more deeply the concept of politics and political contestation. In its treatment of democratization specifically, IPE also needs a greater sensitivity to the particular realities of developing states, given that it is in these that most experiments in democratization have been and are taking place.

The task is thus to rethink the status of the political within IPE and, in so doing, to seek to deepen IPE's analytical purchase on questions of democracy and democratization. Rethinking the state is clearly central to this task. Borrowing concepts creatively from other sub-fields of social science, while at the same time holding on to particular and defining tenets of IPE, is also important. A strong case has already been made both here in this volume and elsewhere (Hettne 1995a; Payne 1998) for creative trespassing into area and development studies. Inspired by Underhill's (2000a: 806) call for 'disciplinary ecumenism' within IPE, this chapter argues that, as far as the study of democratization is concerned, much can be learned from engagement with the rich field of political theory, with meta-theories of social change (especially those that analyse the role of the state and possibilities of collective agency, such as historical sociology) and with the expanding literature on civic and social action in conditions of globalization.

Mainstream approaches to democratization

Democratization reemerged as an important area for study in the 1980s with the aim of exploring the politics of post-authoritarian regimes in Southern Europe and Latin America. The collapse of the Soviet bloc after 1989 enlarged the field of study and, at the same time, increased the visibility of democratization studies within politics and IR. Yet the study of democratization has, in fact, a rather longer history. Its origins lie in mainstream political sociology and development studies in the 1960s. Lipset (1959) and Rostow (1960) both argued that economic development conditions or determines political institutions, the result being that democracy came to be seen as an outcome of capitalist development, the triumph of the middle class and the supremacy of middle-class cultural and political values. These are the basic assumptions of the 'modernizationist' school of democratization. Modernization theorists reached similar conclusions to the political culture school (Almond and Verba 1963; Pye 1966) and suggested that democracy was a rare occurrence, possible only under particular economic circumstances which, furthermore, were to be found almost exclusively in the Anglo-American world and Western Europe. Where democracy was thought to exist in the developing world, as in Chile until 1973, it was usually explained with reference to the spread of European values, European-influenced political elites and a European-style party system (Angell 1993).

Some intellectual issue was taken with these gloomy assumptions and closed paradigms. Rustow (1970) argued controversially that democracy did not require objective structural conditions beyond the existence of a unified nation-state. He stressed instead agency, leadership and the role of elite choice. But, by the early 1970s, this had largely become a sterile debate in any case, authoritarian rule, not democracy, being the lot of the much of the developing world. As a result, Huntington's (1968) view came to prevail: that social science should try to explain the political processes at work in non-democracies, especially in developing countries, rather than to explain why they were not or could not become democracies. Indeed, Huntington went on to suggest, the West's geopolitical interests *required* an understanding and even a rapprochement with some forms of authoritarianism as a bulwark against communism.

This, then, was the state of play in the study of democratization when the dictatorships began to collapse, one after the other, in Portugal, Spain and Greece, then a few years later in Argentina, Brazil and other Latin American countries. In the rush to explain these sudden transformations, Huntington (1991) argued that political change operated as a 'wave' spreading outwards to neighbouring or culturally connected countries. Other scholars revisited Rustow's rather neglected paradigm, which now seemed more apposite precisely because it stressed the role of elite agency. Hence the revival of democratization studies began with a dual focus. One line of analysis followed Huntington and focused on the extent to which pressures for democratization were generated outside the country experiencing political change (Pridham 1991; Nagle and Mahr 1999). The second analytical trend, inspired by Rustow, emphasized the dynamic process of iterated elite interactions in building new democratic institutions and the micro-politics of transitions (Schmitter *et al.* 1986). On the whole, the latter, agency-centred, focus came out on top. More than any other approach, it seemed to capture the trend of global political events. New democracies clearly required a settling of scores or a burying of differences between competing political elites; social and political stability following the end of dictatorship manifestly depended on elite accommodation and compromise. A fascinating and detailed literature was thus produced which examined how these agreements were built, why they succeeded or failed and how these pacts or deals shaped the new political order that was being created (for overviews, see Potter *et al.* 1997; Grugel 2002).

But, despite this exciting and promising start, democratization studies once more began to run out of steam by the middle of the 1990s. It was not that democratization itself was off the political agenda – in fact, far from it. Democratization had gradually come to be seen as the 'normal' framework for politics. Even for those countries where democracy was poor or non-existent, by the 1990s democratization had become an important goal and international bodies were increasingly identifying democratization as a key to political, social and economic development. Yet the field of democratization studies could be said to have reached something of an intellectual impasse, as it notably failed to analyse the impact of the globalization of democratization discourses on political processes on the ground. Mainstream theories of democratization, based on the view that national structures or actors either produce the conditions for the emergence of democracy or, at least, make the deals that bring it into being, were rooted in an assumption of the sealed and sovereign nation-state, thereby making it difficult – perhaps even impossible – to address the global dimensions of democratization. Huntington's notion of the wave, meanwhile, operated at best as an engaging but ultimately entirely descriptive metaphor.

A further problem lay in the mainstream's view that, in addressing democratization, *only* politics mattered. Speaking for agency-based scholarship in general, Przeworski (1999) insisted on a rigid separation of the political order from the economic system. Democracy should be understood as a 'contingent institutional compromise' that left economic relations intact (Przeworski 1986: 59). Democratization processes were undermined, he argued, when social movements pressed for a redistribution of power. According to Gideon Baker (1999), this contributed to the mainstream view that 'actually existing democracies' are the only form of democracy possible. Analytically, it led to a narrow understanding of power, interests and the state and a consequent inability to explain what happens after the initial process of democratic transition is over. Why did some (most?) experiments in democratization lead to limited or illiberal democracies? Why do unsatisfactory and substandard democracies persist, despite popular rejection or apathy and poor performances? What possibilities are there for democratization in externally dependent states? Do levels of development or the global political economy influence outcomes? If so, how? These questions could not and still cannot be satisfactorily explained in mainstream paradigms of democratization.

Finally, mainstream democratization theory tended to ignore the question of who exactly the 'bearers' of democracy were supposed to be. There was an assumption that (national) elites are crucial and some discussion of the impact of elite-led transitions on post-transition politics. Democracy was viewed as a set of contingent political compromises; no class or social group was seen as inherently more democratic than any other. This had the virtue of capturing some of the day-to-day mechanics of democratic politics, but it also separated accounts of contemporary democratization from democracy-building in the past by ignoring the rich sociological and historical vein of analysis which, informed by variants of Marxist, structuralist and Weberian thought, has always paid detailed attention to class conflict, collective action and state transformation (Mann 1993). In the end, agency-centred approaches rejected the theoretical baggage used to analyse the grand socio-political transformations of the past, including sociological class analysis and historically informed studies of economic and social change, in favour of a narrow, behavioural methodology.

IPE and democratization

The 'conceptual mess' (Kopecky and Mudde 2000: 519) in which mainstream democratization studies thus found itself in the 1990s opened the way for approaches that have, in different ways, emphasized the centrality of the concept of the 'global' for understanding democratization. IPE has made a particularly significant contribution to explaining how and why democratization fits within the liberal global architecture, entering the debate as a perspective that views democratization as an integral part of the prevailing world order, the transnationalization of class structures and the transformation of the state. By extension, all discussion of democratization from within IPE assumes that the core of an explanation lies in the unfolding of the global political economy. Democratization processes are, in other words, located in the context of:

- the linkages between the market and states/societies;
- the identification of the relationship between ideas (such as democracy) and material change;
- the transnationalization of public spheres of authority;

- the growing institutionalization of authoritative forms of global governance; and
- the rise of globalized social movements or transnationalized civil society.

At the risk of simplifying the field, three distinct IPE-based approaches to democratization can be discerned: a largely Marxist-inspired account of democratization as hyperliberalism; a critique of global governance and liberal-influenced scholarship that links democratization to global governance; and a rather less well-delineated literature, the inspiration for which derives ultimately from Gramscian concepts of civil society and hegemony, that sees transnational civil society as a source of democratization 'from below'. These three literatures are surveyed briefly below.

Democratization as hyperliberalism

Susan Strange (1992) was amongst the first to suggest, early in the 1990s, that democratization should be understood quite simply as a reflection of the formation of an increasingly liberal global political economy. Democratization emerged in developing and post-communist countries as a result of the hegemony of the capitalist West. In this view, democracy – understood quite simply as the introduction of a set of formal procedures for elected government and the gradual diffusion of liberal values – was functional for capitalist growth and, as such, should be seen as its corollary. Democratization thus becomes a symbol of the triumph of free-market capitalism; it is part of the 'seemingly monolithic conformity' that emerged in the world order in the 1980s and 1990s which Robert Cox (1987) calls 'hyperliberalism'. Hyperliberalism assumes that the force behind the wave of democratization in the 1980s and 1990s is the emergence of global free-market capitalism. This new form of capitalism has negative implications for the quality of democracy in the established democracies as well as defining the terms of democratization in peripheral and post-communist societies. Because it strengthens global capital at the expense of both national producers and labour, it also weakens states and increases competition between states. Deploying the much-quoted Coxian phrase (Cox 1996a: 302), states become 'transmission belts' for decisions taken elsewhere under conditions of global capitalism. Hence the emergence of a liberalized global economy signifies the end of national development projects and the Keynesian welfare state and erodes democracy in the West as well as across the developing world.

One interesting feature of the hyperliberal approach is that its arguments are at odds with some of the scholarship that had become part of the established canon of IPE at the end of the 1990s, namely the view that states retain capacity and 'agential power', notwithstanding the pressures of globalization (Hobson and Ramesh 2002: 5; also Cerny 1993; Weiss 1998). Indeed, there is even now a view that, after all, social democracy can survive in one form or another, at least in Western Europe (Martell 2001; also Garrett 1998; Hay 2000b; Rhodes 2001). Hyperliberalism draws instead on the view that the embrace of liberal globalization dooms genuinely progressive politics in the West and condemns the developing and post-communist worlds to weak versions of democracy, the main purpose of which is to provide a structure for the spread of capitalist norms and practices. Democratization is thus seen as part of an attempt to establish a stable political framework through which to bind the poor into competitive nodes of a globalized capitalist economy. Democratization, in other words, becomes straightforwardly a cover for economic liberalization. Perhaps not surprisingly, this scholarship focuses mainly on democratization in the developing world where there is an abundance of evidence linking the introduction of democratic regimes in the 1980s and 1990s to the onset of liberal economic reform.

The aim of the hyperliberal school, then, is to establish a causal link between liberal politics and economics and to uncover the hidden face of economic exploitation that is allegedly masked by the language of rights, citizenship and freedom. Democratization, in fact, is conceptualized as something of a dystopia: it cannot be understood as a project of emancipation, as mainstream analyses of democratization imply, for political rights are subordinated to and curtailed by marketization. It is reflective of a deeper reality in which a marketized global polity subjects states and citizens alike to the dehumanizing rationale of capitalist production. It acts as a political cover that serves to legitimize this state of affairs. It is to be understood simply – and only – as part of what Gill (1992) has referred to as 'the new constitutionalism' of liberalism that governs the market-led globalized polity.

Clearly, hyperliberalism offers a structuralist account of democratization. Emphasis is squarely placed, in terms of explaining why democratization happens, on economic transformation rather than on political will. Nevertheless, there is still seen to be some role for agency. A new transnational elite (or class) is usually conceptualized as the 'bearer' of this project of transformation (van der Pijl 1995). Robinson (2002: 226) neatly summarizes this view:

> Transnational fractions of local elites have ascended politically in countries around the world, clashing in their bid for hegemony with nationally-based class fractions. They have increasingly captured local states – or key institutions within those states, such as Central Banks and foreign ministries – and used national and state apparatuses to advance globalisation. An increasingly class-conscious transnational capitalist class has become a hegemonic class fraction globally.

More than perhaps anyone else, Robinson (1996, 2002, 2004) has attempted to establish the empirical evidence to sustain the idea of democratization as a project of global capitalism transmitted by globalized elites. Using examples drawn from Latin America, he offers an in-depth analysis of how transnational elites – composed of actors from within the US state and the IFIs – promote a twin agenda of 'polyarchy and neoliberalism'. Seen as extreme by some, this approach is nevertheless strengthened by area studies scholarship, especially on sub-Saharan Africa, frequently carried out by academics who do not themselves draw on the theoretical baggage of either Marxism or IPE (Clapham 1996; van Cranenburgh 1999; Harbeson 2000).

Nevertheless, the idea that class formation is now effectively globalized, as Robinson implies, is difficult fully to sustain in the face of evidence of the continuing salience of states and national classes, despite globalization, especially in the West. Moreover, the complexity of democratization is simplified to the extent that it is depicted merely as a crude tool of management from above. As a result, the hyperliberal thesis has failed as yet to convince the academy as a whole, despite the existence of some highly grounded research, that states are everywhere redundant and that liberal democracy has little more emancipatory promise than authoritarian rule.

Critiques of democratization as global governance

The liberal literature on global governance tends to assume that its introduction will lead to more democratic governance (Falk 1995). As a result, there is a growing assumption within liberal scholarship that the expanding responsibilities of global governance institutions and networks lead to a greater appreciation of the values of democracy and to a commitment to supporting and extending democratic practices globally. Much of this research remains at the level of theoretical conjecture or normative assertion. But there is also an emerging body of empirically grounded work that examines how far governance organizations encourage or promote democratization within the global or regional context, and seeks to identify and assess the models of democracy with which they work (Scholte 1998, 1999, 2001; Casaburi *et al.* 2000; O'Brien *et al.* 2000; Woods 2000, 2001).

Institutions of global governance that declare an absolute preference for democracy include the IMF, the World Bank and the UN. These organizations see themselves as responsible to the 'international community' for the promotion of peace, stability and the conditions for (liberal) economic growth. The huge 'third sector' of think tanks and large NGOs working in development, human rights, gender and environmental issue areas that operate at the interface between international organizations, states and communities also forms a key part of governance structures because it implements, designs and coordinates policies in conjunction with governance agencies. As a result, increasingly robust lines of interdependence can be traced between global organizations and the non-governmental sector. These, it is argued, serve both to police and to normalize democratic values. Optimistic readings of the transformatory capacity of transnational civil society point to its role in attaching values such as human rights, the environment and social justice to the global governance agenda (Glasius and Kaldor 2003). Sikkink (2002: 302), for example, has argued that transnational activism is gradually 'altering the norm structure of global governance' and restructuring world politics in a more progressive mould.

Critical IPE enters this debate, as Payne has argued elsewhere in this volume, with the aim of uncovering the liberal biases within the global governance debate. It attempts to reveal the deeper reality behind the governance agenda rather than accepting uncritically the pro-democratization discourse contained within it. Clearly, this issue is central to development studies as well, since governance interventions occur primarily in the developing world. As a result, there is considerable overlap between the critical IPE critique of global governance and that of contemporary development studies, to the point where the two become almost indistinguishable. Key questions of concern to both include the extent to which governance organizations are representative of the global community; whether governance interventions uphold Western power and impose Westernized notions of what constitutes democracy; the nature of power structures within governance networks; and how governance interventions impact on states.

Much has been written about the transformation of institutions of global governance in the 1990s and the impact of a new rhetoric of consultation and openness in particular (World Bank 1992; also Doornbos 2001). Yet, despite undoubted changes, the thrust of global governance is still to uphold and justify an unequal global order (Payne, this volume; also Williams and Young 1994; Williams 1996). If this is the case, encounters between the governance organizations and transnational civil society organizations or NGOs are far more problematic than Sikkink (2002), for example, assumes. Influencing the agenda and practices of governance agencies from below is extremely difficult (O'Brien *et al.* 2000). Discourses have changed much more than policy. Moreover, organizations such as the World Bank or the UN are dominated by the big donors – the Western states. Meanwhile Scholte's (1998, 1999) detailed research on the World Bank confirms the view that governance institutions are intellectually fixed in a liberal mould and ultimately remain closed to alternative models of democracy, such as those articulated by sectors of transnational civil society (see also Casaburi *et al.* 2000).

In this sense, rather than being seen as neutral agencies promoting democracy, global governance organizations should be regarded as irredeemably Western in their constitution and approaches, with democratization as pursued through governance agencies understood in that context. Whatever the rhetoric, democratization through global governance is a liberal project of world (re)ordering based around the diffusion of Western values and the construction of a global consensus that assumes Western leadership, normatively and strategically. As Cox (1997) has highlighted, the power wielded by governance agencies is a reflection of the fact that they ultimately represent Western geostrategic and economic interests.

As such, they are unreflexively liberal and elitist. This would not be so problematic if exported liberalism were not so tarnished, in the developing world at least, by its historical associations with global inequality and cultural arrogance. Rita Abrahamsen (2000) has pulled out the full significance of this perhaps most effectively. Using examples drawn from sub-Saharan Africa, she demonstrates that governance interventions do prioritize neoliberal developmental discourses above all other perspectives. As well as leading to development crises, the imposition of neoliberal governance has deprived countries of effective states and disrupted welfare networks. In the process, even the possibility of democracy has been destroyed. Her point is clear: externally induced processes of liberalization, such as those that have taken place in sub-Saharan Africa since the late 1980s, directly contribute to the failed states they are supposed to remedy.

Cammack's (2002) study of the World Bank comes to similarly dramatic conclusions. He argues that no project, political or economic, is really feasible in developing countries other than that endorsed by the Bank. This sort of conclusion was echoed, unexpectedly, by Joseph Stiglitz (2002), Chief Economist at the World Bank in the 1990s. Stiglitz caused a stir in development circles by arguing that imposed democracy cannot be sustained in the developing world because it relies on extensive semi-permanent support from outside agencies such as the Bank. He went on to conclude that its strategy of imposition impacts negatively on democratic transition and consolidation in aid-recipient countries because it undermines the democratic process within fragile states. Woods (2001: 97) agrees: external intervention, she argues, 'risks thwarting the desired processes of "institution-building" and "state modernisation"'. Crawford (1997) and Olsen (1998), meanwhile, suggest that the pro-democracy turn in global governance has been overstated. They point out that interest in democratization was always subordinated to other concerns, such as economic and geostrategic interests. In this light, it is not surprising that many development studies/IPE-based assessments of global governance and democracy in the developing world are sombre (see, for example, Murphy 2000). Certainly, the attempt to spread democracy has 'proven more conflictual than anyone could have imagined when it began' (Luckham *et al*. 2001: 47).

Overall, critical IPE perspectives on global governance have offered a convincing critique of the liberal school on democratization and global governance. On close examination, much of what passes for support for democratization is, in reality, little more than an attempted imposition of Western and liberal values. It is difficult not to conclude that most governance institutions are unaccountable and unrepresentative bodies and that governance interventions are generally ill-considered and unproductive. Moreover, the liberal view of global governance, and in particular the idea that transnational civil society is now sufficiently powerful to influence policy, was further undermined by the consequences of the terrorist attacks of 11 September 2001. As Ayres and Tarrow (2002) point out, the state-centrism that has prevailed in the global order since then has led to a growing distrust of civil society groups and weakened their capacity to shape governance outcomes into a more democratic mould. It may be that transnational civil society linked to the governance institutions will ultimately succeed in pushing for a more sensitive approach to questions of democratization, as Kaldor (2000a, 2000b) argues, but so far the evidence appears scanty.

Democratization as transformation

IPE has set out its stall as a tool for analysing the operation of power within the global polity. As such, it has inevitably tended to focus on the activities, values and ideas of the organizations, elites and structures through which global power most evidently flows. The result has been that rather less attention has been paid to the political activities of those located either at the margins of globalized chains of production or in sites of activity that are only indirectly or weakly tied to the global market. This approach thus tends to miss the potential notion of democratization as a counter-hegemonic project of social change. In fact, there is an expanding field of research loosely attached to democratization studies that sets out to evaluate how far it is possible to 'democratize democratization' (Castañeda 1994: ch. 12) and build substantive democracy based on practices of citizenship and inclusion (Kaldor and Vejvoda 1997; Luckham *et al.* 2001; Grugel 1999, 2003a, 2003b), and asks what exactly these concepts imply in terms of policy.

Some of this research overlaps with an emerging interest within IPE around the notion that a global public sphere or a transnational civil society is beginning to emerge. This arena, at least potentially, operates as a space for the articulation of notions of democracy and democratization that go beyond the standard liberal conceptualizations outlined earlier. In particular, it could be argued that the existence and vitality of civil society organizations, especially if they are genuinely global in membership rather than simply Western, challenge the assumption that democracy is straightforwardly and simply a complement to the market, the globalization of capitalism and the Westernization of the world polity. From within IPE, Hettne (1990, 1995b) has drawn particular attention to the importance of civil society in the global political economy. For Hettne (1995b: 5), this return to 'community' or 'civil society' is the second part of what Polanyi (1957) referred to as the 'double movement' of marketization, the first being the expansion and deepening of market exchange:

> After the present phase of neoliberal hegemony and social marginalization, reciprocity – or what in other theoretical frameworks is called 'community or civil society' – is bound to become more important again, simply as a mode of survival when the protective redistributive political structures break up.

According to Sakamoto (1995: 139), this return to community is the result of the internationalization of the state, the universalization of nationalism and technological advance, as well as the globalization of democracy which tends to 'foster a sense of powerlessness on the part of individual citizens', thereby encouraging membership of localized or particularized group activity.

Despite some attention to the theme of community, contestation and civil society, however, IPE has, on the whole, been quite slow to pick up the significance of the emergence of transnational civil society for democratization or to engage with it in any serious or grounded way. Gills's (2000) work on democratization in Asia after financial crisis, Abbott's (2001) study of Indonesia and Morton's (2002) examination of agency from below and democratization in Mexico are but exceptions to this general neglect. Nevertheless, I shall argue below that this approach offers an important route to deepen IPE studies of democratization, and indeed counter-hegemonic agency more generally.

Taking stock and the way forward: exploring the realm of politics

Mayall (2000: 62) suggests that democratization has come to occupy a prominent position in the agenda of global politics without there being a completely convincing account from within IR of why this should be so. The same could be said of IPE, despite the undoubted insights that can be garnered from the different approaches outlined above. IPE generally has not generated a fully coherent approach to or explanation of democratization that captures its multiple identities as a tool of Western management of developing and post-communist societies, an expression of elite power and an inspiration for social and citizenship movements.

Mainstream IPE starts from the view that 'if there is a global polity, certainly its dominant ideology, now, is liberal, both economic and political' (Murphy 2000: 792). The emphasis on 'disciplinary neoliberalism' (Gill 1995) has sometimes slipped, perhaps unconsciously, into an approach that leaves the realm of the political with little or no life of its own. As a result, democratization becomes essentially uninteresting. For hyperliberals, democratization is a straightforward reflection of economic liberalization, seen as the driver of global transformation. Perspectives associated with the critique of global governance, meanwhile, are certainly more concerned with politics, but at their core are questions of authority and regulation in an era of globalization. As a result, the idea that democracy might be conceived as a radical demand for social change and redistribution from below scarcely finds an echo, even in these parts of critical IPE. In conclusion, it is hard to escape the view that, for most IPE scholars, democratization has so far been a largely second-order research question.

More than most issue areas in the global political economy, democratization is driven by a political, as well as an economic, logic. Most IPE scholarship is at present blinkered in its capacity to theorize and explain self-conscious *political* action as a consequence of some of its ontological and methodological assumptions. This translates into a number of specific difficulties for the study of democratization. First, despite scholars' determination not to do so, IPE research in practice tends to emphasize structure over agency, and thus to argue that democracy is a part of the global agenda because it is functional for liberal economics. As a result, the complex reasons for the ways in which democratization has come to be part of the agendas of governments and societies are oversimplified. Just as importantly, IPE offers no purchase on the differential outcomes generated from pressures for democratization. There is no doubt, as Diamond (1999) argues, that democratization encompasses a range of political transformations, including the emergence of (a few) liberal democracies, sets of cynical experiments by manipulative elites leading to pseudo-democratic systems of rule, and externally driven superstructural reform. IPE, at present, can shed very little light on the nature of these differences or the reasons for them. At the same time, demands for democratization can now be heard from groups that are not rooted solely within one nation-state and, so far, IPE has contributed little to the elaboration of any detailed explanations of either the genesis of these movements or their impact. A more nuanced theoretical focus that pays attention to agency – especially, in my view, the agency of collective actors – is therefore required.

Second, IPE works from a conceptual understanding of democracy that unreflectively draws upon a picture of how it operates in the core countries. In effect, with the exception of the 'democratization as transformation' approach, democracy is understood as something that really exists, or that has existed in the West, in the guise of either pluralism or social democracy. This is maintained despite the body of critical research that suggests that democracy is an unrealized – or at best a partially realized – project even in Europe and the USA (for example, Weir and Beetham 1999). This assumption derives from a world view which extrapolates an understanding of global politics and the politics of developing and non-Western parts of the world from the perceived reality of the West. As a result, democracy is conceptualized simply as a management strategy for capitalism by Western agencies, representatives or transnational elites, to be exported from the 'core' to the rest of the world. Instead, a distinction needs to be made between projects of management concerned with questions of public order or the embedding of liberal norms (a process that could be termed 'hollow' or 'imposed' democratization) and the emancipatory project of genuine democracy, which implies radical social and political change involving the redistribution of power. Gill (1996) does, in fact, make this distinction, but he goes on to assume that neoliberalism makes genuine democratization impossible, condemning *a priori* social activism under capitalism to automatic failure.

Third, there is the problem of the state. It is now broadly recognized that IPE works with an inadequately theorized notion of the state, as discussed by Phillips elsewhere in this volume. This is a particular problem when it comes to understanding democratization, for the transformation of the state and questions concerning its authority, legitimacy, functions and representativeness are at the crux of democracy itself. For Rueschemeyer *et al.* (1992), the essence of democratization is, in fact, reform of the state: democratization is the process through which reforms are imposed on an elitist and unrepresentative state that remake it in an accountable and more wholly representative mould. Moreover, democratic theory assumes that the promises inherent within democracy – equality, justice, citizenship, autonomy – must be made real though the state (Weale 1999). If globalization means that this is no longer possible, then democracy requires the creation of cosmopolitan structures of governance, a sort of global state (Held 1995). To make a serious contribution to questions of democratization, therefore, IPE needs to clarify and probe much more fully its view of the state and address the related question of citizenship.

In this light, the school of critical IPE that derives from the ideas of Robert Cox offers perhaps the most appropriate frame for analyses of democratization in two significant senses: in contrast to mainstream approaches, it is consciously historical in its approach, and it is sensitive to the different ways that the interlinked logics of capitalism and power operate in different spatial localities, as well as the leverage of differently situated local, national and international actors (Sinclair 1996). A *prima facie* assumption of Cox's thought is that global power is played out very differently in the different geographical and productive arenas of the world order. It is thus attuned to realities of the developing world as well as to those of advanced capitalist societies. Moreover, Cox is concerned with how states change 'under pressure from above (the world order) and from below (civil society)' (Sinclair 1996: 3). This suggests potential for the analysis of democratization in the context of the dynamic interaction between a globalized sphere of authority, citizenship movements and states. Again, it promises a richer avenue for research than traditional approaches to democratization that centre almost exclusively on (usually visible) interactions between national elites.

Nevertheless, this potential has yet to be fully realized. Part of the problem lies with the Coxian agenda itself. An extremely ambitious and far-reaching programme, Coxian IPE requires a sense of the big picture combined with sensitivity to very different and changing local realities and the capacity to make linkages between the two. But it is difficult to construct an appropriate methodology for the investigation of the all-important issues it identifies. How, for example, can we understand, measure and compare the impact of world order on the political arrangements in different state–society complexes? How can we investigate agency at the global level? What are the spaces for agency from below and how can the role of subaltern actors in social change be conceptualized and identified? What is the appropriate time frame for analysis? Answers to these questions are simply not clear. The methodological difficulties – which are general to Coxian and critical IPE – are heightened in the study of democratization by some particular obstacles. There is a real normative ambiguity within critical IPE relating to democracy and democratization. Is it merely a cover for capitalism? Or do democratic movements and systems of government have a real potential to deliver human betterment? Muddled thinking about democracy and democratization lies at the heart of critical IPE; as a result, what is actually meant by democracy goes largely unexplained. These difficulties lead to contradictory assumptions about the impact (potential and real) of democratization, both for 'ordinary' people and for the global order.

Yet critical IPE, particularly its Gramscian and Polanyian strands, has inspired the emerging literature on democratization as transformation, much of which is being carried by a new generation of IPE scholars, and it is here that we find a particularly useful starting point for the task of taking the democratization debate beyond many of the deficiencies we have identified. This emerging body of scholarship employs (and deploys) complex notions of democracy, focuses on processes of contestation and explores how ideologies are constructed and transformed. It is thus genuinely opening up alternative visions of what democracy is and can be, incorporating views and approaches from the world outside the 'core' of advanced industrialized democracies. It is thus from here that we need to build.

Specifically, the way forward is to continue to 'politicize' IPE – that is, to bring notions of ideology and agency to the fore. This can be facilitated by looking beyond IPE and creatively appropriating concepts and research tools more usually employed in the fields of democratic theory and transnational studies. This latter area is an emergent, overlapping terrain that focuses on the political possibilities for government, order and action in the face of globalization, composed of scholarship at the interface between political theory, sociology and IR (Held 1996, 1999; Archibugi *et al.* 1998; Keck and Sikkink 1998; Risse *et al.* 1999; Kaldor 2000a, 2000b; Piper and Uhlin 2003). At the same time, IPE can constructively enter a dialogue with historical sociology – along the lines already advocated by Hettne (1995b) – which, like IPE, lays claim to being a holistic and interdisciplinary social science approach which has eschewed positivist research in order to be 'the instrument by which structures are discovered invisible to the unaided eye' (Collins 1999: 1). In a nutshell, according to Skocpol (1984: 4, cited in Hettne 1995b), historical sociology is '[best] understood as a continuing ever-renewed tradition of research devoted to understanding the nature and effects of large-scale structures and fundamental processes of change.' In their subject matter and research orientation, historical sociology and IPE are thus closely related and can be usefully brought into greater contact and dialogue with each other than has hitherto been the case. Where historical sociology differs from IPE, however, is in the centrality it assigns first to states, even in processes of change where the external constitutes an important variable, and second to the relationship between states and class actors (Rueschemeyer *et al.* 1992; Mann 1993). Given that IPE has tended to privilege the analysis of *material* power above all, a dialogue with historical sociology might also contribute more broadly to a reassessment of the core question in IPE of how power itself is understood.

I turn now to look more closely at how IPE could engage with these fields of study in ways that might generate a fuller understanding of the complex meanings that attach to the term 'democratization', building on the three central conceptual issues noted at the start of this section. My aim here is to be speculative and suggestive rather than excessively prescriptive: the idea is to open dialogues and suggest possible routes that might lead to broader understandings of democratization in the future.

Restoring ideology

IPE needs urgently to engage both with the *meanings* of democracy and with the *kinds* of democracy that are possible under conditions of globalization, understood here not just as the creation of a (capitalist) global economy but also as a dramatic transformation in how social life is ordered across time and space and 'the intensification of world-wide social relations which link distant localities in such as way that local happenings are shaped by events occurring many miles away and vice versa' (Giddens 1990: 64). Engagement with these questions requires building bridges with democratic theory in order to develop stronger and more appropriate understandings of what constitutes democracy, and with transnational studies in order to better examine the kinds of democratic projects that can be imagined in the contemporary world order. During the Cold War, especially, the dominant approach within democratic theory was effectively to merge democracy into liberalism, to police rigidly the division between the public and the private and to insist that the 'proper' arena for democracy was the nation-state (Held 1996). Typical assumptions were that the nation-state enclosed the community that was to live in 'democracy' and that the 'proper' form of democracy was liberal democracy. While Marxists and other revolutionary movements continued to invoke direct or participatory traditions of democracy that stretch back to the Renaissance republican tradition and to Rousseau, and to create alternative socialist utopias, these views always lay outside the mainstream.

Democratic theorists have now broken out of this stranglehold. Participatory theories of democracy and notions of democracy as rights, processes of deliberation or citizenship are much more common (Pateman 1970; Macpherson 1977; Phillips 1999; Dryzek 2000). Recently, this vision of democracy as participation and citizenship has come to be seen as part of 'the civil society approach' to democracy. According to Fine (1997: 9),

> the distinguishing mark [of civil society theory] is that it *privileges* civil society over all other moments or spheres of social life, on the grounds that civil society furnishes the fundamental conditions of liberty in the modern world.

Within citizenship and civil society approaches to democracy, there is a divide between theorists who see citizenship as an eminently *political* affair and those that argue that citizenship must be understood to encompass social and economic components as well. Phillips (1999) argues that citizenship can only be made real and be exercised once certain inequalities are addressed. Democracy, in other words, requires social and economic inclusion in order to work. The justification for democracy thus becomes the fact that it necessarily deepens and protects a range of political, economic and social rights. Democracy is legitimized because most citizens experience material, social or psychological benefit from it and because it confers the possibility of making rights real (Hall 1995: 26).

Indeed, the notion that democracy is a revolutionary ideal, rather than a tame recipe for the imposition of liberalism, is one increasingly current within political theory and the social sciences more generally. According to Shaw (1999: 6),

> the real 'revolution in the revolution' was not Che Guevara's updating of Maoist guerrilla tactics, but the transformation of democracy into a popular cause, which threatens to sweep away the Cuban and the Chinese Communist states together with their Soviet counterparts. The significance of this revolution, however, is that its appeal extends across the non-Western worlds, with powerful ramifications within the West as well.

It must make sense for IPE to incorporate these explicitly normative and utopian debates about what constitutes democracy into its analyses of democratization. Not only do these perspectives capture rather better the views of many participants and would-be stakeholders in new democracies than the assumption that democracy necessarily means the triumph of liberalism, political and economic; it is also more in keeping with critical IPE's self-conscious assumption that its role is to encourage progressive change. It fits nicely with what Kees van der Pijl (2001: 380) has called IPE's quest to restore 'the radical imagination in political economy'.

In short, democratization should be understood as the introduction and extension of citizenship, which includes popular consent, participation and accountability and the practice of rights, tolerance and pluralism. Democratic consolidation comprises not only the embedding of governing institutions but also the routinization and deepening of these practices. Understanding democratization in this way enables a clear distinction to be drawn between projects of genuine democratization, on the one hand, and, on the other, projects of political and economic management and manipulation pursued by elites (global or national, or a combination of the two). The 'bearers' of projects of genuine democratization must be sought from outside the dominant structures that govern the global political economy. Genuine democratization thus becomes a counter-hegemonic project with the aim of transforming the present structures of global power.

Conceptualizing new forms of agency and new visions of democracy

All IPE scholarship undoubtedly would agree that democratization is best studied within the context of contemporary processes of globalization. The question is how to engage with democratization in the context of the global reordering and 'shake-out' identified by Held *et al.* (1999: 7) in ways that go beyond the fuzzy assumption that the global political economy somehow shapes or determines democratization processes. One way is to consider the claims made by theorists of transnational democracy that democracy at the level of nation-state is no longer possible, and that democracy must meaningfully be pursued instead through cosmopolitan democracy. A second route is to examine the activities of transnationally active social movements that, by definition, press for global democratization through transnational – rather than national or local – action. Certainly, engagement with how, *exactly*, globalization shapes political action and the real democratic possibilities in a globalized world is essential. Engaging seriously with questions of agency under conditions of globalization is, then, a crucial but huge task. All that can be achieved here is to delineate briefly the contours of and the inspiration behind such an ambition (for a fuller discussion, see Grugel 2003b).

The logic of globalization is to bring scholars interested in the global polity into a deepening dialogue with political theorists. It is certainly striking how, since the 1990s, the combination of marketization, globalization and the end of the Cold War has led to an astonishing eruption of transnational social movement activity, breaking down not only the doors of international institutions but also the boundaries between different disciplines within social science as the academy strives to make sense of it. In the process, scholars from IR, history, sociology and political theory have come together to study one of the major social and political consequences of globalization in a more holistic way than has previously been the case. The result is the development of a new field of study: transnational studies or the study of global (or transnational) civil society. This is based on the recognition that the idea of an international civil society has a long lineage (Colás 2001), but also the assumption that globalization has led to the emergence of a new wave of transnational activism and the development of transnational networks that engage in 'solidarity beyond the state' (Smith *et al.* 1997; Keck and Sikkink 1998; Risse *et al.* 1999). As Scholte (2000a) argues, globalization presages a genuinely new chapter in the history of civil society. Of course, not all transnational networks and engagements are necessarily democratic. But there is a huge democratic potential in these new forms of social activism. It is easy to exaggerate the impact of these movements, and a number of writers undoubtedly do so. As noted earlier, the events of 11 September 2001 have certainly curtailed some of these over-optimistic views of the influence of transnational civil society but, even so, they have not led to the dismemberment of transnational activism. Globally active or concerned individuals and organizations still constitute themselves as citizens in and of the 'world' and express commitment to a range of universal goals and values (Dower 2001).

This agenda of research into democratization through counter-hegemonic organizations maps on to central concerns within IPE regarding emancipation and the 'need to develop a fresh understanding of how to gain control over the forces of capital which are currently driving humanity into the abyss' (van der Pijl 2001: 380). Moreover, it has the virtues of addressing vital and eminently political questions – such as, for example, the possibilities for pro-democratic agency from below in a global political economy – and of being concerned with the important debate regarding what, exactly, constitutes democracy. Additionally, it raises the issue of rights and citizenship: in view of the apparent ineffectiveness of the state in protecting citizens under conditions of globalization, are there other, more appropriate arenas through which the goal of democracy can be pursued?

For an important group of political theorists, the answer to this question is 'yes'. The rise of global civil society and the constraints imposed on states under conditions of globalization mean that only democracy posited at the global level – cosmopolitan democracy – can now deliver rights and citizenship for the global community. For Held (1996), the most articulate and certainly the most influential of the cosmopolitan democrats, globalization poses a number of problems and opportunities for democracy. In particular, globalization challenges the Westphalian model of democracy because it undermines, and even threatens, the sovereign powers of the state.

Globalization leads to what Held (1996: 343–7) sees as a number of 'disjunctures' in the world order. The first, and perhaps the most directly significant, disjuncture he identifies is that which arises between the formal authority of states to manage economic policy-making inside national territories and their actual capacity to do so, given that the main players in the global economy are no longer either states themselves or organizations within the control of states. The second is 'the vast array of international regimes and organizations that have been established to manage whole areas of transnational activity (trade, transportation, the uses of the oceans and so on) and collective policy problems'. This has led to changes in the decision-making structures of world politics and a shift away from state control towards 'new and novel forms of geo-governance'. The third disjuncture arises from the ways in which international law is developing powers which challenge the sovereign immunity of the state. The fourth relates to the undermining by globalization processes of the state as 'an autonomous culture centre', with the result that national cultures are no longer distinct.

At the same time as democracy within nation-states is undermined, the question arises of whether deterritorialization and the consequent emergence of 'supraterritorial' and transborder social spaces (Scholte 2000a: 3) actually signify new opportunities for democracy beyond the state. Held and others champion a cosmopolitan form of democracy that would involve empowering old political institutions such as regional assemblies with new and greater powers and the creation of an authoritative assembly of *all* democratic states and societies at the global level (Held 1996: 355). Alongside this, there would be the elaboration of a set of rights for all global citizens. The power of representative non-state actors (social movements and organizations) would be enhanced at the expense of states and the new global order would be based on extending citizenship rights and redistributing resources (Archibugi *et al*. 1998). Cosmopolitanism thus attempts to solve a range of democratic shortcomings in the present world order, specifically the democratic deficit of liberal democracy, the hollowing out of the state through the erosion of state sovereignty, and the struggles for democratization across the developing world. It has received sustained attention within both political theory and IR, and has been at the centre of a rich debate about the ways in which citizenship and globalization can be reconciled.

This said, the problem, from the perspective of the 'globalizing IPE' project, is that cosmopolitanism carries with it an implicit and embedded set of Western biases and liberal assumptions concerning the nature of citizenship (Sandel 1996; Hutchings 2000). As such, while it is an important point of departure for any debate on how to democratize the global political economy, IPE scholarship must necessarily be wary about precisely how much it takes from cosmopolitanism. IPE needs to draw selectively from this debate and build on work that links the practices and limitations of citizenship to the distribution of (global) social and economic power and stresses the importance of upholding collective and community rights in a globalizing and liberalizing world (Phillips 1999; I. Young 1999, 2000).

The state and democratization

As indicated, cosmopolitanism is an important debate within theories of democracy and transnational studies, but it may exaggerate the degree to which state authority has actually been diminished by globalization. A significant body of IPE theory contests the notion that states have little or no authority and/or capacity to act in the world order. From within political theory, there are also cautious voices. Kymlicka (1999) is sceptical about the extent to which ordinary people are persuaded that cosmopolitan, rather than national or local, democracy is even desirable. First, he argues that the nation state remains an important community of fate. Second, he argues that 'democratic politics is politics in the vernacular' (Kymlicka 1999: 121). Most people, in other words, need to speak in their own tongue, on their own terrain and about issues that concern them, in order to take an active part in politics. These assumptions – that the state is still the authoritative form of organization and that most people do not wish to see it democrat-ically superseded but rather strengthened – suggest a different track for IPE from that outlined above. IPE might explore the extent to which national and local democratic orders are possible in a more systematic, historicized, comparative and detailed way than has hitherto been the case. To put it differently and in language more commonly deployed within political economy: do some societies generate states that are capable of genuine democratization? Which ones? Why? What are the constraints and opportunities that are presently opening and closing at the level of state–society complexes for democratization? Who are the agents that can drive forward national/local projects of democratization?

These are research questions typical of fields of study such as CPE and development studies (Hettne 1995b). But they are also the staple fare of historical sociology which, in matters relating to states, aims to shed light on the different trajectories of the development of states through war, revolution or class conflict (Skocpol 1979; Tilly 1990; Mann 1993). Historical sociology analyses how the changing relationship between classes and the state – the latter understood in the Weberian sense of 'a human community that (successfully) claims the *monopoly of the legitimate use of physical force* within a given territory' (Skocpol 1985: 7) – shapes political orders. It therefore admits an important role for collective actors. There are clear commonalities with political economy in that changes in the economy – for example, the expansion of production for the market – are regarded as central in the generation of social or class conflict, although economic change is not, on its own, seen to determine political outcomes.

Indeed, Rueschemeyer *et al.* (1992: 40) locate their groundbreaking historical/sociological account of democratization precisely as a part of what they call a 'new comparative political economy', defined as the study of political systems in relation to broader questions of power. They do so through the analysis of three 'power structures', namely, relative class power, the role of the state and the impact of transnational power. In particular, they argue that, whilst states have a special dependence upon capitalists under capitalism, this has not always prevented subaltern groups from reforming the state. They thus envisage democracy as a system of rule compatible in principle with capitalism, although they question how far it is feasible in dependent parts of the global political economy (see also Huber *et al.* 1997). This kind of work provides a starting point for detailed engagement with democratization for IPE. It offers an account of political change that attempts to fuse structure and agency into a holistic framework, and it assumes that a permanent tension exists between democracy and the market. Nevertheless, Rueschemeyer *et al.* stop short of identifying in any detailed way the interrelationship between the three constellations of power and are unable to specify how far external linkages actually support or hinder democratization. Moreover, their work geographically encompasses Europe and the Americas, omitting most of the developing world, and is built on Westernized notions of the state. This is perhaps its central problem: in offering narratives of the modern state as the establishment of sovereignty through the centralization of military and political power, historical sociology ignores the vast swathes of the globe where sovereignty is fragile, fractured or failed. Perhaps there is a perfect agenda here for future IPE studies of democratization: a detailed and comparative examination of the different forms of state in the global political economy and the very different meanings that attach to democratization as a result.

Conclusion

This chapter has discussed the range of perspectives from which IPE scholarship has conceptualized and studied democratization. It has argued that IPE has generated significant insights regarding democratization, especially concerning the ways in which the 'global' impacts and interacts with the 'national' and the links between economic and political liberalization. It has also offered an important critique of democratization as liberal global governance. Nevertheless, the chapter has also identified serious shortcomings within IPE approaches. A central problem relates to questions of agency and social power. Not all IPE accounts of democratization subordinate democratization to economic change and the creation of global capitalism. But agency is, on the whole, poorly conceptualized. Moreover, attention is paid mainly to the actions of those groups that possess considerable resources of power. Marginalized groups in the global political economy, by contrast, are seen as having little capacity for resistance or innovation. Like dependency theory before it, IPE comes perilously close to offering a one-class theory of politics.

As a way forward, I have suggested that IPE scholarship builds on the 'democratization as transformation' school now emerging within it. This would mean embracing a range of literatures with the aim of bringing in more sophisticated notions of agency, especially collective agency and agency from below. IPE could then focus on a notion of democracy as a project of radical political and social change, as well as a strategy for Western and elite control of the developing world. After all, it makes sense to engage seriously with what ordinary people mean by and want from democracy. Ultimately, this may also imply the necessity of reevaluating, normatively and analytically, the place of the state in the global order. It may be that, together, these inputs could contribute to the further development of a critical and emancipatory IPE.

Chapter 9

The International Political Economy of Regionalism

Fredrik Söderbaum

Regionalism has been 'brought back in' since the late 1980s. There has been an intense and indeed refreshing debate on the origins, dynamics, institutionalization and effects of regional integration processes, offering considerable insights into the contemporary dynamics of structural change in the global political economy. Yet, with only a few exceptions, the discussion has been dominated, on the one hand, by theoretical orthodoxy and, on the other, by a narrow empirical focus on Europe and, more recently, comparisons with North America and Asia-Pacific. The global applicability of the theories of regionalism that have been developed on this basis is thus notably limited, preventing an understanding of the full complexities of contemporary regionalism across the various parts of the world. There consequently has arisen a pressing need to rethink the ways in which the debate about the international political economy of regionalism is conducted, and, in so doing, to enable it to contribute more fully to the broader 'globalization' of IPE as proposed in this volume.

The central purpose of this chapter is thus twofold: first, to review some of the most important approaches in the field, in terms of their theoretical and conceptual formulations as well as empirical focus; and, second, to build on this analysis in order to consider the way forward for developing approaches to the study of regionalism that are more 'globally' applicable and analytically useful. In order to do so, the chapter takes as its point of departure the fundamental distinction between what Cox (1981: 129) labels 'problem-solving' theory, which is positivist and rationalist theory that takes the world as given and on the whole as good, and 'critical' theory, which is concerned with how the existing order came into being and what the possibilities are for structural and social change. Problem-solving approaches are here grouped as (i) neorealism, (ii) liberal institutionalism and

221

(iii) liberal economic integration, while the principal critical approaches are identified as (iv) the world order approach (WOA), (v) the new regionalism approach (NRA) and (vi) the new regionalisms/new realist approach (NR/NRA). Together, these reflect the most important approaches to regionalism that have emerged in IPE and the principal frameworks within which the debate has unfolded, as well as indicating the contours of many of the key controversies in the field. The 'problem-solving' approaches were designed first and foremost for the study of regionalism in the core regions of the global political economy, especially Western Europe, and thus reflect the preeminence in these regions of a context of state-building. They deploy a narrow world view in which regionalism is conceived as a means of facilitating distinctively Western and Westphalian political projects and mitigating the areas of dysfunction in the global economy or security system. By contrast, the critical approaches are theoretically and conceptually more nuanced and offer significantly more capital for the study of areas of the world that have customarily been excluded and ignored in the debate. As such, this chapter will argue that critical approaches constitute a solid foundation from which to build a more globally applicable IPE of regionalism.

Before moving on to this discussion, however, a brief specification of the core concepts of regionalism and regionalization is in order. I take the concept of regionalism to refer in the first instance to the phenomenon of regionalism in its broadest sense – the formal projects and the broader regional processes that give rise to the phenomenon of regional integration – manifest more or less across all the regions of the contemporary global political economy. These projects and processes together constitute what is generally termed the 'new regionalism'. In a more operational sense, however, 'regionalism' represents the body of ideas, values and concrete objectives that seek to create, maintain or modify the provision of security, wealth and other goals within a particular region or as a type of world order. In this particular sense, regionalism is usually associated with a formal project and often generates a process of institution-building. I understand 'regionalization', conversely, to denote the substantive processes that lead to patterns of cooperation, integration, complementarity and identity within a particular cross-national geographical space. It implies an activist element, a strategy of regionalization, which can be pursued by both state and non-state actors. This conceptualization differs slightly from definitions offered by, for instance, Payne and Gamble (1996: 2), for whom regionalism constitutes 'a state-led or states-led project' whereas regionalization is seen as a non-state and social process (also see Hurrell 1995). The distinction between various types of actors is crucial and must be made. However, the definition advanced here makes it possible to integrate the notion of regionalism as a set of ideas, values and objectives with understandings of active regionalization strategies and broader patterns of regionalization.

Problem-solving approaches

We turn first, then, to the three approaches to regionalism that rest on the articulation of problem-solving theory: neorealism, liberal institutionalism and liberal economic integration. At least in terms of research output, problem-solving approaches have dominated the debate and, notwithstanding the preference for critical approaches that we will advance in the course of the chapter, there have been some notably useful developments within the problem-solving camp. There has emerged, for instance, a productive debate between various associated approaches on a range of key issues, particularly the relationship between multilateralism and regionalism and the widening and deepening of regional arrangements. This said, these theories are limited in their ability to contribute to a more globally applicable IPE in view of the fact that they have been developed first and foremost for the study of Western Europe. Attention to North America and Asia-Pacific has indeed been significant, but has been marked by a dominant concern simply to explain variation from the 'standard', European, case (Breslin and Higgott 2000: 343). In addition, little attention is given to historical context or the particular position of states and regions within the global political economy from which distinctive processes and patterns of regionalism arise. Critical and reflective approaches are conveniently ignored (as by Mansfield and Milner 1997) or regarded as 'non-scientific' and speculative (Mattli 1999: 3–16), the discursive hegemony of problem-solving approaches being thereby maintained.

Neorealism

Neorealist analyses of regionalism and the formation of regions deploy an 'outside-in' perspective. In this view, as is well-known, the structural features of the anarchical system predispose states towards competition and conflict, with states furthermore conceived as unitary and rational egoists. While conflict is thus seen to prevail over cooperation as the norm of international behaviour, neorealist perspectives concede that processes of regionalism may arise under certain circumstances, such as when cooperation is deemed necessary for geopolitical reasons or through the politics of alliance formation, especially in order to counter the power of another state or group of states within or outside the region (Waltz 1979; Gilpin 1987; Buzan 1991). These propositions are supplemented by the central neorealist contention – encapsulated in its variant of hegemonic stability theory – that a hegemon or 'stabilizer' state can stimulate the emergence of regional cooperation and regional institutions in a variety of ways, and indeed is necessary for this to happen (Hurrell 1995: 51–3).

Recent variations on these neorealist themes have sought to enhance their applicability to the study of regionalism. In an attempt to lend nuance to some of the above arguments, Grieco (1997: 175–9) argues that a regional hegemon is neither a necessary nor a sufficient condition for the development of regional economic institutions. Through his 'relative disparity shift' hypothesis, Grieco argues that when there is relative stability of capabilities – which depends in part on the relative gains from regional cooperation and the expect- ation of a continuation of this stability – then there is a likelihood of a deeper institutionalization of economic relations (Mansfield and Milner 1997: 10). Conversely, instability of relative capabilities limits the likelihood of regional institutionalization. These arguments complement those advanced in other recent neorealist studies. Mansfield and Milner (1997: 11), for instance, seek to show that economic regionalism might prosper within political–military alliances, in that the efficiency gains stemming from trade flows can be used to enhance political–military capacity. This suggests that states are concerned not with absolute and collective power within alliances, but with relative power in relation to outsiders.

Yet, despite these contributions, the overall neglect within neorealism of the regional level of analysis has been frequently noted as one of its major shortcomings. Barry Buzan (1991, 2003) challenges conventional neorealism persuasively on these grounds. His notion of a 'regional security complex' has had a profound and largely positive impact on the field. Originally, he defined this as 'a set of states whose major security perceptions and concerns are so interlinked that their national security problems cannot reasonably be analysed or resolved apart from one another', but he later redefined it as 'a set of units whose major processes of securitization, desecuritization, or both, are so interlinked that their security problems cannot reasonably be analysed or resolved apart from one another' (Buzan 2003: 141). Within this framework, Buzan's arguments reveal several important similarities with his neorealist colleagues. For instance, security complexes are seen as miniature anarchies, with states taken more or less as given and seen as the main units in the international system. Although Buzan acknowledges other units than states in his newer, updated conceptualization of a regional security complex, states continue to dominate his analysis, analytically as well as prescriptively. In this sense, Buzan shares the conventional neorealist conviction that strong states make strong and mature regions (cooperative anarchies), whereas weak states, in their quest for power and security, tend to create (regional) conflicts and immature regions, or indeed are considered so weak that they do not form a region at all. Not surprisingly, Western Europe – in particular the EU – is viewed as an example of the former, whereas weak states/regions in Africa are deemed to be representative of the latter.

Both neorealism and – although perhaps to a lesser extent – the security complex framework are thus founded on a central preoccupation with the 'core' regions of the world in their approaches to regionalism; furthermore, their central research concern with states derives from the Westphalian processes of state-building that prevail in those regions. The exclusion of other regions from consideration is thereby fully facilitated. It is also justified by neorealists' claim to construct a general theory of international politics that is unashamedly and necessarily based around the great powers. According to Waltz (1979: 72), 'it would be...ridiculous to construct a theory of international politics on Malaysia and Costa Rica'. The resulting emphasis on the great powers and state-centric utilitarianism has been challenged from many quarters. At an empirical level, one critique has contended that the theory is developed from a selective reading of the postwar experience of the USA, often with additional reference to nineteenth-century Britain (Payne and Gamble 1996: 5). At a more general level, it has been contended that the centrality of power politics in neorealism tends towards their reproduction and a reinforcement of the existing structure, as well as a reinforcement of the dominance of the great powers. In other words, neorealist theory and its particular problematique is not only a social construction (Wendt 1992), but has also been designed 'for someone and for some purpose' (Cox 1981: 128).

Liberal institutionalism

The heading 'liberal institutionalism' collects together a variety of functionalist and institutionalist theories, both 'old' and 'new', which are characterized by an 'inside-out' approach to the analysis of regions and an emphasis on the institutional aspects of regional integration. In spite of important differences, liberal institutionalist theories share a number of key assumptions, such as those of the rationality of actors, the existence of pluralist environments, and a distinctively liberal view of both the nature of the state and the role of institutions in the process of regionalization. The first approach to emerge within this school – functionalism – represented a strategy, or normative method, designed to build peace, constructed around the proposition that the provision of common goods and functions can unite people across state borders (Mitrany 1966). For functionalists, in this sense, 'form should follow function' and cooperation should concentrate on technical and basic functional programmes and projects within clearly defined sectors, without challenging national sovereignty or disturbing existing power structures within each country.

Neofunctionalism built upon the functionalist method, but challenged its assumption that politics could be separated from economics. It claimed a greater concern for the centres of power (Haas 1958, 1964) and introduced a utilitarian concept of interest politics, whereby 'function follows interests' and 'ruthless egoism does the trick by itself' (Mattli 1999: 23). Neofunctionalists emphasized the deliberate design and construction of institutions, seen as the most effective means for solving common problems. These in turn were seen as instrumental for the creation of functional as well as political 'spillovers' and ultimately for a redefinition of group identity around the regional unit (Hurrell 1995: 59). During the 1960s, neofunctionalism quickly came to enjoy an enormous intellectual and political reputation and became seen as the paradigm of the European Community. It was also seen as the model of regional integration to be followed in other parts of the world, such as Africa and Latin America (Haas and Schmitter 1965; Nye 1965, 1971; Haas 1967). Yet, in retrospect, it seems that the neofunctionalists expected rather too much. They underestimated the anti-pluralist, centralist and nationalist orientations of many politicians of the time – that is, they neglected core issues of domestic politics (Breslin and Higgott 2000: 335). At the same time, the theory always paid little attention to exogenous and extra-regional forces (see Hansen 1969). Its assumptions proved to be false in Europe and even more irrelevant and misleading in other regions.

As a result – and without ignoring the rich variety of reformulated functionalist and neofunctionalist theories (Ashworth and Long 1998) – neoliberal institutionalism has become the dominant approach to regionalism within the wider liberal paradigm. Like neorealists, neoliberal institutionalists deploy the idea of an anarchical system in which states are the most important actors (Keohane 1984; Mansfield and Milner 1997). But their understandings of states' behaviour and motives for engaging in international affairs are different: neoliberal institutionalists argue that the state will act as negotiator at the intergovernmental level, limited by national political considerations, firms and pressure groups. Regionalism is conceived as motivated by the procurement of public goods, the avoidance of negative externalities from interdependence, cooperation and the acquisition of the absolute gains arising therefrom. Regionalism is thus expected to be an incremental problem-solving process, driven mainly by formal and informal institutions. In essence, efficient regionalism is expected to become increasingly institutionalized.

The widening and deepening of particular regional organizations and their institutional variation are undoubtedly important research topics, but the central weakness of this line of thinking is that regionalism is reduced to a process taking place within particular formal states-led regional organizations – such as the EU, the NAFTA, the Southern Common Market (Mercosur) in South America and the Asia-Pacific Economic Cooperation (APEC) forum – rather than through formal and informal institutions in a broader sense (Fawcett and Hurrell 1995; Mansfield and Milner 1997; Mattli 1999; Telò 2001). This bias is accentuated by the fact that regional organizations are put forward as the point of reference for understanding the global phenomenon of regionalism, compounded by the tendency to derive understandings of them from the European case. Christiansen (2001: 517) illustrates the dangers of this privileging of Eurocentric understandings of regionalism in his assertion that 'on the whole, these forms of regionalism [in the rest of the world] differ from European integration in only focusing on economic matters and relying on a very limited degree of institutionalization'. In other words, regionalism in (Western) Europe is considered multidimensional and highly institutionalized – both a descriptive and prescriptive contention – whereas regionalism in the rest of the world is seen as only weakly institutionalized and reduced to an economic phenomenon. These types of generalizations are problematic and often misleading, and indeed ignore crucial issues concerning the power asymmetries that run through the global political economy.

Liberal regional economic integration

In the academic field of Economics, as opposed to Political Science and IR, by far the dominant approach to the study of regionalism has been the theory of regional economic integration. This 'theory' is in reality a body of theories built around the notions of customs unions and optimal currency areas. Advocates posit that regional integration advances in a linear series of stages: namely, from a preferential trade area through a free trade area, customs union, common market, monetary union, culminating in complete economic union (Balassa 1962). The market forces that are set in train at one stage are anticipated to have a spillover effect to the next stage, so that progression becomes an economic necessity. Equally, as economic integration has its own costs, resources will be misallocated if a more 'advanced' stage is embarked upon before a lower stage is completed. The theory of regional economic integration is not concerned with institutional dynamics or the political dimensions of regionalism, and focuses solely on the welfare effects that result from economic interaction and policy change, particularly in terms of trade creation and trade diversion. Although heated discussion surrounds the applicability of this approach beyond the 'core' regions of the world, where environments of pluralism and competition are supposed to prevail, as a body of theory it continues to have an enormous influence in the debate on regional economic integration all over the world, amongst academics as well as policy-makers (de Melo and Panagariya 1993; Cable and Henderson 1994).

Nevertheless, there have also been other important developments within Economics during the last decade. The new insights can be divided into two main categories: first, those concerned with the impact of economic regionalism on the world trading system; and,

second, those concerned with the economic blocs themselves
(Robson 1993: 330). The first category is dominated by the emergence
of a notion of 'open regionalism', which prescribes that policy should
be directed towards the elimination of obstacles to trade (and to
a lesser extent investment) within a region, while at the same time
doing nothing to raise external barriers to the rest of the world
(Cable and Henderson 1994: 8). The key question is whether the
formation of regional trading blocs are 'stumbling blocks' or 'stepping
stones' towards an open world economy. In good problem-solving
fashion, open regionalism thus seeks to synchronize the global and
the regional levels, the normative concern being with the smooth
functioning of a multilateral trading system and the somewhat
ambiguous notion of world welfare. According to this perspective,
there is no need to replicate the EU (which is often seen as protec-
tionist) and there can be different routes to open regionalism in
Africa, the Americas and Asia. Indeed, it is interesting that open
regionalism has come to be associated with the neoliberal economic
paradigm being pushed and encouraged by the IFIs and large
parts of the (Western) donor community. In the case of Africa, it
seeks to tie into and reinforce structural adjustment programmes
(Haarløv 1997). In Latin America, the long-standing resistance of
the USA to the formation of regional blocs has meant that the
promotion of regionalism by the IFIs was traditionally more muted.
Nevertheless, as that resistance softened through the 1980s and
1990s, open regionalism became the template explicitly favoured
for the Latin American context and promoted by the IFIs in the
same ways as elsewhere. In short, notions of open regionalism have
been developed primarily in order to integrate developing regions
into the global economy in accordance with neoliberal ideology.

Conversely, the second category identified above has been
developed in and for the core countries and regions, particularly
Europe. Somewhat ironically, this thinking has some potential
to contribute to a more globally applicable IPE of regionalism. It
transcends the almost exclusive focus in the orthodox framework
and in the debate about open regionalism on discriminatory trade
policies in favour of a wide range of non-orthodox and dynamic
economic benefits. These include domestic and foreign investment
creation, production and employment creation, political and socio-
economic stability and credibility, economies of scale, avoidance of
the costs of non-integration, development of infrastructure and
other services as well as structural transformation (Robson 1993;

Padoan 2001). At the same time, it seeks to dispense with the sets of unrealistic assumptions inherent in the standard framework, which have limited its applicability even to Europe. This revised perspective is built instead on a recognition that, in the real world, there often exist underdeveloped, distorted factor and goods markets and production structures, market and government failures, transportation costs, imperfect and asymmetric information and competition, an array of externalities, and so on. These reformulated assumptions, together with the focus on a broader set of dynamic benefits, thus make this perspective considerably more 'globally' relevant to the study of regionalisms in Europe and North America as well as in other parts of the world than its counterparts in Economics.

Summary

The three problem-solving schools of thought have had a profound impact on the study of regionalism, and indeed there is no need to deny that they have contributed to the understanding of regionalism and regionalist projects. In spite of important differences and the often competing explanations they offer, these three approaches share significant common ground. What in the broader field of IR/IPE is generally referred to as the neo–neo synthesis – the synthesis of neorealism and neoliberal institutionalism – is also visible in the study of regionalism. Not only do the two 'neo' approaches share an epistemology and a range of core assumptions, but both are also to a large extent focused on variations of institutionalized forms of regionalism or specific issues of regionalism such as trade, finance and security (see Mansfield and Milner 1997; Moravcsik 1998). The main difference is that neorealists emphasize structural and power-oriented variables, while institutionalists give more weight to the regulating influence of regional institutions.

Some interaction has also emerged between political economists and economists. The theorists in various camps do not necessarily reject one another's explanations but seek instead to introduce specific sets of variables into the broader picture. Just as in the era of 'old regionalism', when there was an interesting dialogue between neofunctionalist and orthodox regional economic integration approaches, so the main dialogue with 'outsiders' in contemporary theorizing is when neo–neo approaches integrate problem-solving economic variables into their frameworks, such as strategic trade theory (Milner 1997b; Padoan 2001) or broader market logics (Mattli 1999). From the point of view of Economics, the most important and interesting theorizing arises when economists transcend their own discipline by taking political, institutional and at times even security variables into account (Robson 1993; Mistry 2000; Page 2000).

These debates and theoretical developments are productive and have the potential, especially if and when they lead to a transcendence of rigid disciplinary boundaries, to further a critical questioning of the assumptions on which understandings of regionalism are based. Consequently, they are potentially useful in the elaboration of fuller and better comparisons of regional processes and arrangements in different parts of the world. In short, problem-solving theories *can* contribute to a more globally applicable IPE of new regionalism. The problem is that in their current form they do not. To the extent the problem-solving theories venture at all beyond the European case, their empirical focus only stretches to North America and, occasionally, Asia-Pacific. It is revealing that one of the core problem-solving contributions to regionalism, that of Mansfield and Milner (1997), entirely ignores Africa and all regional organizations on that continent. The assumption made in this volume, and indeed elsewhere, appears to be that meaningful and efficient regionalism is happening only, or primarily, in the 'core' regions of Europe and North America. Apart from the inherent problems of drawing upon such a narrow empirical selection for theorizing about regionalism, the problem lies in the ways that the underlying assumptions and understandings about the nature of regionalism, which stem from a particular reading of European integration, influence the description of what regionalism in the rest of the world does – and, moreover, should – look like. It bears reiterating, as well, that the overwhelming majority of problem-solving scholars maintain a limiting focus on states as aggregated and unitary units, and/or on formal regional intergovernmental organizations. This is highly problematic, as Bach (1999: 1) points out, in that 'Outside Europe, the rebirth of regionalism during the late 1980s often had little to do with the numerous international organizations that were supposed to promote its development'. In sum, problem-solving approaches can be characterized as introverted, ignorant of critical and reflective approaches and, at worst, largely irrelevant to an analysis and understanding of regionalisms outside Western Europe and North America.

Critical approaches

The series of critical IPE approaches to regionalism that has developed since the mid-1990s emerged directly as a response to these shortcomings of problem-solving theory, challenging such core features as its separation of subject and object and of fact and value, its state-centric ontologies and its rational choice epistemology. All of the diverse approaches to regionalism that belong to this critical camp cannot be accounted for here, but the ones selected for closer analysis – that is, the WOA, the NRA and NR/NRA – are some of the most influential. As noted earlier, the central argument advanced in this chapter is that a critical approach is an essential platform from which to launch an effort to 'globalize' the debates surrounding regionalism in IPE. Critical approaches move beyond the narrow and unproblematized conceptualizations of the problem-solving approaches we have just surveyed, thereby challenging in turn the view of the state as a unitary entity and as the most important actor in the international system, the analytical prioritization of regional organizations and the vision of openness as a precondition for achieving economic development in a globalizing world economy. In so doing, critical approaches are able to integrate an understanding of both top-down and bottom-up processes of regionalization, and both formal and informal dimensions of regional processes, in a single analytical framework. Furthermore, they proffer a more nuanced understanding of the relationship between globalization and regionalization, which crucially does not conceive of the reproduction of globalization simply as a Western project.

World order approach

The WOA is heavily indebted to the critical IPE associated with Robert Cox and has been advanced most notably by a group of scholars concentrated in and around the Political Economy Research Centre at the University of Sheffield in the UK (Gamble and Payne 1996a; Hook and Kearns 1999; Breslin and Hook 2003; also, to an extent, Grugel and Hout 1999). This approach is based above all on a commitment to integrate both the domestic and global and the structural and agential dimensions of regionalism within a coherent critical framework. Building thus on the Coxian (and neo-Gramscian) analysis of historical structures, state–society complexes, the social forces engendered in production and types of world order, the key focus of the WOA is the relationship between globalization, regionalization and the development of world orders. It is emphasized that globalization and the ideological preeminence of liberalism have established a new context within which regionalism has to be rethought. The central question for the WOA is to what extent and in what ways states and particular state–society complexes have sought to respond to globalization by building states-led regionalist schemes. Contrary to (realist) fears that regionalism leads to a new era of trade wars and even military conflict between the great powers, the WOA claims that current regionalism – based on open regionalism – emerges from and reinforces the structural and political processes associated with the globalization of the world economy. Regionalism is thus conceived as a strategy for 'managing' a country's or region's insertion into the contemporary world order: 'regionalist projects emerge as a means to help achieve the globalist project in a world where there is no longer a single state with the authority and capacity to impose its leadership' (Gamble and Payne 1996b: 252–3).

The WOA seeks, in addition, to understand regionalism as a manifestation of power in the global political economy. Its proponents claim that regionalism originates in discussions and negotiations within policy-making elites and that it forms part of the hegemonic ideology of free-market capitalism and liberal democracy that in turn constitutes the basis of the contemporary world order. Kearns and Hook (1999: 249–50) conclude that regional cooperation 'is fundamentally an elite-led process wherever one looks around the world and, indeed…it is often used in its own right to outmanoeuvre and stifle popular opposition to the kind of politics and neoliberal economy which it itself represents'. According to the WOA, region-alism both is part of and reinforces the prevailing hegemonic order, based on the neoliberal project, and 'there is very little evidence to suggest that new identities are challenging old, or that cultural barriers and stereotypes are being broken down'.

WOA theorists argue, finally, that unless questions of inequality and uneven development are addressed, regionalist projects are likely to lead to increasing problems and polarization within, as well as between, the regions (Gamble and Payne 1996b: 258). There is a potential for state-led regional projects to mitigate the negative effects of globalization and contribute to a new era of social regulation and community, especially if managed in an enlightened way and opened up to the wider influence and participation of civil society. However, elites have devised these regionalist projects with little such participation. According to Kearns and Hook (1999: 257), if regionalism

> continues to use the public face of international cooperation to mask the needs of a few private interests, particularly amongst the elite, then it may well become one of the targets for any future radical challenge to capitalist civilization. There is a way to go yet before today's subregionalism can be wholeheartedly welcomed.

New regionalism approach

The NRA was initially developed within the United Nations University/ World Institute for Development Economics Research (UNU/ WIDER) research project on new regionalism, and early statements of this approach were set out in a series of volumes edited by Björn Hettne, András Inotai and Osvaldo Sunkel (1999, 2000a, 2000b, 2000c, 2001). The approach starts from the proposition that in order to understand regionalism today it is essential to realize that we are dealing with a qualitatively *new* phenomenon. The new regionalism needs to be understood in the context of the current structural transformation of the global political economy. Regions, in a nutshell, are not formed in a vacuum: globalization and regionalization are intimately connected and together shape the emerging world order, and thus require the construction of a single, conducive framework within which to analyse and understand them.

Contrary to the essentially fixed and static definitions of regions and states characteristic of problem-solving approaches, the NRA is more eclectic and more concerned with the processes and consequences of regionalization in various spheres of political and economic activity and at various levels. The NRA by no means suggests that regions will be unitary, homogeneous or discrete units. Instead, there are understood to exist many varieties of regional subsystem marked by different degrees of what has been called 'regionness' (Hettne and Söderbaum 2000). There are no 'natural' or 'given' regions; rather, regions are constructed, deconstructed and reconstructed – intentionally or otherwise – by collective human agency. Regionalism is understood as a heterogeneous, comprehensive, multidimensional phenomenon, manifesting itself across a wide variety of sectors and 'pushed', or constructed, by a variety of state, market, society and external actors both within and outside formal regional organizations. We are likely to encounter regionalization processes advancing at various speeds in various sectors, and need equally to be sensitive to parallel processes of 'de-regionalization'.

The NRA shares several features with the WOA, especially an overall commitment to a critical IPE and a challenge to problem-solving methodology. Like the WOA, it views globalization as a strong force, perhaps irreversible in some of its dimensions, that carries significant implications for regionalism. Both approaches view economic globalization as a highly uneven process and both seek to reveal the underlying power relations that define and propel it. However, while the WOA sees regionalism primarily as a manifestation of economic globalization and prevailing forms of hegemony, the NRA could be said to adopt a rather more optimistic view of the potential of regional phenomena. The NRA suggests that regionalism should be seen as the 'return of the political' in a globalized world (Hettne 2003: 53). Hettne (1997b: 86) revisits Karl Polanyi in order to make this point:

> The current phenomenon of regionalism could be seen as the manifestation of the second movement, the protection of society, on the level of the macroregion, as a political reaction against the global market expansion which gained momentum in the 1980s. Thus we can speak of a 'Second Great Transformation'.

Seen from this perspective, the new regionalism becomes a way to overcome the contradiction between a Westphalian and a post-Westphalian rationality, a *via media*, between the obsolete nation state approach and the immaturity of predatory globalization (Hveem 1999; Falk 1999; Schulz *et al.* 2001a, 2001b). Specifically, at the level of world order it forms the basis for an improved and better functioning multilateral system – a 'regional multilateralism' (Hettne 2003: 37).

The NRA's interpretation of the role of the state is also somewhat different from that of the WOA. In contrast to the emphasis in the latter on states-led regionalist projects, the NRA highlights the weakened capacity of the state and the consequent improbability of a conventional redistributional solution at the national level and within particular state–society complexes. The NRA extends the Polanyian ideas about the (potential) political role of civil society as a means for the weak and the poor to protect themselves: what Polanyi himself calls the 'self-protection' of society (Hettne 2003: 30–3). Not only economic but also social and cultural regional networks and projects may develop more quickly than the formal states-led regionalist projects (Hettne 1994: 3). From this perspective, it is particularly important to identify and encourage the counter-forces and agents of transformation in the context of globalization (Mittelman 2000: 225). This means grasping the alternative and bottom-up forms of cultural identity and regional self-organization, such as pro-democracy forces, women's movements, environmentalist movements and so on. 'At the end of the day, the possibilities and limitations of transformative regionalism rest on the strength of its links to civil society' (Mittelman 1999: 48).

New regionalisms/new realist approach

The NR/NRA (see Bøås *et al.* 1999a; also Shaw 1998, 2000) acknowledges the contributions made by the NRA and other critical approaches to the study of regionalism. Its proponents seek, however, to integrate into their framework a variety of other perspectives and influences – notably post-structural, political anthropological, realist and postmodernist analytical trends. In so doing, they claim to develop a more historicized, contextualized, agency-oriented approach which provides a more comprehensive understanding of the multiplicities, complexities, contradictions and diversities of regions and regionalization processes in the developing world (Marchand *et al.* 1999). The label 'regionalisms' signifies the pluralistic nature of the regional phenomenon, as opposed to the perceived 'singularity' of other approaches. Although never closely defined in their texts, the 'realist' label is supposed to denote that this is the most 'realistic' account of regionalisms in the developing world, reflected *inter alia* in the call for a reattachment of regional organizations to the 'realities' of the underlying fabrics of the regions. According to one of its architects, the realist label is deliberately defined loosely because 'it is meant to be a state of mind; a way of thinking that encourages innovation rather than closure' (Bøås, personal communication with author; Hentz and Bøås 2002).

Other approaches, including the NRA, are challenged because they are seen as 'singular' (in the sense noted above), too concerned with states, and overly optimistic about regional organizations and institutions. According to the NR/NRA, much more emphasis needs to be placed on what are broadly referred to as 'informal regionalisms from below'. This includes a wide range of non-state actors and informal activities, such as TNCs, ecologies, ethnicities, civil societies, private armies, *maquiladoras*, export-processing zones, growth triangles, development corridors, diasporas from the South in the North, track-two diplomacy, and the informal border politics of small trade, smuggling, mafias and crime (Marchand *et al.* 1999: 905–6; Shaw 1998, 2000). Thus:

> It is only when we make deliberate attempts to connect the two broad processes of formal and informal regionalisms that we can get a clearer picture of the connections between them...The point is that the outcome of these processes is highly unpredictable, and most often there is more to these issues than meets the eye. (Marchand *et al.* 1999: 905–6)

In common with the other critical approaches outlined thus far, the NR/NRA puts heavy emphasis on the relationship between globalization and regionalization. But, again, these theorists claim to emphasize much more the diversities and nuances of this relationship, whereby globalization/regionalization nexuses create a wide range of complex patterns of interaction and response at various levels. Globalization not only has different and uneven impacts between countries and regions but also, perhaps even more so, within them. This leads to a number of diverse local-, national- and regional-level responses to globalization/regionalization nexuses. According to the NR/NRA, it leads also to a rejection of the notion of 'interdependence' between the various actors and units and the system at large, at least as understood by most liberal theorists. The NR/NRA argues, rather, that 'what we are confronted with are juxtaposition, contradictory processes and simultaneous cooperation and conflict interwoven into streams of ideas, identities and more tangible resource. This is the *weave-world of regionalization and globalization at the dawn of the next millennium*' (Bøås *et al.* 1999b: 1062–3; emphasis in original).

Summary

The three approaches outlined above share a critical foundation. As such, they challenge the ontology, epistemology and assumptions, as well as the methodological orthodoxy, of mainstream problem-solving approaches. They take to task the rigid and problematic conceptualizations of states, regions and regional organizations inherent in neorealism and liberal institutionalism, as well as the overriding preoccupation with specifically trade relations in economic integration theory. From an empirical point of view, the critical approaches are not biased in favour of a particular type of regionalism in the core, and indeed some of them have been developed specifically for the purpose of analysing regionalism in the developing world. They refrain from simply juxtaposing European institutionalization and uniquely deep levels of trade and monetary integration found in the EU with regionalism 'elsewhere'. In this way, the critical research programmes to which they lead are genuinely more 'global' in their concerns and their applicability. Nevertheless, as we will elaborate shortly, the comparative dimension of this work needs to be strengthened further.

There are, however, important differences among the various critical approaches. Both the WOA and to some extent the NRA (especially the studies undertaken within the UNU/WIDER project) view regionalism primarily from the systemic vantage point of world order. In so doing, they emphasize the structural features of regionalism. By comparison, the NR/NRA rejects any universalistic logic and places primary emphasis on agency and the contradictory nature of the informal regionalisms from below in particular regions in what it tends to refer to as 'the South'. By the same token, even if the critical approaches correctly distinguish between state and non-state actors and analytically integrate these, in practice there is a tendency still to favour *either* state *or* non-state actors. That is, the WOA and the NR/NRA have radically different understandings of the role and capacity of the state and non-state actors, whereas the NRA tends to float around somewhere in between. As will be seen shortly, however, in the real world both state and non-state actors tend to be grouped together in specific modes of governance, and other collectives and networks.

Yet there is no need for far-reaching theoretical standardization in order to build a 'globalizing' IPE; moreover, a more globally applicable IPE of regionalism should not be, and need not be, reserved for either the North or the South. Even if the culturally skewed 'universalism' of many problem-solving approaches must be transcended, there is no reason to construct *a priori* a particular regionalism theory only for the South, as the NR/NRA seeks to do. We turn, then, to the question of how theories of regionalism can be reframed in order to further the elaboration of the more 'globally' applicable IPE of concern to us in this volume.

Towards a 'global' IPE of regionalism

Comparative regionalism

As we have established, critical approaches constitute fertile foundations for further research, but there is nevertheless a need to move beyond the initial, largely exploratory and often systemic phases of research on regionalism, which tended to be dominated by attention to individual case studies. Indeed, this focus on single cases remains a characteristic of much of the literature. Often scholars do seek to draw broader comparative and theoretical lessons from their case study, and cases are frequently placed within a comparative context. However, too often this constitutes an exercise in juxtaposition rather than genuine comparison. Furthermore, although exceptions exist, there continues to be a narrow empirical focus on Europe, North America and Asia-Pacific, whereas Africa, the Middle East and Latin America tend largely to be overlooked. The EU is put forward as the model and other looser and informal forms of regionalism, wherever they appear, are characterized merely as 'different' or 'weaker'. Thus, as Breslin and Higgott (2000: 343) point out, 'ironically, the EU as an exercise in regional integration is one of the major obstacles to the development of analytical and theoretical comparative studies of regional integration'. What we require now, therefore, are more concrete and theoretically informed comparative studies, and indeed more *genuinely* comparative work on regionalism.

Yet, at the same time, comparative studies are often criticized by area specialists, postmodernists and others, who emphasize cultural differences and the importance of a deep multidisciplinary knowledge of various contexts and people. Part of this critique is well-taken. There are undoubtedly too many culturally skewed comparative frameworks and, if not placed in proper historical context, many comparisons are misleading and perhaps, when overtly prescriptive, dangerous. Comparative analysis should thus be used with care in the social sciences. This said, the comparative method is certainly needed in the construction of a more 'global' IPE of regionalism. Comparative analysis helps to guard against ethnocentric bias and culture-bound interpretations that can arise in too specialized or isolated an area study. Since theory necessarily relies on some generalizations, comparative analysis is also crucial for theory-building. As Breslin and Higgott (2000: 341) go on to argue:

> when conducted properly, the comparative approach is an excellent tool... In particular, it is a key mechanism for bringing area studies and disciplinary studies together, and enhancing both. It provides new ways of thinking about the case studies whilst at the same time allowing for the theories to be tested, adapted and advanced.

Here it should be pointed out that, because regions are usually carefully situated within their historical and structural context, critical research programmes do not fall so easily into the trap of reinforcing Eurocentrism in the analysis of regionalism, or of advancing a particular 'model' of regional integration derived from this experience. However, although the critical approaches tend to deploy a wide empirical selection, they remain primarily based on single case studies or a series of case studies within a rather 'exploratory' framework. In conducting more genuine comparisons, a 'global' IPE of new regionalism should seize the middle ground between holistic case studies and area studies, on the one hand, and, on the other, 'hard' social science as reflected in the use of excessively structured comparisons. In other words, it should seize what has been referred to as the 'eclectic centre' of comparative studies (*World Politics* 1995; also Axline 1994; *Africa Today* 1997; Payne 1998). It should then become possible to avoid both exaggerated and excessively specific contextualization *and* the trap of ethnocentric universalism. This approach to comparative regionalism is compatible with both the WOA and the NRA. In sum, it is crucial to move beyond the false universalism inherent in a selective reading of regionalism in the core, and in the EU in particular, and instead to engage in genuinely comparative analysis.

Towards regional governance and regional networks

Many IPE approaches (both problem-solving and critical) tend to overemphasize the role of the state in the process of regionalization. Critical approaches have indeed done a great deal to transcend rigid and problem-solving state-centrism and to unpack the state–society complex. However, the critique raised by the NR/NRA – that top-down and states-led regional projects continue to be over-emphasized and that market/society-based regionalization is reduced to being understood solely as an outcome of state-led regionalism – should not be ignored. Indeed, we have seen that the WOA is primarily concerned with states-led regionalism and, in summing up the UNU/WIDER project, Hettne *et al.* (2001: xxxii) admitted that 'our project, in spite of good intentions to the contrary, has been too state-centric and too focused on formal organizations rather than pinpointing the processes of more informal regionalization that take place on the ground'. The problem is that the NR/NRA falls into the opposite trap and tends, if not to exaggerate 'regionalisms from below', then at least to fail to specify the scope and density of these processes, the ways in which these influence and shape political economies, and their relationship with more formal regionalist processes.

An important advance in recent research in both IR and IPE has been the wider move away from a traditional Westphalian focus on states, sovereignty, supranationality and intergovernmentalism towards a concern with the close relationship between state and non-state actors. In the study of regionalism, the concern has come to rest with the ways in which state and non-state actors are grouped and tied together in a variety of complex modes of regional *govern-ance*, regional networks and coalitions (Payne, this volume; also Breslin and Higgott 2000; Jönsson, Tägil and Törnqvist 2000; Jayasuriya 2004). The political and institutional landscape is being transformed fundamentally and there is a need to think in terms of more complex, multi-level political structures in which the state is 'unbundled', reorganized and redeployed, and in which non-state actors are also seen as contributing to and shaping the emerging modes of governance and networks.

The point is that much of the reality of today's regionalism is not adequately captured by an exclusive focus on states-led regional projects and regional organizations, but nor is its understanding well-served by a dichotomization of state and non-state actors. The road ahead for an IPE of new regionalism is to avoid *a priori* assumptions of who or what is the dominating and 'driving' actor in the process of regionalization and instead to subject this question to empirical research. The emphasis placed on 'regionalisms from below' in the NR/NRA must be taken seriously, the current tendency to dichotomize state and non-state actors should be transcended, and our study of regionalism could usefully be reconceptualized with reference to modes of regional governance and regional networks.

Indeed, such a shift of focus from states-led regionalism to modes of regionalist governance has been advocated by Anthony Payne (2000) as the best means of recognizing and understanding the rich variety of forms of regional governance and regional networks that are emerging in the contemporary global political economy. This sort of agenda has generated important recent research identifying their forms and substance across regions, from multilayered governance in Europe to 'hub-and-spoke' governance in North America, micro-regions and networks in Europe, spatial development initiatives and corridors in southern Africa, neoliberal regional governance in Africa, 'trans-state governance' in Africa, networks of power and identity in Asia, 'growth triangles' in Southeast Asia, and emerging hemispheric forms of regionalist governance in the Americas (*inter alia*, Mittelman 2000; Payne 2000; Telò 2001; Söderbaum and Taylor 2001; Perkmann and Sum 2002; Söderbaum 2002; Phillips 2003a, 2003b; Rosamond forthcoming). Focusing in this way on governance and networks makes it possible not only to transcend an excessively narrow focus on 'government', but also to integrate informal and private aspects of governance and networks into the same analytical framework.

We have noted that problem-solving research has some potential to contribute to this project of 'globalizing' the study of regionalism. A fundamental problem, however, is that several of the problem-solving approaches – especially those associated with and encouraging processes such as 'open regionalism', regional policy networks, regional public goods, growth triangles and spatial development initiatives – are in reality particular projects of regional governance with a highly political content. As Payne pointed out earlier in this volume, these constitute 'distinctive ideological projects fashioned and pursued by identifiable institutions and interests'. By extension, these 'projects' of regional governance, to borrow his term, are primarily concerned with incremental regionalization processes without attention to the power structures that underpin them and the inegalitarian structures and patterns of dominance which are consolidated and reproduced in the global political economy. Henrikson (1995: 166) is correct in pointing out that 'there are, at bottom, just two kinds of institutions: those that have money (e.g. NATO and the European Union) and those that do not (e.g. most agencies of the UN system and also many Chapter VIII regional organizations)'. Since the problem-solving approaches and the projects of regional governance usually favour 'more of the same' and do not challenge the existing problems of power and dominance in the world, they are also poor participants in a more genuinely 'global' IPE.

Bringing in development

One weakness in mainstream IPE is that it has been excessively structuralist in orientation and concerned primarily with order, power, stability and hegemony, addressed largely through problem-solving theory. Critical IPE has responded to the shortcomings of this sort of mainstream theory and, among other contributions, has highlighted the importance of historical power structures and the contradictions inherent in them, as well as normatively driven notions of change and transformation. As James Mittelman (1999: 44) observes of neoliberalism, in a comment which is also broadly applicable to other liberal problem-solving theories,

> Concerned as it is with purportedly universal laws of development, neoliberal theory posits that, in principle, the same rules of economic development can be applied across the board from the most developed to the least developed countries. As such, the theory is overly mechanical and represents a slot machine approach to regionalism [and to development]. Taking an individualist approach, it is silent about deep structural inequalities, especially the qualitative aspects of underdevelopment lodged in the blockage of highly inegalitarian social systems... What is more, neoliberals' vision of a frictionless world of shared meanings, the uncontested adaption of the ideology of capitalism, is structurally blind to patterns of domination and hegemony.

This critical and structural perspective has contributed to addressing the absence of an emancipatory dimension to international theory (Smith *et al.* 1996), and as such is capable of linking up to the central concerns of development studies with global poverty and social exclusion. A 'global' IPE of regionalism must necessarily take a 'global' perspective on development, poverty and exclusion. Critical IPE has done good work in questioning existing power structures and patterns of domination. But it is not enough to understand development within the framework of (critical) IPE *per se*. There should be a more explicit concern with development itself rather than simply the patterns of power and domination in a structural and global perspective. In other words, it is necessary to 'bring in development' to the discussion on IPE in a more concrete manner, and in so doing to transcend the disciplinary boundaries of IPE and reach towards perspectives from development studies (see Hettne 1995a; Hettne *et al.* 1999; Payne 1999).

In this respect, however, it is important that we return to our earlier arguments concerning the reconceptualization of the state, both in understandings of regionalism and in the ways in which we approach questions of development. The combination of globalization and the various challenges to the nation-state lead to a need for a reconceptualization of development as a national phenomenon. Globalization implies that a blurring takes place between the international and domestic realms, this being a distinction which is often artificially upheld by problem-solving theories and conventional development thinking. Problem-solving theory has focused almost exclusively on the nation state and aggregated national 'welfare'. It does not unpack or problematize the state in development. A conventional state-centric approach 'legitimates states' policies with respect to citizens by placing the domestic domain beyond the parameters of inquiry...what happens to the state matters and what happens to the people within is of second-order importance' (Poku and Edge 2001: 4–5). A revised development theory would transcend this prevailing state-centrism. In particular, it would problematize the role of the state and pay attention to the content of development rather than merely the form, implying a critical questioning of what type of development occurs, for whom, and with what consequences.

In this way, both IPE and studies of regionalism can maintain a core concern for the excluded, poor and marginalized, implying a move towards human and 'alternative' development. Although this idea has a long intellectual history, in the early to mid-1990s a paradigmatic shift occurred wherein the individual became the locus of human development concerns in terms of economic, food, health, environmental, personal, community and political considerations. In effect, the focus shifted from the state level and government authorities to the individual level, and to people's capacity to make and implement choices. Popular participation in economic and political life is regarded not merely as an instrument to further development goals of a particular state, but as a goal in and of itself. Significantly, this renewed focus on human development and human needs has meant that development theory itself has become more 'globally' relevant. As Hettne points out, the revival of development theory is of relevance also in the advanced industrial countries, which means that it has gradually acquired an increasingly universal quality, that is, 'authentic universalism in contradistinction to the false universalism that characterized the Eurocentric phase of development thinking' (Hettne 1995a: 15). In a similar vein, as set out in the introduction to this volume, Payne (1999, 2004, 2005) has produced a body of work setting out the argument that development is in fact a process common to *all* countries and societies, not just to those traditionally understood as 'developing' in the old terminology, and mapping out a future agenda for the study of development which reflects this reality.

These arguments extend very usefully to the study of regionalism inasmuch as they indicate that the relationship between regionalism and development is an issue which is just as pertinent to the European and North American regional projects as it is to, say, African and Latin American ones. In readjusting our conceptual lenses in the way suggested by Hettne and Payne, development becomes a theme capable of pulling together the study of regionalism across the various parts of the world and as such is capable of fostering the construction of a more coherent and unifying framework – as well as a more 'globally' relevant one – within which to conduct the study of regionalism in IPE.

Chapter 10

Whither IPE?

Nicola Phillips

In the introductory chapter, we outlined the rationale for a project of 'Globalizing IPE', which this volume aims to take a first step towards articulating and pushing forwards. The task of this concluding chapter, then, is to attempt to set out what might be the core foundations and ingredients of an IPE of the sort we have aspired to advocate. What I do not wish to suggest for a moment, however, is that there is or can be a single, simple recipe for the rethinking and reworking of the field that this involves. The project of Globalizing IPE is conceived as identifying an agenda and a direction for its further development, but not as requiring or inviting a single strategy for doing so. Indeed, there are potentially a variety of paths which can very profitably be taken towards rebuilding the field in the manner we have identified here as desirable and necessary. The preceding chapters attest amply to this. They demonstrate that the concrete steps we can and should take towards realizing this project will necessarily depend on the particular debates or areas of study in question, as well as on the particular inclinations of individual scholars working in different parts of the field. In short, identifying the means of 'globalizing' IPE will require collective debate and engagement between scholars with a wide range of theoretical inclinations, empirical interests and regional expertise. It is hoped that this volume will contribute, in its small way, to sparking such a debate.

At the same time, I wish to suggest in this concluding essay that there are several base ingredients of a more 'globalized' IPE that together, in my view, could constitute a broad platform from which such a project might be pushed forwards. These involve a redefinition of how we conceive of IPE and the intellectual endeavour it represents, as well as a rethinking of its core organizing concepts. In this sense, the arguments advanced here will be oriented around broad reflections on the field as a whole, while drawing out many of the insights and

246

perspectives advanced in the pages of this volume on particular areas of interest within it. Indeed, these critical interrogations of specific debates have been crucial for gaining a sufficiently wide-ranging impression of the contours of the field in order to begin to construct ideas about the core foundations on which a 'reworked' IPE might come to rest.

Recapturing 'political economy' in IPE

The first element of a more suitably 'globalized' IPE relates to the intellectual foundations of the field itself. We argued in the introductory chapter that these foundations reflect two distinct traditions – that of IR and that of political economy. IPE, as it has evolved since the 1970s, has come to be rooted primarily within the discipline of IR, and it has been from IR that it has inherited both its primary theoretical apparatus and the scope of its empirical concerns. It is this location of IPE within IR that has, I suggest, served in important respects to take the field in an unhelpful direction and engender many of the limitations that we have aimed to expose in this volume.

This 'unhelpful direction' takes two principal forms. The first is that IPE has inherited from IR a body of theory and an empirical remit that have privileged the advanced industrialized world as the focus and the foundation of the field. Just as IR was constructed as a discipline both for and about the 'great powers', so IPE has crystallized as a field in which the primary concerns and theoretical frameworks are both derived from the experiences of the advanced industrialized powers and built for the principal purpose of analysing the particular political economy of advanced capitalism that knits them together. The 'rest of the world' is frequently deemed to matter little to this 'proper' business of IPE, and to carry little relevance for the theorization or empirical study of the global political economy. Furthermore, the manner in which mainstream IPE has sought to stipulate the identity and boundaries of the field has rested on an assumption that those parts of the world located outside the advanced industrialized triad are the *specialized* preserve of scholars associated with 'area studies' or comparative analysis, while the study of the advanced industrialized powers remains entirely the valid preoccupation of international political economists studying broad themes such as capitalism, globalization, finance or global governance. It must be recognized that those with particular national or regional interests are also frequently guilty of cordoning off their own endeavours by focusing closely on local particularities and specificities with only limited attention to the broader global structures into which the countries or regions of interest are inserted (Mittelman 2000: 3; Phillips 2004: 14–15). Yet it remains the case that mainstream IPE has been marked by a generalized demeaning of the importance of regions or countries outside the 'core', a ring-fencing of the so-called 'developing' world as the domain of area 'specialists', and a sense in which the study of those parts of the world is dabbling in detail rather than addressing the big questions that should preoccupy international political economists.

Yet we have argued that this has not only limited the purchase that IPE offers on those parts of the world and those political economies that are not encompassed within the advanced industrialized world, but also disabled the analysis and understanding of the advanced industrialized world itself, the nature of the global political economy and the issues and processes that are of central concern in the field. It has led to a neglect of a number of issues – such as democratization, inequality or development – that are, in different ways, as important in the political economy of the advanced industrialized world as they are in the political economy of regions and countries traditionally classified as 'developing'. It has also led to an excessively partial approach to the study of other core processes and phenomena, such as globalization or capitalism, the nature and dynamics of which cannot be grasped with attention solely to the advanced industrialized world. Understanding the nature and constitution of the global political economy itself also requires due attention to the ways in which, and bases upon which, the various constituent political economies are inserted and integrated into it, as well as the structures of inequality on which it intrinsically rests. We have formulated the project of Globalizing IPE, in this light, not merely as one which aims to build an IPE that better travels outside the advanced industrialized world, as in the body of related work which has aimed either to habilitate the 'Third World' more firmly within IR or else to build a 'multi-hub' discipline in which there exist various 'IRs' developed specifically for different parts of the world. Rather, it is framed as one of building a field of study that is better able to cater for and stretch across the various political economies (including that of advanced capitalism) that constitute the contemporary world order, and is thus capable of offering greater capital and insight for the study of global political economy.

Second, the rooting of IPE firmly within IR has meant the displacement of an appropriate 'idea of political economy' as the foundation for much of the field, and an enduring neglect of the insights offered by the 'political economy' tradition from which IPE takes the other part of its intellectual provenance. The close association of IPE with mainstream IR has meant that it has been the first of the two schools identified by Murphy and Nelson (2001) – the IO school rooted in US scholarship – that has dominated the mainstream of the field. The manner in which IPE has unfolded has reflected the theoretical dominance in mainstream IR of liberalism and neoliberal institutionalism, such that the basis of mainstream IPE scholarship has been shaped by the classical liberal conceptualization of politics and economics as intrinsically separate spheres. IPE has thus been framed by the mainstream as the study of the relationship between the (separate) spheres of politics and economics, states and markets, and public and private. Equally, as Colin Hay and David Marsh (1999a: 7) pointed out, the unfolding of IPE has privileged a particular understanding of 'the political' inherited from the realist tradition in IR, and in large part sustained in neoliberal institutionalist approaches, which has acted to narrow the conceptions of both politics and power predominantly to their formal and public manifestations and their exercise by and within states. It would not be much of an exaggeration, indeed, to claim that a good deal of the mainstream has failed to move far beyond framing IPE, as in its early days, as the study of 'international economic relations' organized around the core question of the relationship between 'states and markets'. In large part, it has remained concerned primarily to insert an account of 'the economic' into IR, and to move beyond the latter's traditionally statist, territorialist and politico-military orientations. Certainly, in the mainstream, there has been little significant innovation in the dominant theoretical apparatus of a sort which would distinguish IPE as a distinct theoretical enterprise from its 'parent' discipline – that is, as an enterprise which founds itself on a tradition of political economy and seeks to engage with IR on that basis. In short, as a result of the dominance of the IO school in IPE, a genuine idea of political economy has been largely lost as a founding concern and enterprise for the field.

It is in this failure to develop or privilege a genuine conceptualization of political economy that what Murphy and Nelson termed the 'British' school of IPE locates its principal critique of the mainstream. It is largely in radical political economy traditions that the British school – the critical, 'new political economy' project – has put down its primary theoretical and analytical roots. The critique of liberal IPE is founded on the contention that, contrary to liberal thinking, politics and economics are intrinsically inseparable, and that this inseparability must be represented in the primary theoretical and methodological approaches to the study of IPE. Thus, as we have seen, a critical agenda advocates an integrated theorization of political economy, which invites an appropriate integration of, on the one hand, politics and economics and, on the other, structure and agency. These particular metatheoretical priorities form the basis of a field of study capable of mitigating the shortcomings imposed by the liberal, problem-solving biases that are deemed to permeate mainstream scholarship. It also allows, as the chapters collected here have shown, for a further reconceptualization of IPE in line with the project of 'globalizing' the field of study, in the sense that it gives greater weight to the idea of a *global* political economy, allows more space for the study of the diverse ways in which the different parts of the global political economy are drawn together, and offers much more purchase on the structures of inequality that define both the contemporary world order and the central processes that constitute it. Indeed, it is in this critical agenda that many of the chapters in this volume have found particular capital and insight for the further development of the debates with which they are concerned.

A freeing of IPE from its excessively restrictive roots in mainstream IR and a more satisfactory capturing of an idea of political economy are, then, the necessary foundations for a field of study which is able more adequately to account for the whole of the global political economy and its various constituent parts. In this, the agenda of critical IPE would appear to offer many fruitful resources. Yet, as already noted, the critical branches of IPE are by no means exempt from the critique we have put forward of the field as a whole. Indeed, in the introductory chapter and throughout the volume, we have been at pains to stress that the problems which animate the project of Globalizing IPE stretch across the field, encompassing both the British and IO schools, and both the corresponding intellectual traditions from which IPE takes its inspiration. Both mainstream and critical IPE, in different ways and to different extents, have manifested the various tendencies and shortcomings that we have identified here as standing in need of remedy.

One obvious example highlighted in several chapters is the pervasive tendency in IPE towards economism. In some approaches, this springs from the dominant liberal biases inherited by mainstream IPE from mainstream IR, and from the understanding of the contemporary world order as constituted primarily by a set of economic globalization processes which function according to an inevitable 'logic' of market integration. In others, it stems from the parallel economistic biases manifest in Marxist and neo-Marxist theories, in which global capitalism is understood to develop according to a logic of capitalist expansion, and structures of politics and class to derive from – in some accounts, be determined by – the economic structure. In a related vein, various chapters have highlighted the ways in which elements of both traditions in IPE suffer from an excessive degree of structuralism, which manifests itself in a variety of ways: for example, as an analytical privileging of structure and world order; as a tendency to focus on the ways in which states and agents are affected by and respond to globalization processes (conceived as structure) rather than the manner in which they are fundamentally constitutive of it; or as a form of structural determinism which affords little intrinsic interest to politics or agency, and little place for notions of contingency and diversity. Thus, despite its aspirations, much of IPE still remains some way from achieving a political economy which privileges neither politicism nor economism, and adequately conceptualizes the integration of structure and agency.

Perhaps most importantly, however, the 'idea of political economy' in IPE has been distorted and displaced by the ways in which the field has been organized since its inception. In what we argued was a significant break with the study of classical political economy in the nineteenth century, the contemporary study of political economy has been founded upon and organized around a clear distinction between levels of analysis. Consequently, the field of 'political economy' has suffered a splintering and fragmentation into the branches that are concerned with the international or global level of analysis and those that are concerned with the comparative study of national (or indeed regional) political economy. The evolution of IPE, despite its multidisciplinary pretensions, has thus been characterized by a process of distancing from other approaches to the study of political economy – particularly those associated with CPE and the political economy of development (PED). The limitations imposed by this split, and non-communication, between international and comparative political economists have been demonstrated clearly in the chapters in this volume, and many of the authors have advocated for IPE a much closer engagement with comparative analysis, as well as with perspectives from PED.

The point of importance in a preliminary agenda for 'globalizing' IPE is that the recapturing of an appropriate idea of 'political economy' as the foundation for the field involves returning to an idea of political economy that is not unduly encumbered by prefixes. It involves, I suggest, a much greater acknowledgement that what we are engaged in is, in essence, the study of *political economy*, and as such that drawing excessively stark boundaries between the various branches of the social sciences concerned with political economy is neither helpful nor appropriate. Across these branches – whether located in IPE, CPE, development studies or elsewhere – the central concerns are essentially shared ones, relating to processes of structural change, forms of social organization, capitalism, processes and models of development, and so on. Moreover, neither national, regional nor global political economy can be understood through the deployment of one 'level of analysis' in isolation from others: the global political economy is fundamentally constituted by regional and national political economies, regional political economies are fundamentally constituted by their relationships with both the global political economy and the national political economies encompassed within them, and so on.

In other words, modern IPE might have found fertile ground in radical political economy's fidelity to the inseparability of politics and economics, but it has largely abandoned the second key insight of the political economy tradition: the notion that *all* political economy is, *by definition*, international. All good political economy is also necessarily comparative. The attachment of the 'C' and the 'I' to a term that already, by definition, encompasses both of these is thus, in the first place, unnecessary and, in the second place, counterproductive in the sense that it limits the theoretical and empirical insight that is necessary for understanding the constitution of political economy at the variety of different levels (Phillips 2004). It is also counterproductive in that it invites and reinforces the narrow focus on the advanced industrialized world, as highlighted above. Strange's concern with the wood rather than the trees – a vision of IPE shared by a significant proportion of scholars working in the field – is not only unhelpful in that it overlooks the ways in which all of the different parts of the global political economy are fundamentally constitutive of it, but also in effect a licence to focus solely on the regions and countries of the advanced industrialized world.

Therefore, IPE has unfolded in a way which both privileges structure (the study of the wood) and assumes, as amply demonstrated in the preceding chapters, that only a small handful of the trees matter for understandings of structure and the central processes under way in the global political economy.

A rebuilding of the field around a more satisfactory idea of political economy, and asserting for it a disciplinary identity that revolves more centrally around the study of political economy, would thus appear to offer a signally conducive foundation for our project of Globalizing IPE. I have placed particular emphasis here on the value of a critical framework, but would reiterate that the project of Globalizing IPE neither requires nor invites a single strategy. Recapturing an idea of political economy involves an engagement with liberal political economy traditions as well as radical ones, and is a project amenable to pursuit within both mainstream and critical IPE. In short, it is a project that aims to entrench political economy traditions (plural) far more firmly and visibly as the intellectual foundation for the field, and to advocate the rebuilding of IPE and its theoretical apparatus and conceptual concerns on this basis. It would also seem to be potentially more faithful to the project that IPE has traditionally aimed to espouse, namely, one based on receptiveness to intellectual perspectives from various disciplines and fields of study. A reformulation of the idea of political economy that underpins IPE – that is, doing away with the unnecessary strictures imposed by prefixes and recapturing a more integrated conception of political economy – invites and facilitates a much greater and more construct- ive engagement with other disciplines and fields, particularly those concerned directly with the study of political economy, in a manner which enhances and facilitates the project of building a field which is more able to stretch across the whole of the global political economy and its constituent parts. Yet it must be stressed that this does not constitute a call for doing away completely with either international or comparative political economy. Clearly, the compara- tive and international branches of the study of political economy construct themselves usefully around different questions, offer different approaches and perspectives and are defined by their distinctive analytical methods. Nor is it a call for scholars to abandon their particular areas of interest within IPE. It is not, in short, an argument for an end to any form of scholarly specialization. It is, instead, a contention that the distinctions between IPE and other areas of the social sciences concerned with the study of political economy have been drawn excessively sharply, at the expense of many avenues of potentially constructive and fruitful engagement. Recapturing an idea of political economy as the central intellectual project for IPE, in this sense, is crucial to broadening the theoretical purchase, conceptual remit and empirical horizons of the field.

The structure–agency question

The issue of the relationship between structure and agency has become well-established in IPE, as in other parts of the social sciences, as one of the overarching metatheoretical questions. It is a relationship which is understood in different ways across the various IPE traditions. As noted in the introductory chapter, most of these have reflected the structuralist inclination which has always permeated the enterprise of political economy: they have arisen from the notion that, as summarized by Andrew Gamble (1995: 517) in his commentary on an influential survey of the field (Caporaso and Levine 1992), 'a proper understanding of the politics [in political economy] requires giving special explanatory weight to economic structures and processes'. In much of IPE, then, the relationship between structure and agency is either one which privileges accounts of structure and pays little *attention* to agency, or alternatively one which privileges structure as the core explanatory variable, thereby affording little *intrinsic interest* to politics and agency in understanding the global political economy. We saw these structuralist tendencies to have been particularly marked in, for example, the 'hyperglobalization' school of thought within globalization studies, both the liberal and Marxist versions of which rest upon a pronounced structural determinism in their depiction of the inexorable logic of market integration and the triumph of markets over political authority. In response, the project of 'new political economy' has founded itself on the core contention that structure and agency are, in essence, mutually constitutive and therefore require an appropriate analytical meshing. Critical currents in IPE have been pivotal in propelling the question of structure and agency to a position of centrality within the core concerns of the field, and in highlighting the importance of politics and agency in understanding the constitution of the global political economy. Thus, as noted and indeed exemplified in many of the chapters here, strident calls have been issued from critical IPE quarters for both the injection of more appropriate attention to 'the political' – the 'P' – into IPE and a more considered account of agency and its relationship with structure.

Yet what I wish to suggest here, as presaged in the introductory chapter, is that the question of structure and agency goes to the heart of ideas of 'political economy' and the possibilities for their entrenchment as the foundation for the field. As such, they are central to the rebuilding and reworking of IPE that this volume has aimed to advocate. A project of meshing structure and agency offers an important means of circumventing many of the shortcomings manifest in the way that IPE debates have unfolded. It has been argued at various points in the preceding chapters that the proper integration of structure and agency is essential for overcoming the excessive structuralism and economism that have widely been deemed to be characteristic of IPE and in ample evidence across liberal, Marxist and critical scholarship. Injecting a more adequate and sustained conceptualization of agency into IPE and its various debates invites a keener sense of 'the political' in political economy and an understanding of the political contingency of structural change. It is also crucial from a normative point of view, in the sense that this emphasis on contingency and political choice serves to open up possibilities within IPE for elaborating a more considered theory of structural change. Indeed, this is one of the core propositions of critical IPE: that by adopting a critical, as opposed to problem-solving, approach to studying world order, we are more able to think in an appropriately historicized manner about how world orders come into being, how they evolve and how the dynamics of challenge and resistance – in some accounts, counter-hegemony – affect the possibilities for emancipatory change. These twin emphases on the analytical and normative importance of an appropriate focus on agency and politics in IPE find continual refrain in the chapters in this volume.

Yet there are a number of striking – and problematic – characteristics of the ways in which questions of structure and agency have generally been addressed in IPE, many of which have served to reinforce its theoretical, conceptual and empirical rooting in the political economy of the advanced industrialized world. The project of meshing structure and agency is usually formulated in a manner which emphasizes the need for affording a greater salience to agency in IPE theory and analysis. It appears frequently to be assumed that we have a field which gives due, and indeed satisfactory, account of structure; what is missing is adequate attention to agency and, by extension, politics.

Therefore, the task for those of us who object to an excessive degree of structuralism in IPE is to temper this with a greater focus on agency and its relationship with (existing) structures. Formulated slightly differently, the project is articulated as one of reinstating 'the political' in IPE by inserting a more sustained focus on agency, and thereby overcoming the field's economistic tendencies. A greater attention to agency is deemed to be the appropriate means of recapturing the political in IPE.

Framing the issue in this way is, however, problematic, inasmuch as it permits and reinforces the pronounced tendency to correlate structure and agency with, respectively, economics and politics. The structure is usually assumed to be of an economic nature; agency is considered to be the 'politics' that requires greater representation in the enterprise of IPE. This formulation of structure as fundamentally economic in nature finds clear expression in the historical character of the field of political economy, as noted above; in modern IPE, it is expressed variously through the privileging of economistic definitions and understandings of globalization, market-based understandings of capitalism, forms of (socio-)economic determinism, and so on. We have seen that all of these tendencies, in their different ways, are central to both liberal and critical schools in IPE. As a result, even within critical IPE, we are led directly back to the formulation of the field as the study of a putative dualism of politics and economics: the way in which the study of structure and agency has been framed fits tightly with this duality and indeed serves to reinforce it. In other words, the predominant formulation of the structure–agency question in IPE is one-sided (focusing on agency), indirectly reinforces an economism in understandings of structure which overlooks its fundamentally political and ideological character, and frequently tends to lapse back into a dichotomization of the political and the economic that is unhelpful for the project of meshing that the 'new political economy' project, in particular, as been so active in advocating.

At the same time, various chapters here have demonstrated the ways in which dominant understandings of agency are equally problematic. They are constructed primarily with reference to organized, formal forms of agency with a strong transnational articulation, with the assumption that the political context in which agency is exercised is one of liberal democracy with representative, participatory and legitimate characteristics. Apart from narrowing – or reinforcing the narrowness of – the conception of the political that prevails in much of IPE (to which we drew attention earlier), the study of agency on this basis invites and reinforces the prevailing conceptual and empirical focus on the advanced industrialized world and the building of theory on this limited basis. Consequently, as we have seen throughout the volume, it offers only limiting perspectives on a range of central questions in IPE, such as those concerning the nature of resistance politics, the nature of globalization or the dynamics of power and inequality in the global political economy. It also distorts and restricts our understanding of the relationship between structure and agency. In effect, it calls forth an interpretation and theorization of this relationship which relies upon the *particular* form it can be said to take when the agents in question are influential economic actors (such as financial agents or corporations), formal and organized groups, groups with strong transnational linkages and considerable access to arenas of policy-making authority, and so on. The relationship between structure and agency looks very different when the agents in question are those unorganized, informal and disenfranchised actors who have few or no possibilities for influence or participation, face a very different set of political realities, and operate primarily in local and 'private' (including domestic) contexts. So too, therefore, does the basis on which we can seek to theorize the relationship between structure and agency.

However, as long as we continue to privilege particular conceptions of agency – those primarily relevant in the contexts of advanced capitalism and liberal democracy – we are left *not only* with unsatisfactory notions of agency built on excessively narrow conceptualizations of politics, but also with compromised understandings of *structure*, inasmuch as it is with these forms of agency that the structure is considered to exist in a relationship of mutual constitution. In other words, it is a focus which invites only a partial account of the constitution of the contemporary world order and a partial representation of the range of constitutive forces within it. The task is thus not only one of injecting agency and politics into IPE in order to arrive at a better conceptualization of 'the political'; it is also one of arriving at a more adequate understanding and theorization of structure itself. This argument can also be framed from a more comparative angle, inasmuch as the nature and implications of structure vary according to the particular part of the world in question. The question of the relationship between structure and agency depends fundamentally on the particular constellation of structural forces which prevail in particular political economies, the specific constraints represented by various ideological, political and economic structures for different parts of the world, and the particular capacities of agents (particularly states) to respond to and shape them effectively. This, again, is a point that has been elaborated at various points in the pages of this volume.

In this sense, the theoretical and empirical basis on which the structure–agency question has been addressed points precisely to the shortcomings we have identified here in IPE's purchase on the nature of the global political economy. It is part and parcel of the ways in which a rooting of the theoretical and empirical enterprise of IPE in the political economy of the advanced industrialized world restricts full understandings of both that political economy and the global political economy as a whole, as well as the various political economies that exist outside this 'core' grouping. It is on this basis, then, that we can begin to address more fruitfully the question of the meshing of structure and agency, which constitutes one of the surest routes to achieving the sort of genuine political economy – one which escapes the strictures of both excessive economism and excessive politicism – that could fruitfully form the foundation of a reoriented field of IPE.

The final, related argument to make in this regard is that the question of structure and agency has been formulated predominantly in a manner which draws an inappropriately stark distinction between structure and agency as two separate spheres. That is, approaches to the structure–agency question frequently rest on an assumption that structure and agency are clearly delineated categories that must be analytically integrated with one another in a satisfactory manner. We have already noted that the dualism between structure and agency corresponds tightly with a distinction between economics and politics, and this forms part of the way in which, problematically, structure and agency are distinguished from each other. In other part, the debate has largely tended to overlook the ways in which the dividing lines between structure and agency, as analytical or conceptual 'categories', are by no means clear. Much of IPE has afforded insufficient attention to the ways in which various entities or phenomena represent at once structures and forms of agency, and has not yet fully come to grips with the challenges – or, I suggest, opportunities – thereby presented for the project of analytical integration. The most obvious example is that of states, which in the field of political economy have traditionally been of central concern both as structure and as agency (Gamble 1995: 517). States exist as a structure, both in a national and in a 'global', systemic context, and as agents within the world order. State debates in modern IPE have rarely reflected (or reflected upon) this duality in the character of states and its significance for, for instance, interpretations of their relationship with globalization. Similarly, economic entities such as TNCs, banks, individual financiers or national central banks can be seen as representing both forms of agency and central elements of the global structure, and there have been few concrete considerations of the implications of this ambiguity. Other examples abound.

Yet this blurring of the dividing lines between structure and agency is not necessarily a problem; on the contrary, it deserves more recognition than it has hitherto received, precisely because it facilitates the project of meshing structure and agency in IPE analysis. By doing away with the tendency to draw an excessively stark dualism between structure and agency, we take a huge stride towards being able to appreciate the dynamics of their mutual constitution and complex enmeshment, as well as the bases on which an effective analytical integration might be achieved.

Rethinking the understandings of both structure and agency with which we work, then, is a crucial first step in addressing questions of structure and agency in IPE debates. The general shortcomings that we have identified as limiting the 'global' relevance and insight of IPE are clearly in evidence in the ways in which the structure–agency question has most frequently been addressed. Such a rethinking also provides a conducive avenue for approaching the question of their relationship and the manner in which they can be integrated appropriately, inasmuch as it goes a good way towards mitigating the artificial dichotomization of both politics and economics and structure and agency. Sustaining a dualism of structure and agency – even when attention to both is fully advocated – in effect serves to entrench the analytical separation of politics and economics that has long characterized the social sciences. Moreover, as Gamble (1995: 517) has noted, it has both reflected and reinforced the disciplinary separation of Economics and Political Science. It is this disciplinary separation which has been pivotal in distorting and diverting the classical political economy traditions in the ways we identified in the introductory chapter, as well as hindering the continued evolution of an integrated field of political economy. It is in these senses that the question of structure and agency goes to the heart of a project of recapturing and entrenching political economy as the foundation for the field and, consequently, is central to the project of Globalizing IPE.

Organizing concepts: power and development

The third ingredient of 'globalizing' IPE is a rethinking of the core concepts around which the field is organized. What is required for the field is an organizing concept, or concepts, capable of pulling together the various theoretical orientations, empirical concerns and regional interests, lending to IPE a coherence and cohesion as an intellectual endeavour and furthering the priorities for 'globalizing' IPE that we have outlined in this volume. The organizing concepts of states and markets have, for some time now, been only poorly indicative of the scale and scope of the field's concerns; in any case, the formulation has been widely criticized, including by Strange herself, for the ways it apparently reduces notions of power and the 'political' to the activities, arenas and authority of states. The concepts that Strange (1995) substituted – authority and markets – were undoubtedly an improvement inasmuch as they allowed us to focus more widely on who and what holds and wields power (more broadly conceived) in the global political economy. Yet once again they tended to reflect the dualisms that have pervaded IPE since its inception: politics on one side and economics on the other. The time would appear to be ripe, therefore, for considering whether a rethinking of the organizing concepts of IPE is in order and, if so, which of these could most profitably be for the purposes of pushing the field in the direction that we have advocated in this volume. I suggest, then, that there are two concepts which pull together the study of IPE and could profitably define the enterprise for the next phase of the field's evolution – namely, power and development.

Power

In some ways, locating power as one of the core organizing concepts in IPE is simply a restatement of a concern which has always under-pinned and animated the field. The study of power has consistently been depicted, in many different guises, as essentially what IPE is all about. Power is everywhere in IPE and runs through virtually all of the work that goes on within the field. The ways we think about power and the questions we ask about it are shaped by two particularly influential frameworks, which are associated most immediately with Susan Strange and Robert Cox, but have been developed widely across the field and pushed in many valuable and interesting directions. The first revolves around the notion of structural power, defined as 'the power to shape and determine the structures of the global political economy... the power to decide how things shall be done' (Strange 1988: 24–5). It is from this platform that much of IPE has sought to propel itself beyond the restrictive conceptions of 'relational' power, of a politico-military nature, that prevail in traditional IR theories. Strange's notion of structural power, which echoed the sociologist Steven Lukes's (1974) similar formulations, was pivotal not only in widening the understanding of the ways in which power is *exercised* in the global political economy, but also in introducing the idea that power is multifaceted and located in a range of structures. These she identified, as is well-known, as the production, finance, security and knowledge structures. The second framework was put forward by Cox (1987) in his elaboration of an agenda for critical IPE. It made a seminal contribution in three senses: first, inasmuch as it again drew attention to the multiple forms and arenas of power in the global political economy (material, ideological and political), placing particular emphasis on ideology as a structure of power and the ideational foundations of the world order; second, in its deployment of neo-Gramscian understandings of a transnational neoliberal elite (or historic bloc) crystallizing around and embodying that ideological structure; and, third, in its further elaboration of Gramscian ideas of hegemony as based on a blend of coercion and consent. From these foundations, as all the chapters collected here have revealed, important and insightful subsequent work in IPE has sought to elaborate understandings of private authority in the global political economy, the power of ideas and ideology, the ways in which power permeates the contemporary politics of development and global governance, the notion of 'soft power' (Nye 1990, 2004), the disciplining power of markets and neoliberalism, the changing nature of state power, and so on.

Yet it is still worth observing that, despite the long-standing centrality of power to IPE, there has been surprisingly little work in IPE that concretely attempts to push forward our conceptualization and theorization of the forms of power that permeate the world order and are exercised within it. To be clear, this is emphatically not to say that there has been none, as just noted, but rather that the body of such work has been surprisingly slight *in comparison with* the centrality and salience of the concept of power in IPE. Despite the fact that virtually all work that is done within IPE is permeated by questions of power, and these questions are inherent in all of the major issue areas and debates which concern us, there has been strikingly little conceptual and theoretical work which seeks explicitly to address our understandings of power in IPE and push forward the debate about the nature and exercise of authority. Indeed, it would be probably accurate to say that since Strange and Cox laid out the above frameworks, and despite their enormously valuable subsequent development, there have been few innovations in the way we understand and theorize power. This is perhaps even clearer in the case of the debate about hegemonic power. Since the late 1980s, when the 'declinist' debate about US hegemony was beginning to run out of steam and, indeed, substantiation, the study of hegemony seems to have experienced something of a lull and has yielded surprisingly little original work, particularly of a conceptual or theoretical nature. The debate has, nevertheless, been somewhat reanimated since the start of the 2000s in the burgeoning literature on 'empire', sparked in part by the changes observed in the exercise of US power under the George W. Bush administration, in ways which have drawn new and interesting linkages between notions of power and contemporary forms of imperialism (*inter alia*, along political economy lines, Hardt and Negri 2000; Harvey 2003; Mann 2003; Falk 2004; Johnson 2004).

Yet repositioning power as one of the central organizing concepts of IPE also requires some attention to the ways in which we formulate the relevant questions. A good deal of energy in IPE has been expended thinking about who or what possesses power in the global political economy. We have by now accommodated fully the notion that power is both public and private, legal and illegal, formal and informal, and so on. There are a range of questions which, however, have been asked and addressed a little less robustly and deserve even more salience in IPE. The first set of questions concerns the ways in which the nature and exercise of power constitute a structure of inequality, how that structure is produced and reproduced, and what its consequences are. This is not only an issue of the exercise of hegemonic power in the global political economy – whether hegemony is understood to be articulated by a single state, a group of social forces, a class alliance or an ideological *nébuleuse* (to coin

Cox's (1996a: 301) expression). Rather, it concerns the hierarchies of power that exist at all levels of social organization and the structures of inequality – material, political, ideational, socio-economic and so on – that they produce and reproduce. These questions have found very valuable representation in a good deal of IPE scholarship, especially, it should be said, from those of a critical bent and those with an interest in questions of development. A positioning of these questions more firmly at the centre of debates about power in IPE therefore offers significant capital for the broader study of the structures of inequality that underpin and define the contemporary world order. It would, in this sense, be particularly conducive to the project of Globalizing IPE.

The second set of questions invites a sort of 'comparative' analysis of power. What has been largely neglected in IPE is investigation into the different forms of power that exist in different parts of the world, and how the relevant questions about power vary accordingly. Attention to the various structures and manifestations of power that exist within and constitute different political economies would shed interesting and useful light on a range of core issues and concepts. For instance, the questions that we ask about the evolution of state power under conditions of globalization necessarily vary according to the particular state in question, the structures of power on which it rests, the nature of its relationship with society, and the forms of power that it exercises. The analysis of many political economies, particularly in parts of Africa, Asia and Latin America, invites close attention to illegal, illegitimate and illicit forms of power and agents that exercise it; equally, it throws into clear relief the limitations of focusing on formal power relationships as well as drawing clear distinctions between public and private forms of power, both of which characterize a good deal of IPE scholarship. Although the importance of the illegal and illicit dimensions of global political economy is established in the literature (*inter alia*, Strange 1996; Friman and Andreas 1999; Andreas 2004), the issues have rarely been addressed with reference to the nature of power in particular national or regional settings, and the wider implications of these comparative perspectives for our understandings of power in IPE have been rather neglected. Asking these more 'comparative' questions about power also carries important consequences for our thinking about the nature of and relationship between structure and agency. It facilitates wider consideration of the structures of power that define the contemporary world order and the possession and exercise of power by particular agents, and in that light invites a reformulation of questions of structure and agency in a vein consistent with that advocated earlier in this chapter.

Development

The second core organizing concept of a reoriented IPE is that of development – or, better said, a concept of development that has been appropriately reworked and redefined for the purpose. Traditional conceptions of development are clearly of slight utility, either in their own right or for the purposes of lending cohesion to the intellectual endeavours of IPE. It is those conceptions, indeed, that inform the frequent assumptions (and assertions) that development is a specific and specialized area of interest in IPE, which is of little relevance to those concerned with the political economy of the advanced industrialized world or the study of many of the broader 'themes' in IPE. But, since the 1980s, there has emerged a range of interesting reformulations of the concept of development which, I suggest, imbue it with a highly significant relevance and utility as an organizing concept around which a reworked field of IPE can cohere.

The means of achieving this reordering of development depends, in the first instance, on a certain clearing of the decks. The traditional connotations of the term 'development', which reverberate through IPE, indicate a dominant teleological understanding of development processes which are captured in the prevailing territorialist distinction between 'developed' and 'developing' parts of the world. Those countries and regions which constitute the 'advanced industrialized' parts of the world are considered to be 'developed'; the rest of the world is usually collected together under the umbrella 'developing'. In the conventional terminology of development theory and international studies, the study of development has thus been encapsulated within a 'North–South' framework, in which the concept is deemed relevant only to the 'South'. It is assumed, by extension, that the 'North' can comfortably and legitimately be excluded from the study of development. The theoretical apparatus and empirical remit of 'development studies' have never been deemed applicable or relevant for the study of the political economy of advanced capitalism, these countries not being considered to be in the process of developing, nor to be engaged in the articulation of development strategies.

Given the leanings and characteristics of IPE that we have identified in this volume, it consequently comes as little surprise that the study of development – and perspectives from the field of development studies – should have enjoyed so little representation within the primary concerns in mainstream IPE. Yet this is also a curious state of affairs. It has been noted that the old field of 'North–South relations' was strikingly 'IPE-like' before IPE came formally into being (Underhill 2000a: 806). It has also been noted that the field of development studies bequeathed to IPE a 'key vocabulary' – that of world systems, developmental states, imperialism, neo-colonialism and so on (Harrison 2004: 156). Development studies was historically responsible for many of the theoretical frameworks – such as those relating to dependency, world systems, imperialism and structuralism – that have left a deep imprint on IPE and remain of central importance in its critical strands. The key classical political economists are, without exception, key theorists of *development* – whether those thinkers associated with the study of early industrialization, such as Marx, Smith, Ricardo, Weber and so on, or such later figures as Wallerstein, Friedman, Hayek and others. In a nutshell, the study of political economy has always been synonymous with the study of development and concretely articulated as such in its classical traditions.

It is only in modern IPE that the study of political economy and the study of development have been separated from one another. Development has come to be understood as the study of 'late industrialization' – of what is generally referred to as the 'developing world' – rather than being, as in its earlier incarnations, fundamentally about the study of the evolution of capitalism and capitalist development in various historical contexts. This can be traced in large part to the organization of the field according to levels of analysis. Despite being the source of seminal theories of global capitalism, development studies has traditionally featured a nationalist bias and a sustained focus on national political economies; consequently the study of development has been closely linked with the field of 'area studies' and the comparative branches of the field of politics, from which IPE has sought systematically to distance itself. In other part, it can be traced to the concomitant articulation of IPE as concerned primarily with the study of advanced capitalism, and the widespread rejection of the relevance of a concept of development in the study of this particular political economy. But the point of importance is that the divorce of the study of political economy from the study of development is a recent phenomenon which reflects the fragmentation of the field of political economy. The marginalization of development in modern IPE is, in this sense, indicative of the absence of a strong idea and tradition of political economy as the foundation for the field. It is here, then, that the threads of the agenda laid out in this chapter come together: the recapturing of political economy in IPE invites a privileging of development and its historicized study; a positioning of an appropriate idea of development as the central organizing concept in IPE constitutes an invaluable means of recapturing political economy as the foundation for the field.

A greater fidelity to this intrinsic enmeshment of political economy and development is, then, a first step towards reordering the concept of development and freeing it from its disabling association with only particular parts of the (developing) world. Leaning on this more historicized interpretation of the place of development in the study of political economy, we can introduce the idea that development stretches across the various parts of the world, is as relevant to the advanced industrialized world as it is to those conventionally labelled 'developing', and is about the political economy of *capitalism* in all of its various manifestations, stages and contexts. By extension, however, it is not valid to claim that development 'happened' in Western Europe and the USA at a particular historical moment and that development processes are now occurring in the contemporary period in other parts of the world. Such a formulation relies on a traditional teleological understanding of development – that is, as a linear and finite process – which is ultimately highly misleading. Into a historicized study of development we need to insert an awareness that development is not 'reached' as an end point, but rather that development is an ongoing process which is common to *all* countries of the world. As Anthony Payne (1999, 2004, 2005) has argued at length, all countries and societies are engaged in a continuing search for development and the elaboration of development strategies for this purpose. It is not the case, as is frequently implied, that governments of the advanced industrialized countries engage in formulating 'public policy' while governments elsewhere engage in formulating 'development strategies'. Policy is inherently about formulating strategies which are deemed to be most conducive to the achievement of continued development, whether this is in the context of advanced capitalism in the USA or Germany, so-called 'late industrialization' in Mexico or Singapore, or entrenched poverty and stagnation in Ivory Coast or Haiti. These development strategies can be of the more 'active' variety often associated with Asian developmentalism or European welfarism, or of the more market-driven variety associated with orthodox forms of neoliberalism. Formulated in this way, then, the concept of development is able to capture the wide range of development experiences, problems and strategies that prevail in the various parts of the global political economy. A greater engagement with PED perspectives, of the sort advocated earlier and in several of the preceding chapters, offers a reservoir of concepts and frameworks for the study of these distinctive and varied political economies of development.

Drawing all countries and parts of the world into an enlarged understanding of development, however, is not in itself sufficient for the full reordering of the concept. It offers only a partial basis on which to think about the nature of the global political economy, inasmuch as it continues to rely on problematic territorialist understandings of its organization. Ultimately, development remains conceptualized through territorialist and nationalist lenses, in a manner which complicates a full understanding of the contemporary social dimensions of development and, moreover, the global political economy of inequality which we have identified as central to the concerns of a 'globalized' IPE. The second step is thus to do away more emphatically with the exclusively territorialist biases that continue to permeate IPE, and in so doing to give greater impetus and space for a concept of development capable of pulling together the study of the *whole* of the global political economy. Rather than carving up the world into countries and regions, we can usefully reformulate our questions about development from a basis which emphasizes the social, *as well as* the territorial, nature of the key fault-lines in the global political economy. This has been elaborated in various parts of this volume. In one formulation, as we have seen, it involves attention to the ways in which classes and social groups are 'transnationalized' in their nature and articulation, and the principal lines of inequality in the global political economy lie not primarily between states but rather between these transnationalized social and class formations. In another, it requires a reformulation of our frameworks for thinking about inequality, such that we take much fuller account of the fact that the primary lines of inequality exist *within* societies, not only between them. These formulations are clearly conducive to a reframing of ideas about development in IPE and an extension of their relevance to the study of the global political economy *as a whole*, not simply to clearly demarcated (and ring-fenced) parts of it.

Having cleared away the territorialist, nationalist and teleogical biases in understandings of development, then, the third step is to rethink the basic issues which we associate with the study of development. We need to insert a concept of development into IPE that is understood not to be about industrialization, growth and national economic performance, but rather one which is capable of encapsulating these issues within a much wider set of questions that revolve around (in)equality and (in)justice in all of their various guises. Conceived in this way, the basic concerns of IPE and development intersect intimately with one another, to the point where there is little sense in talking about two separate fields or, indeed, of development as a 'specialized' area of interest within IPE. All of the various debates in IPE are intrinsically founded upon and pulled together by ideas about development in the global political economy – whether they rest on questions about the nature of development itself; the politics of development; the power structures that condition processes of development and prospects for development strategies; policy-making and economic strategies; multilateralism and international organizations; the public and private agents involved in the elaboration and pursuit of developmental goals and the global framework within which they are articulated; ideas and ideologies of development; the workings of markets and their implications for societies and social groups; the reorganization and redefinition of states; the nature of capitalism; the nature and organization of the capitalist world system and the various ways in which different social groups, economies, states, regions and societies are inserted into it; forms of contemporary imperialism and dependency; and so on.

Such a reworking thus assists the project of bringing the study of development much more centrally into the concerns and remit of IPE (and out of what Robert Bates (1998: 6) has called its 'bondage' in comparative analysis), and also establishes firmly its relevance and utility as an organizing concept for the field as a whole. A reordered concept of development, in this sense, lays a useful foundation for a more 'globalized' IPE which privileges a set of questions, concepts and theoretical perspectives that are relevant not to a single political economy of advanced capitalism but rather the range of political economies and processes that are constitutive of the contemporary world order. Moreover, it is signally conducive to the recapturing of political economy as the foundation for the field. In reorganizing the field in this way, I suggest, we open up very fertile ground on which to advance the next phase of the evolution of IPE.

References

Abbott, Jason (2001) 'Fall from Grace: The Political Economy of Indonesian Decay and Decline', paper presented to the conference on 'The Global Constitution of "Failed States": The Consequences of a New Imperialism?', University of Sussex, 18–20 April.

Abrahamsen, Rita (2000) *Disciplining Democracy: Good Governance and Development Discourse in Africa* (London: Zed Books).

Africa Today (1997) Special Issue: *The Future of Regional Studies* 44:2.

Albert, Michel (1993) *Capitalism against Capitalism* (London: Whurr).

Almond, Gabriel and Sidney Verba (1963) *The Civic Culture: Political Attitudes and Democracy in Five Nations* (Princeton, NJ: Princeton University Press).

Amoore, Louise (2000) 'International Political Economy and the Contested Firm', *New Political Economy* 5:2, pp. 183–204.

——(2002) *Globalization Contested: An International Political Economy of Work* (Manchester: Manchester University Press).

Amoore, Louise and Paul Langley (2004) 'Ambiguities of Global Civil Society', *Review of International Studies* 30:1, pp. 89–110.

Amoore, Louise, Richard Dodgson, Barry K. Gills, Paul Langley, Don Marshall and Iain Watson (1997) 'Overturning "Globalisation": Resisting the Teleological, Reclaiming the "Political"', *New Political Economy* 2:1, pp. 179–95.

Amsden, Alice (2001) *The Rise of 'the Rest': Challenges to the West from Late-Industrializing Economies* (Oxford: Oxford University Press).

Anderson, James and James Goodman (1995) 'Regions, States and the European Union: Modernist Reaction or Postmodern Adaptation?', *Review of International Political Economy* 2:4, pp. 600–31.

Andreas, Peter (2004) 'Illicit International Political Economy: The Clandestine Side of Globalization', review article, *Review of International Political Economy* 11:3, pp. 641–52.

Andrews, David (1994) 'Capital Mobility and State Autonomy: Toward a Structural Theory of International Monetary Relations', *International Studies Quarterly* 38:2, pp. 193–218.

Angell, Alan (1993) 'Chile since 1958', in Leslie Bethell (ed.) *Chile since Independence* (Cambridge: Cambridge University Press), pp. 162–223.

Archibugi, Daniele (1998) 'Principles of Cosmopolitan Democracy', in Daniele Archibugi, David Held and Martin Kohler (eds) *Re-imagining Political Community: Studies in Cosmopolitan Democracy* (Stanford, CA: Stanford University Press), pp. 198–228.

270

Archibugi, Daniele, David Held and Martin Kohler (eds) (1998) *Re-imagining Political Community: Studies in Cosmopolitan Democracy* (Stanford, CA: Stanford University Press).

Armijo, Leslie Elliott (ed.) (1999) *Financial Globalization and Democracy in Emerging Markets* (London: Macmillan).

Arrighi, Giovanni (1994) *The Long Twentieth Century: Money, Power, and the Origins of Our Times* (London: Verso).

Arrow, Kenneth J. (1963) *Social Choice and Individual Values* (New Haven, CT: Yale University Press).

Asher, Mukul (2002) 'Social Security Institutions in Southeast Asia After the Crisis', in Mark Beeson (ed.) *Reconfiguring East Asia: Regional Institutions and Organisations After the Crisis* (London: Curzon Press), pp. 83–98.

Ashworth, Lucian and David Long (eds) (1998) *New Perspectives on International Functionalism* (London: Macmillan).

Axline, Andrew W. (ed.) (1994) *The Political Economy of Regional Co-operation: Comparative Case Studies* (London: Pinter Publishers).

Ayoob, Mohammed (1998) 'Subaltern Realism: International Relations Theory Meets the Third World', in Stephanie Neumann (ed.) *International Relations Theory and the Third World* (London: Macmillan), pp. 31–54.

Ayres, Jeffrey and Sidney Tarrow (2002) 'The Shifting Ground for Transnational Civic Activity', Social Science Research Council: Terrorism and Democratic Virtues (http://www.ssrc.org/sept11/essays/ayres/htm).

Bach, Daniel C. (1999) 'Revisiting a Paradigm', in Daniel C. Bach (ed.) *Regionalisation in Africa: Integration and Disintegration* (London: James Currey), pp. 1–14.

Bache, Ian (2001) 'Different Seeds in the Same Pot? Competing Models of Capitalism and the Incomplete Contracts of Partnership Design', *Public Administration* 79:2, pp. 337–59.

Bagchi, Amiya Kumar (2000) 'The Past and the Future of the Developmental State', *Journal of World Systems Research*, Summer/Fall, pp. 398–442.

Baker, Andrew (1999) 'Nébuleuse and the "Internationalization of the State" in the UK? The Case of HM Treasury and the Bank of England', *Review of International Political Economy* 6:1, pp. 79–101.

Baker, Gideon (1999) 'The Taming of the Idea of Civil Society', *Democratization* 6:3, pp. 1–29.

Balassa, Bela (1962) *The Theory of Economic Integration* (London: Allen & Unwin).

Bates, Robert (1998) 'The Future in Comparative Politics', *Journal of Chinese Political Science* 4:2, pp. 1–18.

Bayart, Jean-François (1993) *The State in Africa: The Politics of the Belly* (London: Longman).

Beeson, M. (1998) 'Indonesia, the East Asian Crisis, and the Commodification of the Nation-State', *New Political Economy* 3:3, pp. 357–74.

——(1999) *Competing Capitalisms: Australia, Japan and Economic Competition in the Asia Pacific* (London: Macmillan).

——(2000) 'Mahathir and the Markets: Globalisation and the Pursuit of Economic Autonomy in Malaysia', *Pacific Affairs* 73:3, pp. 335–51.

——(2001) 'Globalisation, Governance, and the Political-Economy of Public Policy Reform in East Asia', *Governance: An International Journal of Policy, Administration and Institutions* 14:4, pp. 481–502.

——(2002) 'Theorising Institutional Change in East Asia', in Mark Beeson (ed.) *Reconfiguring East Asia: Regional Institutions and Organisations After the Crisis* (London: Curzon Press), pp. 7–27.

Beeson, Mark and Ann Capling (2002) 'Australia in the World Economy: Globalisation, International Institutions, and Economic Governance', in Stephen Bell (ed.) *Economic Governance and Institutional Dynamics* (Melbourne: Oxford University Press), pp. 285–303.

Bell, Stephen (1995) 'The Collective Capitalism of Northeast Asia and the Limits of Orthodox Economics', *Australian Journal of Political Science* 30:2, pp. 264–87.

——(2002) 'Institutionalism', in Dennis Woodward, Andrew Parkin and John Summers (eds) *Government, Politics, Power and Policy in Australia* (Melbourne: Longman), pp. 363–80.

Berger, Mark (ed.) (2004) *After the Third World?*, Special Issue, *Third World Quarterly* 25:1.

Berger, Suzanne (1996) 'Introduction', in Suzanne Berger and Ronald Dore (eds) *National Diversity and Global Capitalism* (Ithaca, NY: Cornell University Press), pp. 1–25.

Bernard, Mitchell and John Ravenhill (1995) 'Beyond Product Cycles and Flying Geese: Regionalization, Hierarchy, and the Industrialization of East Asia', *World Politics* 47:2, pp. 171–209.

Bhagwati, Jagdish (2004) *In Defense of Globalization* (New York: Oxford University Press).

Bieler, Andreas (2000) *Globalisation and the Enlargement of the EU: Austrian and Swedish Social Forces in the Struggle over Membership* (London: Routledge).

Bilgin, Pinar and Adam David Morton (2002) 'Historicising Representations of "Failed States": Beyond the Cold-War Annexation of the Social Sciences', *Third World Quarterly* 23:1, pp. 55–80.

Birnbaum, Norman (1999) 'Is the Third Way Authentic?', *New Political Economy* 4:3, pp. 437–46.

BIS (Bank for International Settlements) (2002a) 'Triennial Central Bank Survey of Foreign Exchange and Derivatives Market Activity 2001 – Final Results', http://www.bis.org/publ/rpfx02.htm, 18 March.

——(2002b) *Quarterly Review: International Banking and Financial Market Developments*, March.

Block, Fred (1977) *The Origins of International Economic Disorder* (Berkeley, CA: University of California Press).

Blyth, Mark and Hendrik Spruyt (2003) 'Our Past as Prologue: Introduction to the Tenth Anniversary Issue of the *Review of International Political Economy*', *Review of International Political Economy* 10:4, pp. 607–20.

Bøås, Morten, Marianne H. Marchand and Timothy M. Shaw (eds) (1999a) *New Regionalisms in the New Millennium*, Special Issue, *Third World Quarterly* 20:5.

——(1999b) 'The Weave-World: Regionalisms in the South in the New Millennium', *Third World Quarterly* 20:5, pp. 1061–70.

Boli, John and George Thomas (eds) (1999) *Constructing World Culture: International Nongovernmental Organizations since 1875* (Stanford, CA: Stanford University Press).

Bordo, Michael D., Barry Eichengreen and Douglas A. Irwin (1999) *Is Globalization Today Really Different than Globalization a Hundred Years Ago?*, NBER Working Papers, No. 7195.

Boyer, Robert (1996) 'The Convergence Hypothesis Revisited: Globalization but still the century of nations?', in Suzanne Berger and Ronald Dore (eds) *National Diversity and Global Capitalism* (Ithaca, NY: Cornell University Press), pp. 29–59.

——(2000) 'Is a Finance-Led Growth Regime a Viable Alternative to Fordism?', *Economy and Society* 29:1, pp. 111–45.

Boyer, Robert and Daniel Drache (eds) (1996) *States Against Markets: The Limits of Globalization* (London: Routledge).

Brady, Rose (1999) *Kapitalizm: Russia's Struggle to Free Its Economy* (New Haven, CT: Yale University Press).

Braudel, Fernand (1992) *The Structures of Everyday Life: The Limits of the Possible* (Berkeley, CA: University of California Press).

Brenner, Robert (1977) 'The Origins of Capitalist Development: A Critique of Neo-Smithian Marxism', *New Left Review* 104:1, pp. 25–93.

Breslin, Shaun (2000) 'Decentralisation, Globalisation, and China's Partial Re-engagement with the Global Economy', *New Political Economy* 5:2, pp. 205–26.

——(2002) 'IR, Area Studies and IPE: Rethinking the Study of China's International Relations', mimeo, University of Warwick.

Breslin, Shaun and Richard Higgott (2000) 'Studying Regions: Learning from the Old, Constructing the New', *New Political Economy* 5:3, pp. 333–52.

Breslin, Shaun and Glenn D. Hook (eds) (2003) *Microregionalism and World Order* (Basingstoke: Palgrave Macmillan).

Brown, Chris (2000) 'Cosmopolitanism, World Citizenship and Global Civil Society', *Critical Review of International Social and Political Philosophy* 3:1, pp. 7–26.

Broz, Lawrence (1997) 'The Domestic Politics of International Monetary Order: The Gold Standard', in David Skidmore (ed.) *Contested Social Orders and International Politics* (Nashville, TN: Vanderbilt University Press), pp. 53–91.

Brune, Nancy, Geoffrey Garrett, Alexandra Guisinger and Jason Sorens (2001) 'The Political Economy of Capital Account Liberalization', paper presented at the Annual Meeting of the American Political Science Association, San Francisco, CA, 31 August.

Bull, Hedley (1977) *The Anarchical Society: A Study of Order in World Politics* (New York: Columbia University Press).

Burnham, Peter (1999) 'The Politics of Economic Management in the 1990s', *New Political Economy* 4:1, pp. 37–54.

——(2001) 'Marx, International Political Economy and Globalisation', *Capital and Class* 75, pp. 7–16.

Buzan, Barry (1991) *People, States and Fear: An Agenda for International Security Studies in the Post-Cold War Era*, second edition (London: Longman).

——(2003) 'Regional Security Complex Theory in a Post-Cold War World', in Fredrik Söderbaum and Timothy M. Shaw (eds) *Theories of New Regionalism: A Palgrave Reader* (Basingstoke: Palgrave Macmillan), pp. 140–59.

Buzan, Barry and Richard Little (2000) *International Systems in World History: Remaking the Study of International Relations* (New York: Oxford University Press).

Cable, Vincent and David Henderson (eds) (1994) *Trade Blocs? The Future of Regional Integration* (London: Royal Institute of International Affairs).

Cairncross, Frances (1997) *The Death of Distance: How the Communications Revolution Will Change Our Lives* (Boston, MA: Harvard Business School Press).

Calder, Kent (1997) 'Assault on the Bankers' Kingdom: Politics, Markets, and the Liberalization of Japanese Industrial Finance', in Michael Loriaux, Meredith Woo-Cumings, Kent E. Calder, Sylvia Maxfield and Sofia A. Perez, *Capital Ungoverned: Liberalizing Finance in Interventionist States* (Ithaca, NY: Cornell University Press), pp. 17–56.

Calvo, Guillermo A. and Carmen M. Reinhart (2000) *Fear of Floating*, NBER Working Papers, No. 7993, November.

Camilleri, Joseph and Jim Falk (eds) (1992) *The End of Sovereignty? The Politics of a Shrinking and Fragmented World* (Brookfield, VT: Edward Elgar).

Cammack, Paul (2002) 'The Mother of All Governments: The World Bank's Matrix for Global Governance', in Rorden Wilkinson and Steve Hughes (eds) *Global Governance: Critical Perspectives* (London: Routledge), pp. 36–53.

——(2004) 'What the World Bank Means by Poverty Reduction, and Why It Matters', *New Political Economy* 9:2, pp. 189–211.

Caporaso, James A. (1997) 'Across the Great Divide: Integrating Comparative and International Politics', *International Studies Quarterly* 41:4, pp. 563–92.

Caporaso, James A. and David P. Levine (1992) *Theories of Political Economy* (Cambridge: Cambridge University Press).

Cardoso, Fernando Henrique and Enzo Faletto (1979) *Dependency and Development in Latin America* (Berkeley, CA: University of California Press).

Casaburi, Gabriel, María Pia Riggirozzi, María Fernanda Tuozzo and Diana Tussie (2000) 'Multilateral Development Banks, Governments and Civil Society: Chiaroscuros in a Triangular Relationship', *Global Governance* 6:4, pp. 25–47.

Castañeda, Jorge (1994) *Utopia Unarmed: The Latin American Left after the Cold War* (New York: Vintage Books).

Castles, Stephen and Alastair Davidson (2000) *Citizenship and Migration: Globalization and the Politics of Belonging* (Basingstoke: Palgrave Macmillan).

Centeno, Miguel (1994) *Democracy Within Reason: Technocratic Revolution in Mexico* (University Park, PA: Penn State University Press).

Cerny, Philip G. (1993) 'Plurilateralism, Structural Differentiation and Functional Conflict in the Post-Cold War World Order', *Millennium: Journal of International Studies* 22:1, pp. 27–51.

——(1994) 'The Infrastructure of the Infrastructure? Toward "Embedded Financial Orthodoxy" in the International Political Economy', in Ronen P. Palan and Barry Gills (eds) *Transcending the State–Global Divide: A Neostructuralist Agenda in International Relations* (Boulder, CO: Lynne Rienner), pp. 223–49.

——(1995) 'Globalization and the Changing Logic of Collective Action', *International Organization* 49:4, pp. 595–626.

——(1997a) 'Communications: R. A. W. Rhodes, "The New Governance: Governing without Government", *Political Studies* (1996), XLIV, 652–67', *Political Studies* 45:1, pp. 1–4.

——(1997b) 'Paradoxes of the Competition State: The Dynamics of Political Globalisation', *Government and Opposition* 32:2, pp. 251–74.

——(1997c) 'International Finance and the Erosion of Capitalist Diversity', in Colin Crouch and Wolfgang Streeck (eds) *Political Economy of Modern Capitalism: Mapping Convergence and Diversity* (London: Sage), pp. 173–81.

——(2000) 'Political Agency in a Globalizing World: Toward a Structu-rational Approach', *European Journal of International Relations* 6:4, pp. 435–63.

Chan, Gerald (1999) *Chinese Perspectives on International Relations* (London: Macmillan).

Chandler, Alfred (1990) *Scale and Scope: The Dynamics of Industrial Capitalism* (Cambridge, MA: Harvard University Press).

Chang, Ha-Joon (2002) *Kicking Away the Ladder: Development Strategy in Historical Perspective* (London: Anthem Press).

Charnovitz, Steve (1997) 'Two Centuries of Participation: NGOs and International Governance', *Michigan Journal of International Law* 18:2, pp. 183–286.

Christiansen, Thomas (2001) 'European and Regional Integration', in John Baylis and Steve Smith (eds) *The Globalization of World Politics: An Introduction to International Relations* (Oxford: Oxford University Press), pp. 495–518.

Clapham, Christopher (1996) *Africa and the International System* (Cambridge: Cambridge University Press).

——(2002) 'The Challenge to the State in a Globalized World', *Development and Change* 33:5, pp. 775–95.

Clark, Cal and Steve Chan (1995) 'MNCs and Developmentalism: Domestic Structure as an Explanation for East Asian Dynamism', in Thomas Risse-Kappen (ed.) *Bringing Transnational Relations Back In* (Cambridge: Cambridge University Press), pp. 112–45.

Clark, Ian (1998) 'Beyond the Great Divide: Globalization and the Theory of International Relations', *Review of International Studies* 24:4, pp. 479–98.

——(1999) *Globalization and International Relations Theory* (Oxford: Oxford University Press).

Clarke, Colin and Anthony Payne (eds) (1987) *Politics, Security and Development in Small States* (London: Allen & Unwin).

Coates, David (2000) *Models of Capitalism: Growth and Stagnation in the Modern Era* (Cambridge: Polity Press).

Cohen, Benjamin J. (1993) 'The Triad and the Unholy Trinity: Problems of International Monetary Cooperation', in Richard Higgott, Richard Leaver and John Ravenhill (eds) *Pacific Economic Relations in the 1990s: Cooperation or Conflict?* (London: Allen & Unwin), pp. 133–58.

——(1996) 'Phoenix Risen: The Resurrection of Global Finance', *World Politics* 48:2, pp. 268–96.

——(1998) *The Geography of Money* (Ithaca, NY: Cornell University Press).

Colás, Alejandro (2001) *International Civil Society: Social Movements in World Politics* (Cambridge: Polity Press).

Coleman, William D. and Anthony Perl (1999) 'Internationalized Policy Environments and Policy Network Analysis', *Political Studies* 47:4, pp. 691–709.

Collins, Randall (1999) *Macrohistory: Essays in the Sociology of the Long Run* (Stanford, CA: Stanford University Press).

Commission on Global Governance (1995) *Our Global Neighbourhood: The Report of the Commission on Global Governance* (Oxford: Oxford University Press).

Cooper, Frederick and Randall Packard (1997) 'Introduction', in Frederick Cooper and Randall Packard (eds) *International Development and the Social Sciences: Essays on History and Politics of Knowledge* (Berkeley, CA: University of California Press), pp. 1–41.

Cooper, Richard N. (1968) *The Economics of Interdependence* (New York: Columbia University Press).

Cox, Robert W. (1981) 'Social Forces, States and World Orders: Beyond International Relations Theory', *Millennium: Journal of International Studies* 10:2, pp. 126–55.

——(1983) 'Gramsci, Hegemony and International Relations: An Essay in Method', *Millennium: Journal of International Studies* 12:2, pp. 162–75.

——(1987) *Production, Power, and World Order: Social Forces in the Making of History* (New York: Columbia University Press).

——(1996a) 'Global *Perestroika*', in Robert W. Cox with Timothy J. Sinclair, *Approaches to World Order* (Cambridge: Cambridge University Press), pp. 296–313.

——(1996b) *Approaches to World Order* (Cambridge: Cambridge University Press).

——(1997) 'Democracy in Hard Times: Economic Globalization and the Limits to Liberal Democracy', in Anthony McGrew (ed.) *The Transformation of Democracy? Globalization and Territorial Democracy* (Cambridge: Polity Press), pp. 49–72.

——(2004) 'Beyond Empire and Terror: Critical Reflections on the Political Economy of World Order', *New Political Economy* 9:3, pp. 307–23.

Crawford, Gordon (1997) 'Foreign Aid and Political Conditionality', *Democratization* 4:3, pp. 69–108.

Crawford, Robert and Darryl Jarvis (eds) (2001) *International Relations – Still an American Social Science: Towards Diversity in International Thought* (Albany, NY: State University of New York Press).

Cronin, James E. (1996) *The World the Cold War Made: Order, Chaos, and the Return of History* (New York: Routledge).

Crouch, Colin and Wolfgang Streeck (eds) (1997) *Political Economy of Modern Capitalism: Mapping Convergence and Diversity* (London: Sage).

Cutler, A. Claire (1995) 'Global Capitalism and Liberal Myths: Dispute Settlement in Private International Trade Relations', *Millennium: Journal of International Studies* 24:3, pp. 377–97.

Cutler, A. Claire, Virginia Haufler and Tony Porter (eds) (1999) *Private Authority and International Affairs* (Albany, NY: State University of New York Press).

de Melo, Jaime and Arvind Panagariya (eds) (1993) *New Dimensions in Regional Integration* (Cambridge: Cambridge University Press).

della Porta, Donatella and Mario Diani (1999) *Social Movements: An Introduction* (Oxford: Blackwell).

Demirguc-Kunt, Asli and Ross Levine (1999) *Bank-Based and Market-Based Financial Systems: A Cross-Country Comparison*, World Bank Research Papers, June.

Dia, Mamadou (1991) 'Development and Cultural Values', *Finance and Development* 28:4, pp. 10–13.

Diamond, Larry (1999) *Developing Democracy: Toward Consolidation* (Baltimore, MD: Johns Hopkins University Press).

Dicken, Peter (1992) *Global Shift: The Internationalization of Economic Activity* (London: Paul Chapman).

Ding, X. L. (2000) 'Informal Privatisation Through Internationalisation: The Rise of *Nomenklatura* Capitalism in China's Offshore Business', *British Journal of Political Science* 30:1, pp. 121–46.

Dirlik, Arif (1999) 'Formations of Globality and Radical Politics', *The Review of Education Pedagogy/Cultural Studies* 21:4, pp. 301–38.

Domínguez, Jorge I. (1996) *Technopols: Freeing Politics and Markets in Latin America in the 1990s* (University Park, PA: Penn State University Press).

Doornbos, Martin (2001) ' "Good Governance": The Rise and Decline of a Policy Metaphor?', *Journal of Development Studies* 37:6, pp. 93–108.

——(2002) 'State Collapse and Fresh Starts: Some Critical Reflections', *Development and Change* 33:5, pp. 797–815.

Dore, Ronald, William Lazonick and Mary O'Sullivan (1999) 'Varieties of Capitalism in the Twentieth Century', *Oxford Review of Economic Policy* 15:4, pp. 102–20.

Doremus, Paul, William Keller, Louis Pauly and Simon Reich (1998) *The Myth of the Global Corporation* (Princeton, NJ: Princeton University Press).

Dos Santos, Theotonio (1970) 'The Structure of Dependency', *American Economic Review* 60:21, pp. 231–6.

Dower, Nigel (2001) 'Citizenship in a Global Context', paper presented to the conference 'Global Civil Society: Critical Engagements', University of Aberystwyth, 11 September.

Drainville, André (1994) 'International Political Economy in the Age of Open Marxism', *Review of International Political Economy* 1:1, pp. 105–32.

Dryzek, John (2000) *Deliberative Democracy and Beyond: Liberals, Critics, Contestations* (Oxford: Oxford University Press).

Dunleavy, Patrick and Brendan O'Leary (1987) *Theories of the State: The Politics of Liberal Democracy* (London: Macmillan).

Dunlop, Claire (2000) 'Epistemic Communities: A Reply to Toke', *Politics* 20:3, pp. 135–44.

Dunn, Kevin C. and Timothy M. Shaw (eds) (2001) *Africa's Challenge to International Relations Theory* (Basingstoke: Palgrave Macmillan).

Dwivedi, O. P. and Jorge Nef (1982) 'Crises and Continuities in Development Theory and Administration: First and Third World Perspectives', *Public Administration and Development* 2:1, pp. 59–77.

Edwards, Sebastian (1999) 'How Effective Are Capital Controls?', *Journal of Economic Perspectives* 13:4, pp. 65–84.

——(2001) *Capital Mobility and Economic Performance: Are Emerging Economies Different?*, NBER Working Papers, No. 8076, January.

Eichengreen, Barry J. (1992) *Golden Fetters: The Gold Standard and the Great Depression, 1919–1939* (New York: Oxford University Press).

——(1996) *Globalizing Capital: A History of the International Monetary System* (Princeton, NJ: Princeton University Press).

——(1999) *Toward a New International Financial Architecture: A Practical Post-Asia Agenda* (Washington, DC: Institute for International Economics).

Eichengreen, Barry and Peter B. Kenen (1994) 'Managing the World Economy Under the Bretton Woods System: An Overview', in Peter B. Kenen (ed.) *Managing the World Economy: Fifty Years After Bretton Woods* (Washington, DC: Institute for International Economics), pp. 3–57.

Eichengreen, Barry J. and Michael Mussa (1998a) 'Capital Account Liberalization and the IMF', *Finance and Development* 35:4, from website; http://www.imf.org/external/pubs/ft/fandd/1998/12/eichen.htm.

——(1998b) *Capital Account Liberalization: Theoretical and Practical Aspects*, IMF Occasional Papers, No. 172.

Elias, Juanita (2004) *Fashioning Inequality: The MNC and Gendered Employment in a Globalising World* (Aldershot: Ashgate).

Ellison, Christopher and Gary Gereffi (1990) 'Explaining Strategies and Patterns of Industrial Development', in Gary Gereffi and Donald L. Wyman (eds) *Manufacturing Miracles: Paths of Industrialization in Latin America and East Asia* (Princeton, NJ: Princeton University Press), pp. 368–403.

Elson, Diane (1998) 'The Economic, the Political and the Domestic: Business, States and Households in the Organisation of Production', *New Political Economy* 3:2, pp. 189–208.

Ernst, Dieter and John Ravenhill (2000) 'Convergence and Diversity: How Globalization Reshapes Asian Production Networks', in Michael Borrus, Dieter Ernst and Stephan Haggard (eds) *International Production Networks in Asia: Rivalry or Riches?* (London: Routledge), pp. 226–56.

Escobar, Arturo (1995) *Encountering Development: The Making and Unmaking of the Third World* (Princeton, NJ: Princeton University Press).

Esping-Andersen, Gosta (1990) *The Three Worlds of Welfare Capitalism* (Princeton, NJ: Princeton University Press).

Evans, Peter (1995a) *Embedded Autonomy: States and Industrial Transformation* (Princeton, NJ: Princeton University Press).

——(1995b) 'Predatory, Developmental and Other Apparatuses: A Comparative Political Economy Perspective on the Third World State', *Sociological Forum* 4:4, pp. 561–87.

——(1997) 'The Eclipse of the State? Reflections on Stateness in an Era of Globalization', *World Politics* 50:1, pp. 62–87.

Evans, Peter, Dietrich Rueschemeyer and Theda Skocpol (eds) (1985) *Bringing the State Back In* (Cambridge: Cambridge University Press).

Falk, Richard (1995) *On Humane Governance: Towards a New Global Politics* (Cambridge: Polity Press).

——(1999) *Predatory Globalization: A Critique* (Cambridge: Polity Press).

——(2003) 'Globalization-from-below: An Innovative Politics of Resistance', in Richard Sandbrook (ed.) *Civilizing Globalization: A Survival Guide* (Albany, NY: State University of New York Press), pp. 191–205.

——(2004) *The Declining World Order: America's Imperial Geopolitics* (New York: Routledge).

Fawcett, Louise and Andrew Hurrell (eds) (1995) *Regionalism in World Politics. Regional Organization and International Order* (Oxford: Oxford University Press).

Feldstein, Martin and Charles Horioka (1980) 'Domestic Savings and International Capital Flows', *Economic Journal* 90:358, pp. 314–29.

Fine, Robert (1997) 'Civil Society Theory, Enlightenment and Critique', *Democratization* 4:1, pp. 7–28.

Finkelstein, Lawrence S. (1995) 'What is Global Governance?', *Global Governance* 1:4, pp. 367–72.

Finnemore, Martha (1996a) 'Norms, Culture and World Politics: Insights from Sociology's Institutionalism', *International Organization* 50:2, pp. 349–67.

——(1996b) *National Interests in International Society* (Ithaca, NY: Cornell University Press).

Finnemore, Martha and Kathryn Sikkink (1998) 'International Norm Dynamics and Political Change', *International Organization* 52:4, pp. 887–917.

Fleury, Sonia (1999) 'Reforma del Estado en América Latina: ¿Hacia Dónde?', *Nueva Sociedad* 160, pp. 58–80.

Frank, André Gunder (1969) *Capitalism and Underdevelopment in Latin America: Historical Studies of Chile and Brazil* (New York: Monthly Review Press).

——(1998) *ReOrient: Global Economy in the Asian Age* (Berkeley, CA: University of California Press).

Frieden, Jeffry A. (1991) 'Invested Interests: The Politics of National Economic Policies in a World of Global Finance', *International Organization* 45:4, pp. 425–51.

Frieden, Jeffry A. and Ronald Rogowski (1996) 'The Impact of the International Economy on National Policies: An Overview', in Robert O. Keohane and Helen V. Milner (eds) *Internationalization and Domestic Politics* (Cambridge: Cambridge University Press), pp. 25–47.

Friman, H. Richard and Peter Andreas (eds) (1999) *The Illicit Global Economy and State Power* (Lanham, MD: Rowman & Littlefield).

Frobel, Friedrich, Jurgen Heinrichs and Otto Kreye (1978) 'The New International Division of Labour', *Social Science Information* 17:1, pp. 123–42.

Fukuyama, Francis (1992) *The End of History and the Last Man* (New York: Penguin).

Gale, Fred (1998) 'Cave "Cave! Hic Dragones": A Neo-Gramscian Deconstruction and Reconstruction of International Regime Theory', *Review of International Political Economy* 5:2, pp. 252–83.

Gamble, Andrew (1995) 'The New Political Economy', *Political Studies* 43:3, pp. 516–30.

——(2000) 'Economic Governance', in Jon Pierre (ed.) *Debating Governance: Authority, Steering, and Democracy* (Oxford: Oxford University Press), pp. 110–37.

Gamble, Andrew and Anthony Payne (eds) (1996a) *Regionalism and World Order* (London: Macmillan).

——(1996b) 'Conclusion: The New Regionalism', in Andrew Gamble and Anthony Payne (eds) *Regionalism and World Order* (London: Macmillan), pp. 247–64.

Gamble, Andrew, Anthony Payne, Ankie Hoogvelt, Michael Kenny and Michael Dietrich (1996) 'Editorial: New Political Economy', *New Political Economy* 1:1, pp. 5–11.

Garrett, Banning (2001) 'China Faces, Debates, the Contradictions of Globalization', *Asian Survey* 41:3, pp. 409–27.

Garrett, Geoffrey (1998) *Partisan Politics in the Global Economy* (Cambridge: Cambridge University Press).

——(2000a) 'Capital Mobility, Exchange Rates and Fiscal Policy in the Global Economy', *Review of International Political Economy* 7:1, pp. 153–70.

——(2000b) *The Causes of Globalization*, Leitner Working Paper, 2000–02, available at http://www.yale.edu/leitner/papers.htm.

Gereffi, Gary (1995) 'Global Production Systems and Third World Development', in Barbara Stallings (ed.) *Global Change, Regional Response: The New International Context of Development* (Cambridge: Cambridge University Press), pp. 100–42.

Gereffi, Gary and Miguel Korzeniewicz (eds) (1994) *Commodity Chains and Global Capitalism* (London: Greenwood Press).

Germain, Randall (2000a) 'Globalization in Historical Perspective', in Randall Germain (ed.) *Globalization and Its Critics: Perspectives from Political Economy* (Basingstoke: Palgrave Macmillan), pp. 67–90.

——(2000b) 'Introduction: Globalization and its Critics', in Randall Germain (ed.) *Globalization and Its Critics: Perspectives from Political Economy* (Basingstoke: Palgrave Macmillan), pp. xiii–xx.

Germain, Randall and Michael Kenny (1998) 'Engaging Gramsci: International Relations Theory and the New Gramscians', *Review of International Studies* 24:1, pp. 2–21.

Gerschenkron, Alexander (1966) *Economic Backwardness in Historical Perspective* (Cambridge: Belknap Press).

Giddens, Anthony (1984) *The Constitution of Society: Outline of the Theory of Structuration* (Cambridge: Polity Press).

——(1990) *The Consequences of Modernity* (Cambridge: Polity Press).

Gill, Stephen (1990) *American Hegemony and the Trilateral Commission* (Cambridge: Cambridge University Press).

——(1992) 'Economic Globalization and the Internationalization of Authority', *Geoforum* 23:3, pp. 269–83.

——(ed.) (1993) *Gramsci, Historical Materialism and International Relations* (Cambridge: Cambridge University Press).

——(1995) 'Globalisation, Market Civilisation, and Disciplinary Neo-liberalism', *Millennium: Journal of International Studies* 24:3, pp. 399–423.

——(1996) 'Globalization and the Politics of Indifference', in James Mittleman (ed.) *Globalization: Critical Reflections* (Boulder, CO: Lynne Rienner), pp. 205–23.

——(2000) 'Toward a Postmodern Prince? The Battle in Seattle as a Moment in the New Politics of Globalisation', *Millennium: Journal of International Studies* 29:1, pp. 131–40.

Gill, Stephen and David Law (1988) *The Global Political Economy* (Baltimore, MD: Johns Hopkins University Press).

——(1989) 'Global Hegemony and the Structural Power of Capital', *International Studies Quarterly* 33:4, pp. 475–99.

Gills, Barry (1997) 'Editorial: "Globalisation" and the "Politics of Resistance"', *New Political Economy* 2:1, pp. 11–15.

——(2000) 'The Crisis of Postwar East Asian Capitalism: American Power, Democracy and the Vicissitudes of Globalisation', *Review of International Studies* 26:3, pp. 381–403.

Gilpin, Robert (1987) *The Political Economy of International Relations* (Princeton, NJ: Princeton University Press).

——(2001) *Global Political Economy: Understanding the International Economic Order* (Princeton, NJ: Princeton University Press).

Glasius, Marlies and Mary Kaldor (2003) 'The State of Global Civil Society: Before and After September 11', in Marlies Glasius, Mary Kaldor and Helmut Anheir (eds) *The Global Civil Society Yearbook 2003* (London: Centre for the Study of Global Governance, London School of Economics), pp. 1–34.

Goldstein, Joshua (1988) *Long Cycles: Prosperity and War in the Modern Age* (New Haven, CT: Yale University Press).

Gordon, David (1994) '"Twixt cup and the lip": Mainstream Economics and the Formation of Economic Policy', *Social Research* 61:1, pp. 1–29.

Gourevitch, Peter (1978) 'The Second Image Reversed: The International Sources of Domestic Politics', *International Organization* 32:4, pp. 881–912.

Granovetter, Mark (1992) 'Economic Institutions as Social Constructions: A Framework for Analysis', *Acta Sociologica* 35, pp. 3–11.

Gray, John (1998) *False Dawn: The Delusions of Global Capitalism* (London: Granta).

Greider, William (1997) *One World, Ready or Not: The Manic Logic of Global Capitalism* (New York: Simon & Schuster).

Grieco, Joseph M. (1997) 'Systemic Sources of Variation in Regional Institutionalization in Western Europe, East Asia and the Americas', in Edward D. Mansfield and Helen V. Milner (eds) *The Political Economy of Regionalism* (New York: Colombia University Press), pp. 164–88.

Groom, A. J. R. and Dominic Powell (1994) 'From World Politics to Global Governance: A Theme in Need of a Focus', in A. J. R. Groom and Margot Light (eds) *Contemporary International Relations: A Guide to Theory* (London and New York: Pinter), pp. 81–90.

Grote, Jürgen R. and Philippe C. Schmitter (1999) 'The Renaissance of National Corporatism: Unintended Side-effect of European Economic and Monetary Union or Calculated Response to the Absence of European Social Policy?', *Transfer: European Review of Labour and Research* 5:1–2, pp. 34–63.

Grugel, Jean (ed.) (1999) *Democracy Without Borders: Transnationalization and Conditionality in New Democracies* (London: Routledge).

——(2002) *Democratization: A Critical Introduction* (Basingstoke: Palgrave Macmillan).

——(2003a) 'Democratization Studies and Globalization: The Coming of Age of a Paradigm', *British Journal of Politics and International Relations* 5:2, pp. 258–83.

——(2003b) 'Democratization Studies: Globalization, Governance and Citizenship', *Government and Opposition* 38:2, pp. 238–64.

Grugel, Jean and Wil Hout (eds) (1999) *Regionalism Across the North–South Divide: State Strategies and Globalization* (London: Routledge).

Haarløv, Jens (1997) *Regional Co-operation and Integration within Industry and Trade in Southern Africa* (Aldershot: Avebury).

Haas, Ernst B. (1958) *The Uniting of Europe: Political, Social and Economic Forces 1950–57* (Stanford, CA: Stanford University Press).

——(1964) *Beyond the Nation-State: Functionalism and International Organization* (Stanford, CA: Stanford University Press).

——(1967) 'The Uniting of Europe and the Uniting of Latin America', *Journal of Common Market Studies* 5, pp. 315–45.

Haas, Ernst B. and Philippe C. Schmitter (1965) *The Politics of Economics in Latin American Regionalism: The Latin American Free Trade Association after Four Years of Operation* (Denver, CO: University of Denver).

Haas, Peter M. (1992) 'Introduction: Epistemic Communities and International Policy Coordination', *International Organization* 46:1, pp. 1–35.

Haggard, Stephan (2000) *The Political Economy of the Asian Financial Crisis* (Washington, DC: Institute for International Economics).

Haggard, Stephan and Sylvia Maxfield (1996) 'The Political Economy of Financial Internationalization in the Developing World', in Robert O. Keohane and Helen V. Milner (eds) *Internationalization and Domestic Politics* (Cambridge: Cambridge University Press), pp. 209–39.

Haggard, Stephan, Chung Lee and Sylvia Maxfield (eds) (1993) *The Politics of Finance in Developing Countries* (Ithaca, NY: Cornell University Press).

Hall, Derek (2004) 'Japanese Spirit, Western Economics: The Continuing Salience of Economic Nationalism in Japan', *New Political Economy* 9:1, pp. 79–99.

Hall, John (1995) 'In Search of Civil Society', in John Hall (ed.) *Civil Society, Theory, History and Comparison* (Cambridge: Cambridge University Press), pp. 1–31.

Hall, Peter A. (ed.) (1989) *The Political Power of Economic Ideas: Keynesianism Across Nations* (Princeton, NJ: Princeton University Press).

——(1999) 'The Political Economy of Europe in an Era of Interdependence', in Herbert Kitschelt, Peter Lange, Gary Marks and John D. Stephens (eds) *Continuity and Change in Contemporary Capitalism* (Cambridge: Cambridge University Press), pp. 135–63.

Hall, Peter A. and David W. Soskice (2001a) 'An Introduction to Varieties of Capitalism', in Peter A. Hall and David Soskice (eds) *Varieties of Capitalism: The Institutional Foundations of Comparative Advantage* (Oxford: Oxford University Press), pp. 1–68.

——(eds) (2001b) *Varieties of Capitalism: The Institutional Foundations of Comparative Advantage* (New York: Oxford University Press).

Hall, Rodney Bruce and Thomas J. Biersteker (eds) (2002) *The Emergence of Private Authority in Global Governance* (Cambridge: Cambridge University Press).

Halliday, Fred (1986) *The Making of the Second Cold War* (London: Verso).

Hansen, Roger (1969) 'Regional Integration: Reflections on a Decade of Theorising', *World Politics* 21:2, pp. 242–56.

Haq, Mahbub ul, Richard Jolly, Paul Streeten and Khadija Haq (eds) (1995) *The UN and the Bretton Woods Institutions* (London: Macmillan).

Harbeson, John (2000) 'Externally-Assisted Democratization: Theoretical Issues and African Realities', in John Harbeson and Donald Rothchild (eds) *Africa in World Politics: The African State System in Flux* (Boulder, CO: Westview Press), pp. 235–59.

Hardin, Garrett (1968) 'The Tragedy of the Commons', *Science* 162, pp. 1243–8.

Hardt, Michael and Antonio Negri (2000) *Empire* (Cambridge, MA: Harvard University Press).

Harrison, Graham (2001) 'Post-Conditionality Politics and Administrative Reform: Reflections on the Cases of Uganda and Tanzania', *Development and Change* 32:4, pp. 657–81.

——(2004) 'Introduction: Globalisation, Governance and Development', *New Political Economy* 9:2, pp. 155–62.

Harvey, David (2003) *The New Imperialism* (Oxford: Oxford University Press).

Hasenclever, Andreas, Peter Mayer and Volker Rittberger (1997) *Theories of International Regimes* (Cambridge: Cambridge University Press).

Hay, Colin (1999) 'Marxism and the State', in Andrew Gamble, David Marsh and Tony Tant (eds) *Marxism and Social Science* (London: Macmillan), pp. 152–74.

——(2000a) 'Contemporary Capitalism, Globalisation, Regionalisation and the Persistence of National Variation', *Review of International Studies* 26, pp. 509–31.

——(2000b) 'Globalization, Social Democracy and the Persistence of Partisan Politics: A Commentary on Garrett', *Review of International Political Economy* 7:1, pp. 138–52.

——(2004a) 'Common Trajectories, Variable Paces, Divergent Outcomes? Models of European Capitalism under Conditions of Complex Economic Interdependence', *Review of International Political Economy* 11:2, pp. 231–62.

——(2004b) 'Re-Stating Politics, Re-Politicising the State: Neoliberalism, Economic Imperatives and the Rise of the Competition State', in Tony Wright and Andrew Gamble (eds) *Restating the State?*, Special Issue of *The Political Quarterly*.

——(2005) 'Globalisation's Impact on States', in John Ravenhill (ed.) *Global Political Economy* (Oxford: Oxford University Press), pp. 235–62.

Hay, Colin and David Marsh (1999a) 'Introduction: Towards a New (International) Political Economy', *New Political Economy* 4:1, pp. 5–22.

——(eds) (1999b) *Demystifying Globalisation* (London: Macmillan).

Hay, Colin and Ben Rosamond (2002) 'Globalization, European Integration and the Discursive Construction of Economic Imperatives', *Journal of European Public Policy* 9:2, pp. 147–67.

Hay, Colin and Matthew Watson (1999) 'Globalisation: 'Sceptical' Notes on the 1999 Reith Lectures', *The Political Quarterly* 70:4, pp. 418–25.

Heilbroner, Robert L. (1985) *The Nature and Logic of Capitalism* (New York: W. W. Norton).

Held, David (1995) *Democracy and Global Order: From the Modern State to Cosmopolitan Governance* (Cambridge: Polity Press).

——(1996) *Models of Democracy*, second edition (Cambridge: Polity Press).

——(1999) 'The Transformation of Political Community', in Ian Shapiro and Casiano Hacker-Cordón (eds) *Democracy's Edges* (Cambridge: Cambridge University Press), pp. 226–36.

——(2004) *Global Covenant: The Social Democratic Alternative to the Washington Consensus* (Cambridge: Polity).

Held, David, Anthony McGrew, David Goldblatt and Jonathan Perraton (1999) *Global Transformations: Politics, Economics and Culture* (Stanford, CA: Stanford University Press).

Helleiner, Eric (1994) *States and the Re-emergence of Global Finance: From Bretton Woods to the 1990s* (Ithaca, NY: Cornell University Press).

Henderson, Jeffrey, Peter Dicken, Martin Hess, Neil Coe and Henry Wai-Chung Yeung (2002) 'Global Production Networks and the Analysis of Economic Development', *Review of International Political Economy* 9:3, pp. 436–64.

Henning, C. Randall (1994) *Currencies and Politics in the US, Germany, and Japan* (Washington, DC: Institute for International Economics).

Henriksen, Alan (1995) 'The Growth of Regional Organizations and the Role of the United Nations', in Louise Fawcett and Andrew Hurrell (eds) *Regionalism in World Politics: Regional Organization and International Order* (Oxford: Oxford University Press), pp. 122–68.

Hentz, James J. and Morten Bøås (eds) (2002) *New and Critical Security and Regionalism: Beyond the Nation State* (Aldershot: Ashgate).

Heron, Tony (2004a) 'Commodity Chains and Global Capitalism: A Theoretical Critique', mimeo, University of Sheffield.

——(2004b) 'Regionalisation Across the North–South Divide? EU Trade Preferences, Outward Processing and the Mediterranean Rim', paper presented at the annual workshop of the BISA International Political Economy Group, 11 June.

Hettne, Björn (1990) 'The Contemporary Crisis: The Rise of Reciprocity', in Kari Polanyi-Levitt (ed.) *The Life and Works of Karl Polanyi* (Montreal: Black Rose Books), pp. 121–30.

——(1993) 'Neo-Mercantilism: The Pursuit of Regionness', *Cooperation and Conflict* 28:3, pp. 211–32.

——(1994) 'The New Regionalism: Implications for Development and Peace', in Björn Hettne and András Inotai (eds) *The New Regionalism: Implications for Global Development and International Security* (Helsinki: UNU/WIDER), pp. 1–49.

——(1995a) *Development Theory and the Three Worlds: Towards an International Political Economy of Development* (London: Longman).

——(1995b) 'Introduction: The International Political Economy of Transformation', in Björn Hettne (ed.) *International Political Economy: Understanding Global Disorder* (London: Zed Press), pp. 3–30.

——(1997a) 'The Double Movement: Global Market versus Regionalism', in Robert W. Cox (ed.) *The New Realism: Perspectives on Multilateralism and World Order* (Tokyo: United Nations University Press), pp. 223–44.

——(1997b) 'Development, Security and World Order: A Regionalist Approach', *European Journal of Development Research* 9:1, pp. 83–106.

——(1999) 'Globalization and the New Regionalism: The Second Great Transformation', in Björn Hettne, András Inotai and Osvaldo Sunkel (eds) *Globalism and the New Regionalism* (London: Macmillan), pp. 1–24.

——(2003) 'The New Regionalism Revisited', in Fredrik Söderbaum and Timothy M. Shaw (eds) *Theories of New Regionalism: A Palgrave Reader* (Basingstoke: Palgrave Macmillan), pp. 22–42.

Hettne, Björn and Fredrik Söderbaum (2000) 'Theorizing the Rise of Regionness', *New Political Economy* 5:3, pp. 457–73.

Hettne, Björn, András Inotai and Osvaldo Sunkel (eds) (1999) *Globalism and the New Regionalism* (London: Macmillan).

——(eds) (2000a) *National Perspectives on the New Regionalism in the North* (Basingstoke: Palgrave Macmillan).

——(eds) (2000b) *National Perspectives on the New Regionalism in the South* (Basingstoke: Palgrave Macmillan).

——(eds) (2000c) *The New Regionalism and the Future of Security and Development* (Basingstoke: Palgrave Macmillan).

——(2001) *Comparing Regionalisms: Implications for Global Development* (Basingstoke: Palgrave Macmillan).

Hettne, Björn, Anthony Payne and Fredrik Söderbaum (eds) (1999) *Rethinking Development Theory*, Special Issue, *Journal of International Relations and Development* 2:4.

Hewison, Kevin (2001) *Nationalism, Populism, Dependency: Old Ideas for a New Southeast Asia?*, Working Paper Series, No. 4, City University of Hong Kong.

Hewson, Martin and Timothy J. Sinclair (1999) 'The Emergence of Global Governance Theory', in Martin Hewson and Timothy J. Sinclair (eds) *Approaches to Global Governance Theory* (Albany, NY: State University of New York Press), pp. 3–22.

Higgott, Richard (1998) 'The Asian Economic Crisis: A Study in the Politics of Resentment', *New Political Economy* 3:3, pp. 333–56.

——(1999) Economics, Politics and (International) Political Economy: The Need for a Balanced Diet in an Era of Globalisation', *New Political Economy* 4:1, pp. 23–36.

Hirst, Paul and Grahame Thompson (1999) *Globalization in Question: The International Economy and the Possibilities of Governance*, second edition (Cambridge: Polity Press).

——(2000) 'Globalization in One Country? The Peculiarities of the British', *Economy and Society* 29:3, pp. 335–56.

Hobden, Stephen (1998) *International Relations and Historical Sociology* (London: Routledge).

Hobden, Stephen and John M. Hobson (eds) (2001) *Historical Sociology of International Relations* (Cambridge: Cambridge University Press).

Hobsbawm, Eric (1987) *The Age of Empire, 1875–1914* (London: Weidenfeld & Nicolson).

Hobson, John M. (1997) *The Wealth of States: A Comparative Sociology of International Economic and Political Change* (Cambridge: Cambridge University Press).

——(1998) 'The Historical Sociology of the State and the State of Historical Sociology in International Relations', *Review of International Political Economy* 5:2, pp. 284–320.

——(2000) *The State and International Relations* (Cambridge: Cambridge University Press).

Hobson, John M. and Mark Ramesh (2002) 'Globalisation Makes of States What States Make of It: Between Agency and Structure on the State/Globalisation Debate', *New Political Economy* 7:1, pp. 5–22.

Hoffman, Stanley J. (1977) 'An American Social Science: International Relations', *Daedalus* 106:3, pp. 41–60.

Hollingsworth, J. Rogers and Robert Boyer (eds) (1997a) *Contemporary Capitalism: The Embeddedness of Institutions* (Cambridge: Cambridge University Press), pp. 1–54.

——(1997b) 'Coordination of Economic Actors and Social Systems of Production', in J. Rogers Hollingsworth and Robert Boyer (eds) *Contemporary Capitalism: The Embeddedness of Institutions* (Cambridge: Cambridge University Press), pp. 1–47.

Holloway, John (1994) 'Global Capital and the National State', *Capital and Class* 52, pp. 23–49.

Holsti, Kalevi J. (1985) *The Dividing Discipline: Hegemony and Diversity in International Theory* (London: Allen & Unwin).

Hongyi, Harry Lai (2001) 'Behind China's World Trade Agreement with the USA', *Third World Quarterly* 22:2, pp. 237–55.

Hood, Christopher (1991) 'A Public Management for All Seasons?', *Public Administration* 69, pp. 3–19.

Hooghe, Liesbet and Gary Marks (2001) *Multi-level Governance and European Integration* (Lanham, MD: Rowman & Littlefield).

Hoogvelt, Ankie (2001) *Globalization and the Postcolonial World: The New Political Economy of Development*, second edition (Basingstoke: Palgrave Macmillan).

Hook, Glenn and Ian Kearns (eds) (1999) *Subregionalism and World Order* (London: Macmillan).

Huber, Evelyn, Dietrich Rueschemeyer and John Stephens (1997) 'The Paradoxes of Contemporary Democracy: Formal Participatory and Social Dimensions', *Comparative Politics* 29:3, pp. 323–42.

Hunt, E. K. (1979) *History of Economic Thought: A Critical Perspective* (Belmont, CA: Wadsworth).

Huntington, Samuel P. (1968) *Political Order in Changing Societies* (New Haven, CT: Yale University Press).

——(1991) *The Third Wave: Democratization in the Late Twentieth Century* (Norman, OK: University of Oklahoma Press).

Hurrell, Andrew (1995) 'Regionalism in Theoretical Perspective', in Louise Fawcett and Andrew Hurrell (eds) *Regionalism in World Politics: Regional Organization and International Order* (Oxford: Oxford University Press), pp. 9–73.

Hurrell, Andrew and Ngaire Woods (1995) 'Globalisation and Inequality', *Millennium: Journal of International Studies* 24:3, pp. 447–70.

——(eds) (1999) *Inequality, Globalization and World Politics* (Oxford: Oxford University Press).

Hutchings, Kimberley (2000) 'Modelling Democracy', in Hazel Smith (ed.) *Democracy and International Relations: Critical Theories/Problematic Practices* (Basingstoke: Palgrave Macmillan), pp. 31–50.

Hveem, Helge (1999) 'Political Regionalism: Master or Servant of Economic Internationalization?', in Björn Hettne, András Inotai and Osvaldo Sunkel (eds) *Globalism and the New Regionalism* (London: Macmillan), pp. 85–115.

IMF (International Monetary Fund) (1997) *World Economic Outlook: May 1997* (Washington, DC: IMF).

——(2000) *Country Experiences with the Use and Liberalization of Capital Controls* (Washington, DC: IMF).

——(2001) *World Economic Outlook* database, at http://www.imf.org/external/pubs/ft/weo/2001/03/data/index.htm#1.

Jackson, Robert H. (1990) *Quasi-States: Sovereignty, International Relations and the Third World* (Cambridge: Cambridge University Press).

Jackson, Robert H. and Alan James (eds) (1993) *States in a Changing World: A Contemporary Analysis* (Oxford: Oxford University Press).

James, Paul (1997) 'Postdependency? The Third World in an Era of Globalism and Late-Capitalism', *Alternatives* 22:2, pp. 205–26.

Jayasuriya, Kanishka (2001) 'Globalisation and the Changing Architecture of the State: Regulatory State and the Politics of Negative Coordination', *Journal of European Public Policy* 8:1, pp. 101–23.

——(ed.) (2004) *Asian Regional Governance: Crisis and Change* (London: Routledge).

Jessop, Bob (2002) *The Future of the Capitalist State* (Cambridge: Polity Press).

Johnson, Chalmers (1982) *MITI and the Japanese Miracle: The Growth of Industrial Policy, 1925–1975* (Stanford, CA: Stanford University Press).

——(2004) *The Sorrows of Empire: Militarism, Secrecy, and the End of the Republic* (New York: Metropolitan Books).

Johnson, R. Barry and Natalia T. Tamirisa (1998) *Why Do Countries Use Capital Controls?*, IMF Working Papers, WP/98/181, December.

Johnson, Simon and Todd Mitton (2001) 'Cronyism and Capital Controls: Evidence from Malaysia', unpublished paper, 20 August.

Johnston, José and Gordon Laxer (2003) 'Solidarity in the Age of Globalization: Lessons from the Anti-MAI and Zapatista Struggles', *Theory and Society* 32:1, pp. 39–91.

Jönsson, Christer, Sven Tägil and Gunnar Törnqvist (2000) *Organizing European Space* (London: Sage).

Jørgensen, Knud Erik (2003) 'Towards a Six-Continents Social Science: International Relations', *Journal of International Relations and Development* 6:4, pp. 330–43.

Kahler, Miles (1990) 'Orthodoxy and its Alternatives: Explaining Approaches to Stabilization and Adjustment', in Joan Nelson (ed.) *Economic Crisis and Policy Choice: The Politics of Adjustment in the Third World* (Princeton, NJ: Princeton University Press), pp. 33–61.

——(2000) 'The New International Financial Architecture and Its Limits', in Gregory Noble and John Ravenhill (eds) *The Asian Financial Crisis and the Structure of Global Finance* (Cambridge: Cambridge University Press), pp. 235–60.

Kahler, Miles and David A. Lake (eds) (2003) *Governance in a Global Economy: Political Authority in Transition* (Princeton, NJ: Princeton University Press).

Kaldor, Mary (2000a) 'Transnational Civil Society', in Tim Dunne and Nicholas J. Wheeler (eds) *Human Rights in Global Politics* (Cambridge: Cambridge University Press), pp. 195–213.

——(2000b) 'Civilising Globalisation? The Implications of the "Battle in Seattle"', *Millennium: Journal of International Studies* 29:1, pp. 105–14.

Kaldor, Mary and Ivan Vejvoda (1997) 'Democratization in Central and East European Countries', *International Affairs* 73:1, pp. 59–82.

Kaplan, Ethan and Dani Rodrik (2001) *Did the Malaysian Capital Controls Work?*, NBER Working Papers, No. 8142, February.

Kaplinsky, Raphael (2000) 'Globalisation and Unequalisation: What Can Be Learned from Value Chain Analysis?', *Journal of Development Studies* 37:2, pp. 117–46.

Kapstein, Ethan B. (1994) *Governing the Global Economy* (Cambridge, MA: Harvard University Press).

Katzenstein, Peter J. (1985) *Small States in World Markets: Industrial Policy in Europe* (Ithaca, NY: Cornell University Press).

Katzenstein, Peter J. and Yutaka Tsujinaka (1995) '"Bulling", "Buying", and "Binding": US–Japanese Transnational Relations and Domestic Structures', in Thomas Risse-Kappen (ed.) *Bringing Transnational Relations Back In* (Cambridge: Cambridge University Press), pp. 79–111.

Kaul, Inge, Isabelle Grunberg and Marc A. Stern (eds) (1999) *Global Public Goods: International Cooperation in the 21st Century* (New York: Oxford University Press for the United Nations Development Programme).

Keane, John (2003) *Global Civil Society?* (Cambridge: Cambridge University Press).

Kearns, Ian and Glenn Hook (1999) 'Conclusion: Subregionalism – An Assessment', in Glenn Hook and Ian Kearns (eds) *Subregionalism and World Order* (London: Macmillan), pp. 247–58.

Keck, Margaret and Kathryn Sikkink (1998) *Activists Beyond Borders: Advocacy Networks in International Politics* (Ithaca, NY: Cornell University Press).

Keohane, Robert O. (1984) *After Hegemony: Cooperation and Discord in the World Political Economy* (Princeton, NJ: Princeton University Press).

Keohane, Robert O. and Joseph S. Nye (eds) (1972) *Transnational Relations and World Politics* (Cambridge, MA: Harvard University Press).

——(1977) *Power and Interdependence* (Boston, MA: Little, Brown).

——(1987) '*Power and Interdependence* Revisited', *International Organization* 41:4, pp. 725–53.

——(2000) 'Globalization: What's New? What's Not? And So What?', *Foreign Policy* 118, pp. 104–19.

Khagram, Sanjeev, James V. Riker and Kathryn Sikkink (eds) *Restructuring World Politics: Transnational Social Movements, Networks, and Norms* (Minneapolis, MN: University of Minnesota Press).

Khilnani, Sunil (2001) 'The Development of Civil Society', in Sudipta Kaviraj and Sunil Khilnani (eds) *Civil Society: History and Possibilities* (Cambridge: Cambridge University Press), pp. 11–32.

Kickert, Walter J. M. (1997) 'Public Governance in the Netherlands: An Alternative to Anglo-American "Managerialism"', *Public Administration* 75:4, pp. 731–52.

Kindleberger, Charles P. (1986) *The World in Depression 1929–39* (Berkeley, CA: University of California Press).

King, Alexander and Bertrand Schneider (1991) *The First Global Revolution: A Report by the Council of the Club of Rome* (New York: Simon & Schuster).

Kitching, Gavin (2001) *Seeking Social Justice through Globalization: Escaping a Nationalist Perspective* (University Park, PA: Penn State University Press).

Kitschelt, Herbert, Peter Lange, Gary Marks and John D. Stephens (eds) (1999) *Continuity and Change in Contemporary Capitalism* (Cambridge: Cambridge University Press).

Kooiman, Jan (1993) 'Findings, Speculations and Recommendations', in Jan Kooiman (ed.) *Modern Governance* (London: Sage), pp. 249–62.

Kopecky, Petr and Cas Mudde (2000) 'What Has Eastern Europe Taught Us about the Democratization Literature (and vice versa)?', *European Journal of Political Research* 37:4, pp. 517–39.

Krasner, Stephen D. (ed.) (1983) *International Regimes* (Ithaca, NY: Cornell University Press).

——(1994) 'International Political Economy: Abiding Discord', *Review of International Political Economy* 1:1, pp. 13–19.

——(1995) 'Power Politics, Institutions, and Transnational Relations', in Thomas Risse-Kappen (ed.) *Bringing Transnational Relations Back In* (Cambridge: Cambridge University Press), pp. 257–79.

——(1999) *Sovereignty: Organized Hypocrisy* (Princeton, NJ: Princeton University Press).

——(ed.) (2001) *Problematic Sovereignty: Contested Rules and Political Possibilities* (New York: Columbia University Press).

Krugman, Paul (1999) *The Return of Depression Economics* (New York: W. W. Norton).

Kurtz, Marcus (2001) 'State Developmentalism Without a Developmental State: The Public Foundations of the "Free Market Miracle" in Chile', *Latin American Politics and Society* 43:2, pp. 1–25.

Kurzer, Paulette (1993) *Business and Banking: Political Change and Economic Integration in Western Europe* (Ithaca, NY: Cornell University Press).

Kymlicka, Will (1999) 'Citizenship in an Era of Globalization: Commentary on Held', in Ian Shapiro and Casiano Hacker-Cordón (eds) *Democracy's Edges* (Cambridge: Cambridge University Press), pp. 112–26.

Lake, David A. (2003) 'The New Sovereignty in International Relations', *International Studies Review* 5:3, pp. 303–23.

Lambert, Rob and Eddie Webster (2003) 'Transnational Union Strategies for Civilizing Labour Standards', in Richard Sandbrook (ed.) *Civilizing Globalization: A Survival Guide* (Albany, NY: State University of New York Press), pp. 221–35.

Latham, Robert (1997) *The Liberal Moment: Modernity, Security, and the Making of Postwar International Order* (New York: Columbia University Press).

Lavigne, Marie (1995) *The Economics of Transition: From Socialist Economy to Market Economy* (London: Macmillan).

Leftwich, Adrian (1994) 'Governance, the State and the Politics of Development', *Development and Change* 25:2, pp. 363–86.

——(2000) *States of Development: On the Primacy of Politics in Development* (Cambridge: Polity).

Levi, Margaret (1981) 'The Predatory Theory of Rule', *Politics and Society* 10:4, pp. 431–63.

——(1989) *Of Rule and Revenue* (Berkeley, CA: University of California Press).

Lindblom, Charles E. (1977) *Politics and Markets: The World's Political and Economic Systems* (New York: Basic Books).

Lipschutz, Ronnie D. (1992) 'Reconstructing World Politics: The Emergence of Global Civil Society', *Millennium: Journal of International Studies* 21:3, pp. 389–420.

Lipset, Seymour Martin (1959) 'Some Social Requisites of Democracy: Economic Development and Political Legitimacy', *American Political Science Review* 53:1, pp. 69–105.

Lodge, George C. and Ezra F. Vogel. (eds) (1987) *Ideology and National Competitiveness* (Boston, MA: Harvard Business School).

Loriaux, Michael (ed.) (1996) *Capital Ungoverned: Liberalizing Finance in Interventionist States* (Ithaca, NY: Cornell University Press).

Luckham, Robin, Anne Marie Goetz and Mary Kaldor (with Alison Ayers, Sunil Bastian, Emmanuel Gyimah-Boadi, Shireen Hassim and Zarko Puhovski) (2001) *Democratic Institutions and Politics in Contexts of Inequality, Poverty and Conflict*, IDS Working Paper 104, University of Sussex.

Lukes, Steven (1974) *Power: A Radical View* (London: Macmillan).

Luttwak, Edward N. (1990) 'From Geopolitics to Geo-economics', *The National Interest* 20, pp. 17–23.

McGinnis, Michael D. (1999) 'Rent-seeking, Redistribution, and Reform in the Governance of Global Markets', in Aseem Prakash and Jeffrey A. Hart (eds) *Globalization and Governance* (London: Routledge), pp. 54–76.

McGowan, Francis and Helen Wallace (1996) 'Towards a European Regulatory State', *Journal of European Public Policy* 3:4, pp. 560–76.

McMichael, Philip (2000) *Development and Social Change: A Global Perspective*, second edition (Thousand Oaks, CA: Pine Forge).

Macpherson, C. B. (1977) *The Life and Times of Liberal Democracy* (Oxford: Oxford University Press).

Mahoney, James (2000) 'Path Dependence and Historical Sociology', *Theory and Society* 29, pp. 507–48.

Mann, Michael (1993) *The Sources of Social Power, Volume 2: The Rise of Classes and Nation States, 1760–1914* (Cambridge: Cambridge University Press).

——(1997) 'Has Globalization Ended the Rise and Rise of the Nation-State?', *Review of International Political Economy* 4:3, pp. 472–96.

——(2003) *Incoherent Empire* (London: Verso).

Mansfield, Edward D. and Rachel Bronson (1997) 'The Political Economy of Major-Power Trade Flows', in Edward D. Mansfield and Helen V. Milner (eds) *The Political Economy of Regionalism* (New York: Columbia University Press), pp. 188–208.

Mansfield, Edward D. and Helen V. Milner (eds) (1997) *The Political Economy of Regionalism* (New York: Colombia University Press).

Manzetti, Luigi (2002) *The Argentine Implosion*, North–South Agenda Papers, No. 59, North–South Center, University of Miami, November.

Marchand, Marianne H., Morten Bøås and Timothy M. Shaw (1999) 'The Political Economy of New Regionalisms', in Morten Bøås, Marianne H. Marchand and Timothy M. Shaw (eds) *New Regionalisms in the New Millennium*, Special Issue, *Third World Quarterly* 20:5, pp. 897–910.

Marks, Gary, Liesbet Hooghe and Kermit Blank (1996) 'European Integration from the 1980s: State-Centric v. Multilevel Governance', *Journal of Common Market Studies* 34:3, pp. 341–78.

Martell, Luke (2001) *Capitalism, Globalisation and Democracy: Does Social Democracy Have a Role?*, available at www.theglobalsite.ac.uk.

Mastanduno, Michael (2000) 'Models, Markets, and Power: Political Economy and the Asia-Pacific, 1989–1999', *Review of International Studies* 26:4, pp. 493–507.

Mattli, Walter (1999) *The Logic of Regional Integration: Europe and Beyond* (Cambridge: Cambridge University Press).

Maxfield, Sylvia (1990) *Governing Capital: International Finance and Mexican Politics* (Ithaca, NY: Cornell University Press).

——(1991) 'Bankers' Alliances and Economic Policy Patterns: Evidence from Mexico and Brazil', *Comparative Political Studies* 23:4, pp. 419–58.

——(1997) *Gatekeepers of Growth: The International Political Economy of Central Banking in Developing Countries* (Princeton, NJ: Princeton University Press).

——(1998) 'Understanding the Political Implications of Financial Internationalization in Emerging Market Countries', *World Development* 26:7, pp. 1201–19.

Mayall, James (2000) 'Democracy and International Society', *International Affairs* 76:1, pp. 61–75.

Mayntz, Renate (1993) 'Governing Failures and the Problem of Governability', in Jan Kooiman (ed.) *Modern Governance* (London: Sage), pp. 9–20.

Médard, Jean-François (1982) 'The Underdeveloped State in Tropical Africa: Political Clientelism or Neo-patrimonialism?', in Christopher

Clapham (ed.) *Private Patronage and Public Power: Political Clientelism in the Modern State* (London: Pinter), pp. 177–92.

Meesook, Kanitta, Il Houng Lee, Olin Liu, Yougesh Khatri, Natalia Tamirisa, Michael Moore and Mark H. Krysl (2001) *Malaysia: From Crisis to Recovery*, IMF Occasional Papers, No. 207, 27 August.

Michie, Jonathan and John Grieve Smith (eds) (1999) *Global Instability: The Political Economy of World Economic Governance* (London: Routledge).

Migdal, Joel (1988) *Strong Societies and Weak States: State–Society Relations and State Capitalism in the Third World* (Princeton, NJ: Princeton University Press).

——(2001) *State in Society: Studying How States and Societies Transform and Constitute One Another* (Cambridge: Cambridge University Press).

Migdal, Joel, Atul Kohli and Vivienne Shue (eds) (1994) *State Power and Social Forces: Domination and Transformation in the Third World* (Cambridge: Cambridge University Press).

Milliken, Jennifer and Keith Krause (2002) 'State Failure, State Collapse, and State Reconstruction: Concepts, Lessons and Strategies', *Development and Change* 33:5, pp. 753–74.

Milner, Helen V. (1997a) *Interests, Institutions, and Information* (Princeton, NJ: Princeton University Press).

——(1997b) 'Industries, Governments, and the Creation of Regional Trade Blocs', in Edward D. Mansfield and Helen V. Milner (eds) *The Political Economy of Regionalism* (New York: Colombia University Press), pp. 77–106.

Milner, Helen V. and Robert O. Keohane (1996) 'Internationalization and Domestic Politics: A Conclusion', in Robert O. Keohane and Helen V. Milner (eds) *Internationalization and Domestic Politics* (Cambridge: Cambridge University Press), pp. 243–58.

Mistry, Percy S. (2000) 'Regional Integration and Economic Development', in Björn Hettne, András Inotai and Osvaldo Sunkel (eds) *The New Regionalism and the Future of Security and Development* (Basingstoke: Palgrave Macmillan), pp. 26–50.

Mitrany, David (1966) *A Working Peace System* (Chicago, IL: Quadrangle Books).

Mittelman, James H. (1999) 'Rethinking the New Regionalism in the Context of Globalization', in Björn Hettne, András Inotai and Osvaldo Sunkel (eds) *Globalism and the New Regionalism* (London: Macmillan), pp. 25–53.

——(2000) *The Globalization Syndrome: Transformation and Resistance* (Princeton, NJ: Princeton University Press).

——(2004) 'What Is Critical Globalization Studies?', *International Studies Perspectives* 5:3, pp. 219–30.

Moore, Mick (2002) '"Bad Governance" or the Underdevelopment of Political Underdevelopment?', paper presented at the conference 'Towards a New Political Economy of Development: Globalisation and Governance', Political Economy Research Centre, University of Sheffield, 4–6 July.

Moran, Michael (2003) *The British Regulatory State: High Modernism and Hyper-Innovation* (Oxford: Oxford University Press).

Moravcsik, Andrew (1998) *The Choice for Europe: Social Purpose and State Power from Messina to Maastricht* (Ithaca, NY: Cornell University Press).

Morton, Adam (2002) 'La Resurreción del Maíz: Globalisation, Resistance and the Zapatistas', *Millennium: Journal of International Studies* 31:1, pp. 27–54.

——(2003) 'Structural Change and Neoliberalism in Mexico: "Passive Revolution" in the Global Political Economy', *Third World Quarterly* 24:4, pp. 631–53.

——(2004) 'New Follies on the State of Globalisation Debate?', review article, *Review of International Studies* 30:1, pp. 133–47.

Morton, Adam David and Pinar Bilgin (2004) 'From "Rogue" to "Failed" States? The Fallacy of Short-termism', *Politics* 24:3, pp. 169–80.

Mosley, Layna (2003) *Global Capital and National Governments* (Cambridge: Cambridge University Press).

Muñoz Gomá, Oscar (ed.) (1996) *Después de las Privatizaciones: Hacia el Estado Regulador* (Santiago: CIEPLAN/Dolmen Ediciones).

Murphy, Craig N. (1994) *International Organization and Industrial Change: Global Governance since 1850* (Cambridge: Polity Press).

——(2000) 'Global Governance: Poorly Done and Poorly Understood', *International Affairs* 76:4, pp. 789–803.

——(ed.) (2003) *Egalitarian Politics in the Age of Globalization* (Basingstoke: Palgrave Macmillan).

Murphy, Craig N. and Douglas R. Nelson (2001) 'International Political Economy: A Tale of Two Heterodoxies', *British Journal of Politics and International Relations* 3:3, pp. 393–412.

Mussa, Michael (2002) 'Argentina and the Fund: From Triumph to Tragedy', Institute of International Economics, 25 March, from http://www.iie.com.

Myrdal, Gunnar (1968) *Asian Drama: An Inquiry into the Poverty of Nations*, 3 volumes (New York: Pantheon).

Nagle, John and Alison Mahr (1999) *Democracy and Democratization: Post-Communist Europe in Comparative Perspective* (London: Sage).

Nelson, Paul (1995) *The World Bank and Non-Governmental Organizations: The Limits of Apolitical Development* (London: Macmillan).

Neumann, Stephanie (ed.) (1998) *International Relations Theory and the Third World* (London: Macmillan).

Niskanen, William A. (1971) *Bureaucracy and Representative Government* (Chicago, IL: Aldine Atherton).

Nordlinger, Eric A. (1981) *On the Autonomy of the Democratic State* (Cambridge, MA: Harvard University Press).

North, Douglass (1990) 'Institutions and Their Consequences for Economic Performance', in Karen S. Cook and Margaret Levi (eds) *The Limits of Rationality* (Chicago, IL: Chicago University Press), pp. 383–401.

North, Douglass C. and Robert P. Thomas (1973) *The Rise of the Western World: A New Economic History* (Cambridge: Cambridge University Press).

Nye, Joseph (1965) *Pan-Africanism and the East African Integration* (Cambridge: Cambridge University Press).

——(1971) *Peace in Parts: Integration and Conflict in Regional Organization* (Boston, MA: Little, Brown).

——(1990) *Bound to Lead: The Changing Nature of American Power* (New York: Basic Books).

——(2004) *Soft Power: The Means to Success in World Politics* (New York: PublicAffairs Ltd).

Oatley, Thomas and Robert Nabors (1998) 'Market Failure, Wealth Transfers, and the Basle Accord', *International Organization* 52:1, pp. 35–54.

O'Brien, Robert (1995) 'International Political Economy and International Relations: Apprentice or Teacher?', in John MacMillan and Andrew Linklater (eds) *Boundaries in Question: New Directions in International Relations* (London: Pinter), pp. 89–106.

——(2000a) 'Workers and World Order: The Tentative Transformation of the International Union Movement', *Review of International Studies* 26:4, pp. 533–56.

——(2000b) 'Labour and IPE: Rediscovering Human Agency', in Ronen Palan (ed.) *Global Political Economy: Contemporary Theories* (London: Routledge), pp. 89–99.

——(2004) 'Continuing Incivility: Labor Rights in a Global Economy', *Journal of Human Rights* 3:2, pp. 203–14.

O'Brien, Robert, Anne Marie Goetz, Jan Aart Scholte and Marc Williams (2000) *Contesting Global Governance: Multilateral Economic Institutions and Global Social Movements* (Cambridge: Cambridge University Press).

Odell, John S. (2002) 'Bounded Rationality and the World Political Economy', in David M. Andrews, C. Randall Henning and Louis W. Pauly (eds) *Governing the World's Money* (Ithaca, NY: Cornell University Press), pp. 168–93.

O'Donnell, Guillermo (1973) *Modernization and Bureaucratic-Authoritarianism: Studies in South American Politics* (Berkeley, CA: University of California Press).

Ohmae, Kenichi (1990) *The Borderless World: Power and Strategy in the Interlinked Economy* (London: HarperCollins).

——(1995) *The End of the Nation State: The Rise of the Regional Economies* (London: HarperCollins).

Olsen, Gorm Rye (1998) 'Europe and the Promotion of Democracy in Post-Cold War Africa: How Serious is Europe and for What Reason?', *African Affairs* 97, pp. 343–67.

Olson, Mancur (1971) *The Logic of Collective Action* (Cambridge, MA: Harvard University Press).

Orrù, Marco, Nicole Woolsey Biggart and Gary G. Hamilton (1991) 'Organizational Isomorphism in East Asia', in Walter W. Powell and Paul J. DiMaggio (eds) *The New Institutionalism in Organizational Analysis* (Chicago, IL: University of Chicago Press), pp. 361–89.

Osborne, David and Ted Gaebler (1992) *Reinventing Government* (Reading, MA: Addison-Wesley).

Osiander, Andreas (2001) 'Sovereignty, International Relations, and the Westphalian Myth', *International Organization* 55:2, pp. 251–87.

Padoan, Pier Carlo (2001) 'Political Economy of New Regionalism and World Governance', in Mario Telò (ed.) *European Union and New Regionalism: Regional Actors and Global Governance in a Post-hegemonic Era* (Aldershot: Ashgate), pp. 39–58.

Page, Sheila (2000) *Regionalism in the Developing Countries* (Basingstoke: Palgrave Macmillan).

Palan, Ronen and Jason Abbott with Phil Deans (1996) *State Strategies in the Global Political Economy* (London: Pinter).

Panitch, Leo (1996) 'Rethinking the Role of the State', in James H. Mittelman (ed.) *Globalization: Critical Reflections* (Boulder, CO: Lynne Rienner), pp. 83–113.

——(2000) 'The New Imperial State', *New Left Review* 2, pp. 5–20.

Pantojas-García, E. (2001) 'Trade Liberalization and Peripheral Postindustrialization in the Caribbean', *Latin American Politics and Society* 43:1, pp. 57–77.

Pateman, Carole (1970) *Participation and Democratic Theory* (Cambridge: Cambridge University Press).

Pauly, Louis (1997) *Who Elected the Bankers? Surveillance and Control in the World Economy* (Ithaca, NY: Cornell University Press).

Payne, Anthony (1998) 'The New Political Economy of Area Studies', *Millennium: Journal of International Studies* 27:2, pp. 253–73.

——(1999) 'Reframing the Global Politics of Development', *Journal of International Relations and Development* 2:4, pp. 369–79.

——(2000) 'Globalization and Modes of Regionalist Governance', in Jon Pierre (ed.) *Debating Governance: Authority, Steering, and Democracy* (Oxford: Oxford University Press), pp. 201–18.

——(ed.) (2004) *The New Regional Politics of Development* (Basingstoke: Palgrave Macmillan).

——(2005 forthcoming) *The Global Politics of Unequal Development* (Basingstoke: Palgrave Macmillan).

Payne, Anthony and Andrew Gamble (1996) 'Introduction: The Political Economy of Regionalism and World Order', in Andrew Gamble and Anthony Payne (eds) *Regionalism and World Order* (London: Macmillan), pp. 1–20.

Payne, Anthony and Paul Sutton (eds) (1993) *Size and Survival: Politics of Security in the Small Island and Enclave Developing States of the Caribbean and the Pacific* (London: Frank Cass).

——(2001) *Charting Caribbean Development* (Basingstoke: Palgrave Macmillan).

Perina, Rubén (ed.) (1985) *El Estudio de las Relaciones Internacionales en América Latina y el Caribe* (Buenos Aires: GEL).

Perkmann, Markus and Ngai-Ling Sum (eds) (2002) *Globalization, Regionalization and the Building of Cross-Border Regions* (Basingstoke: Palgrave Macmillan).

Perraton, Jonathan, David Goldblatt, David Held and Anthony McGrew (1997) 'The Globalisation of Economic Activity', *New Political Economy* 2:2, pp. 257–77.

Peters, B. Guy (2000) 'Governance and Comparative Politics', in Jon Pierre (ed.) *Debating Governance: Authority, Steering, and Democracy* (Oxford: Oxford University Press), pp. 36–53.

Peterson, M. J. (1992) 'Transnational Activity, International Society and World Politics', *Millennium: Journal of International Studies* 21:3, pp. 371–89.

Philip, George (1999) 'The Dilemmas of Good Governance: A Latin American Perspective', *Government and Opposition* 34:2, pp. 226–42.

——(2003) *Democracy in Latin America: Surviving Conflict and Crisis?* (Cambridge: Polity).

Phillips, Anne (1999) *Which Equalities Matter?* (Cambridge: Polity).

Phillips, Nicola (2003a) 'The Rise and Fall of Open Regionalism? Comparative Perspectives on Regional Governance in the Southern Cone of Latin America', *Third World Quarterly* 24:2, pp. 217–34.

——(2003b) 'Hemispheric Integration and Subregionalism in the Americas', *International Affairs* 79:2, pp. 257–79.

——(2004) *The Southern Cone Model: The Political Economy of Regional Capitalist Development in Latin America* (London: Routledge).

——(2005) 'Latin America in the Global Political Economy', in Richard Stubbs and Geoffrey R. D. Underhill (eds) *Political Economy and the Changing Global Order*, third edition (Oxford: Oxford University Press).

Pierre, Jon (2000) 'Introduction: Understanding Governance', in Jon Pierre (ed.) *Debating Governance: Authority, Steering, and Democracy* (Oxford: Oxford University Press), pp. 1–10.

Piper, Nicola and Anders Uhlin (eds) (2003) *Transnational Activism, Power and Democracy: Contextualising Networks in East and Southeast Asia* (London: Routledge).

Poku, Nana and Wayne Edge (2001) 'Introduction', in Nana Poku (ed.) *Security and Development in Southern Africa* (Westport, CT: Praeger Publishers), pp. 1–12.

Polanyi, Karl (1944/1957) *The Great Transformation: The Political and Economic Origins of Our Time* (Boston, MA: Beacon Press).

Pollitt, Christopher (1990) *Managerialism and the Public Services: The Anglo-American Experience* (Oxford: Basil Blackwell).

Porter, Michael E. (1990) *The Competitive Advantage of Nations* (London: Macmillan).

Potter, David, David Goldblatt, Margaret Kiloh and Paul Lewis (eds) (1997) *Democratization* (Cambridge: Open University/Polity Press).

Prakash, Aseem and Jeffrey A. Hart (eds) (1999) *Globalization and Governance* (London: Routledge).

Pridham, Geoffrey (ed.) (1991) *The International Context of Regime Transition in Southern Europe* (London: University of Leicester Press).

Przeworski, Adam (1986) 'Some Problems in the Study of Transition to Democracy', in Guillermo O'Donnell, Philippe Schmitter and Laurence Whitehead (eds) *Transitions from Authoritarian Rule: Comparative Perspectives* (Baltimore, MD: Johns Hopkins University Press), pp. 47–63.

——(1999) 'Minimalist Conceptions of Democracy: A Defense', in Ian Schapiro and Casiano Hacker-Cordón (eds) *Democracy's Value* (Cambridge: Cambridge University Press), pp. 47–63.

Puig, Juan Carlos (1980) *Doctrinas Internacionales y Autonomía Latino-americana* (Caracas: Universidad Simón Bolívar).

Pye, Lucian (1966) *Aspects of Political Development* (Boston, MA: Little, Brown).

Quinn, Dennis P. (1997) 'The Correlates of Change in International Financial Regulation', *American Political Science Review* 91:3, pp. 531–52.

Quinn, Dennis P. and Carla Inclán (1997) 'The Origins of Financial Openness: A Study of Current and Capital Account Liberalization', *American Journal of Political Science* 41:3, pp. 771–813.

Radice, Hugo (2000) 'Globalization and National Capitalisms: Theorizing Convergence and Differentiation', *Review of International Political Economy* 7:4, pp. 719–42.

Reich, Robert (1991) *The Work of Nations: Preparing Ourselves for 21st Century Capitalism* (New York: Simon & Schuster).

Rhodes, Martin (2001) 'Globalization, Welfare States and Employment: Is There a European "Third Way"?', in Nancy Bermeo (ed.) *Unemployment in the New Europe* (Cambridge: Cambridge University Press), pp. 87–120.

Rhodes, R. A. W. (1996) 'The New Governance: Governing without Government', *Political Studies* 44:4, pp. 652–67.

Richards, David and Martin Smith (2002) *Governance and Public Policy in the United Kingdom* (Oxford: Oxford University Press).

Riggs, Fred (1964) *Administration in Developing Countries: The Theory of Prismatic Society* (Boston, MA: Houghton Mifflin).

Risse, Thomas (2002) 'Transnational Actors and World Politics', in Walter Carlsnaes, Thomas Risse and Beth A. Simmons (eds) *Handbook of International Relations* (London: Sage), pp. 255–74.

Risse, Thomas and Stephen C. Ropp (1999) 'International Human Rights Norms and Domestic Change: Conclusions', in Thomas Risse, Stephen C. Ropp and Kathryn Sikkink (eds) *The Power of Human Rights: International Norms and Domestic Change* (Cambridge: Cambridge University Press), pp. 234–78.

Risse, Thomas, Stephen Ropp and Kathryn Sikkink (eds) (1999) *The Power of Human Rights: International Norms and Domestic Change* (Cambridge: Cambridge University Press).

Risse-Kappen, Thomas (ed.) (1995) *Bringing Transnational Relations Back In: Non-state Actors, Domestic Structures and International Institutions* (Cambridge: Cambridge University Press).

Robinson, William I. (1996) *Promoting Polyarchy: Globalization, US Intervention and Hegemony* (Cambridge: Cambridge University Press).

——(2001) 'Transnational Processes, Development Studies, and Changing Social Hierarchies in the World System: A Central American Case Study', *Third World Quarterly* 22:4, pp. 529–63.

——(2002) 'Globalisation as a Macro–Structural–Historical Framework for Analysis: The Case of Central America', *New Political Economy* 7:2, pp. 221–50.

——(2004) *A Theory of Global Capitalism: Production, Class, and State in a Transnational World* (Baltimore, MD: Johns Hopkins University Press).

Robinson, William I. and Jerry Harris (2000) 'Towards a Global Ruling Class? Globalization and the Transnational Capitalist Class', *Science & Society* 64:1, pp. 11–54.

Robson, Peter (1993) 'The New Regionalism and Developing Countries', *Journal of Common Market Studies* 31:3, pp. 329–48.

Rodrik, Daniel (1997) *Has Globalization Gone Too Far?* (Washington, DC: Institute for International Economics).

——(2000) 'Exchange Rate Regimes and Institutional Arrangements in the Shadow of Capital Flows', mimeo, September.

Rosamond, Ben (2003) 'Babylon and On? Globalization and International Political Economy', *Review of International Political Economy* 10:4, pp. 661–71.

——(forthcoming) *Globalization and the European Union* (Basingstoke: Palgrave Macmillan).

Rosenau, James N. (1980) *The Study of Global Interdependence: Essays on the Transnationalization of World Affairs* (London: Pinter).

——(1992) 'Governance, Order, and Change in World Politics', in James N. Rosenau and Ernst-Otto Czempiel (eds) *Governance without*

Government: Order and Change in World Politics (Cambridge: Cambridge University Press), pp. 1–29.

——(1995) 'Governance in the Twenty-first Century', *Global Governance* 1:1, pp. 13–43.

——(1997) *Along the Domestic–Foreign Frontier: Exploring Governance in a Turbulent World* (Cambridge: Cambridge University Press).

Rosenau, James N. and Ernst-Otto Czempiel (eds) (1992) *Governance without Government: Order and Change in World Politics* (Cambridge: Cambridge University Press).

Rostow, W. W. (1960) *The Process of Economic Growth* (Oxford: Clarendon Press).

Rueschemeyer, Dietrich, Evelyne Huber Stephens and John D. Stephens (1992) *Capitalist Development and Democracy* (Cambridge: Polity Press).

Ruggie, John Gerard (1982) 'International Regimes, Transactions, and Change: Embedded Liberalism in the Postwar Economic Order', *International Organization* 36:2, pp. 379–415.

——(ed.) (1983) *Multilateralism Matters: The Theory and Praxis of an Institutional Form* (New York: Columbia University Press).

——(1993) 'Territoriality and Beyond: Problematizing Modernity in International Relations', *International Organization* 47:1, pp. 139–74.

——(1998) *Constructing the World Polity: Essays on International Institutionalism* (New York: Routledge).

Ruigrok, Winfried and Rob van Tulder (1995) *The Logic of International Restructuring* (London: Routledge).

Rupert, Mark (1995) *Producing Hegemony: The Politics of Mass Production and American Global Power* (Cambridge: Cambridge University Press).

——(2000) *Ideologies of Globalization: Contending Visions of a New World Order* (London: Routledge).

Russett, Bruce (2003) 'Reintegrating the Subdisciplines of International and Comparative Politics', *International Studies Review* 5:4, pp. 9–12.

Rustow, Dankwart (1970) 'Transition to Democracy: Toward a Dynamic Model', *Comparative Politics* 2:3, pp. 337–63.

Sakamoto, Yoshikazu (1995) 'Democratisation, Social Movements and World Order', in Björn Hettne (ed.) *International Political Economy: Understanding Global Disorder* (London: Zed Press), pp. 129–43.

Samuelson, Paul A. (1954) 'The Pure Theory of Public Expenditure', *Review of Economics and Statistics* 36, pp. 387–9.

Sandel, Michael (1996) *Democracy's Discontent* (Cambridge, MA: Harvard University Press).

Sassen, Saskia (1991) *The Global City: New York, London, Tokyo* (Princeton, NJ: Princeton University Press).

——(1995) 'The State and the Global City: Notes towards a Conception of Place-centered Governance', *Competition and Change* 1:1, pp. 31–50.

——(1998) *Globalization and its Discontents* (New York: The New Press).

Sayer, Derek (1991) *Capitalism and Modernity: An Excursus on Marx and Weber* (London: Routledge).

Schaffer, Bernard (1969) 'The Deadlock in Development Administration', in Colin Leys (ed.) *Politics and Change in Developing Countries* (Cambridge: Cambridge University Press), pp. 177–211.

Scharpf, Fritz (1991) *Crisis and Choice in European Social Democracy* (Ithaca, NY: Cornell University Press).

Schmitter, Philippe (1979) 'Still the Century of Corporatism?', in Philippe Schmitter (ed.) *Trends Toward Corporatist Intermediation* (Beverly Hills, CA: Sage), pp. 7–48.

Schmitter, Philippe, Guillermo O'Donnell and Laurence Whitehead (eds) (1986) *Transitions from Authoritarian Rule: Comparative Perspectives* (Baltimore, MD: Johns Hopkins University Press).

Schneider, Volker (2000) 'Global Economic Governance by Private Actors: The International Chamber of Commerce', in Justin Greenwood and Henry Jacek (eds) *Organized Business and the New Global Order* (New York: St Martin's Press), pp. 223–40.

Scholte, Jan Aart (1997) 'Global Capitalism and the State', *International Affairs* 73:3, pp. 427–52.

——(1998) 'The IMF Meets Civil Society', *Finance and Development* 25:3, pp. 42–5.

——(1999) 'Civil Society and a Democratisation of the International Monetary Fund', in Sarah Owen Vandersluis and Paris Yeros (eds) *Poverty in World Politics: Whose Global Era?* (London: Macmillan), pp. 91–116.

——(2000a) *Globalization: A Critical Introduction* (Basingstoke: Palgrave Macmillan).

——(2000b) 'Global Civil Society', in Ngaire Woods (ed.) *The Political Economy of Globalization* (Basingstoke: Palgrave Macmillan), pp. 173–201.

——(2001) *Civil Society and Democracy in Global Governance*, CSGR Working Paper No. 65/01, Centre for the Study of Globalisation and Regionalisation, University of Warwick.

Schulz, Michael, Fredrik Söderbaum and Joakim Öjendal (eds) (2001a) *Regionalization in a Globalizing World: A Comparative Perspective on Actors, Forms and Processes* (London: Zed Books).

——(2001b) 'Key Issues in the New Regionalism: Comparisons from Asia, Africa and the Middle East', in Björn Hettne, András Inotai and Osvaldo Sunkel (eds) *Comparing Regionalisms: Implications for Global Development* (Basingstoke: Palgrave Macmillan), pp. 234–76.

Searle, John R. (1995) *The Construction of Social Reality* (New York: Free Press).

Sell, Susan (1999) 'Multinational Corporations as Agents of Change: The Globalization of Intellectual Property Rights', in A. Claire Cutler, Virginia Haufler and Tony Porter (eds) *Private Authority and International Affairs* (Albany, NY: State University of New York Press), pp. 169–97.

Sell, Susan and Aseem Prakash (2004) 'Using Ideas Strategically: The Contest Between Business and NGO Networks in Intellectual Property Rights', *International Studies Quarterly* 48:1, pp. 143–75.

Sen, Gautam (2003) 'The United States and the GATT/WTO System', in Rosemary Foot, S. Neil MacFarlane and Michael Mastanduno (eds) *US Hegemony and International Organizations* (Oxford: Oxford University Press), pp. 115–38.

Sen, Jai, Anita Anand, Arturo Escobar and Peter Waterman (eds) (2004) *The World Social Forum: Challenging Empires* (Delhi: Viveka Foundation).

Shaw, Martin (1994) *Global Society and International Relations: Sociological Concepts and Political Perspectives* (Cambridge: Polity Press).

——(1999) 'The Historical Transition of Our Times: The Question of Globality in Historical Sociology', paper presented to the conference 'Historical Sociology and International Relations', University of Aberystwyth, July.

——(2000) *Theory of the Global State: Globality as an Unfinished Revolution* (Cambridge: Cambridge University Press).

Shaw, Timothy M. (1998) 'African Renaissance/African Alliance: Towards New Regionalisms and New Realism in the Great Lakes at the Start of the Twenty-first Century', *Politeia* 17:3, pp. 60–74.

——(2000) 'New Regionalisms in Africa in the New Millennium: Comparative Perspectives on Renaissance, Realisms, and/or Regressions', *New Political Economy* 5:3, pp. 399–414.

Shields, Stuart (2003) 'The "Charge of the Right Brigade": Transnational Social Forces and the Neoliberal Configuration of Poland's Transition', *New Political Economy* 8:2, pp. 225–44.

Siffin, William J. (1976) 'Two Decades of Public Administration in Developing Countries', *Public Administration Review* 36:1, pp. 61–71.

Sikkink, Kathryn (2002) 'Restructuring World Politics: The Limits and Asymmetries of Soft Power', in Sanjeev Khagram, James V. Riker and Kathryn Sikkink (eds) *Restructuring World Politics: Transnational Social Movements* (Minneapolis, MN: University of Minnesota Press), pp. 301–34.

Simmons, Beth A. (1999) 'The Internationalization of Capital', in Herbert Kitschelt, Peter Lange, Gary Marks and John D. Stephens (eds) *Continuity and Change in Contemporary Capitalism* (Cambridge: Cambridge University Press).

Sinclair, Timothy J. (1994) 'Passing Judgement: Credit Rating Processes as Regulatory Mechanisms of Governance in the Emerging World Order', *Review of International Political Economy* 1:1, pp. 133–59.

——(1996) 'Beyond International Relations Theory: Robert W. Cox and Approaches to World Order', in Robert Cox with Timothy Sinclair, *Approaches to World Order* (Cambridge: Cambridge University Press), pp. 3–18.

Sklair, Leslie (2000) *The Transnational Capitalist Class* (Oxford: Blackwell).

Skocpol, Theda (1979) *States and Social Revolutions* (Cambridge: Cambridge University Press).

——(1984) *Vision and Method in Historical Sociology* (Cambridge: Cambridge University Press).

——(1985) 'Bringing the State Back In: Strategies of Analysis in Current Research', in Peter Evans, Dietrich Rueschemeyer and Theda Skocpol (eds) *Bringing the State Back In* (Cambridge: Cambridge University Press), pp. 3–37.

Skogstad, Grace (2001) 'The WTO and Food Safety Regulatory Policy in the EU', *Journal of Common Market Studies* 39:3, pp. 485–505.

Slater, David (1998) 'Post-Colonial Questions for Global Times', *Review of International Political Economy* 5:4, pp. 647–78.

Slaughter, Anne-Marie (1997) 'The Real New World Order', *Foreign Affairs* 76:5, pp. 183–97.

Smith, Jackie, Charles Chatfield and Ron Pagnucco (eds) (1997) *Transnational Social Movements and Global Politics: Solidarity Beyond the State* (Syracuse, NY: Syracuse University Press).

Smith, Steve (2000) 'The Discipline of International Relations: Still an American Social Science?', *British Journal of Politics and International Relations* 2:3, pp. 374–402.

——(2002) 'The United States and the Discipline of International Relations: "Hegemonic Country, Hegemonic Discipline"', *International Studies Review* 4:2, pp. 67–85.

Smith, Steve, Ken Booth and Marysia Zalewski (eds) (1996) *International Theory: Positivism & Beyond* (Cambridge: Cambridge University Press).

Smouts, Marie-Claude (1998) 'The Proper Use of Governance in International Relations', *International Social Science Journal* 155:1, pp. 81–9.

Söderbaum, Fredrik (2001) 'Modes of Regional Governance in Africa: By Whom, For Whom and For What Purpose?', mimeo, Department of Peace and Development Research, Göteborg University.

Söderbaum, Fredrik and Ian Taylor (2001) 'Transmission Belt or Facilitator for Development – Problematising the Role of the State in the Maputo Development Corridor', *Journal of Modern African Studies* 29:4, pp. 675–95.

Soederberg, Susanne (2002) 'A Historical Materialist Account of the Chilean Capital Control: Prototype Policy for Whom?', *Review of International Political Economy* 9:3, pp. 490–512.

Sørensen, Georg (2001) *Changes in Statehood: The Transformation of International Relations* (Basingstoke: Palgrave Macmillan).

Soskice, David (1999) 'Divergent Production Regimes: Coordinated and Uncoordinated Market Economies in the 1980s and 1990s', in Herbert Kitschelt, Peter Lange, Gary Marks and John D. Stephens (eds) *Continuity and Change in Contemporary Capitalism* (Cambridge: Cambridge University Press), pp. 101–34.

Spruyt, Hendrick (1994) *The Sovereign State and its Competitors: An Analysis of Systems Change* (Princeton, NJ: Princeton University Press).

Steans, Jill (1998) *Gender and International Relations: An Introduction* (Cambridge: Polity).

——(1999) 'The Private is Global: Feminist Politics and Global Political Economy', *New Political Economy* 4:1, pp. 113–28.

Stevis, Dimitris and Terry Boswell (1997) 'Labour: From National Resistance to International Politics', *New Political Economy* 2:1, pp. 93–104.

Stiglitz, Joseph E. (2000) 'Capital Market Liberalization, Economic Growth, and Instability', *World Development* 28:6, pp. 1075–86.

——(2002) *Globalization and Its Discontents* (London: Penguin).

Stopford, John and Susan Strange (1991) *Rival States, Rival Firms: Competition for World Market Shares* (Cambridge: Cambridge University Press).

Strange, Susan (1970) 'International Economics and International Relations: A Case of Mutual Neglect', *International Affairs* 46:2, pp. 304–15.

——(1988) *States and Markets* (London: Pinter).

——(1990) 'The Name of the Game', in Nicholas X. Rizopoulos (ed.) *Sea-Changes: American Foreign Policy in a World Transformed* (New York: Council on Foreign Relations), pp. 238–73.

——(1992) 'States, Firms, Diplomacy', *International Affairs* 68:1, pp. 1–15.

——(1994) 'Wake Up, Krasner! The World *Has* Changed', *Review of International Political Economy* 1:2, pp. 209–19.

——(1995) '1995 Presidential Address: ISA as a Microcosm', *International Studies Quarterly* 39:3, pp. 289–95.

——(1996) *The Retreat of the State: The Diffusion of Power in the World Economy* (Cambridge: Cambridge University Press).

——(1997) 'The Future of Global Capitalism; Or Will Divergence Persist Forever?', in Colin Crouch and Wolfgang Streeck (eds) *Political Economy of Modern Capitalism: Mapping Convergence and Diversity* (London: Sage Publications), pp. 182–91.

——(1998) *Mad Money* (Manchester: Manchester University Press).

Streeck, Wolfgang (1997) 'German Capitalism: Does It Exist? Can It Survive?', *New Political Economy* 2:2, pp. 237–56.

Sum, Ngai-Ling (1999) 'Politics of Identities and the Making of the "Greater China" Subregion in the Post-Cold War Era', in Glenn Hook and Ian Kearns (eds) *Subregionalism and World Order* (London: Macmillan), pp. 197–221.

Sunkel, Osvaldo (1972) 'Big Business and "Dependencia": A Latin American View', *Foreign Affairs* 50:3, pp. 517–31.

Szeftel, Morris (2000) 'Clientelism, Corruption and Catastrophe', *Review of African Political Economy* 27:85, pp. 427–41.

Tabb, William K. (1995) *The Postwar Japanese System: Cultural Economy and Economic Transformation* (New York: Oxford University Press).

Tarrow, Sidney (2000) 'Beyond Globalization: Why Creating Transnational Social Movements is so Hard and When is it Most Likely to Happen', posted at Global Solidarity Dialogue: www.antenna.nl/~waterman/tarrow.html.

Taylor, Ian and Peter Vale (2000) 'South Africa's Transition Revisited: Globalisation as Vision and Virtue', *Global Society* 14:3, pp. 399–414.

Taylor, Paul (1999) 'The United Nations in the 1990s: Proactive Cosmopolitanism and the Issue of Sovereignty', *Political Studies* 47:3, pp. 538–65.

Telò, Mario (ed.) (2001) *European Union and New Regionalism: Regional Actors and Global Governance in a Post-Hegemonic Era* (Aldershot: Ashgate).

Thiele, Leslie Paul (1993) 'Making Democracy Safe for the World: Social Movements and Global Politics', *Alternatives* 18, pp. 273–305.

Thomas, Caroline and Peter Wilkin (2004) 'Still Waiting after All These Years: The "Third World" on the Periphery of International Relations', *British Journal of Politics and International Relations* 6:2, pp. 241–58.

Tickner, Arlene B. (2002) *Los estudios internacionales en América Latina: ¿Hegemonía intelectual o pensamiento emancipatorio?* (Bogotá: Alfaomega).

——(2003a) 'Seeing IR Differently: Notes from the Third World', *Millennium: Journal of International Studies* 32:2, pp. 295–324.

——(2003b) 'Hearing Latin American Voices in International Relations Studies', *International Studies Perspectives* 4:4, pp. 325–50.

Tilly, Charles (1990) *Coercion, Capital and European States, AD 990–1990* (London: Blackwell).

Toke, Dave (1999) 'Epistemic Communities and Environmental Groups', *Politics* 19:2, pp. 97–102.

Turner, Mark and David Hulme (1997) *Governance, Administration and Development* (London: Macmillan).

Tussie, Diana (2004) 'Of Reason and Purpose: Re-thinking the Study of International Relations in Latin America', paper presented at the Annual Convention of the International Studies Association, Montréal, 17–20 March.

Underhill, Geoffrey R. D. (2000a) 'State, Market, and Global Political Economy: Genealogy of an (Inter-?) Discipline', *International Affairs* 76:4, pp. 805–24.

——(2000b) 'Conceptualizing the Changing Global Order', in Richard Stubbs and Geoffrey Underhill (eds) *Political Economy and the*

Changing Global Order, second edition (Oxford: Oxford University Press), pp. 4–5.

Valdés, Juan Gabriel (1995) *Pinochet's Economists: The Chicago School in Chile* (Cambridge: Cambridge University Press).

van Apeldoorn, Bastiaan (2002) *Transnational Capitalism and the Struggle Over European Integration* (London: Routledge).

van Cranenburgh, Oda (1999) 'International Policies to Promote African Democratization', in Jean Grugel (ed.) *Democracy without Borders: Transnationalization and Conditionality in New Democracies* (London: Routledge), pp. 92–105.

van der Pijl, Kees (1995) 'The Second Glorious Revolution: Globalizing Elites and Historical Change', in Björn Hettne (ed.) *International Political Economy: Understanding Global Disorder* (London: Zed Books), pp. 100–28.

——(1998) *Transnational Classes and International Relations* (London: Routledge).

——(2001) 'Restoring the Radical Imagination in Political Economy', *New Political Economy* 6:3, pp. 380–90.

Wade, Robert (1990) *Governing the Market: Economic Theory and the Role of Government in East Asian Industrialization* (Princeton, NJ: Princeton University Press).

——(1996a) 'Globalization and its Limits: Reports of the Death of the National Economy are Greatly Exaggerated', in Suzanne Berger and Ronald Dore (eds) *National Diversity and Global Capitalism* (Ithaca, NY: Cornell University Press), pp. 60–88.

——(1996b) 'Japan, the World Bank, and the Art of Paradigm Maintenance: *The East Asian Miracle* in Political Perspective', *New Left Review* 217, pp. 3–36.

——(1998–9) 'The Coming Fight over Capital Controls', *Foreign Policy* 113, pp. 41–54.

Wade, Robert and Frank Veneroso (1998) 'The Asian Crisis: The High Debt Model vs. the Wall Street–Treasury–IMF Model', *New Left Review* 228, pp. 3–27.

Waever, Ole (1998) 'The Sociology of a Not So International Discipline: American and European Developments in International Relations', *International Organization* 52:4, pp. 687–727.

Wallerstein, Immanuel (1979) *The Capitalist World-Economy* (Cambridge: Cambridge University Press).

——(ed.) (2004) *The Modern World System in Longue Durée* (Boulder, CO: Paradigm).

Waltz, Kenneth (1959) *Man, the State, and War* (New York: Columbia University Press).

——(1979) *Theory of International Politics* (Reading, MA: Addison-Wesley).

——(2000) 'Globalization and American Power', *The National Interest* 59, pp. 46–57.

Wapner, Paul (1995) 'Politics Beyond the State: Environmental Activism and World Civic Politics', *World Politics* 47:3, pp. 311–40.

Watson, Matthew (1999) 'Re-thinking Capital Mobility: Re-regulating Financial Markets', *New Political Economy* 4:1, pp. 55–75.

——(2003) 'Constructing and Contesting Orthodoxies: General Equilibrium Economics and the Political Discourse of Globalisation', paper presented at the Annual Convention of the International Studies Association, Portland, OR, 26 February–1 March.

Weale, Albert (1999) *Democracy* (London: Macmillan).

Weber, Max (1964) *The Theory of Social and Economic Organization* (New York: Free Press).

——(1972) 'Politics as a Vocation', in H. H. Gerth and C. W. Mills (eds) *From Max Weber* (New York: Oxford University Press), pp. 77–128.

——(1974) *The Protestant Ethic and the Spirit of Capitalism* (London: Allen & Unwin).

——(1978) *Economy and Society*, 2 volumes (Berkeley, CA: University of California Press).

Weir, Stuart and David Beetham (1999) *Political Power and Democratic Control in Britain* (London: Routledge).

Weiss, Linda (1997) 'Globalization and the Myth of the Powerless State', *New Left Review* 225, pp. 3–27.

——(1998) *The Myth of the Powerless State* (Ithaca, NY: Cornell University Press).

——(ed.) (2003) *States in the Global Economy: Bringing Domestic Institutions Back In* (Cambridge: Cambridge University Press).

Weiss, Thomas W. and Leon Gordenker (eds) (1996) *NGOs, the UN, and Global Governance* (Boulder, CO: Lynne Rienner).

Wells, Louis T. (1972) 'The Multinational Business Enterprise: What Kind of International Organization?', in Robert O. Keohane and Joseph S. Nye Jr (eds) *Transnational Relations and World Politics* (Cambridge, MA: Harvard University Press), pp. 97–128.

Wendt, Alexander (1992) 'Anarchy is What States Make of It: The Social Construction of Power Politics', *International Organization* 46:2, pp. 391–425.

——(1999) *Social Theory of International Politics* (Cambridge: Cambridge University Press).

Wenli, Zhu (2001) 'International Political Economy from a Chinese Angle', *Journal of Contemporary China* 10:26, pp. 45–54.

Whitley, Richard (1992a) *Business Systems in East Asia: Firms, Markets and Societies* (London: Sage).

——(1992b) *European Business Systems: Firms and Markets in their National Contexts* (London: Sage).

Wilkinson, Rorden (2000) *Multilateralism and the World Trade Organisation: The Architecture and Extension of International Trade Regulation* (London: Routledge).

——(2002) 'The World Trade Organisation', *New Political Economy* 7:1, pp. 129–41.

Wilks, Stephen (1996) 'Regulatory Compliance and Capitalist Diversity in Europe', *Journal of European Public Policy* 3:4, pp. 536–59.

Willetts, Peter (1999) 'Transnational Actors and International Organizations in Global Politics', in John Baylis and Steve Smith (eds) *The Globalization of World Politics* (Oxford: Oxford University Press), pp. 287–310.

Williams, David G. (1996) 'Governance and the Discipline of Development', *European Journal of Development Research* 8:2, pp. 157–77.

——(1999) 'Constructing the Economic Space: The World Bank and the Making of Homo Economicus', *Millennium: Journal of International Studies* 28:1, pp. 79–99.

Williams, David and Thomas Young (1994) 'Governance, the World Bank and Liberal Theory', *Political Studies* 42:1, pp. 84–100.

Williams, Karel (2000) 'From Shareholder Value to Present Day Capitalism', *Economy and Society* 29:1, pp. 1–12.

Williamson, John (2003) 'Overview: An Agenda for Restarting Growth and Reform', in John Williamson and Pedro-Pablo Kuczynski (eds) *After the Washington Consensus: Restarting Growth and Reform in Latin America* (Washington, DC: Institute for International Economics), pp. 1–19.

Williamson, John and Pedro-Pablo Kuczynski (eds) (2003) *After the Washington Consensus: Restarting Growth and Reform in Latin America* (Washington, DC: Institute for International Economics).

Winters, Jeffrey (2000) 'The Financial Crisis in Southeast Asia', in Richard Robison, Mark Beeson, Kanishka Jayasuriya and Hyuk-Rae Kim (eds) *Politics and Markets in the Wake of the Asian Crisis* (London: Routledge), pp. 34–52.

Woo-Cumings (ed.) (1999) *The Developmental State* (Ithaca, NY: Cornell University Press).

Woods, Ngaire (2000) 'The Challenge of Good Governance for the IMF and the World Bank Themselves', *World Development* 28:5, pp. 823–41.

——(2001) 'Making the IMF and the World Bank More Accountable', *International Affairs* 77:1, pp. 83–100.

——(2003) 'The United States and the International Financial Institutions: Power and Influence Within the World Bank and the IMF', in Rosemary Foot, S. Neil MacFarlane and Michael Mastanduno (eds) *US Hegemony and International Organizations* (Oxford: Oxford University Press), pp. 92–114.

Woodward, Bob (1994) *The Agenda: Inside the Clinton White House* (New York: Simon & Schuster).

World Bank (1992) *Governance and Development* (Washington, DC: World Bank).

World Politics (1995) Special Issue: *The Role of Theory in Comparative Politics: A Symposium*, 48:1.

WSF (World Social Forum) (2004) 'Charter of Principles', available at http://www.wsfindia.org/charter.php. Accessed 21 January 2004.

Xinning, Song (2001) 'Building International Relations Theory with Chinese Characteristics', *Journal of Contemporary China* 10:26, pp. 61–74.

Young, Iris Marion (1999) 'State, Civil Society and Social Justice', in Ian Shapiro and Cassiano Hacker-Cordon (eds) *Democracy's Value* (Cambridge: Cambridge University Press), pp. 163–89.

——(2000) *Inclusion and Democracy* (Oxford: Oxford University Press).

Young, Oran R. (1999) *Governance in World Affairs* (Ithaca, NY: Cornell University Press).

Zartman, I. William (ed.) (1995) *Collapsed States: The Disintegration and Restoration of Legitimate Authority* (Boulder, CO: Lynne Rienner).

Zysman, John (1983) *Governments, Markets, and Growth: Financial Systems and the Politics of Industrial Change* (Ithaca, NY: Cornell University Press).

——(1994) 'How Institutions Create Historically Rooted Trajectories of Growth', *Industrial and Corporate Change* 3:1, pp. 243–83.

——(1996) 'The Myth of a "Global" Economy: Enduring National Foundations and Emerging Regional Realities', *New Political Economy* 1:2, pp. 157–84.

Index

CPSIA information can be obtained
at www.ICGtesting.com
Printed in the USA
LVHW060026020922
727362LV00008B/197

9 780333 965054